Catholicism, Politics and Society in Twentieth-Century France

Catholicism, Politics and Society in Twentieth-Century France

edited by Kay Chadwick

LIVERPOOL UNIVERSITY PRESS

First published 2000 by
Liverpool University Press
4 Cambridge Street
Liverpool
L69 7ZU

British Library Cataloguing-in-Publication Data
A British Library CIP Record is available

ISBN 0–85323–974–6 hardback
       0–85323–984-3 paperback

Typeset in Plantin by Koinonia, Bury
Printed and bound in Great Britain by
Bell and Bain Ltd, Glasgow

Contents

Editor's preface

This volume represents the fruit of a cross-national project involving British and French academics who work on issues related to the vast and complex theme of Catholicism in twentieth-century France. Each contributor is a specialist in the subject area of their chapter; together they possess an impressive body of knowledge, aspects of which this collection sets out to capture and present to the reader. The volume was completed as the twentieth century ended and the twenty-first began, a period coloured by themes of reassessment and evaluation, and an effective moment for a reconsideration of the twentieth century from all manner of angles. The purpose of this book is to offer a timely, end-of-century analysis of certain key themes and events crucial to an understanding of the role played by French Catholics and their Church throughout the twentieth century.

As editor of the volume, my thanks go out to all the contributors not only for their willing participation in this project, but also for their commitment, patience and co-operation at all its stages. My thanks are due also to the team at Liverpool University Press.

Kay Chadwick

Notes on contributors

Nicholas Atkin is Lecturer in History at the University of Reading. His research interests lie in the field of French history. He is the co-editor, with Frank Tallett, of *Religion, Society and Politics in France since 1789* (1991) and *Catholicism in Britain and France since 1789* (1996), and author of *Church and Schools in Vichy France, 1940–1944* (1991) and *Pétain* (1997).

Nicholas Beattie is Reader in Education at the University of Liverpool. His research interests lie in the politics of education in western Europe. His book *Professional Parents: Parent Participation in Four Western European Countries* (1985) won the Standing Committee on Studies in Education prize as the best education book of that year. He is at present working on a book on the Freinet movement in France, Germany and Italy.

Kay Chadwick is Lecturer in French at the University of Liverpool. Her research interests cover modern French studies and twentieth-century French history. She is co-editor, with Paul Cooke, of *Religion in Modern and Contemporary France* (1998), and the author of articles on French secularism and education, Catholicism and the French Catholic Church since 1789, Catholic collaborators and the legacy of Vichy in history, literature and film. She is currently writing a book on the collaborator Alphonse de Châteaubriant.

David Curtis is Senior Lecturer in French at the University of Hull. He has published articles on French seventeenth-century thought, on the history of modern Catholic social teaching and on inter-war Catholic thought in its relationship to Marxism. He is the author of *The French Popular Front and the Catholic Discovery of Marx* (1997).

Jean-Claude Delbreil is Professor of Contemporary History at the University of Metz. His research interests include twentieth-century French Christian Democracy and French political and religious life. He is the author of *Les Catholiques français et les tentatives de rapprochement franco-allemand dans l'entre-deux-guerres* (1972) and *Centrisme et démocratie chrétienne en France. Le Parti Démocrate Populaire des origines au MRP, 1919–1944* (1990). He is currently preparing a book on Marc Sangnier.

Danielle Delmaire is Lecturer in Contemporary History at the University of Lille III. Her research interests cover Catholic anti-Semitism, Jewish communities and Jewish youth movements in nineteenth- and twentieth-century France as well as the Shoah in northern France. Her publications include *Antisémitisme et catholiques dans le Nord pendant l'affaire Dreyfus* (1991), and she is currently preparing a *thèse d'État* on the Jewish communities of northern France (1791–1948).

Evelyne Diébolt has taught at the University of Paris VII and currently teaches in continuing education. Her research interests focus on the history of associations. She is the co-author, with Marie-Hélène Zylberberg-Hocquard, of *Marcelle Capy-Aline Valette: femmes et travail au dix-neuvième siècle* (1984), and the author of *La Maison de santé protestante de Bordeaux (1863–1934)* (1990).

Yves-Marie Hilaire is Professor of History at the University of Lille III. His research interests focus on Catholic religious sociology. He is the co-author (with Gérard Cholvy et al.) of *Histoire religieuse de la France contemporaine* (3 vols, 1986–-88) and editor of *Matériaux pour l'histoire religieuse du peuple français* (1986). His authored books include *La Religion populaire* (1981).

Michael Kelly is Professor of French at the University of Southampton. He has written monographs on Emmanuel Mounier (1979), Modern French Marxism (1982) and Hegel in France (1993), and edited several books, including *French Cultural Studies: An Introduction* (1995, with Jill Forbes). He is currently completing a book on French culture at the Liberation and preparing a monograph on Henri Lefebvre. He is an Associate Editor of the journal *French Cultural Studies*.

Kevin Passmore is Lecturer in History at the University of Wales at Cardiff. His research interests lie in the field of twentieth-century French history, especially the political groups of the 1920s and 1930s. He is the author of *From Liberalism to Fascism: The Right in a French Province, 1928–1939* (1997), and is currently working on a history of the French Right since 1870.

Émile Poulat is Director of the École des Hautes Études en Sciences Sociales in Paris. He is the author of several books on religion in modern France, including *Naissance des prêtres-ouvriers* (1965), *Liberté, laïcité. La Guerre des deux France et le principe de modernité* (1988) and *L'Ère postchrétienne. Un monde sorti de Dieu* (1994).

Colin Roberts is Subject Leader in French at Coventry University. His publications include monographs on the novelists Gilbert Cesbron and Marie Cardinal, as well as articles on aspects of French Catholicism and of contemporary French thought (especially Paul Ricœur). He is currently researching into discourses of secularisation in France.

Abbreviations

ACA	Assemblée des cardinaux et archevêques
ACGF	Association catholique générale féminine
ACI	Action catholique indépendante
ACJF	Action catholique de la jeunesse française
ACRIF	Association contre le racisme et pour le respect de l'identité française et catholique
ADAP	Assemblées dominicales en l'absence de prêtre
AF	Action française
ALP	Action libérale populaire
ANIDEF	Association nationale des infirmières diplômées de l'État français
AOCV	Association de l'œuvre des catéchistes volontaires
ASF	Action sociale de la femme
BAC	Bureau d'action civique
BBC	British Broadcasting Corporation
CDJC	Centre de documentation juive contemporaine
CDS	Centre démocratique et social
CED	Communauté européenne de défense
CERES	Centre d'études de recherche et d'éducation socialiste
CFDT	Confédération française démocratique du travail
CFTC	Confédération française des travailleurs chrétiens
CGE	Comité général d'études
CGQJ	Commissariat général aux questions juives
CGT	Confédération générale du travail
CGTU	Confédération générale du travail unitaire
CIMADE	Comité inter-mouvements auprès d'évacués
CNAL	Comité national de l'action laïque
CNI	Centre national des indépendants
CNR	Conseil national de la résistance

CSCV	Confédération syndicale du cadre de vie
CSF	Confédération syndicale des familles
DRAC	Droits du religieux ancien combattant
EEC	European Economic Community
ENS	École normale supérieure
FNC	Fédération nationale catholique
FNF	Fédération nationale des femmes
INC	International Nurses' Council
JAC(F)	Jeunesse agricole chrétienne (féminine)
JCC	Jeunes chrétiens combattants
JEC(F)	Jeunesse étudiante chrétienne (féminine)
JIC(F)	Jeunesse indépendante chrétienne (féminine)
JOC(F)	Jeunesse ouvrière chrétienne (féminine)
JR	Jeune république
LDN	Ligue des droits de la nation
LFF	Ligue des femmes françaises
LICRA	Ligue internationale contre le racisme et l'antisémitisme
LND	Ligue nationale de la démocratie
LOC	Ligue ouvrière chrétienne
LOC–MPF	Ligue ouvrière chrétienne–Mouvement populaire des familles
LPF	Ligue patriotique des Françaises
LSA	Ligue sociale d'acheteurs
LVF	Légion des volontaires français contre le bolchevisme
MLO	Mouvement de libération ouvrière
MLP	Mouvement de libération du peuple
MPF	Mouvement populaire des familles
MRAP	Mouvement contre le racisme et pour l'amitié entre les peuples
MRL	Mouvement républicain de libération
MRP	Mouvement républicain populaire
MUR	Mouvements unis de la résistance
NEF	Nouvelles équipes françaises
NEI	Nouvelles équipes internationales
OSE	Œuvre de secours aux enfants
PCF	Parti communiste français
PDP	Parti démocrate populaire
PPF	Parti populaire français
PPI	Parti populaire italien

PS	Parti socialiste
PSF	Parti social français
PSU	Parti socialiste unifié
RDR	Rassemblement démocratique révolutionnaire
RHEF	Revue d'histoire de l'Église de France
RISS	Revue internationale des sociétés secrètes
RPF	Rassemblement du peuple français
SDN	Société des nations
SFIO	Section française de l'internationale ouvrière
SIPDIC	Secrétariat international des partis démocratiques d'inspiration chrétienne
SNI	Syndicat national des instituteurs
SS	Schutzstaffel
STO	Service du travail obligatoire
TOM	Territoires d'outre-mer
UAS	Union des auxiliaires sociales
UCISS	Union catholique internationale de service social
UCSS	Union catholique des services sanitaires et sociaux
UDSR	Union démocratique et socialiste de la résistance
UFC	Union française des consommateurs
UFCS	Union féminine civique et sociale
UNAF	Union nationale des associations familiales
UNAPEL	Union nationale des associations de parents d'élèves
UNIOPSS	Union nationale interfédérale des œuvres privées sanitaires et sociales
UPRA	Union populaire républicaine d'Alsace
URL	Union républicaine de Lorraine

Introduction

Kay Chadwick

Before the 1789 Revolution, national and religious identity in France were closely linked, and the mutual dependency of the French monarchy and the Catholic Church largely guaranteed religious unity. Following the definitive recognition of Protestantism in the eighteenth century and Napoleon's Concordat with Pope Pius VII in 1801, Catholicism was confirmed as the religion of the majority of French people but was no longer the official State religion. Then, on 9 December 1905, the promulgation of the *loi de séparation des Églises et de l'État* designated France a *laïque* (or secular) Republic, one where no religion is either publicly recognised or subsidised by the State, but where freedom of religious expression is guaranteed provided this occurs as a private act. Pluralist France was born alongside the formalisation of the secular principle for, by dint of officially not recognising any single faith, the State effectively permitted all faiths. Contemporary France's complex, heterogeneous society is mirrored in her diversified religious framework, where Catholicism now co-exists with the nation's other representative faiths, including Protestantism and Judaism (both long-established in France) as well as Islam, a more recent arrival but now France's second religion in terms of the numbers of practising faithful.

The twentieth century began with bitter conflict between the Catholic Church and the French State, based on an original definition of *laïcité* (secularism) in combative, separatist terms. Although the 1905 law formally concerned all faiths, the Catholic Church (rightly) considered itself the principal target. Suspicion and hostility coloured the Church's attitude, while themes of exclusion and oppression littered its discourse. The State's response was equally hostile, coupled with a determination to complete the secular programme begun with the Third Republic in 1870, namely to remove the hold which anti-revolutionary, intransigent Catholicism had long had over French society. But, as the twentieth century progressed, the Catholic Church itself came to find positive value in secularism. The loss of its public status as majority religion in 1905 was, after all, matched by its acquisition of social and political independence from the State. This, the Church argues, has granted it a free voice on matters of public interest and concern. In the interests of its own role and status in contemporary France, the Catholic Church therefore now accepts and will even defend secularism, because of the guarantee it offers in respect of the Church's own rights.

Throughout the twentieth century, the Catholic Church was a significant actor on the French public stage and Catholicism functioned as a notable component of French identity. Catholics and their Church played a visible and sometimes arguably questionable role in such periods of tension as the Second World War and the Vichy regime (1940–44), the Algerian conflict (1958–63) and the events of May 1968. Institution and faithful responded variously to twentieth-century political developments and to the ideologies of both Left and Right inspired and sustained within France, including Marxism, Communism, Nationalism and Socialism. They also played their part in the Jewish question, where prejudice and a clear commitment to convert have tempered, and where there is now evidence of an evolution towards understanding. The period also saw the diversification of Catholic political practice, with Catholics represented across the whole range of the political spectrum by the end of the century. After 1900, numerous Catholic-inspired movements, leagues and associations attempted, in diverse ways and with various ends in mind, to mobilise and promote Catholic action, although at the end of the century there was no specifically Catholic political party in existence.

In the social sphere, the Catholic Church was prominent in the twentieth-century education debate, defending the individual's freedom to choose private (and largely Catholic) education, and finding compromises with the State in order to ensure its own continued existence as an educational provider while, at the same time, retaining something of its specific character. Elsewhere, the Church emerged as a major participant in the debate on immigration and integration in the post-1945 period. In this domain, it became and remains especially active in the promotion and defence of human rights, choosing also to involve itself in the issue of the rights and status of Islam in secular France, itself an indicator of how the Church sees the modern relationship between religions and the State. In addition, the Church was forced to consider the question of the role and status of women both within the institution itself (where they form the majority of the faithful and lay workers) and in society at large, with issues of responsibility and participation, as well as of personal health and welfare (especially birth control, abortion and artificial fertilisation) high on the agenda in an age of social and moral evolution. The drugs issue and the AIDS question, symptomatic of *fin de siècle* society in particular, extended the Church's interest in social issues beyond gender-specific themes, an interest matched by its commitment to a general defence of the disadvantaged, including the homeless, the unemployed and the poor. Indeed, the twentieth century saw few, if any, issues of social concern on which the Church failed to pronounce.

The twentieth century was nonetheless a period of general crisis and division for French Catholics and their Church. In some domains, the Church evolved to embrace the modern world (as in its defence of human rights) while in others (especially those pertaining to sexuality) its discourse remains inflexible and, for many Catholics (although not all), inadequate. The century bore witness not only to the continuing strength of the conservative Catholic mainstream, but also to the not insignificant impact of the intransigent, integrist current and to the growth of Catholicism's progressive and charismatic strands. It was a time when the relationship of many Catholics to their Church altered beyond recognition, when traditional Catholic observance declined, when many sought and found different ways of belonging to the faith and living as Catholics and when fewer followed Rome's dictates to the letter.

Despite, or even precisely because of, the influence and effect of secularism, religious issues have persisted on the political agenda, and the 'guerre des deux France' (the opposition of France's secular and clerical – that is, Catholic – camps) sporadically still impacts on the French national consciousness.[1] At the end of the century, hardline secularists still held to a combative definition of secularism, as witnessed by the demonstration in Paris on 9 December 1995, when ten thousand French marched to commemorate the birth of the secular State exactly ninety years before, attacking Pope John Paul II as 'l'assassin par opium du peuple'.[2] Subsequent events revitalised the issue. In January 1996, for instance, some chose to interpret the burial of former President François Mitterrand by the French Catholic Church as the symbolic interment of secularism and the reinstatement of Catholicism as the official State religion.[3] And, later the same year, debate raged in the French press at the time of John Paul II's visit to France to celebrate the fifteen-hundredth anniversary of the Catholic baptism of Clovis, King of the Franks. Emphasising, as it did, France's long-standing Catholic culture (itself controversially acknowledged by President Jacques Chirac), the event was viewed in some quarters as an attempt by the Church to re-appropriate part of French national identity for itself, and thereby to regain some of its lost influence.[4] Such occasional skirmishes do not, in the end, detract from the fact that the secular–clerical war is over and that a peace has been reached. Secularism is firmly established as the guiding principle of modern, republican France. The French Catholic Church has broadly accommodated to its requirements and has thereby managed to carve out a role for itself which will carry it forward through the twenty-first century. Catholicism may no longer be the protean monster it once was, but no consideration of modern French culture and identity would be complete without serious reference to its continuing impact and influence on the life of the nation. Furthermore, the scale and import of its evolution since 1900 in particular indicates that the twentieth century is a valuable and effective window through which to view the Catholic phenomenon.

This volume sets out to capture some of the variety and significance of that phenomenon, and to express something of its extraordinary vitality and interest. No volume could satisfactorily claim to address all facets of the topic, given its breadth and intensity, and the intention here is not to provide an exhaustive account but rather to focus on specific issues and moments crucial to an understanding of the role played by French Catholics and their Church throughout the twentieth century. The volume is, therefore, necessarily selective in its choice both of the themes for inclusion and in the aspects of each theme identified for analysis. Each contribution represents one piece in the mosaic that is the overall collection: each has its own particular 'colour' and 'shape' in the form of an individual author and a clearly identifiable theme; and each can be read independently as a self-contained analysis which enables the reader to focus on a key theme or period which interested and concerned French Catholics and their

Church during the century. As a collection, the chapters represent a composite entity which in its very structure reflects the fragmentation of Catholic activity and attitudes in the twentieth century, and which invites the reader to appreciate that variety by tracking the progression and evolution of the French Catholic Church and French Catholics over that period. As with a mosaic, no two 'patterns' are ever fully alike. Another volume on the same topic could be constructed differently; it could highlight other themes or periods, or choose to focus on different aspects of themes also treated here. But, in all probability, it would exhibit a similar thematic variety, equally justifiable and significant in its approach, indicating that there are numerous ways to read and write about Catholicism in France.

The authors of this volume, diverse though their interests and specialities are, share a common aim: namely, to create an opportunity for a reading of Catholicism in twentieth-century France. Their contributions offer a collage of insights and reflections rather than a definitive assessment of the subject which, it is hoped, will function to encourage the reader to explore this vast and complex topic further. To that end, suggestions for further reading on individual topics and for wider reading around and beyond the scope of this collection can be found in the Select bibliography at the end of the volume (p. 280). The chapters combine background information with critical analysis and debate. Some concentrate on an assessment of their theme at a certain moment in the century, which permits detailed discussion of issues of particular significance at the time; others adopt a broader perspective, enabling the reader to trace Catholic activity in a specific area over a period of time and thereby to understand and evaluate its development. In terms of the organisation of the volume, the chapters broadly proceed from the more specifically political to a consideration of themes located principally in the societal domain. Most contributions, however, inevitably include both political and societal elements, suggesting that it is ultimately impossible, and even undesirable, to order them into a fixed structure and thereby impose a particular reading of the subject. For the same reasons, the volume avoids compartmentalisation of theme and period. The chapters deliberately overlap in terms of the period studied, while themes connect and echo across the volume, thereby emphasising the variety of Catholic activity throughout the century, as well as the interplay of certain themes and events which lie at the very heart of the evolution of Catholics and their Church. The purpose of the following pages of this introduction is to offer a preview of the main contents of the collection, to highlight some of the principal topics discussed and to offer one possible 'route' through the volume, with a view to facilitating the reader's own choices and decisions about how best to make use of this book.

Secularism is a major theme raised in various ways by many of the contributors to this volume. Émile Poulat's opening chapter presents secularism as a paradoxical principle, inextricably linked with the evolution of the Catholic Church in France. Poulat disputes a common definition of secularism as religious neutrality, arguing that its very guarantee of religious existence and expression, in the name of the freedom of conscience, links rather than separates Churches and State. This guarantee is seen to have cost the Republic dear in terms of principle. But the Catholic Church has also had to pay a price, since it has had to learn to operate as one religion among many in accordance with the principle of the equality of religions as laid down by the 1905 Separation. True equality may not always operate in practice, since the Republic can be seen to favour the nation's principal Churches over her smaller sects, but there can be no doubt that one significant effect of the 1905 Separation is that the Catholic Church can no longer legitimately claim special status.

The advantages of secularism for the Catholic Church are such that the principle is no longer in dispute, although some minor contentious points may remain. Indeed, in her contribution on the Church and the immigration question, the editor of this volume argues that the Church has not only come to acknowledge secularism and the construction of France as a modern, pluralist society, but will also use secularism's guarantees to its own advantage and even plead for its respect, this in order to safeguard its own rights and status in matters of existence and expression, and as a means of handling other religions, especially Islam. The Church's ability to function on a largely successful basis within the secular State underpins its call for Islam similarly to adapt to secular circumstances, and thereby to come into line with Catholicism in terms of status and operation within the State. Promoted as a means to integration, the Church's message to Islam carries a sub-text, as revealed by its response to the 1994 *affaire du foulard*: namely that, like itself, Islam cannot and should not claim special status and treatment. Integration means incorporation, and adaptation to the French context is the key.

A further important meeting between the Catholic Church and

secularism in the twentieth century can be found in the domain of education, as illustrated by Nicholas Beattie's discussion of recent developments in Catholic schooling in France. Beattie examines how Catholic education has evolved in the secular context in order to survive, focusing on the financial benefits afforded by the December 1959 *loi Debré*, provided that schools comply with certain State requirements concerning curriculum content, educational standards and pupils' individual freedom of conscience. As a result, the survival of the Catholic system is no longer in question, for its numbers have grown to such an extent that it is now widely considered to represent a public service. It offers parents a choice, although one rarely made on purely religious grounds. It has become a professionalised alternative to the over-stretched State system, identical to its public counterpart in its day-to-day operation but, for many, different in style and attitude towards pupils. Its existence is therefore defended on the grounds of freedom of choice, as during the secular–clerical confrontation of 1981–84, when the current Socialist government proposed but failed to create a single, unified, secular education system. Choice, of course, implies the provision of something different, and Beattie goes on to assess the 'separateness' of Catholic schooling, examining what is uniquely Catholic about the schools (their 'caractère propre', as Debré described it) and how they conceive their role in modern, secular France. He provides convincing evidence of the Church's broad accommodation to the demands of secularism in the educational context of the Fifth Republic, since the mainstream identity which emerges is one of an educative community which strives to develop the moral personality within the rules provided by the State. Nevertheless, as Beattie argues, Catholic schools sustain and promote specifically Catholic values simply through their presence as separate, associate providers in the education system rather than as fully integrated elements, and accommodation to secularism would seem, then, to have its accepted limits. Beyond the mainstream, however, small groups of Catholics such as the *Équipes enseignantes* argue for an alternative approach. For them, compromise is insufficient, while 'separateness' risks producing closed, militant principles. Secularism is neither an enemy to be fought (as traditionalists claim) nor a principle which has to be tolerated in the name of survival. It creates a proper, open environment for religious faith to flourish, and the Church must therefore further engage seriously and positively both with secularism and with the

complex, pluralist society in which Christians live and work, since it
has much to learn from both.

The Church's meeting with secularism in the twentieth century,
then, was characterised by a shift towards dialogue and understanding which may lead the way to further engagement in the third
millennium. A similar shift can be identified in respect of the Church
and the Jewish question. Danielle Delmaire's analysis of this theme
indicates that French Catholics were almost unanimously anti-
Semitic at the end of the nineteenth century, as the Dreyfus Affair
illustrates, although by the end of the twentieth century few held
such views. In between, the Catholic–Jewish relationship experienced a difficult progression hampered by long-standing popular
prejudices and a series of acutely sensitive events. Indeed, although
examples of Catholic–Jewish dialogue and co-operation can be
identified as early as the inter-war period, these were limited in
existence and scope, and Catholicism's goal remained the conversion
of the Jews. Then the Second World War, remembered for the
Holocaust, raised further problematic issues for Catholics and their
Church. In particular, Delmaire calls into question the hierarchy's
timid objections or, worse still, its silence in the face of Vichy's anti-
Jewish legislation. Nicholas Atkin suggests in his study of Catholics
in Vichy France that the bishops may have acted as they did out of
devotion to Pétain, or because they did not appreciate the full horror
of racial persecution; their response, however, also plainly revealed
that – apart from a few notable exceptions – they were largely not free
of prejudice and they failed to give a clear lead to the faithful. Not all
Catholics, of course, supported Vichy, and both Atkin and Delmaire
are careful to reference Catholic activity in the Resistance and to
detail a Catholic defence of Jews on the grounds of simple humanity,
especially in the final two years of the war. As Atkin concludes, the
épuration of the Church after the war would undoubtedly have been
more extensive but for the actions of those rank-and-file Catholics
who defied Vichy and the Nazis.

The war represented the point of genesis for the most significant
subsequent issues of tension and sensitivity between Catholics and
Jews in France, as highlighted by Delmaire: most notably, the *affaire
Finaly* which revitalised the thorny issue of conversion; the infamous
affaire Touvier, which forced the nation to face Vichy's anti-Semitic
behaviour; and the question of the location of a Catholic convent
close to the former Auschwitz concentration camp, which Jewish

groups feared would lead to an unwelcome 'christianisation' of the Holocaust. That such events hampered Catholic–Jewish relations is beyond doubt. But Delmaire points out that other more positive events must also be remembered, such as the creation of pro-active Christian/Catholic–Jewish groups, or Vatican II's removal of anti-Jewish phraseology from Catholic prayers, or the French Church's apology for its silence under Vichy, all designed to promote mutual respect and to further understanding. Some reticence and mistrust may remain on both sides, but dialogue continues.

Catholic response to the twentieth century became particularly varied on a political level as the years progressed. The early decades, however, were marked by a natural affinity between Catholics and the political Right, a theme developed by Kevin Passmore in his study of the *Fédération républicaine* – chosen for analysis on the grounds that it was the largest party on the Right in the 1920s and 1930s, and had a strong Catholic following – and echoed in Nicholas Atkin's discussion of Catholics under the Vichy regime. Both chapters testify to the strength of the contemporary conservative Catholic view which did not accept secularisation as an inevitable historical process to which the Church had to adapt if it was to survive. The *Fédération républicaine* was regarded as the unofficial agent of the Church in Parliament. As Passmore's contribution argues, its support bore witness to the strength and vitality of a popular Catholic nationalism that was at once anti-socialist, anti-feminist and anti-capitalist in response to the 'threat' posed by the Left (as particularly represented by the Popular Front from 1936–38) to religious, patriarchal and economic hierarchies. The party called for the union and mobilisation of all Catholics around a programme of social conservatism within a Christian society, and used a populist discourse which aimed to counteract the 'danger' represented by socialist and feminist movements, and which found real support among Catholic women and workers. But it is suggested that the party's populism was repeatedly eclipsed by its basic distrust of the masses, coupled with its obvious preference for an elite leadership which would provide the supervision and direction it believed the people needed, and its support drifted as other groups emerged to offer increased autonomy to their grass-roots members. The *Fédération républicaine* may have declined, but Passmore believes that Catholic nationalism itself remained a potentially viable political programme, needing only the right circumstances for execution.

These, he contends, dawned with the Vichy regime in 1940, for no party or programme better prefigured the National Revolution in its social conservatism than the *Fédération républicaine*.

Connections between the two can be readily identified, as revealed by Nicholas Atkin's assessment of Vichy and its appeal for French Catholics and their Church. Vichy's programme, encapsulated in its slogan *travail, famille, patrie*, echoed that of the *Fédération républicaine* in its attack on the secular Third Republic and the Left, and its emphasis on an ordered society, based on traditional and stable family, property and gender roles. A majority of bishops embraced this programme, acknowledging Vichy as the legitimate power and acclaiming Pétain as France's providential man, and most ordinary Catholics followed their lead. Vichy, it was thought, would enable a spiritual revival and a reconversion of France to Catholicism. The regime certainly seemed to value clerical support, at least in the early days, when some prominent Catholics held posts in the administration. By 1942, however, most had left office, and Catholic influence at Vichy declined. Atkin records that the Church did make some gains under Vichy, especially in respect of educational grants and family legislation, but it failed to obtain the ultimate concession to which it aspired since no definitive religious settlement was offered by Vichy. The Vichy regime would prove to be the Church's last potential opportunity for such an agreement in the twentieth century.

The *Fédération républicaine* and the Vichy regime stand as just two of many influential outlets for Right-wing Catholicism in the first half of the century, in a list which also includes Charles Maurras's *Action française*, Général de Castelnau's *Fédération nationale catholique* and Colonel de la Rocque's *Croix de Feu*.[5] On the other hand, as Michael Kelly points out, it is anachronistic to talk in terms of Catholic involvement on the Left at least in the first quarter of the century, although its ancestors date from that period, particularly in the shape of Marc Sangnier's *Sillon* movement. Kelly argues that the 1926 papal condemnation of *Action française* for subordinating religion to politics represents a defining moment in changing the political face of French Catholicism, since it diverted some away from their traditional Right-wing political affiliations towards an exploration of the Centre and the Left, and opened a period of questioning on the nature of Catholic political and social action. This process was accelerated, Kelly contends, by younger Catholics who were less influenced than their parents by fundamentalist teaching and awake as never before to democratic and socialist ideas. From the later 1920s, many joined the specialised youth movements established around this time within the official *Action catholique de la jeunesse française* (ACJF), which intended through its programme of *catholicisme intégral* to involve Catholics in public life outside the influence of *Action française* and its programme of *nationalisme intégral*.

In the 1930s, traditional Catholic teaching found it difficult to engage with the many weighty and crucial social, economic and political problems posed by the modern world, and the Catholic hierarchy remained overwhelmingly conservative. In the early 1930s, Catholics within groups such as *Esprit* treated both Right and Left with equal reserve in their search for a fresh response to the modern world. Drawing on the theory of the primacy of the spiritual, formulated in the 1920s by Jacques Maritain, they put forward an intellectual response which promoted a 'third' way, or a 'true' modernity, critical of what David Curtis calls the 'false' modernity of capitalist democracy or Communist totalitarianism, and defined as a *nouvelle chrétienté* – in other words, a reconquest of the modern world and the establishment of a new culture and civilisation of Christian inspiration. At the time considered to be avant-garde on an intellectual level, Curtis indicates that *nouvelle chrétienté* represented not so much a concrete programme as a spiritual aspiration and, as such, was limited in its potential for implementation. *Esprit* eventually declared openly for the Left, in a reluctant move which, Kelly argues, both entailed a contraction of its wider project and undermined its 'third-way' approach.

In the mid-1930s, *Esprit* was just one of several minority groupings with diverse aims and objectives which represented channels for Catholic Left-wing activity. Largely located outside the main parties, they shared a willingness to dialogue with the modern world, driven by their moral and spiritual concerns, coupled with an awareness of the dangers of censure by the Church for their activities. Among their number, Kelly identifies other intellectual reviews (such as *Terre nouvelle*), as well as groupings directly involved in electoral politics, including the Christian Democratic *Jeune république* (JR) (a Centre-Left party run by Sangnier of *Sillon* fame), widely regarded as the *frère ennemi* of the Christian Democratic *Parti démocrate populaire* (PDP) (a Centre-Right party), both discussed at length by Jean-Claude Delbreil in the context of his study of the evolution and impact of Christian Democracy in France. Delbreil holds, in agreement with

Curtis, that differences between the two parties were encapsulated in their response to the Popular Front. For, while the larger PDP endorsed a reformist social programme, it did not support the Popular Front; on the other hand, JR chose actively to defend Catholic interests in a Left-wing environment by forming part of the Popular Front majority, a landmark move in the history of relations between Catholics and the Left.

The Catholic discovery of Communist Marxism represents one of the most significant developments of the 1930s, as the chapter by David Curtis demonstrates, doubly important since it shaped post-1945 Catholic approaches to Marxism. The Roman Catholic Church's anti-Communism is well-documented, as exemplified by the May 1931 encyclical *Quadragesimo anno*, which denounced Communism as impious, unjust and barbarous. Most Catholics in 1930s France were diehard anti-Communists. They identified the Popular Front with Communism and were suspicious of the Communists' decision to court them with the offer of the *main tendue* in April 1936. This was actually accepted by very few Catholics but, according to Curtis, that fact is much less important in terms of the evolution of Catholicism in France than the nature of the refusal articulated. For a minority of Catholics, their response to the *main tendue* entailed what Curtis calls a 'positive' anti-Communism, which meant they could condemn Communism as a political system but nonetheless appreciate Communists as persons with fair social aspirations and objectives. This meant in practice that a minority of Catholics not only refused to denounce measures taken by the Popular Front (in which Communists were represented), on the grounds that these corresponded with aspects of Catholic social teaching, but were also even prepared to give the Popular Front their critical support in spite of Pius XI's further denunciation of Communism in the 1937 encyclical *Divini redemptoris*. Compelled to formulate a direct response to the challenge of Communist Marxism, Curtis shows that both Churchmen and lay Catholics played an important role in the 1930s analysis and critique of Marxism, as the quantity and quality of their writing on the theme testifies. While a definition and a rejection of Marxism as pseudo-religion held fast, it is clear that some were interested by Marxism as a potential stimulus to Catholic social thought, particularly in its interpretation of capitalism. Such evidence of intellectual engagement and discovery, Curtis contends, represented a remarkable *aggiornamento* for Catholics and their Church.

With the benefit of hindsight, it is persuasive to see the *main tendue* as the root of major long-term ideological developments in the relationship between Catholics and the Left, an argument developed and illustrated in Michael Kelly's complementary chapter. This shows that the 1930s shift towards a Catholic–Marxist dialogue was given fresh impetus after the Second World War, with many priests and theologians increasingly convinced that Christians had much to learn from Marxist ideas. Although slowed by the onset of the Cold War and by interventions from Rome, the 1970s finally saw the culmination of this encounter in the foundation of a Christian–Marxist movement, unthinkable fifty years before.

The post-war period was a time when many of the barriers between Catholics and the Left were lowered and a significant degree of social militancy was added to Catholicism. Kelly tracks this evolution from the early days of the Fourth Republic to the final years of the century, providing evidence of an increasing pluralism of approach to social issues and the espousal of a social agenda which highlighted common interests (such as the struggle against exploitation and oppression, as well as a call for justice and fraternity), and which prompted a substantial number of ordinary French Catholics to join a range of Left-inspired groupings. The Church's initial missionary and emancipatory aspirations are evidenced by the worker-priest movement at home, which aimed to reach out to the working class, and by Catholic action in mission fields abroad, principally the Third World. But, as Kelly records, it was the process of *aggiornamento* undertaken by Vatican II (1962–65) which – while proclaiming doctrinal continuity – opened up Catholic thinking to an unprecedented degree in many areas of activity. In respect of the Church's internal practices, audible changes to liturgy and ceremony were combined with visible changes to religious dress and life in a modernisation process welcomed by many, but disapproved of by others. A new spirit of dialogue and respect was employed in the Church's relations with other faiths and non-believers, and led to its participation in a range of joint committees which, within France, took shape particularly in the form of Catholic–Protestant and Catholic–Muslim groups. And, in its response to the complex social and economic issues of the modern world, the Church focused on a rejection of discrimination and a defence of the disadvantaged, illustrative of an acceptance of values normally associated with the Left.

In her chapter on immigration, integration and the French Catholic Church, the volume editor focuses on one effective example of the Church's defence of the disadvantaged through a study of its espousal of a human rights policy in its response to the immigration question. The Church's adoption of the universal Declaration of Human Rights in 1948 made it a late but keen convert to a cause in process since 1789. Largely equipped to cope with France's Catholic immigrants on the basis of religious similarity, the Church also revealed itself concerned to address the question of non-Catholic (principally Muslim) immigrants – for the most part, settled families unable to envisage life elsewhere, many of whom possess French nationality. The Church, it seems, has accepted the fact that the days when being French meant being white, Catholic and European are long gone. It regards exclusion as the enemy, and contends that humanitarian concerns set in a context of equality outweigh differ- ence in the quest for integration. Such statements testify to the Church's evolution in terms of its social militancy, and examples abound of its interventions on behalf of France's 'other' commun- ities as governments of both Right and Left adopted increasingly hardline immigration policies.

The Church's involvement in the immigration issue, coupled with its action on behalf of other socially disadvantaged groups (for example, the poor, the unemployed and the homeless) stand, then, as evidence of an opening-up to the Left in the later years of the twentieth century. But, in contrast, the Church also retained an inflexible discourse on other social questions, notably those relating to sexual health and reproduction, male–female relationships and matters of bioethical concern. Some Catholics, of course, accepted and followed the Church's dictates on these as on other matters. But, over the years, its stance alienated many Catholics who acknow- ledged the Church's involvement in wider social issues but who did not appreciate what was seen as its dogmatic and often insensitive intervention in matters considered to relate to personal morality. Indeed, in his assessment of modern Catholic identity, Colin Roberts indicates that, after the condemnation of artificial birth control and abortion in *Humanae vitae* (1968), many younger Catholics began to modify their identification with both institution and faith and to relativise the Church's teachings on these issues, claiming greater freedom to decide for themselves what was morally right and wrong in different situations.

Consideration of the Church's stance on sexual issues also features in Evelyne Diébolt's overview of women and the French Catholic Church, which contends that Church dictates caused many younger Catholic women – less conservative in social and political terms than ever before – to leave the Church from the 1960s. This was clearly a matter of some consequence for an institution which, as revealed by Diébolt's broader exploration of her theme, was so heavily dependent on women for its grass-roots operation and following. The twentieth century saw significant structural changes to society which revolutionised women's lives and choices, and offered new opportunities for greater participation and responsibility in public life. In religious life, Catholic women had long played a significant role as parishioners and nuns, forming the greater part of the conservative mass within the Church. Diébolt details how that role expanded over the century as women became increasingly involved in Church activities as lay workers, catechism teachers, members of Catholic associations and charity and youth workers. As such, they represented the majority of salaried and voluntary workers within the institution. Few would dispute that women form the backbone of the Church and contribute massively to its organisation and operation, although the question of function and responsibility has become a source of difficulty for some women in their relationship with the male hierarchy. After Vatican II, in particular, many women actively committed to the Church aspired to greater levels of institutional responsibility and involvement, only to be disappointed by an ongoing lack of progress on this point.

In the later years of the century, lay workers – whether male or female – were accorded more extensive pastoral responsibilities which permitted wider participation in Church life and ceremony, a move generally welcomed by French Catholics. Women and married men, however, remained barred from the priesthood. Greater reliance on the laity, coupled with the development of the role of deacons (open to married men), reflected an attempt to respond to the *crise des vocations* affecting the Catholic Church, since in France, as elsewhere, fewer young men were attracted to the priesthood, while fewer men and women together were drawn to monastic life. Such internal institutional decline went hand in hand with a wider decline in the appeal of institutional Catholicism. Yves-Marie Hilaire's survey of religious sociology in France confirms that, by the end of the century, traditional Catholic observance had fallen significantly and numerous parishes were obsolete. Hilaire argues persuasively in terms of the ebb and flow of religious practice within an overall general decline, rather than in terms of a continuous linear decline, and demonstrates that the level of religious practice across the century (and, indeed, further back) was influenced by a range of factors, including not only the common variables of gender, age and geographical location, but also various socio-historical influences such as the implantation of an increasingly dominant secular climate or specific occurrences such as the events and aftermath of May 1968. The case study of religious belief and practice in the Breton parish of Limerzel summarised by Roberts complements and corroborates Hilaire's conclusions, since it delineates the advance of secular ideas in a previously staunchly Catholic parish and highlights the extent to which younger people especially deserted the Church and adopted a more personal and private relationship with religion. Indifference towards Church and institutional religious practice does not, of course, necessarily mean a loss of faith. As Roberts demonstrates, in the later years of the century a good number of Catholics began to seek and find different ways of being Catholic, illustrative not only of the declining social and moral influence of the Church but also of the fragmentation of Catholic identity in the modern secular age. Some chose to express their faith privately, requiring no fixed external outlet in order to live as Catholics. Others joined one of the many small but fervently committed progressive and charismatic groups which sprang up in France after Vatican II, and which emphasised the subjective experience of the individual believer rather than formal, traditional practice.

These new and different Catholic identities were met with moves to reaffirm traditional identity. Roberts details the assertive and conservative Catholic backlash which emerged with the papacy of John Paul II, and which was spearheaded in France by the Archbishop of Paris, Cardinal Lustiger. The theme is echoed by Kelly, who notes a range of papal interventions against the Catholic Left in France – including sympathisers with Marxism and Liberation Theology – and highlights the systematic appointment of conservative prelates who, by the end of the century, had largely replaced the supporters of Vatican II. But Roberts indicates that even the conservatism of John Paul II was insufficient for the minority breakaway integrist current in France, the *Fraternité Saint-Pie X*, set up by the late Marcel Lefebvre in reaction to the reforms of Vatican

II and its compromises with secular principles, demanding instead the restoration of a specifically Catholic social order and a return to traditional Catholic doctrine.

These different groups stand as evidence of what Roberts calls the 'blurring' of Catholic identity at the end of the twentieth century. Within France, Catholicism no longer represents a national focus, although it still operates as a major component of national identity. Secularism has not eradicated either faith or religious culture, but has instead created a climate in which multiple faiths – Christian and non-Christian – may function. Twenty-first-century French Catholicism is as fragmented as the nation's diversified religious framework. Being Catholic in contemporary France no longer means the espousal of a particular political or social agenda, or regular and traditional religious practice, or even strict adherence to the dictates of the Church. Modern French Catholicism has many mansions, as this volume illustrates.

NOTES

1. The term 'guerre des deux France' is attributed to and discussed at length by Émile Poulat in *Liberté, laïcité. La Guerre des deux France et le principe de modernité* (Paris: Cujas–Cerf, 1988).

2. *Le Monde*, 12 December 1995, p. 8.

3. Danièle Sallenave, 'L'autre enterrement', *Le Monde*, 19 January 1996, p. 5.

4. *Le Monde*, 20 September 1996, p. 1.

5. Both Michael Kelly and Kevin Passmore recognise the appeal of these groups to Right-wing Catholics (see Chapters 3 and 7).

1

La laïcité en France au vingtième siècle

Émile Poulat

Laïcité: comment parler de ce qui se dit avec un mot français intraduisible en anglais et, plus généralement dans toutes les langues du monde, à l'exception des langues latines (et du turc) pour lesquelles suffit une simple transcription? Il existe heureusement un précédent: comment parler aux Français de l'*humour* britannique? Pourtant, à défaut du mot, la réalité qu'il recouvre est loin d'être étrangère aux autres pays en notre siècle. Il suffit de décomposer cette réalité en ses ingrédients: un esprit national, une évolution sociale, une forme institutionnelle.

DU LAÏC AU LAÏQUE

Laïc, adjectif ou substantif, est un très vieux mot de culture chrétienne un terme panchrétien, si l'on peut dire – en opposition au *clerc*, l'un et l'autre d'origine grecque.[1] Il a fallu attendre le dix-neuvième siècle pour que laïc se laïcise, opposant cette fois le *laïque* (une graphie imaginée pour bien marquer la distinction nouvelle) et le *clérical*: celui qui se réclame des Lumières et celui qui les condamne au nom de l'Église.

Tout au long des deux siècles écoulés, on assistera donc à ce que beaucoup appelèrent 'la guerre des deux France'.[2] La victoire était acquise au camp de la raison, de la liberté et du progrès, à la veille de la Grande Guerre, que le mot abstrait *laïcité* était encore considéré par les 'laïques' comme un néologisme: preuve qu'il n'était nécessaire ni à l'esprit nouveau, ni à l'évolution politique pour asseoir l'idéal qu'il désignait. En revanche, il peut devenir un leurre idéologique dont l'évocation ou l'invocation dissimule la réalité sociale et institutionnelle. Même en France, combien sont aujourd'hui en mesure de parler d'elle avec pertinence?[3]

Il y a bien eu en France un *esprit laïque* fort, tout comme un *esprit républicain*,[4] avec deux points d'ancrage: l'*Encyclopédie* et la Révolution. Aujourd'hui, en vérité, nous sommes tous laïques, même les catholiques, et tous républicains, hors quelques groupes royalistes ou traditionalistes. C'est pourquoi la bataille pour la laïcité ne fait plus recette. Esprits laïques et esprits religieux se sont rapprochés par la force d'une situation – d'un état de culture – que tous acceptent. Le contentieux demeure, sur des points mineurs, mais la guerre est finie. Ce qui les mobilise, parfois côte à côte, ce sont les graves problèmes de société qui ont surgi: échec scolaire, violence urbaine, anomie sociale, chômage, exclusion, drogue, sida; autrement dit, les jeunes, les vieux et les inactifs.

On n'en conclura pas que la laïcité est maintenant dépassée, même si l'état d'esprit qu'elle connote s'est profondément modifié. Cette modification, c'est précisément l'œuvre accomplie par ce qui a constitué une véritable *révolution laïque*. On voit mal comment elle aurait pu se faire par consentement mutuel et contrat social. Cette révolution passait par une évolution des mentalités qui ne pouvait se faire sans perturbation, par des étapes dont les acteurs ignoraient tout. Elle a débouché sur un équilibre que personne – pour ou contre – n'avait ni prévu ni voulu.

L'esprit national, ce sont les particularités historiques qui dessinent cette transformation. L'évolution sociale, c'est ce processus de *sécularisation* qui accompagne la *modernité* et qui caractérise le développement des pays occidentaux. La forme institutionnelle, c'est la figure juridique et administrative prise en France par l'équilibre auquel nous sommes parvenus.

La laïcité française est souvent définie comme *neutralité* ou indifférence de l'État à l'égard des religions; ou encore (en référence à la loi de 1905) par la *séparation* des Églises et de l'État. Ces deux définitions, malgré les autorités qui les appuient, sont insuffisantes, superficielles ou en partie erronées. Ce sont des interprétations a priori que n'intéressent guère la connaissance de dossiers. Le fait premier, pour nous tous, est bien qu'aux termes des constitutions de 1946 (Quatrième République) et de 1958 (Cinquième République), la France est une 'République laïque', sans que cette assertion soit autrement définie et alors que les constituants qui l'ont votée ne lui donnaient pas tous le même sens.

Notre laïcité ne se réduit ni aux lois qui la règlent, ni aux idéaux qui la soutiennent. Elle ne se comprend que par la grande transformation qui, sous des noms divers et par des voies diverses, a fait passer l'Occident chrétien d'un état préchrétien à un âge post-chrétien.[5] La démonstration de Fustel de Coulanges qui avait placé la religion au fondement de la cité antique ne valait pas seulement pour la Grèce. La puissance de Rome avait logiquement débouché sur le culte impérial, qui n'excluait pas culte locaux ou religions privées. Puis était venu ce bref moment d'équilibre, l'édit de Milan (313), qui laissait à chacun le choix de son Dieu et le Dieu de son choix. Lui succéda l'édit de Thessalonique (380), qui établissait le christianisme religion d'État.

DE LA TOLÉRANCE À LA LIBERTÉ

La paix de religion d'Augsbourg (1555) s'inscrit dans le prolong-ement de cette histoire. Ce qui est nouveau, ce n'est pas le principe qu'elle rappelle – *cujus regio ejus religio* – et que Montaigne formulait à sa manière,[6] mais le droit d'en jouir reconnu aux dissidents luthériens. C'est l'apprentissage de la coexistence confessionnelle, la tolérance civile voisinant avec l'intolérance religieuse: l'orthodoxie s'inscrit en faux contre l'hérésie, mais, selon Pascal, 'vérité en-deçà des Pyrénées, erreur au-delà'. Un esprit nouveau se forme, dans le sillage des Politiques (Michel de L'Hospital), pour qui 'l'excommunié ne cesse pas d'être citoyen', et de Montaigne s'attachant à penser 'd'une manière laïque, non cléricale, mais religieuse toujours'.[7]

Cette *laïcisation* de la politique, qu'elle soit fondée sur les ambi-tions du pouvoir monarchique ou, comme ici, sur le souci de la paix intérieure, n'entame pas, en France, le *principe de catholicité* – 'une foi, une loi, un roi' – dont les légistes font la première des 'lois fondamentales' du royaume. Ainsi s'explique la conduite d'Henri IV: il abjure le protestantisme pour accéder au trône (1593), puis proclame l'Édit de Nantes en faveur des protestants (1598). Ce principe tient en deux règles majeures: le catholicisme est seule religion publique admise en France (Louis XIV fermera la paren-thèse d'Henri IV en 1685); sa doctrine et sa discipline y sont reçues comme lois civiles.[8]

La Révolution française mettra bas cet édifice: c'est à elle qu'on doit véritablement le *principe de laïcité* qui nous régit, alors même qu'elle ignorait le mot. On peut dire que celui-ci découle de la *Déclaration des droits de l'homme et du citoyen* (1789) et qu'il faudra plus d'un siècle pour expliciter ses prémisses. On peut le formuler ainsi: liberté publique de conscience et d'expression pour tous sans exception. Confiance est faite aux individus pour que l'exercice de leurs libertés concoure au 'bonheur commun', au lieu de se retourner contre l'ordre public et la vie sociale. Un pari audacieux, mais aussi un débat permanent sur ses exigences, étant précisé d'entrée de jeu que 'la liberté consiste à pouvoir faire tout ce qui ne nuit pas à autrui'. Cette liberté n'est pas anarchique: elle a 'pour principe la nature, pour règle la justice, pour sauvegarde la loi'.

Toutes les opinions, 'mêmes religieuses', sont libres de s'exprimer publiquement: en 1789, cela concernait celles qui s'écartaient de l'orthodoxie catholique; aujourd'hui, c'est une garantie offerte contre tout laïcisme ou athéisme d'État. Mais, en toute hypothèse, la Déclaration de 1789 ne visait que de libertés individuelles: elle ne comportait ni liberté de religion, ni liberté d'association. Leur pleine reconnaissance sera longue à s'imposer: 1905 pour la première, 1901 pour la seconde.

Pour Bonaparte, les leçons de l'expérience révolutionnaire étaient claires: une société ne peut vivre sans religion. Sans revenir à l'Ancien Régime et à son principe de catholicité, il conçut donc un régime public des cultes reconnus: catholique (grâce à un concordat avec le pape Pie VII en 1801), luthérien, réformée, puis israélite. La liberté de conscience n'était pas remise en cause et tous en bénéficiaient; en revanche, la liberté de religion était limitée dans son exercice public aux quatre confessions agréées, qui jouissaient d'un statut de droit public. Napoléon III étendit ce statut à l'islam en Algérie.

CINQ PARADOXES

Cette histoire débouche sur quelques paradoxes qui demandent éclaircissement.

1. En un sens, ce statut 'enchaînait' les Églises à l'État, dans la pure tradition régalienne (faut-il dire gallicane ou joséphiste?). Certains laïques s'en réjouissaient et tenaient au concordat. Certains catholiques ou réformés le déploraient et pensaient à Israël en Égypte ou à Babylone. Les deux camps étaient divisés sur l'intérêt de ce régime dit concordataire. L'idée de séparation finit par l'emporter chez les laïques. A Rome, le pape Pie X en condamna le principe, les conditions et les modalités. En 1924, le pape Pie XI accepta un *modus vivendi* qui préservait les droits des évêques et que le temps a consacré. L'Église catholique en France y a gagné une liberté cher payée dont elle goûte aujourd'hui les avantages. La guerre est finie, même si le contentieux n'est pas vidé. La nature de celui-ci l'interdit sur le fond: il ne reste que des dossiers mineurs.

2. En 1793, la Convention avait établi la liberté de l'enseignement. Napoléon la supprima et créa l'Université impériale, détentrice du monopole. L'Église catholique fut au premier rang pour reconquérir cette liberté: 1833 (loi Guizot) pour le primaire, 1850 (loi Falloux) pour le secondaire, 1875 pour le supérieur. Liberté de religion, liberté d'enseignement, le parallélisme de l'expression et la dissymétrie de comportement ne doivent pas abuser. L'Église catholique tient comme à la prunelle de ses yeux à tout ce qui touche la *libertas Ecclesiae*, en matière d'enseignement comme en matière de culte. Le concordat avait établi le culte comme un service public. La République décida de laïciser l'ensemble des services publics. Il était impensable de laïciser les cultes: on ne pouvait que les privatiser, les faire passer du droit public au droit privé. A l'inverse, l'enseignement confessionnel, dit libre, était né privé. Il ne pouvait être concerné par la séparation, et la loi de 1905 n'en parle pas. Quant à l'enseignement, sa 'séparation' remontait aux lois scolaires de 1881–86. Et pourtant, de manière imprévisible, on assiste depuis la loi Debré (1959) à un véritable renversement de situation: l'enseignement privé associé par contrat au service public de l'éducation nationale.

On dira la même chose des congrégations religieuses, régies par la loi de 1901 sur les associations, mais avec un statut vexatoire (Titre III), aboli en 1942. Soumises à autorisation, elles restaient de droit privé; dispensées aujourd'hui d'autorisation, elles peuvent bénéficier de la reconnaissance légale (équivalent de la reconnaissance d'utilité publique).

3. Le principe de catholicité était exclusif: qui n'est pas catholique n'a pas de droits civils. Le principe de laïcité est inclusif: les libertés civiles sont un droit de nature reconnu à tout homme. Il a donc fallu des convictions laïques pour vaincre les résistances catholiques à l'ordre nouveau. En revanche, une fois cet ordre instauré, convictions catholiques et convictions laïques sont égales en droit, également admises au débat public et au forum démocratique. Un ajustement qui ne va pas sans un difficile apprentissage de part et d'autre.

4. La loi de 1905 a reçu un titre qui prête à malentendu: 'loi concernant la séparation des Églises et de l'État'. Elle eût gagné à s'intituler 'loi sur le nouveau régime des cultes' ou 'loi sur la privatisation des établissements publics du culte'. On y eût économisé une fausse querelle autour du mot *séparation*, malsonnant pour la pensée catholique qui préfère, selon la formule de Jacques Maritain, 'distinguer pour unir'. On fût surtout resté plus près de la réalité, qui oblige à nuancer sérieusement les prétentions de la loi. Pour des raisons historiques, validées politiquement, celle-ci ne s'applique pas aux trois départements d'Alsace et Moselle (sous juridiction allemande en 1905), dont le statut local dérive du régime concordataire. Elle ne s'applique pas davantage en Guyane (où tous les cultes sont libres, mais où le catholicisme jouit d'une situation privilégiée), ni dans les territoires d'outre-mer (TOM): leur statut local, particulier, ne relève ni du concordat ni de la séparation.

Le régime général lui-même, tel qu'il est institué et pratiqué, oblige à relativiser l'idée qu'on peut se faire de la séparation. Au nom de la liberté de conscience, des aumôniers publics assurent le service du culte dans les hôpitaux, les hospices, les prisons et les lycées,[9] ainsi qu'aux armées.[10] Au nom de l'inaliénabilité du domaine public, les édifices du culte, nationalisés en 1790 et mis à la disposition du clergé en 1802, sont demeurés en 1905 propriété de l'État ou des communes, à charge pour eux de les entretenir. Par attention pour le particularisme alsacien, l'État entretient à Strasbourg deux facultés de théologie (catholique et protestante), sans lien direct avec le concordat de 1801. On multiplierait les exemples, dont la leçon est claire: en régime de séparation, la liberté de religion coûte cher à la République laïque sans qu'elle s'en offusque.

5. On se souvient de Lamennais et de son *Essai sur l'indifférence en matière de religion* (1817–23), dirigé contre le régime concordataire qui mettait tous les cultes sur pied d'égalité, du moins les quatre cultes reconnus. Il parlerait aujourd'hui de neutralité, une notion qui est elle aussi à relativiser, doublement. En premier lieu parce qu'aux termes mêmes de la loi de 1905, article premier, 'la République assure la liberté de conscience' et 'garantit le libre exercice des cultes'. A la différence de la Belgique et de l'Allemagne, les cultes sont reconnus comme une réalité spécifique de droit privé: leur pratique ne se réduit pas à un simple droit de réunion et une 'conception du monde' ne suffit pas à faire un culte. En second lieu, la pratique administrative nuance sérieusement l'égalité théorique des cultes, sur la base de trois critères: l'enracinement historique, la dimension universelle, l'utilité sociale. En clair, la République préfère les grandes Églises aux groupuscules sectaires.

La laïcité française est à la fois un principe général, un cadre institutionnel et une pratique administrative. La réalité évolue, le principe demeure et rien n'annonce sa fin prochaine. Aujourd'hui, deux faits nouveaux s'imposent à la fois à la République laïque et aux Églises chrétiennes: d'une part, la montée de l'islam, désormais deuxième religion en France; d'autre part, la laïcisation de la vie privée après la laïcisation de la vie publique. Devant l'islam, la difficulté ne tient ni à la laïcité, suffisamment souple, ni aux Églises, courageusement présentes, mais aux réflexes isolationnistes de la société française. La laïcisation de la vie privée pourrait poser des problèmes plus redoutables aux Églises et, à terme, à la République: elle entraîne en effet un effacement de la *morale publique* – 'la morale de nos pères', disait Jules Ferry, celle qui se référait au Décalogue – qui constituait un véritable contrat social, le pacte moral que la guerre des deux France avait toujours respecté.

NOTES

1. On relèvera ici la distinction essentielle entre *laos* et *démos*.

2. Émile Poulat, *Liberté, laïcité. La Guerre des deux France et le principe de modernité* (Paris: Cujas–Cerf, 1988).

3. Jean Boussinesq, *La Laïcité française. Mémento juridique* (Paris: Seuil, 1994).

4. Jacques Viard, éd., *L'Esprit républicain* (Paris: Klincksieck, 1972).

5. Émile Poulat, *L'Ère postchrétienne. Un monde sorti de Dieu* (Paris: Flammarion, 1994).

6. Frappé par 'l'empire de la coutume', Montaigne écrit en 1588 que 'nous sommes chrétiens au même titre que nous sommes ou périgourdins ou allemands' (*Essais*, Livre I, ch. 23, et Livre II, ch. 12, 'Apologie de Raymond Sebond').

7. Montaigne, *Essais*, Livre I, ch. 56. Autrement dit des écrits 'purement humains et philosophiques sans mélange de théologie', contrairement aux théologiens qui 'écrivent trop humainement' (ibid.).

8. La clause française de *réception* visait à récuser tout droit pontifical d'ingérence. Elle était épaulée par les 'libertés de l'Église gallicane' que symbolisa la

Déclaration dite des Quatre articles (1682), devenue loi française par édit royal, confirmée par décret impérial en 1802, demeurée en vigueur jusqu'en 1905.

9. En principe les lycées accueillant des internes. Il s'agit de lieux fermés, où manque la liberté de circulation.

10. L'aumônerie militaire catholique a été érigée, par accord bilatéral, en diocèse aux armées, dirigée par un évêque ayant rang de colonel.

2

Antisémitisme des catholiques au vingtième siècle: de la revendication au refus

Danielle Delmaire

A la fin du dix-neuvième siècle, les catholiques quasi unanimement se proclamaient antisémites et leur presse dénonçait les crimes rituels, la filouterie et la puissance économique des juifs. A la fin du vingtième siècle, ces croyances ne sont partagées que par une infime minorité de catholiques irréductiblement antisémites. Entre les deux, le cataclysme de la Shoah a renversé bien des préjugés: l'antisémitisme puis l'antijudaïsme.

BILAN DE L'AFFAIRE DREYFUS: LA REVENDICATION VIOLENTE PUIS L'OUBLI

Une carte photographique circulant peu de temps après l'affaire Dreyfus représente un prêtre absorbé par la lecture du journal *La Libre Parole*,[1] la feuille antisémite d'Édouard Drumont, l'auteur de *La France juive*. Comme un grand nombre de ses confrères, il y trouve sa ration d'antisémitisme mais il aurait pu aussi s'abreuver à d'autres sources: *La Croix*, des Assomptionnistes, qui se vante d'être 'le journal le plus antijuif de France',[2] ou les *Croix* régionales[3] et autre presse catholique, diocésaine ou non, qui vit assez bien. Ce prêtre est représentatif d'un grand nombre d'ecclésiastiques. Ainsi lorsqu'en 1895, *La Libre Parole* lança un concours sur la question juive, cent cinquante manuscrits lui furent envoyés et le jury distingua huit auteurs parmi lesquels se trouvaient quatre prêtres: l'abbé Jacquet et Mgr Tilloy, pronotaire apostolique et docteur en théologie, se partageaient le premier prix.[4]

Les prêtres étaient, dans leur passion antisémite, largement soutenus par leur hiérarchie; non pas par le pape Léon XIII qui gardait ses distances mais par les évêques et les théologiens. A Lille, par exemple, l'Université catholique rassemblait un aréopage d'enseignants distingués dans les lettres, le droit ou la théologie, tous affichaient leur antisémitisme.[5] A Laon, 'l'évêque laisse annoncer que les auditeurs de M. Brunetière trouveront asile dans une salle dépendant du petit séminaire' alors que ce conférencier anti-dreyfusard s'était vu refuser les locaux de la municipalité.[6] Les catholiques sociaux et démocrates chrétiens n'étaient guère plus tendres envers les juifs. La plupart dénonçait les juifs mauvais patrons qui pressuraient les ouvriers à la différence des catholiques, patrons sociaux, soucieux du bien-être de leurs employés.[7]

L'immense majorité des catholiques suivait le clergé. On peut mesurer les effets néfastes de cet 'enseignement du mépris'[8] en lisant les états d'âme des participants à la souscription en faveur de la veuve de Henry, lancée par *La Libre Parole* en décembre 1898 (Henry avait contrefait de documents afin de prouver la culpabilité de Dreyfus).[9] Certes, seulement quatre cents ecclésiastiques, soit 3,1% des souscripteurs (mais le clergé catholique ne représentait que 0,2% de la population active),[10] ont répondu à cette souscription de la haine mais le commentaire ajouté à l'obole en dit long sur l'antisémitisme: 'pour une descente de lit de peau de youpins, afin de les piétiner matin et soir' ou 'un petit curé poitevin qui chanterait avec plaisir le Requiem du dernier des youpins'[11] ou 'un curé de campagne qui fait les vœux les plus ardents pour l'extermination des deux ennemis de la France: le Juif et le Franc-Maçon', ou encore 'un étudiant en médecine démocrate chrétien antisémite'. Des catholiques notoires versèrent dans les mêmes excès, le député Albert de Mun, des enseignants et des étudiants d'universités catholiques, des élèves d'écoles ou de patronages catholiques, des rédacteurs ou des lecteurs des *Croix* régionales défendaient la veuve Henry en vomissant du juif et l'appartenance au catholicisme était souvent revendiquée. Des ligues antisémites comptaient des catholiques parmi leurs adhérents: *Action française* et la *Ligue antisémitique* recrutaient abondamment chez les étudiants catholiques. Les cercles de la jeunesse catholique diffusaient les *Croix* qui colportaient les pires ragots antisémites.

Au milieu de ce déferlement de sottises une poignée de catholiques honnêtes et lucides refusaient l'aveuglement. Un *Comité catholique pour la défense du droit* naquit, en février 1899, à l'initiative de Paul Viollet; il ne rassembla jamais plus de cent dix-huit adhérents dans tout le pays. Ils étaient peu connus, isolés et suspects au point que le prélat qui renseigna Léon Chaine sur l'existence de ce comité préféra garder l'anonymat![12] Des prêtres ont payé chèrement leur adhésion au dreyfusisme: le courageux abbé Pichot perdit son poste de professeur de mathématiques et l'abbé Birot, d'Albi, vit sa carrière ralentie.[13] Péguy réunit autour de lui un cercle de dreyfusards, peu de catholiques le fréquentaient.

Après l'affaire Dreyfus, la majorité des catholiques de France abordèrent le vingtième siècle avec des sentiments copieusement antijuifs qu'ils revendiquaient bruyamment. Toutefois, cette affaire fut comme un point d'orgue dans cette longue campagne antisémite qui affligea la France durant le dernier quart du dix-neuvième siècle. En effet, auparavant diverses affaires avaient provoqué de vigour-euses manifestations d'antisémitisme auxquelles les catholiques avaient largement participé (le krach de l'Union Générale, le boulangisme, le scandale de Panama, les duels des années 1892–93) mais, au lende-main de la grâce présidentielle qui libéra Dreyfus, les catholiques lâchèrent la cible juive et se rassemblèrent pour un autre combat: l'anticléricalisme des radicaux qui occupaient désormais le pouvoir. L'antisémitisme, sans vraiment disparaître, cessa de nourrir la hargne des catholiques. La réhabilitation du capitaine, obtenue juste après la douloureuse séparation des Églises et de l'État, suscita peu de réactions antisémites chez les catholiques, puis l'ampleur des problèmes sociaux qui précédèrent la guerre fit remiser l'antisémitisme.

La Grande Guerre fut l'occasion pour les juifs de France de manifester pleinement leur 'amour sacré de la patrie'.[14] Dans un grand élan de patriotisme, les juifs originaires d'Alsace ou de Lorraine étaient prêts à la revanche et les juifs récemment immigrés n'hésitèrent pas à voler au secours de la mère patrie adoptive.[15] Dans les tranchées, leurs actes de bravoure impressionnaient favorable-ment les plus antisémites et la souffrance ou le sacrifice tissaient de réels liens d'amitié. L'intimité de la mort, rencontrée quotidienne-ment, renforçait les sentiments religieux du poilu quelle qu'était sa religion et ainsi, face au danger et dans l'enfer des combats, les cultes se mêlaient sans perturber les consciences. Même un Maurice Barrès, si férocement antidreyfusard par le passé, s'en émerveillait et lorsqu'il incluait les israélites dans *Les diverses familles spirituelles de la France*, il se justifiait en citant des lettres de soldats juifs:

> Je suis juif, sincèrement croyant et attaché à ma religion. Chaque fois que je voyais qu'il fallait aller à la mort je pensais à 'Lui', et mon devoir m'appar-aissait naturel, sans mérite. Il m'est arrivé, voulant me recueillir, d'aller m'agenouiller dans une église et je ne crois pas avoir commis un sacrilège.[16]

Et il ne manqua pas de raconter la mort du rabbin Abraham Bloch (fin août 1914):

> Les brancardiers emportent, au milieu des flammes et des éclatements, les cent cinquante blessés. L'un de ceux-ci, frappé à mort, réclame un crucifix. Il le demande à M. Abraham Bloch, l'aumônier israélite qu'il prend pour l'aumônier catholique. M. Bloch s'empresse; il cherche, il trouve, il apporte au mourant le symbole de la foi des chrétiens. Et quelques pas plus loin, un obus le frappe lui-même. Il expire aux bras de l'aumônier catholique, le Père Jamin, jésuite, de qui le témoignage établit cette scène.[17]

Dès octobre 1914 *L'Action française* et *La Croix* avaient oublié leur acrimonie antisémite pour honorer l'abnégation et la bravoure d'un rabbin. L'Union sacrée, expression politique d'abord, prit pleinement son sens religieux sur les champs de bataille: des cérémonies associant tous les cultes se déroulèrent pendant la guerre.[18] En ces mois de souffrance et de mort, les passions 'anti' tombèrent: antisémitisme et anticléricalisme furent gommés.

ENTRE LES DEUX GUERRES: RÉSURGENCE DE L'ANTISÉMITISME MAIS PREMIERS DIALOGUES

Au lendemain de la guerre, certains catholiques irréductibles dans leur antisémitisme oublièrent rapidement cette fraternité religieuse née au front.

Dès 1920, *Les Protocoles des sages de Sion* se diffusèrent aisément dans les milieux catholiques; *Action française*, encore solidement soutenue par des ecclésiastiques, retrouva ses accents antisémites et Mgr Jouin, aidé de l'abbé Boulin, s'activa à nouveau pour sa *Revue internationale des sociétés secrètes* (RISS).[19] Les juifs redevinrent les fauteurs de troubles. Pour Maurras, la Révolution russe comme la SDN des Américains étaient une œuvre néfaste des juifs. Désormais la lutte contre le bolchevisme athée passait par l'antisémitisme, ainsi *Le Bloc catholique* afficha nettement son programme en devenant *Le Bloc antirévolutionnaire* en 1927. Diverses publications régionales prenaient le relais comme *Les Cahiers de l'Ordre*, fondés par l'abbé Duperron avec Jean Drault, qui déjà affutait sa plume contre Dreyfus, Henry Coston et Xavier Vallat. Dans les années trente, la xénophobie s'amplifia sur fond de crise (économique, scandales politiques) et l'antisémitisme s'en trouva fortifié. Des intellectuels catholiques se mirent au service de cette haine: tel Bernanos qui ne quitta *Action française* qu'en 1932, puis attiré par Maritain et Bidault, démocrate chrétien, il conserva un antisémitisme d'une remarquable constance;[20] tel encore Georges Blond qui écrivait dans *Je suis partout*, Henri Ghéon, Henri Massis, Marcel Jouhandeau, Pierre Gaxotte ou Henry Bordeaux. L'avènement du Front Populaire et le gouvernement Blum intensifièrent la rancœur d'hommes politiques catholiques comme Darquier de Pellepoix ou Xavier Vallat, député de l'Ardèche, qui déplorait à l'Assemblée que son vieux pays gaulois fût dirigé par un talmudiste. A la veille de la Seconde Guerre mondiale, des catholiques animaient des conférences pour dénoncer l'emprise des juifs sur la France.[21]

Mais ces passions vécurent plus difficilement qu'avant la Grande Guerre: la quasi unanimité des catholiques communiant dans l'antisémitisme était rompue et *La Libre Parole* ne trouvant plus suffisamment de lecteurs disparut en 1924. La poignée de catholiques à l'écoute du judaïsme était devenue une brassée.

L'amitié née dans la solidarité des tranchées ne déserta pas tous les cœurs sitôt la paix signée. Les cérémonies du souvenir en l'honneur des disparus rassemblaient souvent les représentants des trois cultes (catholique, protestant et juif) permettant ainsi de mieux se connaître et ceci même encore dans la décennie 1930.[22] Les catholiques qui se retrouvaient autour du Général de Castelnau dans la *Fédération nationale catholique* (FNC) ne manifestaient que rarement des sentiments antisémites. Le groupe DRAC (*Droits du religieux ancien combattant*) refusait l'exclusive et admettait dans ses rangs des juifs et des protestants. Ainsi les rabbins Kaplan de Paris ou Poliakoff de Lille répondaient aux invitations de cette ligue où ils côtoyaient le père Dieux ou le pasteur Durrleman.[23] *L'Union des prêtres anciens combattants* et d'autres ligues féminines accueillaient aussi des conférenciers juifs. Ces ligues, il est vrai, voulaient avant tout défendre les intérêts religieux des anciens combattants contre les radicaux anticléricaux. Voilà pourquoi elles restaient imperméables à une quelconque discrimination religieuse; par contre, elles se montraient réceptives au nationalisme.

A partir de 1925–26, après l'expérience d'un gouvernement radical, un certain nombre d'intellectuels catholiques, souvent des religieux, commencèrent à percevoir le judaïsme moins négativement. Dès 1923, dom Donatien de Bruyne, bénédictin de l'abbaye de Maredsous accueillait favorablement l'*Anthologie juive* d'Edmond Fleg et nourrissait l'espoir qu'un tel ouvrage permettrait de mieux appréhender le judaïsme.[24] Comprendre cette religion-mère, telle était la première démarche de ces catholiques précurseurs du rapprochement judéo-chrétien. Et même *La Croix*, au passé terriblement antisémite, révisa sa position par rapport aux juifs grâce à l'influence du père Merklen qui entra au journal en 1927.[25] D'autres publications, comme *La Vie catholique* ou *L'Aube*, dénoncèrent la persécution des juifs en Allemagne. Le père Devaux de Notre-Dame de Sion, ordre qui se consacrait depuis près d'un siècle à la conversion des juifs, pensait sincèrement qu'une meilleure connaissance des juifs devait faciliter sa tâche. La fin semble de nos jours peu recevable mais le moyen, à savoir une véritable rencontre du judaïsme, marquait déjà un immense pas vers un respect des ennemis d'hier. Le jésuite Bonsirven alla jusqu'à affirmer qu'il fallait comprendre le Nouveau Testament à la lumière de l'Ancien. Le père Dieux invitait son auditoire à réviser son attitude envers les juifs. Ces religieux entendaient développer les études juives en milieu catholique. C'est ainsi que la revue *Études*, des jésuites, ouvrit une 'Chronique juive' et que *Le Retour d'Israël* dont la raison d'être était la conversion d'Israël devint le *Bulletin catholique de la question d'Israël*,[26] ce qui indiquait clairement que de l'espoir d'une conversion on passait, timidement certes, à la recherche de la compréhension. Le rôle de quelques juifs convertis, comme Schwob ou Raïssa Maritain, ou fidèles à leur religion comme Edmond Fleg avec son livre bouleversant *L'Enfant prophète*, fut déterminant dans cette évolution d'une partie des intellectuels religieux catholiques. Quant à Aimé Pallière, sa personnalité étonnante rayonna chez les juifs et chez les catholiques ouverts au dialogue. Catholique, il adhéra au judaïsme sans se convertir complètement et il réalisa l'union des deux religions sans aucun syncrétisme.

Face à la persécution, des ecclésiastiques épaulèrent l'action de la *Ligue internationale contre le racisme et l'antisémitisme* (LICRA): le cardinal Liénart, à Lille, et le cardinal Verdier, à Paris, faisaient partie du comité de soutien. En avril 1933, suite à des violences antisémites en Allemagne, le cardinal Verdier écrivit au grand rabbin de France pour lui manifester sa sympathie, le cardinal Maurin fit de même à Lyon.[27] Le 7 février 1934, se déroulait salle Wagram, à Paris, 'un meeting interconfessionnel de protestation contre la suppression des causeries religieuses' à la radio; 'les trois cultes étaient fraternellement représentés' se souvient le grand rabbin Jacob Kaplan[28] qui y rencontra ses amis le père Lhande et le pasteur Durrleman. *L'Union civique des croyants* à laquelle adhéraient des catholiques, des juifs et des protestants, fut créée en 1934. Le 16 mars 1936, une nouvelle manifestation réunissait le grand rabbin Liber, le père Ferrand des Pères de Sion et le pasteur Wautier d'Aygalliers. Un an plus tard, le père Dieux multipliait les rencontres pluriconfessionnelles pour dénoncer vigoureusement les persécutions raciales.[29] Enfin, en janvier 1938, salle Jappy à Paris, se déroula un meeting avec l'abbé Viollet (fils du fameux dreyfusard catholique), le pasteur Cooreman et le rabbin Kaplan. Dans ce sillage, des démocrates chrétiens comme Sangnier ou Bidault à *L'Aube* stigmatisaient l'antisémitisme en Allemagne comme en France. Oscar de Férenzy entreprit de répondre à *La Libre Parole*, reparue en 1930, en lançant *La Juste Parole* à laquelle collaboraient Jacques Maritain, François Mauriac et les pères Devaux, Dieux et Bonsirven.

Les deux années précédant la guerre virent une forte mobilisation pour contrer le fléau antisémite. Il est vrai qu'à partir de 1937, l'exemple venait du Vatican avec l'encyclique *Mit brennender Sorge* du pape Pie XI puis sa fameuse déclaration, le 6 septembre 1938 'spirituellement, nous sommes tous des sémites'. Un projet d'encyclique n'aboutit pas avant sa mort mais depuis sa récente publication, l'on sait qu'il condamnait fermement et sans faiblir toute forme de racisme tout en maintenant un réel antijudaïsme.[30]

PERSÉCUTION ET SOLUTION FINALE PENDANT LA SECONDE GUERRE MONDIALE: INDIFFÉRENCE, AMITIÉ ET SAUVETAGE

L'avènement du gouvernement de Vichy signifiait la fin des principes démocratiques en France ce qui ne pouvait que satisfaire les partisans d'*Action française* qui se trouvèrent nombreux autour de ce gouvernement. Le garde des Sceaux Alibert qui signait, avec Pétain, les lois portant sur les juifs dès octobre 1940[31] était un antisémite proche de l'*Action française*. La mise à l'écart d'une partie des citoyens perturba peu la conscience de la hiérarchie catholique: à la fin de 1940, Mgr Gerlier, archevêque de Lyon, délégua Mgr Guerry auprès du gouvernement de Vichy 'pour protester contre la violation des droits de la personne humaine' et il ajouta que 'les conditions dans lesquelles vingt mille juifs se trouvent entassés au camp de Gurs sont une violation flagrante des règles les plus élémentaires du droit humain'.[32] Mais la protestation manquait encore d'énergie et une question reste sans réponse: les membres de cette hiérarchie condamnèrent la persécution raciale en temps de paix, 'pourquoi alors le silence des débuts de Vichy?'[33] La stupeur après la débâcle et l'occupation empêcha-t-elle de réagir? Pourtant en 1941, le premier effroi avait disparu aussi ce fut plutôt la grande confiance en Pétain qui aveugla plus d'un évêque et de nombreux catholiques. En défendant la famille et la patrie, Pétain représentait des valeurs sûres pour les nationalistes catholiques.

La législation antijuive s'enrichit constamment durant toute l'année 1941 et un *Commissariat général aux questions juives* fut confié au député catholique Xavier Vallat. Le 24 juillet 1941, une timide objection de l'*Assemblée des cardinaux et archevêques* rappela 'le sens du respect de la personne humaine'; elle s'arrêta là. Or les premières rafles touchaient déjà les juifs à Paris et les camps de Drancy, Pithiviers et Beaune-la-Rolande étaient déjà ouverts. Le cardinal Liénart accordait une telle confiance à Pétain qu'il se montra incapable de mesurer les dangers de sa politique antisémite.[34] Il fallut les grandes rafles suivies des drames de la déportation durant l'été 1942 pour que les réprobations publiques condamnent cette politique, et encore elles n'émanent que de cinq évêques.

D'autres catholiques, d'autres prêtres s'engagèrent plus avant dans la voie du soutien à Vichy ou dans la collaboration, au nom même de leur foi, tel Mgr Dutoit, évêque d'Arras, tel le cardinal Baudrillart farouchement anticommuniste, tel Mgr Mayol de Luppé, aumônier dans la *Légion des volontaires français contre le bolchevisme*. Enfin des catholiques ont pleinement consenti à poursuivre les juifs, pour les déporter, pour les tuer: la récente enquête menée par un groupe d'historiens sur Touvier établit clairement les liens entre ce chef milicien et certains prêtres catholiques (voir plus loin).

Toutefois la France entière ne se trouvait pas derrière Vichy. Très tôt, une poignée de Français refusèrent la défaite et rejoignirent le général de Gaulle à Londres. Parmi eux l'on comptait des croyants de toutes confessions: israélites, protestants et aussi catholiques. De Gaulle lui-même, qui bénéficia d'une éducation catholique, s'exprimait ainsi dès le 22 août 1940:

> Le jour de la victoire … la France libérée ne peut manquer d'avoir à cœur de veiller à ce qu'il soit fait justice des torts portés aux collectivités victimes de la domination hitlérienne et, entre autres, aux communautés juives qui, dans le pays momentanément soumis à l'Allemagne, sont malheureusement en butte à l'intolérance et aux persécutions.[35]

Une partie de la France catholique versa spontanément dans la résistance et non seulement par patriotisme mais par opposition formelle au gouvernement de Vichy ou aux occupants qui bafouaient sans vergogne les droits humains. Autour des jésuites de Lyon, cette résistance trouva 'les armes de l'esprit'.[36] Déjà le père Chaillet, et d'autres avec lui, avait lancé un terrible cri d'indignation contre la 'chasse honteuse à l'homme, traqué comme une bête immonde' dans un ouvrage percutant, paru en 1939.[37] En novembre 1940, le père Yves de Moncheuil de l'Institut catholique de Paris et ami du père Chaillet, dans une conférence privée et restreinte à un auditoire catholique, condamna clairement la mise à l'écart des juifs et préconisa de les aider. Puis ce fut au tour du père Fessard de dénoncer le racisme dans une conférence publique, dès le 15 décembre 1940, en l'église St Louis de Vichy.[38] En cette fin d'année 1940, les pères Chaillet et Fessard se retrouvèrent à Lyon avec d'autres jésuites du scolasticat de Fourrière qui partageaient leur aversion pour l'antisémitisme. Le 17 juin 1941, une protestation s'éleva, toujours de Lyon, de la faculté de théologie, pour dénoncer la loi du 2 juin statuant sur les juifs qui niait le principe selon lequel 'nul ne peut être inquiété pour ses opinions religieuses' et qui niait aussi l'identité chrétienne des juifs convertis.[39] Peu de temps après, à l'été 1941, le père Fessard affina sa réflexion sur le sort que Vichy imposait aux juifs dans un texte qui devint le premier numéro des *Cahiers du Témoignage chrétien* et qui portait comme titre *France, prends garde de perdre ton âme*. Il semble bien que ce fut la seule publication clandestine qui, dès son premier numéro, s'est inquiétée pour la vie des juifs. Par la suite d'autres mouvements de résistance se sont élevés contre la législation inique mais peu y songeaient si précisément avant les grandes rafles de l'été 1942. Car, selon Bédarida, 'dès le premier numéro des *Cahiers*, la tactique du *Témoignage chrétien* est donc claire: démontrer que christianisme et antisémitisme sont incompatibles; communiquer des informations authentiques et vérifiées (arrestations, camps de concentration en France tel que Gurs, présentation du *Juif Süss*, etc.)'.[40] A Lyon encore, dès la fin de 1940, se constitua une organisation d'aide aux juifs, réfugiés en grand nombre dans la ville. Peu à peu, en 1941, elle se développa autour du père Chaillet et réunit des catholiques (Jean-Marie Soutou, Germaine Ribière, l'abbé Glasberg), des protestants (le pasteur de Pury) et des juifs (André Weill, Samy Lattès). Ce fut l'*Amitié chrétienne* qui collabora avec d'autres œuvres comme la

CIMADE des protestants et l'OSE des juifs pour cacher ceux que la déportation menaçait, pour mettre en place des filières de passage vers la Suisse, pour tisser un réseau d'assistantes sociales secourant les fugitifs. Le travail fut considérable et nombre d'enfants et d'adultes échappèrent à la mort grâce à cette organisation qui, par sa composition plurireligieuse, jetait les bases d'un rapprochement entre juifs et chrétiens pour l'après-guerre.

Le 22 juillet 1942, la rafle du Vel d'Hiv provoqua 'une protestation en faveur des droits imprescriptibles de la personne humaine'.[41] La déportation, à l'été 1942, des juifs internés dans les camps de la zone non occupée et entièrement contrôlée par le gouvernement de Vichy suscita une lettre véhémente de la part de Mgr Saliège, évêque de Toulouse, que d'autres évêques imitèrent:

> Dans notre diocèse, des scènes émouvantes ont eu lieu dans les camps de Noé et de Récébédou. Les juifs sont des hommes, les juives sont des femmes. Tout n'est pas permis contre eux, contre ces femmes, contre ces pères et mères de famille. Ils font partie du genre humain; ils sont nos frères comme d'autres. Un chrétien ne peut l'oublier. (Saliège, évêque de Toulouse)

> Je fais entendre la protestation indignée de la conscience chrétienne et je proclame que tous les hommes, aryens ou non aryens, sont frères parce que créés par Dieu. (Théas, évêque de Montauban)

> ... nous croyons remplir un grave devoir de notre charge en faisant entendre le cri douloureux de la conscience chrétienne bouleversée par les mesures qui viennent d'être prises et exécutées en ces derniers jours contre des hommes, des femmes, des enfants coupables seulement d'appartenir à la race juive et d'être des étrangers. (Delay, évêque de Marseille)

> L'exécution des mesures de déportation qui se poursuivent actuellement contre les juifs donne lieu sur tout le territoire à des scènes si douloureuses que nous avons l'impérieux et pénible devoir d'élever la protestation de notre conscience. (Gerlier, archevêque de Lyon)

> La religion et l'humanité ne peuvent que protester contre cette violation des droits sacrés de la personne humaine et de la famille et cette méconnaissance de la loi divine de charité. (Moussaron, archevêque d'Albi)[42]

Tandis que la hiérarchie de l'Église catholique de France protestait vigoureusement contre la grande déportation de l'été 1942, des membres de la base de cette même Église agirent pour secourir les familles menacées de mort. Des couvents, des monastères, des institutions religieuses ont caché bien des proscrits, Mgr Gerlier finit par faire lever la clôture des monastères pour mieux dissimuler les juifs et, à Nice, Mgr Rémond fit ouvrir des pensionnats aux enfants juifs traqués. De nombreux exemples pourraient être donnés, deux suffiront: le père Jacques, directeur du petit collège d'Avon près de Fontainebleau, fut emmené en déportation par un froid matin d'hiver 1944 avec les trois enfants juifs qu'il cachait dans son établissement; il avait aussi permis à un professeur de sciences naturelles, radié du corps des enseignants, de continuer ses cours en ce même collège;[43] le père Devaux hébergea puis cacha de nombreux juifs, enfants et adultes, en la maison de sa congrégation, rue Notre-Dame des Champs à Paris. A Grenoble, les sœurs de cette même congrégation secoururent également un grand nombre d'enfants juifs.

Des prêtres n'hésitaient pas à fournir de faux papiers et un précieux certificat de baptême: le jeune Joseph Joffo, avec son frère Maurice, bénéficia de cette aide et il le raconta dans *Un sac de billes*; l'abbé Glasberg et son équipe de prêtres catholiques et d'amis juifs consacra leurs efforts 'à fabriquer des faux papiers, à cacher des gens, à faire relâcher des internés sous divers prétextes et à ouvrir des centres d'accueil pour héberger les détenus libérés, les soigner et les faire disparaître sous une fausse identité'.[44] Le père Marie-Benoît, capucin, engagea des pourparlers avec le Vatican pour obtenir le transfert de juifs réfugiés sur la Côte d'Azur vers l'Italie ou l'Afrique du Nord. L'*Amitié chrétienne* s'activa particulièrement pour favoriser la fuite des juifs vers la Suisse, et, près d'Annemasse, des rédemptoristes 'firent passer des juifs en Suisse'.[45] Les secours dans les camps d'internement sollicitèrent beaucoup d'énergie et de courage: l'abbé Glasberg et Jean-Marie Soutou, encore eux, aidés de Germaine Ribière, de la *Jeunesse étudiante chrétienne*, travaillaient avec la CIMADE protestante pour apporter quelque réconfort aux internés et tenter de les en faire sortir.

Une question se posa vite à ces sauveteurs d'enfants juifs: fallait-il les convertir ou même fallait-il répondre favorablement à une demande de conversion de la part de ces enfants? Beaucoup se refusèrent à prendre une telle initiative et la plupart des sauveteurs préférèrent attendre la fin de la guerre afin d'éviter une conversion motivée par une menace de mort. Certains prêtres même favorisèrent l'enseignement du judaïsme à leurs jeunes protégés, tel l'abbé Vancourt à Lille ou tel Joseph Folliet qui entretint une 'paroisse juive' pour permettre l'étude de l'Ancien Testament à ces enfants juifs.[46]

L'APRÈS SHOAH ET SES SÉQUELLES

Au lendemain de la guerre, le désastre était immense pour la communauté juive de France mais, avec l'épuration, on croyait alors en avoir fini avec l'antisémitisme. C'était oublier le vieux fonds d'antijudaïsme qui refit rapidement surface dans les milieux catholiques.

Mgr Delay avait laissé transparaître des préjugés antisémites dans sa protestation lors des rafles:

> Nous n'ignorons pas que la question juive pose de difficiles problèmes nationaux et internationaux. Nous reconnaissons bien que notre pays a le droit de prendre toutes les mesures utiles pour se défendre contre ceux qui, en ces dernières années surtout, lui ont fait tant de mal et qu'il a le devoir de punir sévèrement tous ceux qui abusent de l'hospitalité qui leur fut si libéralement accordée. Mais les droits de l'État ont des limites.[47]

Néanmoins il s'insurgeait contre les arrestations en masse d'hommes et de femmes dont la seule faute était d'être juifs! Bien des catholiques, tout en condamnant la persécution, acceptaient de croire que la déportation n'était qu'un châtiment mérité: ainsi en septembre 1941, les membres de la bourgeoisie chrétienne de Tourcoing percevaient le problème juif comme 'la conséquence apparente de l'esprit de corps ou plutôt de séparation des Juifs, la conséquence profonde de la malédiction du Christ'.[48]

Après la guerre, cette idée ne disparut pas. En 1945, Daniel-Rops, historien catholique, justifiait 'l'horreur du pogrom' par 'l'insoutenable horreur de la Crucifixion':[49] la mise à mort des juifs par la déportation était la réponse à la mise à mort du Christ par la crucifixion. Quelques juifs qui avaient encore la force de dénoncer de telles iniquités comme le rabbin Jacob Kaplan[50] et surtout l'historien Jules Isaac, l'ami de Charles Péguy, réagirent énergiquement. Par ailleurs, la lenteur avec laquelle les organisations juives récupérèrent des enfants cachés par des catholiques, manifeste la tentative de conserver ces âmes hors du judaïsme malgré l'interdiction de convertir ces enfants prononcée par des évêques.[51]

Jules Isaac entreprit donc de démontrer l'absurdité d'un antisémitisme chrétien dans un ouvrage imposant, *Jésus et Israël*, commencé en 1943 alors que les nazis le traquaient et terminé en 1946. Toutefois démontrer ne suffisait pas, il fallait aussi agir en faveur d'une reconnaissance mutuelle afin que plus jamais un chrétien ne verse dans l'antisémitisme ni même l'antijudaïsme. D'abord, il répondit vigoureusement à Daniel-Rops dans un retentissant article de la revue *Europe* en invitant les chrétiens à ne plus se tromper lorsqu'ils désignaient les bourreaux et à reconnaître la 'meurtrière tradition' de l'Église qui 'mène à Auschwitz'.[52] Ensuite, il commença son long combat pour changer les relations judéo-chrétiennes, entamées avant la guerre et mûries pendant les temps douloureux de la persécution 'mais il s'agit, après la guerre, de [les] revoir fondamentalement'.[53] A la suite d'une première réflexion qui eut lieu à Oxford en 1946, les protagonistes d'une entente entre les chrétiens et les juifs organisèrent une conférence internationale et pluriconfessionnelle à Seelisberg en Suisse, à l'été 1947. Or cette entente ne se fit pas spontanément et il fallut vaincre bien des réticences chez les catholiques. Jules Isaac insistait pour que l'Église catholique abandonnât définitivement l'accusation de déicide qui était source d'une persécution multi-séculaire et terriblement meurtrière. Ses partenaires catholiques acceptaient volontiers la responsabilité de l'enseignement de leur Église dans la propagation de l'antisémitisme mais souhaitaient curieuse-ment que les juifs reconnussent leurs torts envers le christianisme. Le refus de la délégation juive, qui estimait n'avoir rien à reprocher au judaïsme, fut clair et net, ce qui provoqua une suspension de la commission. La proclamation commune que sont les 'Dix points de Seelisberg' fut élaborée dans un débat houleux.[54] Ce dérapage de départ dans le rapprochement judéo-chrétien témoigne d'un antijudaïsme vivace et cinquante ans après, des catholiques pensent encore que les juifs auraient des choses à se reprocher quant à leur perception du christianisme.[55]

Immédiatement après cette importante conférence, Jules Isaac travailla inlassablement à la création, en 1948, puis au développe-ment de l'*Amitié judéo-chrétienne* de France. Le mouvement partit d'Aix-en-Provence où résidait le fondateur, puis il essaima partout en France avec un pôle particulièrement actif à Lille grâce au dynamisme de Geneviève Gendron, salésienne, et du chanoine Renard, professeur en théologie, tous deux soutenus par le cardinal Liénart pourtant méfiant envers ce mouvement œcuménique à ses débuts.[56] Depuis, cette association combat sans répit toute expres-sion d'antisémitisme et son prolongement, l'antisionisme. Elle participa à la confection des dossiers que cardinal Liénart présenta au concile de Vatican II à l'issue duquel l'Église catholique renonçait à l'accusation de déicide portée contre les juifs et supprimait l'outrageante prière du vendredi saint 'pour les juifs perfides'. En avril 1973, le *Comité épiscopal français pour les relations avec le judaïsme* élabora *Les Orientations pastorales sur l'attitude des chrétiens à l'égard du judaïsme*; elles vont plus loin encore que le texte conciliaire dans le respect mutuel entre juifs et catholiques.[57]

Dans le demi-siècle qui suivit la Seconde Guerre mondiale diverses affaires empoisonnèrent les relations entre catholiques et juifs au point de perturber la vie politique du pays.

En 1952, les Français découvraient l'affaire Finaly qui déchirait une famille cruellement éprouvée par la Shoah. En réalité, l'affaire durait depuis plus de six ans: une directrice de crèche, très catholique, refusait de rendre à leurs tantes deux garçonnets juifs qu'elle avait recueillis pendant la guerre, après la déportation de leurs parents. En trompant la justice, cette Melle Brun était parvenue à débouter la famille de sa demande et, en 1948, elle avait pris soin de faire baptiser les bambins. Finalement après maints et maints procès, jugements, provocations et déboires, les deux enfants Finaly purent rejoindre une tante en Israël: c'était en 1953, huit ans après les premières démarches des sœurs de leur père.[58] Comment une simple directrice de crèche municipale était-elle parvenue à tenir tête à la justice et à faire disparaître les enfants en Espagne? En réalité, elle n'était point seule et, en faisant baptiser les enfants, elle pouvait s'assurer le soutien de l'Église pour qui le baptême interdisait toute éducation juive, donc tout retour dans la famille d'origine. Or les parents traqués avaient montré leur attachement au judaïsme en faisant circoncire leurs deux garçonnets en 1941 et en juillet 1942, quelques jours avant les grandes rafles. Malgré cela, des sœurs de Sion, dont le but initial était la conversion des juifs, des franciscains, des prêtres, des couvents en France et en Espagne, voire en Autriche, bref un réseau aux mailles serrées, bravèrent et même bafouèrent la justice de la France républicaine et laïque. L'opinion publique s'enflamma dans cette affaire qui fit renaître un anticléricalisme un peu désuet. Les positions fermes du rabbin Kaplan[59] n'ébranlèrent pas les partisans de la conversion forcée. Mgr Caillot de Grenoble couvrit Melle Brun dont la mauvaise foi et l'antisémitisme étaient pourtant patents, le journal *La Croix* mit en doute les accusations portées par le rabbin Kaplan contre Melle Brun, et le secrétaire particulier de l'archevêque de Paris se trouva fort contrarié par de tels propos qui pourtant clamaient une stricte vérité.[60] Quelques années après la Shoah, c'était encore l'antisémitisme qui habitait Melle Brun et ses défenseurs catholiques: elle insultait les juifs en les traîtant de lâches puisqu'ils abandonnaient leurs enfants pendant la guerre et Maître Givord 'expliqua l'origine de ce procès par l'intérêt que la "judéo-maçonnerie" porta à cette affaire'.[61] Le cardinal Liénart de Lille renonça à une manifestation judéo-chrétienne pour manifester sa désapprobation envers le rabbin Kaplan. Toutefois quelques catholiques prenaient conscience que l'Église catholique se déstabilisait en se plaçant au-dessus du droit commun et surtout en niant avec autant d'impudence le droit des consciences. Le père Demann, appartenant à la congrégation de Notre-Dame de Sion, éleva la voix le premier et mit toute sa connaissance du judaïsme et tout son talent au service de la cause de la famille Finaly. Mais, comme jadis les catholiques antidreyfusards, ces catholiques-là étaient peu nombreux et isolés.

Une autre affaire, secoua l'opinion publique française, à plusieurs reprises après la guerre: l'affaire Touvier. Cet ancien milicien responsable, entre autres, de meurtres de juifs avait été condamné à mort par contumace à deux reprises (septembre 1946 et mars 1947) et était parvenu à se cacher en France jusqu'à ce que le président Pompidou lui accorde une grâce (novembre 1971). Il fallut la dénonciation énergique du journaliste Jacques Derogy dans *L'Express* pour que soit engagée une nouvelle instruction pour crime imprescriptible contre l'humanité. Touvier dut alors reprendre sa vie de clandestin qui prit fin avec son arrestation le 24 mai 1989, à Nice, au prieuré Saint François, connu pour son intégrisme. Comment ce milicien, très recherché après la guerre puis après 1971, avait-il réussi une si longue cavale sans quitter le territoire national? La rumeur d'une généreuse complicité de la part d'ecclésiastiques et de maisons religieuses se répandit rapidement. Aussi immédiatement après l'arrestation de Touvier, le cardinal Decourtray, archevêque de Lyon, décida-t-il dès juin 1989 d'ouvrir les archives de l'archevêché et de confier à une commission d'historiens le soin d'étudier ces documents. Attitude extrêmement courageuse et honnête que le cardinal justifiait de la sorte: 'Je pensais que la vérité était préférable quelle qu'elle soit et moins compromettante que le mensonge ou les rumeurs que l'on a tendance à transformer en vérités. Je continue à penser qu'un tort bien établi et que l'on porte dans la vérité et le courage est préférable à l'innocence suspecte.'[62]

Or cette commission permit de découvrir quel était l'entourage de Touvier: c'étaient essentiellement des catholiques, pétainistes, antisémites et intégristes. Le milieu familial baignait dans le catholicisme le plus réactionnaire de l'entre-deux-guerres: le père lisait Drumont et accepta de s'éloigner de Maurras par obéissance à la condamnation papale mais il approuva l'engagement de son fils dans la Milice et dans la collaboration. Lorsqu'il se réfugia dans la clandestinité pour échapper à la justice, Paul Touvier ne put se cacher qu'avec des complicités catholiques qu'il trouva sans difficultés. Il abusa de 'la tradition hospitalière de l'Église'.[63] Dès septembre 1944, il se réfugia à l'Institut du Prado puis à l'abbaye de Bonnecombe; il sollicita l'aide de prêtres de paroisses en Savoie, dans l'Oise et la région parisienne. Des familles attachées à un catholicisme traditionnel et suranné acceptèrent de le soustraire à la justice.[64] Par la suite, lorsque Touvier, toujours clandestin, tenta d'obtenir réparation des décisions de justice qu'il estimait iniques, il se procura constamment et aisément l'appui efficace de prêtres et même d'ecclésiastiques haut placés comme Mgr Duquaire qui discernait en Touvier 'un homme de foi, un vrai catholique'.[65] De même, au cours de ses cavales répétées il trouva régulièrement refuge dans des monastères connus comme la Grande Chartreuse en Isère (même après l'échec de la grâce présidentielle en 1972) ou auprès des très troublants *Chevaliers de Notre-Dame*.[66] Le philosophe Gabriel Marcel, pressenti pour aider l'ancien milicien, se récusa et refusa énergiquement de tomber dans le panneau de la charité chrétienne. Mais il 'demeure un isolé', même si pourtant il a fait la preuve que, pour un intellectuel catholique, 'l'impératif de charité ne saurait dispenser de l'impératif de vérité'.[67] En fait, les écclésiastiques qui participèrent à ce sauvetage se laissèrent volontairement ou involontairement berner. En octobre 1984, Touvier rencontra Mgr Lefebvre à Ecône.[68] A la fin des années 1980, lorsque l'opinion publique découvrit avec stupeur cette cavale, la majorité des catholiques français désavoua cette frange intégriste qui ne renonçait toujours pas à protéger un ancien milicien, auteur d'un crime contre l'humanité.

L'affaire du carmel d'Auschwitz ébranla le rapprochement judéo-chrétien, semant le doute, chez les juifs, sur la sincérité des catholiques.[69] La maladresse des carmélites polonaises venues s'installer dans l'enceinte du camp Auschwitz I fit craindre aux juifs de France une christianisation de la Shoah. La réaction fut vive dans toutes les communautés et celle de France s'organisa pour protester auprès des dignitaires de l'Église. Les responsables de l'*Amitié judéo-chrétienne*, à commencer par son président, l'historien Pierre Pierrard, associèrent leurs efforts à ceux des représentants de la communauté juive de

France. Une délégation mixte religieusement négocia à Genève et dans l'ensemble l'accord fut unanime, côté français, même si les partenaires juifs s'impatientaient, à juste titre, des lenteurs de réflexion de la hiérarchie catholique. L'affaire mit en évidence l'antisémitisme latent en Pologne mais une large majorité de catholiques français en prit pleinement conscience pour le condamner.

Enfin la récente parution de la *Bible des communautés chrétiennes*, texte biblique agrémenté de commentaires antisémites, provoqua un certain remous.[70] Le retrait de l'imprimatur accordé trop rapidement par l'évêque de Versailles et l'interdiction de vente écourtèrent l'affaire. Quelques catholiques s'agacèrent de tant de bruits car ils n'appréciaient pas l'ingérence, dans leurs affaires, de juifs assez puissants pour obtenir la saisie de la publication. A leurs yeux, le contenu importait peu, la forme de l'interdit déplaisait.

L'antisémitisme, longtemps tabou après la guerre, a repris quelque vigueur depuis vingt à trente ans. Il n'est pas l'apanage des catholiques et bien des athées sont prêts à recevoir ou à colporter tous les ragots hostiles aux juifs, comme les rumeurs d'Orléans (mai 1969) ou d'Amiens (mars 1970) accusant des commerçants juifs de se livrer à la traite des Blanches![71] Dans les troupes du *Front national*, parti d'extrême droite volontiers antisémite, se trouvent des catholiques mêlés à des gens sans foi (et ni loi parfois).[72] En fait, l'antisémitisme latent qui se love dans les consciences puis qui pointe sournoisement au détour d'une phrase pour donner l'impression que les juifs sont toujours responsables des malheurs qui s'abattent sur nous ou sur eux, reste le plus tenace et le plus difficile à vaincre. Il se glissa insidieusement dans la phrase que Raymond Barre, Premier Ministre, lâcha spontanément au lendemain de l'attentat contre la synagogue de la rue Copernic, en octobre 1980: 'Cet attentat odieux qui voulait frapper des Israélites qui se rendaient à la synagogue et qui a frappé des Français innocents qui traversaient la rue Copernic.'

Toutefois, l'amitié entre catholiques et juifs se développe et s'affirme sans arrière-pensée du côté catholique, ce qui ne fut pas toujours clair au début du mouvement. L'*Amitié judéo-chrétienne*, actuellement menée par les pères et sœurs de Notre-Dame de Sion, agit efficacement à tous les niveaux pour l'éradication du mal antisémite. Les facultés de théologie catholiques ont inscrit des cours d'histoire de religion juive et de langue hébraïque à leurs programmes. Une association, *Les Amis des sessions d'Hébreu*, rencontre un certain succès auprès des catholiques qui s'initient et même se spécialisent dans la lecture du texte biblique dans sa langue d'origine, et apprenent à bien connaître le judaïsme.

Enfin, la reconnaissance par les évêques de France de la responsabilité de l'Église dans le développement de l'antisémitisme en France, avant et pendant la Seconde Guerre mondiale, est la preuve éclatante que le catholicisme français a vraiment mis fin à deux millénaires d'incompréhension et de haine à l'égard du judaïsme et du peuple juif.[73]

L'antisémitisme est de moins en moins le fait exclusif des catholiques. Aura-t-il fallu les épisodes douloureux (l'affaire Dreyfus, les sacrifices de la Grande Guerre, la Shoah, les affaires de l'après-guerre) de l'histoire des juifs pour tordre le cou à des préjugés meurtriers?

NOTES

1. Reproduite dans *L'Histoire*, numéro spécial sur l'affaire Dreyfus, janvier 1994, 70.

2. Pierre Sorlin, *La Croix et les Juifs 1880–1899. Contribution à l'histoire de l'antisémitisme contemporain* (Paris: Grasset, 1967), p. 95.

3. Danielle Delmaire, *Antisémitisme et catholiques dans le Nord pendant l'affaire Dreyfus* (Lille: Presses Universitaires de Lille, 1991).

4. Pierre Pierrard, *Juifs et catholiques français* (Paris: Fayard, 1970), pp. 64–70. Ce livre a été réédité et augmenté sous le titre *Juifs et catholiques français: d'Édouard Drumont à Jacob Kaplan, 1886–1994* (Paris: Cerf, 1997).

5. Delmaire, *Antisémitisme et catholiques*, pp. 49–63.

6. Archives Nationales (AN): F 7/12487. Rapport du préfet de l'Aisne, 4 juillet 1900. La conférence devait se dérouler le 11 juillet.

7. Jean-Marie Mayeur, 'Les Congrès nationaux de la Démocratie chrétienne à Lyon 1896–1898', *Revue d'histoire moderne et contemporaine*, 9 (1962), 171–206.

8. L'expression est de Jules Isaac (voir plus loin), titre d'un de ses ouvrages (Paris: Fasquelle, 1962) selon lequel l'Église catholique porte la responsabilité d'une large diffusion de l'antisémitisme.

9. Pierre Quillard les a rassemblés dans *Le Monument Henry* (Paris: Stock, 1899). Stock est l'éditeur des dreyfusards.

10. S. Wilson, 'Le Monument Henry: la structure de l'antisémitisme en France, 1898–1899', *Annales*, 2 (1977), 265–91.

11. Pierrard, *Juifs et catholiques français*, p. 104.

12. Louis Chaine, *Les Catholiques français et leurs difficultés actuelles* (Paris: Stock, 1903), pp. 3–4.

13. Jean-Marie Mayeur, 'Les Catholiques dreyfusards', *Revue historique*, CCLXI

(1979), 337–61; Danielle Delmaire, 'Perception de l'affaire Dreyfus dans le milieu des intellectuels catholiques français: vers une controverse?', dans *Les Intellectuels face à l'affaire Dreyfus, alors et aujourd'hui: perception et impact de l'affaire en France et à l'étranger*, éd. Roselyne Koren et Dan Michman (Paris: L'Harmattan, 1998), pp. 91–107. Cette communication contredit l'article de René Rémond, 'Les Catholiques choisissent leur camp', *L'Histoire*, op. cité, 70–73, qui affirme que les catholiques furent peut-être moins antisémites qu'on ne le pense pendant l'affaire Dreyfus. Voir aussi Danielle Delmaire, 'Innovation et solitude: les catholiques dreyfusards', colloque 'Jalons pour une amitié judéo-chrétienne en France', Université de Lille 3, novembre 1998 (actes à paraître).

14. Citation de la Marseillaise, chant révolutionnaire contemporain de l'émancipation des juifs en France.

15. Paul Landau, *Les Juifs et la Grande Guerre* (thèse soutenue en décembre 1992) et '"La patrie en danger": d'une guerre à l'autre' dans *Histoire politique des juifs de France*, éd. Pierre Birnbaum (Paris: Presses de la Fondation Nationale des Sciences Politiques, 1990), pp. 74–91.

16. p.23 d'un tiré à part du livre publié à la fin de la Première Guerre mondiale. Ce tiré à part est, en fait, une ré-impression du chapitre sur les juifs, réalisée aux États-Unis en 1943, pour témoigner 'avec éclat contre la pseudo "révolution nationale" de 1940, contre le racisme d'importation imposé par l'Allemagne et adopté par des Français indignes' (ibid., p. 4).

17. Ibid., p. 20.

18. Richard Millman, *La Question juive entre les deux guerres: ligues de droite et antisémitisme en France* (Paris: Armand Colin, 1992), pp. 35–38, rappelle notamment que Drumont meurt en 1917, quasiment oublié.

19. Pierrard, *Juifs et catholiques*, pp. 234–35.

20. Lazare Landau, *De l'aversion à l'estime: juifs et catholiques en France de 1919 à 1939* (Paris: Le Centurion, 1980), pp. 216–32.

21. Pierrard, *Juifs et catholiques*, p. 265.

22. Millman, *La Question juive*, donne plusieurs exemples de communions commémoratives.

23. Ibid., p. 58, p. 238.

24. Dans *La Révue bénédictine* de juin 1923; voir Pierrard, *Juifs et catholiques*, p. 249.

25. René Rémond et Émile Poulat (éds), *Cent ans d'histoire de 'La Croix'*, colloque de mars 1987 (Paris: Le Centurion, 1988), cinquième partie: 'La Croix entre les deux-guerres', pp. 187–300.

26. Pierrard, *Juifs et catholiques*, p. 248.

27. Ibid., p. 268.

28. Pierre Pierrard interroge le grand-rabbin Kaplan dans *Justice pour la foi juive* (Paris: Le Centurion, 1977), pp. 46–47.

29. Pierrard, *Juifs et catholiques*, p. 269.

30. Georges Passelecq et Bernard Suchecky, *L'Encyclique cachée de Pie XI. Une occasion manquée de l'Église face à l'antisémitisme* (Paris: La Découverte, 1995).

31. Recueil des textes officiels français et allemands 1940–1944, réédité par l'association *Les Fils et Filles des Déportés Juifs de France* et le *Centre de documentation juive contemporaine* sous le titre *Les Juifs sous l'occupation*, 1982.

32. Mgr Guerry, *L'Église catholique en France sous l'occupation* (Paris: Flammarion, 1947), p. 38.

33. Question judicieusement posée par Jean-Marie Mayeur dans un rapport général lors du colloque organisé par le CDJC en mars 1979: Georges Wellers, André Kaspi et Serge Klarsfeld, *La France et la question juive 1940–1944* (Paris: Messinger, 1979), p. 167.

34. Il ne répondit pas à une demande de secours pendant la rafle qui décima les communautés du Nord. Voir Danielle Delmaire, 'Le cardinal Liénart et la persécution des juifs de Lille', dans *La France et la question juive*, pp. 231–48.

35. Message envoyé à la section britannique du Congrès juif mondial, cité par Georges Wellers, *L'Étoile jaune à l'heure de Vichy, de Drancy à Auschwitz* (Paris: Fayard, 1973), p. 265.

36. Renée Bédarida, *Les Armes de l'esprit, Témoignage chrétien, 1941–1944* (Paris: Éditions ouvrières, 1977). Ce qui suit doit beaucoup à cet excellent travail.

37. Pierre Chaillet, *L'Autriche souffrante* (Paris: Bloud et Gay, 1939); cité par Renée Bédarida, 'Les *Cahiers du Témoignage chrétien* et l'antisémitisme', in *La France et la question juive*, p. 215.

38. Ibid., p. 215. Le Père de Moncheuil mourut fusillé par les Allemands le 11 août 1944. Un colloque lui rendit hommage: *Spiritualité, théologie et résistance, Yves de Montcheuil théologien au maquis du Vercors* (Grenoble: Presses Universitaires de Lyon, 1987).

39. Mgr Guerry, *L'Église catholique*, p. 37.

40. Bédarida, *Les Armes de l'esprit*, p. 218.

41. Mgr Guerry, *L'Église catholique*, p. 40.

42. Ibid., pp. 41–44.

43. Louis Malle, élève de ce collège s'en souvint quarante ans plus tard pour son film *Au revoir les enfants*. Voir Frédéric Viey, *Fontainebleau-Avon, Journal d'une communauté juive de la Révolution à nos jours* (Avon: F. Viey 1991), pp. 69–71.

44. François Delpech, 'La persécution des juifs et l'*Amitié Chrétienne*', dans *Églises et chrétiens dans la IIe guerre mondiale, la région Rhône-Alpes*, Actes du colloque de Grenoble, 1976, sous la direction de Xavier de Montclos, Monique Luirard, François Delpech et Pierre Bolle (Lyon: Presses Universitaires de Lyon, 1978), p. 160.

45. Pierrard, *Juifs et catholiques*, p. 321.

46. Ibid., p. 325. Voir aussi Danielle Delmaire et Yves-Marie Hilaire, 'Chrétiens et juifs dans le Nord/Pas-de-Calais pendant la Seconde Guerre mondiale', *Revue du Nord*, 237 (1978), 454.

47. Mgr Guerry, *L'Église catholique*, p. 42.

48. Archives diocésaines de Lille, 4 K 112.

49. Daniel-Rops, *Histoire Sainte, Jésus en son temps* (Paris: Fayard, 1945), p. 527. A propos du procès de Jésus et de la responsabilité éventuelle de Pilate: 'Les Juifs ont manœuvré avec l'obstination et la cautèle qu'on leur connaît en d'autres circonstances, pour que le Romain se chargeât d'appliquer la sentence' (ibid., p. 529).

50. Pierrard, *Justice pour la foi juive*, pp. 130–35.

51. Ibid., p. 129.

52. Jules Isaac, 'Comment on écrit l'histoire (Sainte)', *Europe*, 7 (1946), 12–25 et cité par Menaham Macina, 'Le "syndrome de Seelisberg", persistance du

soupçon d'un "enseignement du mépris" rabbinique envers le christianisme',
Tsafon, 24 (1995–96), 95–107.

53. Pierrard, *Justice pour la foi juive*, p. 139.

54. Ibid., pp. 139–45.

55. Voir Macina, 'Le "syndrome de Seelisberg"'.

56. Danielle Delmaire, 'Une correspondance inédite de Jules Isaac avec les membres de l'*Amitié judéo-chrétienne* de Lille', *Tsafon*, 4 (1990–91), 3–40.

57. Tous ces textes furent rassemblés par Bernard Dupuy et Marie-Thérèse Hoch, *Les Églises devant le judaïsme, documents officiels 1948–1978* (Paris: Cerf, 1980).

58. M. Keller (mandataire de la tante des enfants), *L'Affaire Finaly telle que je l'ai vécue* (Paris: Librairie Fischbacher, 1960); Pierrard, *Justice pour la foi juive*, pp. 165–205; André Kaspi, 'L'Affaire des enfants Finaly', *L'Histoire*, 3 (1985), 40–53.

59. Notamment son communiqué du 11 février 1953: chaque argument commençait par 'Il est faux …' afin de mettre en évidence les multiples mensonges de Melle Brun. Il est reproduit dans Pierrard, *Justice pour la foi juive*, pp. 176–77.

60. Ibid., pp. 178–79.

61. Keller, *L'Affaire Finaly*, p. 128.

62. Lettre du cardinal Decourtray aux membres de la commission, le 28 juin 1990, et citée par René Rémond, Jean-Pierre Azéma, François Bédarida, Gérard Cholvy, Bernard Comte, Jean Dujardin, Jean-Dominique Durand et Yves-Marie Hilaire, *Touvier et l'Église: rapport de la Commission historique instituée par le cardinal Decourtray* (Paris: Fayard, 1992), pp. 15–16.

63. Ibid., p. 103.

64. Ibid., pp. 95–114. Telle la famille Berthet dont il épousa clandestinement la fille, Monique, et telle encore la famille Storez, dont une des filles vint témoigner en sa faveur lors de son procès en avril 1994.

65. Ibid., p. 165.

66. Ordre fondé au lendemain de la guerre par des partisans de Pétain dans le but de secourir les victimes de l'épuration. Il existe toujours (ibid., p. 142, p. 300).

67. Ibid., pp. 266–67.

68. Ibid., p. 301. 'On conviendra que, d'année en année, Touvier est davantage pris en charge par la fraction catholique qui partage sa vision politique' (p. 302) et particulièrement son défenseur lors de son procès, Me Trémolet de Villers.

69. L'affaire fit couler beaucoup d'encre dans la presse, je limite la bibliographie au témoignage d'un des négociateurs juifs: Théo Klein, *L'Affaire du Carmel d'Auschwitz* (Paris: Éditions Bertoin, 1991).

70. Menaham Macina, 'Faux en "écritures" ou "faux pas" théologique? L'anti-judaïsme de la *Bible des Communautés chrétiennes*', *Ad Veritatem*, 46 (1995), 12–71. L'auteur fut le premier à relever cet 'antijudaïsme'.

71. Voir Edgar Morin, *La Rumeur d'Orléans* (Paris: Seuil, 1970).

72. L'origine juive de l'évêque de Paris, Mgr Lustiger, n'alimente que très faiblement l'antisémitisme d'une extrême droite catholique, elle-même peu représentative des catholiques français.

73. 'Déclaration de repentance', lue par Mgr Olivier de Berranger, évêque de Saint-Denis, devant le mémorial de Drancy, 30 septembre 1997; reproduite dans *Le Monde*, 1 octobre 1997, p. 1.

3

Catholicism and Nationalism
The *Fédération républicaine*,
1927–39[1]

Kevin Passmore

The inter-war years are usually regarded as a watershed in the relationship between the Catholic Church and political life in France. In this period, it is argued, the Church broke its links with the royalist *Action française* (AF) and at last accepted that it must work within the Republic.[2] This rapprochement is said to have been encouraged by the unity of Catholics and anti-clericals during the First World War, and by fear of working-class unrest during the troubled post-war years. Whereas politicians became increasingly preoccupied with economic and social issues, the Church shifted its attention from politics to religious matters – supposedly permitting the emergence of a more 'genuine' Christianity. The Church's goal, as it had always been, remained the re-christianisation of France, but this would now be achieved through evangelisation rather than by political action against the 'atheistic' Republic, and the point of departure of Catholic activity became the parish rather than the political party. The beneficiaries of this reorientation are said to have been social Catholics, who had long held that re-Christianisation depended on severance of the link between Catholicism, social conservatism and Right-wing nationalism. These 'progressives' were particularly active in the Catholic trade union moment, the *Confédération française des travailleurs chrétiens* (CFTC), and the specialist groups of Catholic Action, especially the *Jeunesse agricole chrétienne* (JAC), *Jeunesse ouvrière chrétienne* (JOC) and their feminine counterparts (JACF and JOCF), which sought to involve workers and peasants in the work of proselytism.[3] The new militants usually favoured the moderately conservative *Parti démocrate populaire* (PDP), but they are regarded as having prepared the way for the more Left-wing Catholicism of the later twentieth century.

There are a number of difficulties with this view of the history of Catholicism. To begin with, religion remained an important structurant of political life in France. Practice was still relatively high: as late as 1947, 37% of voters claimed to have attended mass on one of the two previous Sundays. In the 1930s the extent to which voting behaviour was entangled with religious issues was often stressed and, moreover, the flowering of official, semi-official and private associations and interest groups in this period, ranging from school associations to trade unions and welfare organisations, provided whole new areas of conflict between Catholics and anti-clericals.[4] A further difficulty is that the history of political Catholicism has largely been shaped by historians who are sympathetic to the victors in the struggles they describe.[5] They share the conviction of inter-war social Catholics that it was in some way necessary (historically and theologically) for the Catholic Church to embrace the 'modern world' if it was to halt the process of dechristianisation. Drawing implicitly upon modern-isation theory, it is assumed that secularisation is an irresistible historical process to which the Church had to adapt if it was to survive.[6] The danger with this teleology is that the inter-war period will be viewed merely as a stage in the pre-history of late-twentieth-century Catholicism. Thus Étienne Fouilloux sees the condemnation of *Action française* in 1926 as an 'événement fondateur pour un nouveau cours du catholicisme français qui se poursuivra d'une seule traite, en dépit d'accidents finalement secondaires, jusqu'au second concile du Vatican'.[7] The 'accidents' that do not fit in with this narrative include the revival of clerical/anti-clerical conflict under the *Cartel des gauches* in 1924–26,[8] and more importantly from the present perspective, the continuing strength of intransigent Catholic nationalism in the 1930s. This scholarly neglect of nationalism is facilitated by labelling its major political manifestation, the *Fédération républicaine*, as 'traditionalist' – in other words, a backwards-looking movement destined to be beached by the tide of progress.[9]

The purpose of this chapter is to demonstrate the historical importance of the *Fédération républicaine*, with particular emphasis on its dominant nationalist wing.[10] The *Fédération* was the largest party of the parliamentary Right, supported by about eighty to one hundred deputies in the period. It had been founded in 1903 by the Right wing of the moderate republicans, but in subsequent years had become increasingly clerical and nationalist. The final stage in this rightwards *dérive* came in the late 1920s, under the leadership of the deputy for Meurthe-et-Moselle, Louis Marin. At first only a few *Fédération* deputies supported Marin's extreme nationalism, including his friends François de Wendel and Édouard de Warren, both Catholic and conservative steel magnates from the Lorraine. In the course of the 1930s support for Marin grew. A new generation of leaders of more modest origin emerged, including Victor Perret from the Rhône, Philippe Henriot from the Gironde and Xavier Vallat from the Ardèche. We shall see that the re-making of Catholicism, far from marginalising Catholic nationalism, together with broader social and political developments, actually popularised it and contributed to the transformation of the *Fédération républicaine*. We shall also see that the traditional/modern dichotomy is inadequate to the task of making sense of a movement that stood in reality at the intersection of reactionary nationalism and liberal republicanism. The *Fédération*'s distinctive ideological synthesis is better understood as the product of the specific class, gender and religious conflicts of the late Third Republic.

CATHOLIC NATIONALISM AND THE MOBILISATION OF THE FAITHFUL

Nationalists often complained in the 1930s of their exclusion from Catholic *œuvres*. In 1937, for example, Louis Marin protested angrily to Cardinal Valeri, the Papal Nuncio, that the Archbishop of Nancy had forbidden the deputies of the *Fédération* to attend Catholic meetings in Meurthe-et-Moselle, which Marin attributed to the influence of Christian democrats.[11] In the following year Jean Guiter, secretary of the *Fédération*, complained that in Besançon the PDP, the moderate conservative deputy Georges Pernot and the Archbishop had joined forces in order to oblige a pro-*Fédération* journalist to leave his job on a conservative newspaper, *L'Éclair comtois*.[12]

But while it is true that progressives found more openings in Church organisations from the late 1920s, much space remained for nationalists. This was partly because, as James McMillan points out, Pius XI (1922–39) was neither a liberal pluralist, nor a democrat, nor a social reformist. The Pope's growing anti-Communism after 1936 has often been noted, if only to put it down to papal dotage or to changes in his entourage.[13] In fact, even before this date Pius had been willing to collude with dictatorships of the extreme Right, as his conclusion of agreements with Mussolini in 1929 and Hitler in 1933 had shown. Pius XI was, of course, hostile in many respects to Fascism and Nazism, especially to the paganism of the latter, and he was unwavering in his search for international peace. His ultimate goal had always been the reconstruction of a Christian *cité*, in which Catholic principles would be the basis of social organisation, and in which the Church would act as the guide of the State. Political forms were of secondary importance so long as evangelisation was not hindered. Although in France Pius XI sometimes worked with progressives, this was only because the nationalists refused to keep Catholic organisations out of party politics, and above all because they rejected papal pacifism. In reality, both nationalists and progressives could, in certain conditions, count on papal support. Christian Democrats had Pius's ear on questions of international policy, while the Pope shared the aversion of conservatives to political collaboration with the Left.[14] On issues of social policy the situation was more complex, for Pius XI agreed with progressives that the Church must not be seen as an agent of social conservatives, yet viewed with alarm the possibility of collaboration with any of the parties of the Left.

   In these circumstances it was possible for nationalists, whether sympathetic to royalism, the *Action libérale populaire* (ALP) (a confessional party which had flourished in the 1900s), or the *Fédération*, to prosper in the parishes. Paradoxically, a major reason for the survival of nationalism was the Church's new insistence upon apoliticism. The injunction to ignore politics and to place Catholicism first was meant by the hierarchy as a riposte to *Action française*'s insistence upon the primacy of politics. In practice the primacy of Catholicism meant the exclusion of Leftists from Catholic organisations, on the grounds that they were, by definition, political, since they spoke for only a single social group. By the same token, since Right-wingers of any nuance were assumed to place Church and nation above special interests, they were necessarily 'apolitical'. So they were allowed into Catholic organisations on condition that they steered clear of explicitly party politics. The effects of this policy were particularly clear in the case of the *Fédération nationale catholique* (FNC), formed in 1925 in order to defend the interests of Catholics against the religious policies of the *Cartel des gauches*, and which may have enrolled as many as two million members. When the FNC's leader, Général de Castelnau, attempted to use the organisation to intervene in elections, the hierarchy was annoyed. Yet Castelnau's insistence that the need to gather together all Catholics overrode the question of the regime permitted nationalists of various nuances to control the movement. Castelnau himself favoured the *Fédération* Right, while vice-presidents Jean La Cour Grandmaison and Xavier Vallat were privately sympathetic to *Action française*, but became *Fédération* deputies. The two inter-war presidents of the FNC in the Rhône department, Charles Jacquier and Gabriel Perrin, were both royalists.[15]

The case of the FNC shows that the Church's strategy of 'apolitical' mobilisation through the parishes often provided nationalists with an audience of previously unhoped-for proportions. The strength of nationalism was further enhanced by the fact that the FNC recruited many members from organisations formed in the days of militant clericalism. The men of the parish Catholic Unions (*cercles d'hommes* or *cercles paroissiaux*) had been enrolled en masse into Castelnau's organisation. These unions were often affiliated to the *Œuvre des cercles*, heir of the *Œuvre des cercles catholiques ouvriers*, created by the Legitimist and later *rallié*, Albert de Mun in 1872.[16] In the inter-war years the movement had long since dropped any mention of the proletariat from its title, but it remained on the nationalist Right. In the Rhône the eleven-strong bureau of the *Œuvre des cercles* included four nobles, three of whom were prominent members of *Action française*.

The FNC, moreover, remained a force to be reckoned with in the 1930s, even though it was no longer able to draw the massive crowds of its heyday during the campaign against the *Cartel*. In Normandy, for example, the organisation experienced a revival in the middle of the decade, as it mobilised against the suppression of religious broadcasting on Radio Paris–PTT and against co-education in primary schools.[17] In the late 1920s, the Church endeavoured to 'apoliticise' the FNC. Yet Castelnau successfully fought off attempts to create a rival 'committee of civic action' within Catholic Action, and thus ensured that the FNC remained the official arm of the Church in matters concerning the rights of Catholics. As such, in the elections of 1928, 1932 and 1936, the FNC was able to draw up minimum conditions which had to be accepted by candidates desirous of Catholic support.[18] Castelnau's personal influence was reaffirmed in April–May 1936, when the philosopher P.-H. Simon of the Catholic University of Lille suggested that in some circumstances Catholics should vote for a Radical rather than a Catholic nationalist. A series

of articles in *L'Écho de Paris* whipped up Catholic opinion against
Simon, so that Archbishop Liénart, privately sympathetic to Simon,
had to force him to retract.[19] Castelnau's influence, relayed by the
press, backed by the authority of the FNC and made official by the
general's status as mouthpiece of the hierarchy on certain political
issues, represented a major constraint upon the expression of
'progressive' views by Catholics through the late 1920s and 1930s.

What is more, in some parts of France the *Fédération républicaine*
became reliant upon the FNC and parish *cercles* for its popular support. In the 1932 elections in Meurthe-et-Moselle the FNC joined
with *Action française* to support the *Fédération*'s de Warren against a
PDP opponent.[20] In neighbouring Moselle the *Action catholique
populaire de Lorraine*, another FNC affiliate, provided deputy Guy de
Wendel of the *Fédération* with a popular audience.[21] In a bitterly
fought by-election in Mortain in 1937, the *Fédération* struggled with
the *Parti social français* (PSF) for the backing of the *Union catholique
de la Manche*.[22] In the previously mentioned departments there was
no permanent organisation of the *Fédération*, so the FNC appears to
have filled the organisational vacuum.[23] In other areas the (partial)
depoliticisation of the FNC was directly implicated in the emergence
of a populist Catholic nationalism within the *Fédération*. In the late
1920s FNC orators such as Philippe Henriot, Xavier Vallat and
Victor Perret, while continuing to be active in Catholic organisations,
focused their energies on the *Fédération*, contributing thereby to its
transformation in some parts of France from a notable-based party
into a structured political movement. Xavier Vallat, deputy of the
Ardèche, was the best known of the royalists who responded to the
condemnation of *Action française* by concentrating his energies on the
FNC and the *Fédération*, becoming a vice-president of both.[24] In
Lyon, thanks to the eviction of *Action française* supporters from the
local *cercles d'hommes*, Victor Perret, himself vice-president of the
cercle Saint-Bruno in the Croix-Rousse district of the city, was able to
use this organisation as a means of recruitment to the *Fédération*. He
was helped by the fact that the *cercles* had greatly expanded during the
inter-war period, rising from around six hundred members in 1908
to between five and six thousand in 1933. By 1932 Perret had wrested
control of the *Fédération* in Lyon from the deputy, Georges Peissel,
the latter a moderate, favourable to the PDP.[25]

There were similar developments in Bordeaux. Here the nationalist wing of the Catholic movement had in the 1920s been dominated

by the abbé Bergey, first elected to parliament in 1919 as a Clemenciste deputy. A formidable orator, Bergey had been a leading light in the FNC's campaign against the *Cartel des gauches*. Most important from the present perspective is that the overlapping membership of both his religious arm, the *Ligue d'action et de défense religieuse* (an FNC affiliate) and his political movement, the *Union populaire républicaine*, were recruited from the parish. His most devoted followers, a sort of personal security guard, known as the 'volontaires de l'abbé Bergey', were expected to participate in both political and religious demonstrations. Bergey's weekly editorial in *Action catholique de Bordeaux* provided commentaries on both political and religious issues. In 1932, after Bergey's unexpected withdrawal from political life, the torch of the nationalist Right passed to Philippe Henriot, another FNC orator. Whereas Bergey preferred informal links to the *Fédération*, and sat in parliament with the non-affiliated deputies, Henriot was a convinced party man, and became a vice-president of the *Fédération*.

The connection between the *Fédération* and Catholic organisations was reinforced by papal policy towards political parties. Pius XI sought neither to incorporate Catholics and republicans together into a broad conservative party, as Leo XIII had attempted to do in the 1890s, nor to create a confessional party in the style of the ALP. The latter was not revived as a national force after the First World War, although local sections remained active until 1930. Therefore the *Fédération* took over the ALP's role as the unofficial agent of the Church in Parliament, and inherited its electorate and much of its personnel. Joseph Denais (deputy for Paris), Perret and Bergey all had links to the ALP. The *Ligue des droits de la nation* (LDN), founded in 1929, and patronised by the ninety-two-year-old founder of the ALP, Jacques Piou, played a significant role in bringing the *cadres* of the two parties together. The LDN was Catholic and nationalist in inspiration, and campaigned in particular for a strong State.[26] The ALP inheritance also helped to give the nationalism of the *Fédération* a more popular twist. As the title of the party suggests, the ALP was founded upon an appeal to the Catholic people. In the *Fédération* this populism was embodied in organisational terms in an alliance with the parish men's unions (another aspect of the ALP taken over by the *Fédération*). Thus, although the inter-war remaking of Catholicism as an evangelical rather than a political movement often favoured progressive Catholics, it also provided new opportunities for Catholic nationalism – and, indeed, provided it with a more populist twist. These developments were reinforced by the rise of class- and gender-based movements within the Right.

CATHOLIC NATIONALISM AND SOCIETY

The vitality of Catholic nationalism must in part be seen as a response to the threat posed by the Popular Front to conservative views of the social order. But the *Fédération*'s shift to the Right had begun in the late 1920s, at a time when the Left was relatively weak. This indicates that the sources of populist nationalism lay also in the changing nature of the Right. Take first the Catholic elites. It is sometimes forgotten that Catholicism and anti-clericalism were not just 'opinions' or 'mentalities', but were connected to interests. Access to power in inter-war France remained, to a considerable extent, determined by religious affiliation.[27] Wealthy Catholics were still excluded from certain areas of State employment, such as the Prefectoral Corps, the Council of State (with a few exceptions) and the Education ministry. And Catholics rarely became government ministers. Exclusions of this nature fed the *Fédération*'s hostility to the republican elite, and was reflected in its difficult relationship with the main lay conservative party, the *Alliance démocratique*. The *Fédération* backed the *Alliance*'s social conservatism, yet accused its deputies of letting their desire for ministerial office lead them into anti-clerical coalitions with the Radicals, thereby endangering social peace and religion. Some wealthy Catholics were therefore tempted to mobilise the Catholic people as a lever in their own battle for access to State power.

This populism also represented an attempt by the elites to contain a rank and file increasingly inclined to assert its rights as auxiliaries of the clergy, as workers and/or as women, for, in parallel with the rise of feminism and trade unionism on the Left, class- and gender-based movements developed within the popular constituency of the Catholic Right. These sectional movements were, in turn, related to the mobilisation of parishioners previously described. The changing position of women within the bourgeoisie is one such example. For much of the nineteenth century the class and status of bourgeois women had been determined by their subordinate position within the patriarchal family. Beginning at the turn of the century, and especially after the First World War, a greater number of women embarked upon careers, and sometimes, because of the shortage of partners that resulted from high war-time mortality, remained unmarried. A few women entered the liberal professions, but more significant was the entry into the social services of bourgeois women, often unmarried, Catholic and politically conservative. This movement was accelerated by the Social Insurance Acts of 1928 and 1930, and of the Family Allowances Act of 1932. The result was that, for the first time, enterprising middle-class Catholic women came together as distinct occupational groups. Doubtless such women were behind the growth of Right-wing feminist groups such as the *Fédération nationale des femmes* (FNF), formed in 1928. Among other things, the FNF sought ways of reconciling maternal duties with careers in the professions, nursing and civil service.[28] By the 1930s even non-feminist women's groups like the two million-strong *Ligue patriotique des Françaises* (LPF) had begun to take account of issues raised by feminists. The LPF rejected feminism as a product of liberal individualism, yet had long struggled to convince sceptics that women, like men, could aid clergy within Catholic Action. In the 1930s the league also abandoned its blanket hostility to women's participation in the labour force and accepted female suffrage, as long as both could be reconciled with the primary duty of motherhood. The growth of such women's groups had paradoxical effects on Catholic nationalists. The *Fédération* took up the suffrage cause and created women's sections within the party in 1935, yet we shall see that its fundamental misogyny was reinforced and it sought to confine women's equality to the passive exercise of political rights.

Divisions among the white-collar classes that provided so much of the Right's mass support also affected the nature of Catholic nationalism. The key development was the formation of the CFTC in 1919. The latter, whatever its Left-wing rivals alleged, must be understood in terms of a collective antagonism on the part of some Catholic employees to their employers. Yet since the CFTC saw the protection of the promotion prospects of *Catholic* white-collar workers, often against the competition of women and non-Catholics, as intrinsic to their collective interests it remained part of the constituency of the Right. A brief consideration of the Catholic trade unions will therefore illuminate some of the class, religious and gender tensions within the Right, and will help to explain the popularisation of Catholic nationalism in the 1930s.

During and after the war increasing numbers of women, many of them Catholics, were admitted to white-collar employment. This resulted in three kinds of conflict. First, it increased clerical/anti-clerical competition for jobs, thereby reinforcing antagonism between Right and Left. This was particularly evident in the teaching profession. The inter-war years were the heyday of the highly anti-clerical *Syndicat national d'instituteurs* (SNI), which was given a voice in the appointment process in 1924. The SNI was suspicious of all women teachers, especially of those who were Catholic. So the emergence of groups of *institutrices* affiliated to Catholic Action made it doubly fearful. Antagonism to the SNI reinforced the identity of religion and anti-socialism in the minds of rank-and-file Catholics, and potentially provided an impulse for popular Catholic nationalism. Secondly, male Catholic white-collar workers were hostile to both female and non-Catholic male rivals for employment. Although women's promotion prospects were slim, their exclusion from the best jobs required active intervention on the part of men, given that many competitive examinations had been opened to women. So Catholic men, through the CFTC, agitated for the return of women to the home, and urged the recognition of Catholic moral criteria as a means of identifying individuals worthy of promotion. Here too was a stimulus for the emergence of a popular Catholic nationalism, that was at once anti-socialist, anti-feminist and anti-capitalist. Thirdly (and paradoxically), the growth of female employment stimulated consciousness of the separate interests of Right-wing Catholic women which, within limits, sought equality of access to jobs, in opposition to both male Catholic workers and to the Left. The separate identity of women was reinforced by the fact that within the CFTC they joined gender-segregated unions.

Thus the changing employment patterns of white-collar workers exacerbated struggles for jobs between Catholics and non-Catholics and men and women, and thereby contributed to the popularisation of Catholic nationalism and provided a mass audience for the *Fédération*. Moreover, the fact that trade unions and women's groups developed within the audience of the Catholic Right undermined the binary opposition, between nation and Church on the one hand and socialism and feminism on the other, on which the *Fédération* relied. Hence the *Fédération*'s hostility to the PDP. Catholic women and male trade unionists both found allies in the PDP, so that it was accused by *Fédération* politicians of infecting Catholicism with the anti-family and anti-capitalist agenda of the Left. Worse still, Catholic workers' and women's groups penetrated the *Fédération* itself. The new generation of *Fédération* leaders endeavoured to mobilise parishioners within the party as a means of containing the threat from socialism and feminism, yet this, paradoxically, provided organisational and recruitment opportunities for Catholic workers' and women's groups. The FNF cultivated pro-suffrage *Fédération* deputies such as Marin, and in 1935 transformed itself into the women's section of the *Fédération*.[29] In Lyon the membership of the CFTC-affiliated *Corporation des employés de soieries* (a male white-collar union) overlapped with the *Cercles d'hommes* which had provided the basis for Perret's takeover of the *Fédération* in the city.[30] Similarly, in Bordeaux certain CFTC organisations collaborated with Bergey, while the abbé himself sponsored the creation of a *Union féminine d'action sociale*.[31] Thus, the institutional restructuring of the Church, together with the emergence of Catholic women's groups and trade unions, resulted in the popularisation of Catholic nationalism evident in the remaking of the *Fédération*.

DEFENDING FAMILY, PROPERTY AND RELIGION

The nationalism of the *Fédération* derived from a dialectic of pressure from above and below, and was both a reaction against, and a product of, the mobilisation of class- and gender-based movements within the Catholic electorate. As such the *Fédération* represented a highly unstable political synthesis, and struggled to reconcile defence of hierarchy, religion, property and family, at a time when subversive movements seemed to have undermined the Right itself. For these reasons the ideology of the *Fédération* cannot be abstracted from the contradictory pressures to which the movement was subject. The difficulty of assigning a label to the *Fédération* is increased by the fact that it drew upon two different political traditions: the liberal republicanism once represented by the Opportunists, and the confessionalism of the ALP. To categorise the *Fédération* as 'traditionalist' does little justice to its complexities.

The *Fédération*'s journey towards the Right was reflected in the party leadership. The first post-war leader, the Lyonnais businessman Auguste Isaac, was a deeply conservative practising Catholic. Yet he was also an economic liberal, espoused *laïcité* as an essential component of freedom of conscience and thanked the Revolution of 1789 for having abolished the corporations (so dear to nationalists). As contemporaries were fond of saying, Isaac was 'a moderate republican, but not moderately republican'.[32] Isaac withdrew from the leadership of the *Fédération* in 1924; three years later he resigned from the party in protest against its excessive nationalism and the influx of ex-royalists into the party.[33] Isaac's successor, Louis Marin, was also a republican, and partly shared Isaac's liberalism and parliamentarianism. He differed in that Catholicism was explicitly part of his definition of the Right. Although more committed to the parliamentary Republic than Perret, Henriot or Vallat, Marin was one of the prime movers in the development of the populist Catholic nationalism of the inter-war period.

Marin unreservedly endorsed Raymond Poincaré's famous declaration that Left and Right were divided by the 'chasm' of the religious question.[34] One side of this opposition was relatively unproblematic, for *Fédération* writers all agreed that the Left was defined principally by a materialist ideology, of which anti-clericalism was the logical extension. According to Marin the insatiable materialism of the Left readily developed into aggression against the spiritualism manifest in religion and the nation. Similarly, a ceaseless search for novelty and facile satisfaction led to a hatred for the millennial traditions, including Catholicism, from which France had been created. Anti-clericalism was also said to be reinforced by the abstract knowledge inculcated by State primary schools, which falsely led human beings to believe that they possessed the total knowledge that in reality belonged only to God. For Marin, however much they might differ on short-term issues, all Leftists agreed that they must, through control of the education system, ensure that the young were imbued with materialism and hatred for religion and nation, both of which depended on sacrifice of personal interests to the higher good.[35]

Marin's arguments are all the more significant because they date from February 1937, when the Popular Front was still in power, and when it might be expected that class struggle had eclipsed the religious quarrel. In fact, *Fédération* writers had explained the Popular Front electoral victory in terms that demonstrated the continued importance of religion – albeit inseparable from class and gender – in their construction of the Left. Marin's final appeal to the electors in April 1936 argued that they were confronted by two alternatives. The

Fédération represented the 'national and traditional'; its troops included the great mass of believers, who were defended by no other party. On the other side stood the 'comrades' republic', controlled ultimately by the Freemasons, whose historic mission it was to undermine religion and nation.[36] Indeed, some *Fédération* writers regarded the Popular Front merely as another episode in the clerical/ anti-clerical struggle, while Marin saw it as a repeat of Waldeck–Rousseau's ministry of 1899: both were based on the Radicals' mistaken belief that the best way to save the Republic was to bring 'revolutionaries' into the government, and to use anti-clericalism to divide the forces of order. Moreover, the expropriation of Church property in 1905 had set a precedent for the occupation of factories in June 1936.[37] While many conservatives denounced the Popular Front as a Judeo–Bolshevik conspiracy, the *Fédération* did not waver in its belief that Freemasons and the teaching unions provided its backbone.[38]

Indeed, the figure of the *instituteur public* stood for all that the *Fédération* rejected. The primary school teacher was no longer, as he had been before 1914, a pillar of the bourgeois republic. Rather the *Écoles normales* had produced a generation of socialist and Communist teachers, who manned the revolutionary trade unions that were said to have taken over the schools. Meanwhile, in the *Fédération*'s newspaper, *La Nation,* Jean Le Mee denounced feminist teachers for their belief that the liberation of women was dependent on the overthrow of capitalism, and for promoting sex education, thereby tapping into Catholic hostility to the merging of boys' and girls' schools in the inter-war period.[39] Thus the primary school teacher epitomised the Left's threat to religion, property, family and gender roles. During the Popular Front period, two figures symbolised the *Fédération*'s hatred: Marceau Pivert, the pacifist *primaire-supérieur* teacher and leader of the revolutionary wing of the *Section française de l'internationale ouvrière* (SFIO), and Jean Zay, the Radical Minister of National Education in the Popular Front government, never forgiven for having 'insulted' the French flag in his youth and accused of promoting only revolutionary teachers.[40] Le Mee's weekly column on the trade unions was stuffed full of denunciations of teachers and their unions for monitoring the political opinions of parents and pupils, discriminating against Catholics in examinations and for favouring revolutionaries and Freemasons in promotions.[41] These accusations remind us that the ·

popularisation of Catholic nationalism was connected to a battle for jobs and political influence. Far from being pushed into the background by the class struggles of the 1930s, anti-clericalism had been given a new lease of life by the growth of civil service trade unions, for these were seen as the most modern arm of the struggle against Catholicism and the social order.

Catholicism was, then, an essential component of the *Fédération*'s world-view. Yet because the religious quarrel was entangled with class and gender antagonisms, definition of the Left in terms of anti-clericalism presented serious practical problems. In fact, it was difficult for conservative politicians to create a coherent political alignment, whatever criteria were chosen, so the *Fédération*'s conception of the Right was fluid and shifted according to context. Despite claims for the primacy of religion, *Fédération* politicians were uncertain as to whether religion, property or nation should be the starting-point of political action, and they mixed calls for the re-building of the Christian *cité* with endorsement of the liberal principle of freedom of conscience. More precisely, the problem was that if religion were to be made the touchstone of the Right, then the socially conservative, but laïc, *Alliance démocratique* would be excluded, while the reform-ist, but Catholic, PDP, would have to be included. If, on the other hand, defence of property defined the Right, then the *Alliance* would be included and the PDP excluded.

Take first the *Fédération*'s attitude to the PDP. The latter party was the *bête noire* of the *Fédération*, for it was accused of dividing the Catholic vote. Underlying this hostility was the presupposition that Christianity was intrinsically opposed to class and gender conflict. Catholicism was necessarily conservative because only Christian love could provide a secure basis for class collaboration and acceptance of traditional gender roles.[42] The materialism of the Left, in contrast, was blamed for fomenting working-class discontent and for making women more concerned with fashion than with giving birth to children.[43] Marcel Petitjean of the *Fédération* made three accusations against the PDP.[44] First, in foreign policy it supported rapproche-ment with Germany. It was difficult for Petitjean to criticise the Christian Democrats on this score, given that international pacifica-tion was favoured by the Pope. Petitjean therefore contented himself with describing this policy as Leftist in inspiration and implicitly therefore as anti-Catholic. Secondly, and likewise, the PDP was accused of borrowing its social programme from the Left, favouring, amongst other things, the Social Insurance Acts. Revealingly, Petitjean criticised the PDP not just for endorsing Left-wing civil service trade unions, but for supporting the Catholic agricultural syndicates of abbé Mancel in Brittany, which were accused of setting peasants against landowners. Thirdly, Petitjean accused the PDP of unnailing Christ from the cross in order to make of him a party agent. The PDP's rapprochement of theology and revolution was literally blasphemous, for Christianity dictated that relations between classes and individuals should be based on reciprocal love, and that the special interests of women or workers should be sacrificed to the general good. It followed that the PDP could not be truly Catholic, and the definition of the Right as Catholic remained intact.

In its struggle against the PDP, the *Fédération* urged the union of all Catholics around a programme of social conservatism within a Christian society. Such arguments were unlikely to facilitate collaboration with the *Alliance démocratique*, and, indeed, there were cases where religious quarrels had undermined electoral co-operation.[45] In April 1932 Marin, as was his wont, assured his readers that the coming elections would be fought by two blocs. On one side stood the Marxists. On the other stood those with a *national* programme, albeit divided by foreign policy, the social question, and *religion*.[46] Although the cement of the Left remained irreligion, the logic of Marin's position was now different, in that the nation now stood above religion. Still the problem would not go away, for the *Fédération* could not entirely disarticulate nation and religion. The two were assumed to be related by their common roots in the spiritual, by the fact that Catholicism was an indispensable element of the national tradition and, as we have seen, the very notion of order was held to have Catholic roots. Faced with such difficulties, other *Fédération* politicians groped around for alternative constructions of the Right. Victor Perret argued that the protection of private property provided a more neutral ground on which the Right could be united. But Perret's conception of the economic terrain was also freighted with religious assumptions. He held that only Christianity could ensure that all social classes would accept the natural hierarchy of family, profession and nation.[47] Perret also assumed that defence of property required purges of the irreligious personnel of public education, a measure seen as counter-productive by the lay Right, for State schools were regarded by them as a means of promoting the social mobility that would ultimately diffuse the socialist threat. Another way out of the dilemma, this time preserving the primacy of religion, was to assert that the supporters of the *Alliance* were, at heart, Catholic. For Petitjean, *Fédération* and *Alliance* deputies scarcely differed in their social and economic conceptions: most were Catholic educated; the majority endorsed the programme of the FNC and were opposed to the lay laws. *Alliance* deputies, wrote Petitjean, nevertheless verbally endorsed *laïcité* out of fear of being compromised politically and because they did not want to cut themselves off from the Republic.[48] Petitjean salvaged, in theory at least, the Catholic definition of the Right. But as with the other answers to the problem of the *Alliance*, the price was legitimation of practical collaboration with anti-clericals, and acceptance of the liberal principle of freedom of conscience.

The *Fédération*'s debt to liberalism emerges equally clearly from Marin's long explanation, penned for Nuncio Valeri in February 1937, of his views on the relationship between the Church and politics.[49] Marin accepted in principle that it was impossible to distinguish between religious and non-religious issues. Even the question of when the fishing season should end could, he admitted, have a religious dimension. Therefore, the Church's view was potentially relevant to any issue. Marin also accepted Church control of all groups with specifically religious functions. Yet, he argued, Catholic associations needed technical advice that could be provided only by politicians. Even the Church itself, since it was attacked politically, required political defence. Underlying Marin's arguments was the liberal notion of the separation of the religious and secular. Politicians were experts in government, the Church in ethics. Politicians would consult the Church in matters of morality, but would reserve technical matters to themselves. Marin, in fact, was positively opposed to clerical intervention in the political sphere. It would, he said, alienate non-Catholics and foment an anti-clerical reaction.

Thus in attempting to exclude the PDP (and the working-class and women's groups with which it was associated) from the Right, the *Fédération* defined itself in terms that owed something to Catholic traditionalism, in that social order was held to rest upon Christian principles reaffirmed over the centuries. Yet in order to include the *Alliance* in the Right, and to avoid alienating those whose anti-clericalism was believed to be skin-deep, the *Fédération* had to play down Catholicism and concede the liberal principle of freedom of conscience. Whatever principle of unity was chosen tended to melt away in practice because of the impossibility of reconciling the diverse demands upon the *Fédération*. In this respect the party was no different to any other: claims to base political action upon an ultimate ground are intrinsically difficult to sustain. More pertinently, these dilemmas reveal the difficulties inherent in classifying the *Fédération* as traditionalist.

MOBILISING THE CATHOLIC PEOPLE

Both of the traditions upon which the *Fédération* drew combined an elitist social conservatism with an appeal to the people – to popular sovereignty in the case of liberalism, and to the Christian people in that of Catholicism. This populism meant that the *Fédération*'s response to the crisis of the 1930s was not 'reactionary' in a simple sense, for it included an attempt to neutralise challenges to the established order by mobilising them within a framework that preserved (in theory) the hegemony of the social elites. This can be seen in the *Fédération*'s response to challenges in the religious, gender and social spheres.

Taking religion first, Marin's liberal conception of the Church's position in society appears in some respects to match the hierarchy's own desire to withdraw from party politics. In fact, his assessment of the causes of anti-clericalism put him at odds with the Church's re-christianisation project. In Marin's view the anti-clericalism of the great majority stemmed from an irrational fear of the priest that would evaporate were it not fed by the interference of the Church in matters that did not concern it. An identical assumption of the fundamentally Catholic nature of the people underlay the view that anti-clericalism could be attributed to the occult activity of Free-masons. Here *Fédération* writers were in accord with Castelnau, who railed endlessly about the pernicious influence of Freemasons and revolutionary school teachers, yet was confident that the eternal truth would survive, either in those who possessed and lived the faith, or where it dwelled in French hearts because of Christian heredity. In other words, both Marin and Castelnau assumed that dechristian-isation was more apparent than real.[50] It followed that there was no need for re-christianisation, and no need for the public display of faith on the part of Catholic Action militants that was supposed to bring about conversion by example.[51] On the contrary, the people would return to religion if the Church stuck to its allotted role and if the influence of atheistic Marxism and Freemasonry (that is to say the Radical–Socialist Party, Socialists and Communists) were eliminated. Such a project would be pursued by political and administrative methods, such as reform of the electoral system in order to exclude the Left from power, suppression of 'illegal' civil service trade unions and purges of the University. The *Fédération* also pursued vigorously the campaign to end legal discrimination against Catholic associations and teaching orders, while criticising progressives for their supposed willingness to drop these traditional grievances.[52] La Cour Grandmaison's explanation of the role of the FNC confirms nationalist suspicion of specialist Catholic Action. He claimed for the FNC the directing and unifying role within Catholic Action, for specialist groups were too narrowly based for such a task. For La Cour Grandmaison another strength of the FNC was that it was open to all who wanted peace, order and liberty. The implicit inclusion within Catholic Action of non-Catholics demonstrated his lack of sympathy with the desire of the specialist groups to create a Christian elite. The latter conception permitted peasants, workers and women to play a significant role in Catholic organisations, so long as they showed the desired commitment to the faith.[53]

Notwithstanding the elitism of the *Fédération*'s solutions to the religious question, the party remained convinced of the fundamental soundness of the Catholic people. This populism was most evident in the case of Bergey, who contrasted his humble cassock with the frock-coats and smoking jackets of the Chamber of Deputies, and boasted of the dignitaries who had visited his humble presbytery.[54] For Marin the people were much less guilty than the parties or the government. He made a distinction between voters and 'general opinion', the latter being more 'extensive' than (and often very different from) the former. History had shown that voters were often mistaken, and that only in periods of cataclysm (such as 1914) or crisis (such as 1926) would the electorate open its eyes. At the time of writing, in May 1932, voters were unaware of the gravity of the crisis, but opinion was said by Marin to be in a state of anguish.[55] The populism of the *Fédération* was not merely a rhetorical pose. It underlay endorsements of the riots of 6 February 1934, when the far Right had attempted to storm the Chamber of Deputies. For Vallat the riots proved that the French belonged to a race so profoundly honest that they had embarked upon revolution as soon as they discovered that their representatives lacked virtue. At the *Fédération*'s national congress, Perret spoke of 'le réveil de la conscience nationale se traduisant par des manifestations spontanées du peuple de Paris aux côtés des anciens combattants'.[56] Populism was also integral to the organisational remaking of the *Fédération*. Petitjean called for the party to create powerful organisations which would be masters of the fate of deputies.[57] Perret declared his intention to renovate France with the help of the popular classes, against the opposition of the 'established bourgeoisie' and 'certain deputies'.[58]

It is important to highlight the limits of *Fédération* populism. Marin held that public opinion, although finally sovereign, was insufficiently enlightened to speak directly for the national interest. Leaders in the fields of agriculture, industry, education, the arts and religion, who had demonstrated their ability to produce new solutions to new problems, would have to guide the masses.[59] For Perret the masses knew little of politics, and regarded issues in moral terms or as a matter of immediate interest. They were motivated by reflexes and mystiques, and so were open to demagogy. Whereas far-Right organisations such as the *Parti populaire français* (PPF) saw the people in masculine terms, Perret saw it as prone to feminine instability.[60] The role of the party militant, of whom Perret saw himself the spokesman, was therefore to direct the people.[61] The organisational structures set up by the *Fédération* in the late 1920s and early 1930s reflected this desire to mobilise the people from above. Party members did little more than applaud their leaders at meetings and help out at election time. Often the *Fédération* contented itself with *encadrement* of the leisure of the members of parish men's unions. In Lyon, the principal point of contact between the *Fédération* and the men's groups was the *boules* match. In Maine-et-Loire, the Catholic *cercles* on which the Right relied were largely recreational; indeed, priests often complained that their members played *boules* during vespers.[62] Here too, in the notion that the people were at once fundamentally sound yet also in need of elite leadership, it is possible to see the eclectic roots of the *Fédération*'s ideas. The Catholic tradition gave to wealthy *hommes d'œuvres* the task of leading the faithful. Similarly, as Pierre Rosanvallon has argued, moderate republicans had traditionally been ambiguous in their view of democracy, insisting on the need for those with superior 'capacities' to direct the electorate.[63]

The same blend of elitism and populism can be seen in the *Fédération*'s response to feminism. Party spokesmen agreed that the traditional balance between the sexes was changing fundamentally. Bergey argued that Catholics must adapt to the fact that many young women had been obliged to abandon the pleasures of family life and to find a profession. Hence the foundation of Catholic schools and unions for women. Bergey also approved of the Catholic feminist group, the *Fédération nationale des femmes* (FNF). The *Fédération* as a party supported female suffrage. Marcel Petitjean argued that women should possess the right to vote simply by virtue of their humanity; after all, he said, the suffrage had been accorded to recently naturalised foreigners and to natives of the colonies who had barely reached political maturity. Both Bergey and Petitjean emphasised the granting of rights to women as passive members of the political community, where their role was to be balanced by giving extra votes to fathers of families. Care was taken to assert that women participated in the political community on terms different to those of men. Petitjean accepted, somewhat reluctantly, that women possessed a sense of duty, perspicacity, devotion and sacrifice at the *minimum* level, but emphasised that they would bring their special virtues to the electorate, and that both social legislation and the birthrate would benefit. For his part, Bergey stressed the fact that, for better or for worse, women were more likely to go to extremes. Therefore they must be prepared for the vote by religious education.[64] Just as Perret insisted that the electorate required guidance from the elites if it were not to be seduced by demagogues, so Bergey assumed that women required supervision.

Similar ambiguities were present in the *Fédération*'s response to the social question. The party's claim in June 1936 that it had always favoured reforms identical to those enacted by the Popular Front was unconvincing. The party had never offered much to workers beyond paid holidays, salary rises in accordance with 'economic reality', elimination of immigrants from the labour force and the return of working mothers to the home. The great majority of *Fédération* deputies had opposed the Social Insurance Acts of 1928 and 1936, voting instead for a system based on existing mutual aid societies. The Popular Front provoked little change in the *Fédération*'s attitude, for although it voted in favour of paid holidays and collective contracts, it condemned wage rises, the forty-hour week and the negative effects on productivity of trade union activity. But the *Fédération* combined reaction with the notion that the worker must be mobilised in the corporation. This corporatism did not go very far. Perret's call for a return to the 'great corporative family' was designed to remove skilled workers from the influence of revolutionary trade unions and to facilitate class collaboration through the creation of mixed unions where boss and worker could learn to understand each other. Victor Perret played down the theme on his home territory of Lyon because of the continued strength of liberalism there. Unlike the fascist and populist *Croix de Feu* and especially its successor, the *Parti social français* (PSF), the *Fédération* was unwilling to countenance separate workers' and employers' syndicates within the corporation. Neither did the *Fédération* follow the *Croix de Feu*/PSF in creating its own trade union wing. Perret set up a Workers' and Employees' committee in Lyon, but it did not in any respect resemble an autonomous workers' organisation. Instead its two hundred members listened to lectures on Communism, aspects of labour legislation and general politics from *Fédération* dignitaries.[65] But for all the limitations of its programme, the *Fédération* did entice many working-class and especially white-collar workers to its standard. These workers had not been duped by their employers; rather, the *Fédération* attracted those who placed antagonism to rivals in the labour market, whether women or non-Catholics, ahead of grievances against employers. At most they espoused an anti-capitalism consisting in the complaint that employers were insufficiently zealous in promoting Catholics and returning women to the home. Perhaps typical of conservative white-collar workers was Auguste Gruffaz, president of the regional union of the CFTC in the south east, and a member of the *Fédération*. Gruffaz rarely criticised employers, except to urge them to place less emphasis on 'materialism' or technical considerations in deciding promotions, to take more account of 'moral qualities', and to ensure that women were excluded from the workforce. In other words, Gruffaz combined anti-socialism with the defence of the special interests of his male Catholic colleagues.[66]

CONCLUSION

The *Fédération* in the 1930s demonstrated the vitality of Catholic nationalism. The fundamental anti-feminism and anti-socialism of the party had been hardened by the social and political struggles of the period, particularly as they seemed to divide the Right itself. Far from causing religious issues to lose their importance, class and gender conflicts were blamed on the spread of an anti-religious materialism by Freemasons, feminists, trade unionists and Marxists. This conviction was reinforced by the spread to new areas of struggle for jobs, power and influence. These conflicts converged with the Church's mobilisation of the faithful in the parishes and led to a popularisation of Catholic nationalism. The *Fédération*, then, represented a response to the triple threat to religious, patriarchal and economic hierarchies. On the one hand, *Fédération* elites used a populist discourse and practice to neutralise and contain the danger represented by socialist and feminist, class and gender, movements, within and outside of the Right. On the other hand, this populism was the reflection of real aspirations on the part of Catholic women and workers. But it should be stressed that these aspirations barely amounted to a Right-wing socialism or feminism, for the interests of women or workers as a category were rarely evoked. On the contrary, the women and workers defined their interests in terms that excluded non-Catholics.

Nevertheless, the *Fédération* found it difficult to hold on to its increasingly self-conscious rank and file, for party leaders, raised in the liberal–conservative and/or Catholic traditions, were ultimately too distrustful of the masses to allow them much space. The *Croix de Feu* and PSF proved to be a rather more promising vehicle within which conservative women and workers could combine their hostility to socialism and Left-wing feminism with vigorous pursuit of their special interests. Unlike the *Fédération*, the PSF developed a quasi-autonomous trade union wing and allowed women a larger degree of autonomy within the party. Here we touch upon another dimension of the relationship between the Church and the nationalist Right. Whereas the *Fédération* won the support of those Catholics who prioritised political action against the causes of dechristianisation, the *Croix de Feu*/PSF owed as much, if not more, to the evangelism of Catholic Action, and perhaps also to its political allies in the PDP.[67] The reasons for this convergence do not concern us here. Suffice it to say, first, that some Catholic 'progressives' had been ambivalent in their attitude to democracy. Secondly, both *Croix de Feu*/PSF and Catholic progressives promised a 'third way' between socialism and capitalism.[68] Thirdly, the fact that the *Croix de Feu*/PSF claimed to be apolitical in a way that the *Fédération* did not, meant that it was possible for militants of Catholic Action to reconcile involvement in the far Right with the Church's apoliticism. Fourthly, the declining enthusiasm of the Right for war against Germany removed one of the major reasons why progressives, long in favour of peace, had been repelled by the far-Right movements like the *Croix de Feu*/PSF.

Finally, the strength of Catholic nationalism in the 1930s throws new light on the origins of the Vichy experience, for no party better prefigures the National Revolution than the *Fédération*. Louis Marin, of course, was a firm, if qualified, supporter of the Republic, who refused from the beginning to have anything to do with Vichy. Henriot, Perret, Bergey and Vallat had a more positive view. Doubtless they saw the regime's purges of Freemasons and Jews, hostility to trade unions and women's groups, support for Catholic schooling and its combination of tightly controlled popular mobilisation with restoration of the power of the 'natural' elites, as fulfilment of the *Fédération*'s programme. Just as the *Fédération* has been seen by historians as traditionalist, so René Rémond has depicted the Vichy regime as a manifestation of the counter-revolutionary strand in French political history.[69] The view that Vichy was traditionalist has the advantage of permitting a clear distinction between Pétain's dictatorship and the liberal–democratic Fifth Republic. And because traditionalist movements were held to be bound to disappear as modernisation advanced, Vichy can be seen as representing the last stand of the counter-revolutionary tradition, never to reappear as a significant political force. Post-war French conservatism is thereby freed of the taint of Vichy. Yet the interpretation offered here suggests that the *Fédération* represented a synthesis, albeit an unstable one, of Catholic traditionalism with liberal-conservatism. By extension, this chapter suggests that Vichy, too, could be viewed in this way. In this respect its conclusions are compatible with those of Robert Paxton, who argued that Pétain's regime was marked by a similar mixture of traditionalism and liberalism.[70] It would seem, then, that far from being predestined for marginalisation, Catholic nationalism represented in the 1930s a potentially viable political programme, requiring only favourable circumstances for implementation. If Catholic nationalism subsequently expired, it was killed by events, not by the onward march of history.

NOTES

1. The author wishes to thank Garthine Walker for her comments on this chapter.
2. Étienne Fouilloux, '"Fille aînée de l'Église" ou "pays de mission"?', in *Histoire de la France religieuse*, vol. 4, 'Société sécularisée et renouveaux religieux', ed. René Rémond (Paris: Seuil, 1992); René Rémond, *Les Catholiques, le communisme et les crises, 1929–39* (Paris: Armand Colin, 1960); H.W. Paul, *The Second Ralliement: the Rapprochement Between Church and State in France in the Twentieth Century* (Washington: Catholic University of America Press, 1967); James McMillan, 'France', in *Political Catholicism in Europe, 1918–65*, eds Tom Buchanan and Martin Conway (Oxford: Clarendon Press, 1996).
3. The term 'progressive', as used in this chapter, does not imply sympathy for the Left. The great majority of progressives were sympathetic to the PDP or Left wing of the *Fédération*. They were progressive only in relation to Catholic nationalists.
4. *La Vie religieuse des Français à travers les sondages d'opinion (1944–1976)*, ed. Jacques Sutter, 2 vols (Paris: Éditions du CNRS, 1984), p. 815; AN 317 AP 119 (Fonds Marin), Marin to Valeri, 19 February 1937; *L'Union républicaine*, 21 June 1936; Philippe Boutry and Alain-René Michel, 'La religion', in *Histoire des droites en France*, ed. Jean-François Sirinelli, 3 vols (Paris: Gallimard, 1992), III, 687; Kevin Passmore, *From Liberalism to Fascism: The Right in a French Province, 1928–1939* (Cambridge: Cambridge University Press, 1997), pp. 47–48; see *Semaine religieuse de Lyon*, 19 January and 22 March 1929 for the fears of Cardinal Maurin that village schoolteachers would control the new social insurance funds.
5. See, for example, the celebratory tone of Fouilloux, '"Fille aînée de l'Église"'.
6. Rémond, *Les Catholiques*, p. 10.
7. Fouilloux, '"Fille aînée de l'Église"', p. 135.
8. See, for example, Paul, *The Second Ralliement*, pp. 101–39; James McMillan, 'Catholicism and Nationalism in France. The case of the *Fédération nationale catholique*', in *Catholicism in Britain and France since 1789*, eds Nicholas Atkin and Frank Tallet (London: The Hambledon Press, 1996), pp. 151–63 (p. 153).
9. René Rémond, *Les Droites en France* (Paris: Aubier, 1981), p. 189.
10. William D. Irvine, *French Conservatism in Crisis: the Republican Federation in France in the 1930s* (Baton Rouge/London: Louisiana State University Press, 1979); Jean-Noël Jeanenney, *François de Wendel en République: l'argent et le pouvoir 1914–1940* (Paris: Seuil, 1976).
11. AN 317 AP 119, Marin to Valeri, 19 February 1937.
12. AN 317 AP 72, Guiter to Marin, 10 June 1938.
13. Rémond, *Les Catholiques*, p. 11; Paul Christophe, *1936: Les Catholiques et le Front populaire* (Paris: Éditions ouvrières, 1986), pp. 33–60, pp. 139–45.
14. Christophe, *1936*, pp. 71–72.
15. Jean-Claude Delbreil, *Centrisme et démocratie chrétienne: le Parti démocrate populaire des origines aux MRP 1919–1944* (Paris: Publications de la Sorbonne, 1990), pp. 174–87; Général Yves Gras, *Castelnau, ou l'art de commander* (Paris: Denoël, 1990), pp. 349–404; Passmore, *From Liberalism to Fascism*, pp. 150–51; Nadine-Josette Chaline, *Des catholiques normandes sous la Troisième République: crises,*

combats, renouveaux (Le Coteau: Horvath, 1985), pp. 184–87; McMillan, 'Catholicism and nationalism', pp. 159–60.

16. McMillan, 'Catholicism and nationalism', p. 155; Christian Bougeard, 'Bleus, blancs, rouges en Bretagne dans l'entre-deux-guerres', in *Les Bleus de Bretagne de la Révolution à nos jours*, ed. Alain Droguet (Saint-Brieuc: Fédération Côtes-du-Nord, 1991), pp. 407–8.

17. Chaline, *Des catholiques normands*, pp. 182–83.

18. Delbreil, *Centrisme et démocratie chrétienne*, pp. 224–25, p. 301.

19. Christophe, *1936*, pp. 48–61.

20. Jean-Claude Delbreil, 'Les Démocrates chrétiens en Lorraine dans l'Entre-deux-guerres', *Les Cahiers lorrains*, 4 (1987), 414–47 (pp. 430–31, pp. 435–37).

21. AN F7 14 614, various reports of 1934–38.

22. AN 317 AP 72, Alicot to Guiter, 15 February 1937.

23. Irvine, *French Conservatism in Crisis*, pp. 27–48 and map 6.

24. Xavier Vallat, *Le Nez de Cléopatre* (Paris: Seuil, 1957).

25. Passmore, *From Liberalism to Fascism*, pp. 140–62; Jean-Luc Marais, *Les Sociétés d'hommes: histoire d'une sociabilité du 18e siècle à nos jours* (Vauchrétienne: I. Davy, 1986), pp. 139–46; Jean-Luc Marais, 'La Défense de l'Anjou chrétien', in *Le Diocèse d'Angers*, ed. François Lebrun (Paris: Beauchesne, 1981), pp. 235–61.

26. *Action libérale populaire* (Bulletin mensuel du Comité régional du sud-est), January 1927–December 1929.

27. The paragraphs that follow are based on Maurice Larkin, *Religion, Politics and Preferment in France since 1890: la Belle Époque and its legacy* (Cambridge: Cambridge University Press, 1995), pp. 147–73; Siân Reynolds, *France Between the Wars: Gender and Politics* (London: Routledge, 1996), pp. 83–108, pp. 132–55; Odile Sarti, *The Ligue patriotique des Françaises 1902–1933* (New York/London: Garland, 1992); Anne Cova, 'Femmes et catholicisme social: trois mouvements nationaux d'initiative lyonnaise', in *Cent ans de catholicisme social à Lyon et en Rhône-Alpes*, eds Jean-Dominique Durand et al. (Paris: Éditions ouvrières, 1992), pp. 307–22; Michel Launay, *La CFTC: origines et développement 1919–1940* (Paris: Publications de la Sorbonne, 1986), esp. p. 305.

28. Paul Smith, *Feminism and the Third Republic: Women's Political and Civil Rights in France 1918–1945* (Oxford: Clarendon Press, 1996), pp. 52–55.

29. Smith, *Feminism and the Third Republic*, p. 55, pp. 91–93.

30. Passmore, *From Liberalism to Fascism*, pp. 84–85.

31. AN F7 13224, reports of 24 June 1929, 20 November 1929, 9 April 1939.

32. Régis Ladous, 'Auguste Isaac et la tradition républicaine', in *Cent ans de catholicisme social*, pp. 131–58.

33. AN 317 AP 73, Isaac to Guiter, 19 April 1930.

34. AN 317 AP 119, Marin to Valeri, 19 February 1937.

35. *La Nation*, 13 February 1937.

36. *La Nation*, 25 April 1936, 29 August 1936.

37. *La Nation*, 2 May 1936, 20 June 1936.

38. *La Nation*, 28 May 1932, 18 April 1936; Gérard Cholvy, *Géographie religieuse de l'Hérault contemporaine* (Paris: Presses Universitaires de France, 1968), p. 392.

39. *La Nation*, 20 February 1932.

40. *La Nation*, 30 April 1932, 28 May 1932, 4 April 1936.

41. *La Nation*, 30 July 1932, 6 August 1932, 18 April 1936, 14 November 1936,

5 December 1936, 26 December 1936, 6 May 1939.

42. The *Fédération*'s arguments against the PDP owed much to Jean Le Trécorrois (pseudonym of Père Bénigne), *Les Déviations du Parti démocrate populaire* (Paris: Dupré, 1931).

43. *La Nation*, 17 April 1937.

44. *La Nation*, 30 January 1932, 28 May 1932.

45. AN 317 AP 72, undated report on the 1935 municipal elections in Paris; AN 317 AP 119, Marin to Valeri, 19 February 1937 on the Lorraine; *Action catholique de Bordeaux*, 5 September 1931.

46. *La Nation*, 23 April 1932, 20 June 1936.

47. Passmore, *From Liberalism to Fascism*, pp. 153–55.

48. *La Nation*, 16 January 1932, 8 February 1936.

49. AN 317 AP 119, Marin to Valeri, 19 February 1937.

50. *Crédo* (bulletin officiel de la FNC), January 1935. See also Bergey in *Action catholique de Bordeaux*, 5 December 1933.

51. AN 317 AP 119, Marin to Valeri, 19 February 1937. Similarly, Auguste Isaac complained in 1930 that the intervention of Catholic Action caused sensible reforms to be tainted with clericalism (Ladous, 'Auguste Isaac', p. 143).

52. *La Nation*, 30 July 1932, 6 August 1932, 18 April 1936, 14 November 1936, 5 December 1936, 26 December 1936, 6 May 1939. See Tranvouez, *Catholiques d'abord*, pp. 110–12, for an account of this kind of Catholic politics.

53. *Le Figaro*, 7 June 1937.

54. AN 324 AP 4 (Fonds Tardieu), Bergey to Tardieu, 4 April 1932; *Action catholique de Bordeaux*, 20 March 1933.

55. *La Nation*, 2 January 1932, 4 May 1932.

56. *La Nation*, 2 May 1936; AN 317 AP 82/3, *La Politique générale de la Fédération*.

57. *La Nation*, 4 June 1932.

58. AN 317 AP 73, 28 September 1932; Passmore, *From Liberalism to Fascism*, pp. 140–42.

59. *La Nation*, 4 January 1932, 4 May 1932.

60. Kevin Passmore, 'Class, gender and populism: the PPF in Lyon, 1936–39', in *The Right in France since 1789*, eds Nicholas Atkin and Frank Tallett (London: Tauris Press, 1997), pp. 183–214.

61. *La Nation*, 2 January 1932, 9 January 1932.

62. Marais, *Les Sociétés d'hommes*, p. 144; Passmore, *From Liberalism to Fascism*, pp. 155–56.

63. Pierre Rosanvallon, *Le Moment Guizot* (Paris: Seuil, 1985).

64. *Action catholique de Bordeaux*, 5 January 1930; *La Nation*, 2 July 1932.

65. *La Nation*, 22 February 1930, 3 May 1930; Irvine, *French Conservatism*, pp. 75–93; AN 317 AP 82/3, 2 June 1936.

66. Passmore, *From Liberalism to Fascism*, pp. 84–85.

67. For the involvement of PDP and Catholic Action activists in the PSF see Chaline, *Des catholiques normands*, p. 194; Pierre Péan, *Une Jeunesse française* (Paris: Fayard, 1994); Passmore, *From Liberalism to Fascism*, pp. 241–43.

68. See *La Croix du Rhône*, 5 May 1936.

69. Rémond, *Les Droites*, pp. 231–38.

70. Robert Paxton, *Vichy France: Old Guard and New Order 1940–1944* (New York: Morningside, 1972).

4

True and false modernity: Catholicism and Communist Marxism in 1930s France

David Curtis

From the viewpoint of an historian of 1930s France, the most important of the three relationships distinguished by Denis Maugenest[1] – those between Church and Communism, between Christians and Marxists and between Catholic faith and Marxism – is undoubtedly that between Church and Communism; and if the Popular Front years (1934–38) were the most important in the decade, this was, from that viewpoint, because they saw an intensification of a 'lutte d'influence'[2] between Church and Party for the souls and minds of the French people and specifically for those of the working class. However, the third relationship, that between Catholic faith and Communist Marxism, is worthy of attention, and not only because the 1930s Catholic discovery of Marxism–Leninism and of the philosophy of Marx shaped post-1945 Catholic approaches to Marxism. The ambition of *catholicisme intégral* to realise 'tout le christianisme dans toute la vie' involved more than social and political action, more than the creation of Catholic organisations and the permeation of secular organisations and institutions. It involved also a rejection of a dechristianised modern world (and thus a secular-isation theory) and a project of a 'true' modernity. This project was articulated primarily as 'the restoration of the social order', as illustrated by the subtitle of the May 1931 papal social encyclical, *Quadragesimo anno*. But the project found expression too as a 'nouveau Moyen âge' (the title of the Russian Orthodox philosopher Nikolai Berdyaev's seminal 1927 work), a 'nouvelle chrétienté' and a 'human-isme intégral' (the title of the neo-Thomist philosopher Jacques Maritain's influential 1936 book).

In the 1930s, and above all in the Popular Front period, the ideal of a *nouvelle chrétienté* generated powerful critiques of the 'false' modernity embodied in the *frères ennemis* of Western capitalist democracy and Eastern Communist totalitarianism. It especially inspired well-informed *dépassements* of the ideology of Communism, a system that was seen by the Church as an integral anti-Catholicism, a unity of anti-religious theory and practice, a *marxisme intégral.* Since these *dépassements* were elaborated very much in response to the political, social and intellectual challenge posed in the Popular Front period by Communism in general and by the French Communist Party (PCF) in particular, and owed much to the evolution of French intellectual life in the late 1920s and early 1930s, it is with an account of this challenge and of this evolution that we may begin this chapter.

Pius XI's preoccupation with the worldwide Communist 'peril', represented in his eyes not only by the consolidation of Stalinism in the Soviet Union but also by Mexican and Spanish anti-clericalism, was increasingly apparent in his pronouncements from the beginning of the decade: *Quadragesimo anno,* for example, denounced Communism as impious, unjust and barbarous. The growth of Communist influence in France was monitored by the Jesuits of the *Dossiers de l'Action populaire,* by the Dominicans of *La Vie intellectuelle* and of course by *Documentation catholique.* This was especially the case after the Party's momentous 1934 *grand tournant* (the shift from class-against-class sectarianism to a tactic of working-class and middle-class alliance against Fascism) had led it to abandon its policy of a *poing levé* against the Church and to make overtures to young Catholic workers. Nevertheless, Churchmen underestimated both the success of the new Communist tactic in the political and social domains and the growing appeal of a Marxism presented by the PCF as a scientific humanism, the basis of a new culture. The events of 1936 were to take the Church into a 'zone de turbulence'[3] in which, as Jean-Marie Mayeur writes, 'les communistes deviennent même les principaux adversaires ou les principaux interlocuteurs, au point d'éclipser leurs prédécesseurs'.[4] Church–PCF relations were now to be the occasion of increased friction not only between French Catholics already sharply divided over political and social matters, but also between the avant-garde of French Catholicism and Rome.

Of these 1936 events the two most important were the *main tendue* in France and the Civil War in Spain. The Communist Party leader, Maurice Thorez, offered the Party's hand to Catholics in his broadcast election speech of 17 April 1936. Already dramatic in tone, the *main tendue* (which the Party has never withdrawn) was given added force by its social and political context. It was offered to Catholic workers over the heads of the Church's hierarchy one month after the position of the Catholic trade union, the *Confédération française des travailleurs chrétiens* (CFTC), had been weakened by the reuniting of the Socialist-dominated *Confédération générale du travail* (CGT) and the Communist-dominated *Confédération générale du travail unitaire* (CGTU). One month after Thorez's speech, the Party made vast – and to the Church, unexpected – electoral gains which were to be the basis of its influence in the Popular Front coalition of Socialists, Radical Socialists, Communists and others. In this context it was of little importance that the *main tendue* was accepted openly by very few Catholics (prominent amongst whom were the *littérateur* Robert Honnert; the *secrétaire de rédaction* of the pro-Popular Front weekly *Vendredi*, Louis Martin-Chauffier; and the Catholics around the revolutionary interdenominational monthly *Terre nouvelle*). Much more important than the question of the acceptance or refusal of the *main tendue*, both in terms of French political history and of the political, social and intellectual evolution of the Church, was the nature of the anti-Communism involved in its refusal.

The vast majority of Catholics at the time were visceral anti-Communists, readers of *La France catholique* (the organ of the *Fédération nationale catholique* (FNC) which had been set up in 1925 to defend Catholic interests against Édouard Herriot's government, the *Cartel des gauches*), the *Pèlerin* and the Right-wing newspaper *L'Écho de Paris*. They identified Popular Front and Communism and were only too ready to believe that the so-called 'Dimitrov Plan' to destroy the Church and set up a Communist dictatorship was genuine. For such Catholics the *main tendue* was simply further proof, if proof were needed, of Communist duplicity. However, a minority of Catholics rejected this simplistic attitude. Prominent amongst these were the Christian Democrats of the newspaper *L'Aube*, the Dominicans of the weekly *Sept* and the journal *La Vie intellectuelle* and many Catholic contributors to the pluralist, personalist review *Esprit*. For these Catholics the papal strategy to free the faithful from subservience to temporal interests entailed a 'positive' anti-Communism. This strategy had been exemplified most dramatically by the 1926 condemnation of the Right-wing movement *Action française* (AF), which enjoyed the support of leading Catholic intellectuals. Confident in 'la primauté du spirituel' (the title of Maritain's influential 1927 work), in the uniqueness and independence of the Catholic 'third way' which claimed to be 'neither Left nor Right', 'positive' anti-Communists were able to distinguish to varying degrees between Communists as persons with social aspirations that were just and Communism as a political party, and to accept some aspects of the Communist critique of capitalism while condemning the political system of Communism as a virulent atheism and anti-humanism.

However, this minority did not function as a political and ideological bloc able to confront the conservative majority: on the contrary, it exemplified by its diversity the pluralism it advocated. We find therefore that, while *Sept* refused to condemn all the measures taken by the Popular Front government of 1936–37, *Esprit* (whose Catholic editor Emmanuel Mounier had already shown himself ready to dialogue with Party intellectuals at the Party-orchestrated June 1935 International Writers' Conference) was prepared to give the government its critical support. Likewise, while *Sept* condemned the factory occupations of May–June 1936 in the name of Catholic social doctrine, members of the CFTC and the *Jeunesse ouvrière chrétienne* (JOC), the white hope of Social Catholicism, were participating in both strikes and factory occupations. Meanwhile and most significantly, while the Centre–Right Christian Democrat Party the *Parti démocrate populaire* (PDP) did not support the newly elected Socialist-led government, deputies of the Centre-Left Christian Democrat party *Jeune république* (JR) were putting down an important marker in the history of relations between Catholics and the Left by forming part of the Popular Front majority. This was a clear indication that anti-clericalism was no longer a criterion of Left-wing allegiance.

Divisions between Catholics were further accentuated by the Spanish Civil War, which began in July 1936. The war confirmed that there was an unbridgeable gulf between what François Mauriac called 'deux races d'esprit': visceral and 'positive' anti-Communists. While the latter 'race' was often prepared to argue and campaign for international mediation to end the war, the former saw Franco's insurrection as a crusade against Marxist barbarism. And it was the visceral anti-Communists who now had the ear of Rome. Events in France led Rome to place *Terre nouvelle* on the Index in July 1936 and to subject to close examination the positions of *L'Aube* and of *Esprit*. In August 1937, events in France and Spain led to the closure of the Dominican *Sept*, the weekly having shown in Rome's eyes insufficient awareness of the extent and the nocivity of the Communist (and Socialist) role in the French Popular Front and of the Communist role in fomenting Spanish Republican attacks on the Church. The closure of this weekly, which had been set up in 1934 to forward Pius XI's attempt to disengage French Catholicism from the political Right, was symbolic of the 'raidissement'[5] in papal policy during the Popular Front period. In the encyclical *Divini redemptoris* against atheistic Communism, published a few months before the closure of *Sept*, the Pope had condemned the doctrine and social order of Bolshevism, denounced the *main tendue* as hypocritical and forbidden any collaboration in any domain with Communism on the part of those who wished to defend 'Christian civilisation'. Rightwing Catholics, ignoring the encyclical's call to Christian social action and paying little attention to accounts in French newspapers of the condemnation of Nazism by the March 1937 encyclical *Mit brennender Sorge*, saw *Divini redemptoris* as Rome's endorsement of their own type of anti-Communism. The Communist question appeared indeed to be a 'débat clos'.[6]

While drawing attention to Catholic divisions, an historian of the Popular Front period is therefore justified in putting Catholic reactions to the *main tendue* under the general heading of 'The view from the Right'.[7] At this time, 'le repoussoir communiste a ... une fonction de rassemblement, d'unification, d'affirmation d'identité pour toutes les forces politiques non communistes'.[8] To brand as *rouges chrétiens* those members of a pluralistic Church who refused to adopt the anti-Communism of the Right was to attempt to discredit the search for a Catholic 'third way'. Divided politically, those most engaged in this search were obliged to admit that it was a Popular Front government under a Socialist Prime Minister that was implementing aspects of Catholic social teaching, and that the efforts of Maritain and others to combat their co-religionaries' simplistic antirepublican understanding of the Spanish Civil War were doomed to failure.

From the viewpoint of an historian of the intellectual evolution of the 1930s French Church, however, the situation is much less depressing. The Popular Front period saw Churchmen producing 'une abondante littérature d'articles, de brochures et même de livres'[9] on the theory and practice of Communism. In the first instance there was the need to justify the Church's refusal of the *main tendue* to the PCF, to society at large and to the laity. Indeed, since the Party could have expected no other reaction, the laity was the main target audience: the very small minority who, in the words of *Divini redemptoris,* 'either have already fallen victim to this dreadful plague of Communism or are in danger of infection'; those Social Catholics who were sensitive to the justice of some Communist policies; and the large conservative majority who were ignorant of the Church's social teaching. It soon became apparent to Churchmen that it was not enough to denounce the 'équivoques' caused by the similarities in the vocabulary – 'peace', 'social justice', etc. – of Communists and Catholics, nor to pour scorn on the PCF's recent conversion to the values of Country, Army and Family. It was not enough either to remind Catholics that the Church had long possessed its own social doctrine critical of the abuses of the capitalist system. Most Catholics needed to be told that at issue was more than the sincerity or insincerity of Communists, or the attractiveness or otherwise of PCF propaganda: the fundamental question was the nature of Communist doctrine. It was after all the doctrine of what Lenin called 'pure' Communism that was the key to the Party's *grand tournant* and thus to the *main tendue.* Most Catholics needed to be told therefore that this doctrine was a coherent, total philosophy of life and the negation of the Church's view of Man and the world.

For its part the PCF lost no chance to proclaim that it had such a doctrine and that the *main tendue* was inspired by it. In season and out of season the Party claimed that its Marxism–Leninism was the heir of the materialism of the French Enlightenment and of the non-religious strand in Western humanism, and that Marxist historical materialism was an 'application' of philosophical materialism. Furthermore, the Party was engaged on a major publishing enterprise intended to make available the most important texts of Marxism–Leninism (including those on religion) and the works of a new and far from monolithic school of French Marxism; for, behind the Party's ideological propaganda, typified by Paul Vaillant-Couturier's 1936 pamphlet *Au service de l'esprit,* was 'a thriving culture of Marxist philosophy which, for all its faults, was dynamic and productive'.[10] Under these conditions, it was not simply in the Church's political and social interest to elevate its refusal of the *main tendue* onto the plane of mutually exclusive first principles, it was its duty to do so. For, in the words of the Dominican J.-V. Ducattillon, 'le problème du communisme ... est avant tout un problème de vérité'.[11]

As Emmanuel Mounier and other contemporaries noted at the time, Churchmen often carried out this duty very well. Responding in 1936 to the *main tendue,* they updated their knowledge of

Marxism–Leninism, both the classical texts and the texts of the predominantly positivistic strain in French Marxism as exemplified by the 1935 *A la lumière du marxisme*. Alfred Ancel, a priest of the Lyon Prado, and above all J.-V. Ducattillon, provided a powerful counter-offensive.[12] Likewise, in 1937 and 1938, Churchmen such as the Dominican Marie-Dominique Chenu and the Jesuits Gaston Fessard, Jean Daniélou and Henri de Lubac did not share most French Catholics' response to the encyclical *Divini redemptoris*. Far from being a pretext for an 'arrêt de pensée' the encyclical, which reflected the Pope's reluctance to abandon hopes for a *nouvelle chrétienté*, was an 'appel à penser',[13] a stimulus to discover and appropriate the element of truth that Communist Marxism, like any erroneous system of thought, inevitably contained. What is more, *Divini redemptoris*, by distinguishing between the thought of the Bolsheviks and that of Marx and leaving the 'true' interpretation of the latter an open question, served to fuel the controversy on this subject that was raging in 1937. At a time when, as the encyclical bemoaned, Marxism was enjoying growing intellectual prestige amongst the young, and when the Communist Henri Lefebvre and the fellow-traveller Georges Friedmann were presenting Marxism as a Promethean humanism diametrically opposed to any Christian *humanisme intégral*, a sophisticated Catholic response was essential.

This response had to take into account both the Marxism of the Bolsheviks, which was an evolutionary materialism, and the Marxism of Marx, which was in its origins a dialectical humanism. During the Popular Front period the latter was drawn on by Lefebvre and Friedmann, by Socialists and by *non-conformistes* (non-Marxist intellectuals) such as Robert Aron and the Protestant Denis de Rougemont. What is more, very much through the scholarship of the fellow-traveller Auguste Cornu whose *Karl Marx: l'homme et l'œuvre* appeared in 1934, the young Marx's thought was discovered by laymen such as Marcel Moré, Paul Vignaux and Jacques Maritain. In Marx's early writings Churchmen believed that they had found the roots not only of a humanist, or rather would-be humanist, critique of capitalism, but also the roots of Bolshevik anti-religion, inhumanity and totalitarianism. It was by intensifying their counter-offensive against Communist Marxism in this way that Churchmen effected what was indeed a remarkable though underestimated philosophical *aggiornamento*[14] in the history of the Church's published writings on Marxism, remarkable both for its rapidity and for its quality.

The challenge–response model is therefore useful, indeed essential, to explain both the quantity and the quality of Catholic writing on Communist Marxism in the Popular Front period. Certainly, the progress, momentous in the history of Catholic–Communist relations, of the young 'philosophical' Marx from the periphery of the Church (Moré's 1935 series of articles in the review *Esprit*) into its mainstream (the 1937–38 *La Vie intellectuelle* sections on Marxism, for example) is inexplicable without reference to the PCF's claim that Marxism–Leninism was a true humanism. And the dependence on events of the Catholic engagement with Communist Marxism is confirmed by the fact that once the internal Communist 'threat' had receded and had been replaced in 1938 by that of German expansionism, the stream of Catholic anti-Communist literature became a trickle. However, it is a truism that intellectual life does not have the same rhythm as political life and, in this particular case, one may say that events (including an intellectual event like the publication of Cornu's book) first accelerated and then slowed down the Catholic discovery of Communist Marxism. As the term *aggiornamento* implies, they neither began it nor, as the post-war period shows, ended it. And while in the political domain the Church may be seen as forced back onto the defensive by the rise of Communism, this was on the whole far from being the case in the intellectual domain. To explain the quantity and quality of Catholic *dépassements* of Communist Marxism in the Popular Front period we have to take into account also the evolution of the as yet largely unpoliticised French intellectual life of the late 1920s and early 1930s.

It was during this period that Berdyaev published *Un nouveau Moyen âge* (which drew attention to the Feuerbachian origins of Marx's would-be humanism), *Le Marxisme et la religion* and *Le Christianisme et la lutte des classes*, and that the German publicist Waldemar Gurian brought out his *Le Bolchevisme: introduction historique et doctrinale*. Both authors were widely read in Catholic circles. In 1928 the Protestant Socialist André Philip published his *Henri de Man et la crise doctrinale du socialisme*, which spread the Ethical Socialism of this Belgian reviser of Marxism. De Man, who distinguished between the original humanism of Marx and the materialism that Marxism later became, was much read by Catholics. He appealed, for example, to Dominicans and to contributors to the review *Esprit*, and shaped the response to Marx's thought of many of the latter, including Paul Vignaux. By the beginning of the 1930s also, the 'return to Hegel'[15] was well under way and was providing a stimulus to the study of the young Marx's thought, which had of course been elaborated very much in reaction to that of Hegel. Marx's early writings were now being published by the Socialist, and therefore anti-Communist, Costes publishing house, and by the Communists of the short-lived review *Avant-poste*; Moré, for one, set out on his project to *dépasser* Communist Marxism in the early 1930s context of the 'return to Hegel' and of the Costes initiative.

Finally, and most importantly, the late 1920s and the early 1930s saw the first manifestations of what Jean Touchard called 'l'esprit des années trente' (the origins of which are to be found in the 'cultural depression' of the *fin de siècle*). Often influenced by the idiosyncratic revisionist Marxism of Georges Sorel, by the libertarian Socialism of Pierre-Joseph Proudhon and by the philosophy of Henri Bergson, this was a *non-conformiste*, anti-materialist response to what was seen as the crisis of Western capitalist civilisation and the failure of Russian Communism. *Esprit*, which first appeared in October 1932, was a strong voice in what Georges Friedmann called 'le mouvement spiritualiste des intellectuels occidentaux contre la civilisation industrielle [qui] dégrade l'homme, étouffe en lui les "valeurs spirituelles"'.[16] However, one may see 1930s Catholic thought as a whole as influenced by this *zeitgeist*. The influence of Sorel, Proudhon, Bergson, de Man (and Charles Péguy) is apparent in Catholic writing on Marxism, and the formulation of the ideal of a personalist, and therefore anti-materialist, *nouvelle chrétienté* owes much to the spiritualist currents of the 1930s. As de Lubac said: 'Catholicisme et personnalisme s'accordent et se fortifient mutuellement.'[17]

It was very much through this fruitful interaction with the thought and the thinkers of the decade that Catholics were able to play an important part in the 1930s analysis and revision of Marxism, both the 'official' Marxism of Moscow, Marxism–Leninism, and the thought of Marx himself. Ducattillon's study of Marxism–Leninism, published in 1937 and republished in 1946, was an excellent introduction to a tedious subject and was followed by a detailed study of Communist philosophy in the *Archives de philosophie* by Alexandre Marc, Blaise Romeyer and others.[18] Likewise, Gaston Fessard's pioneering exegesis of passages from Marx's 1844 *Economic and Philosophical Manuscripts* was, for all his modest disclaimers, a landmark in Marx scholarship.[19] As for *Esprit*, it was rightly proud of having begun in Catholic circles, with Berdyaev's help, a 'constructive' critique of the theory and practice of Communism. Indeed, *Esprit* arguably did more to make known the thought of the young Marx than did the Communist Party, since it published Moré's (lengthy) 'condensation' of Cornu's seminal work[20] and was prepared to discuss, sometimes with irony, sometimes with sympathy, works by Henri Lefebvre which were inspired by the young Marx's ideas and were ignored by the Party very much for that reason. And Catholic writings on Marx made an important contribution to the ongoing 1930s revision of Marx's thought. Moré's personalist revision, for example, influenced by his contact with surrealism and with the Leftist, anti-Stalinist *La Critique sociale*, fed into the revisionism of *Les Nouveaux Cahiers*. His revision of Marx was consonant with the tendency of Western intellectuals at the time to see 'the breakdown of the hard and fast division between base and superstructure and the emphasis on the latter' as the crucial issues involved in the reformulation of Marxism.[21] As for Gaston Fessard's revision of Marx's thought, this, like the *dépassements* put forward by Jean Daniélou and Henri de Lubac,[22] reflected and contributed to the growing existential current in French thought associated with the great Catholic philosopher of immanence, Maurice Blondel. This current grew stronger in the 1930s very much through the labours of the ubiquitous Jean Wahl (who was in contact with Mounier and Fessard), of Alexandre Kojève (whose seminal course on Hegel's religious thought was attended by Fessard) and of the German existential thinker Max Scheler (whose ideas were spread by Berdyaev and the Catholic Paul-Louis Landsberg and much influenced Emmanuel Mounier's response to Marxism's 'pseudo-values').

However, if we wish to understand more fully how the discovery and the *aggiornamento* we have referred to were possible, we have to take into account more than the reactions of Catholics to the events of the Popular Front period and more than the interaction of Catholic Churchmen and laymen with the intellectual currents of the late 1920s and the 1930s. Applying as far as possible the axiom 'le même s'explique par le même',[23] we need to consider specifically religious preoccupations: *catholicisme intégral*'s rejection of a dechristianised modern world and its project of a 'true' modernity, a new culture and civilisation of Christian inspiration. Both this rejection and this project were apparent in the origins of *Esprit*, and in the thought of men like Maritain, Vignaux and Moré, well before the Great Depression and the PCF's 'humanist' offensive gave them added relevance; and both pre-existed the *non-conformisme* of the 1930s. Indeed, the ideal of a *nouvelle chrétienté* was rooted in nineteenth-century intransigent Catholicism's claim to embody true modernity; in her rejection and critique of 'le monde né de la révolution libérale et de la révolution industrielle';[24] and in her competition with the Socialist movement for the souls of the poor, especially after the publication of the great 1891 social encyclical *Rerum novarum*. In the Church's eyes the crisis of Western civilisation, which *Quadragesimo anno* analysed, and the horrors of Stalinism, which *Divini redemptoris* denounced, were but confirmation of the justice of that claim and of that critique.

For Communism was not the only aberrant form of modernity, though in the 1930s the Church came to see it as the most dangerous. What was specific about the Church's social doctrine was the rejection of *libéral* 'separatism':[25] the attempt, largely successful, to marginalise the Church and privatise religious belief and practice by removing whole zones of activity – economic, political, philosophical, etc. – from the Church's oversight. This apostate and heretical modern Western world, having usurped the authority of God and His Church, was in an advanced state of decomposition and was doomed to end in catastrophe. In the economic domain *libéralisme* stood condemned by its inability to resolve the class conflict that mechanisation had created, to free the working class – itself a creation of mechanisation – from a degrading slavery to the machine, and to avoid the international economic rivalry that was the main cause of war. In the political domain, *libéralisme* stood condemned by its inability to reintegrate the society it had atomised by its purely 'formal' democracy, which was but a cloak for the domination of capital. In the domain of culture, *libéralisme* had engendered an anti-metaphysical, 'functional' rationality which separated means and ends and was therefore impotent to reintegrate an anarchic, centreless, fragmented and confused intellectual and artistic life. To explain how this 'deontologised' world without God had come into being, Catholic writers developed what was in effect an ideological secularisation theory with a medieval 'baseline'. The revolt against the Church was traced by Jacques Maritain and others back to the individualist Protestant Reformation (which some historians see, on the contrary, as *de*-secularising) and the Renaissance, through the eighteenth-century Enlightenment and nineteenth-century *libéralisme* and *libéralisme's* offspring, Socialism and now Communism. The latter was an aggravation of *libéral* materialism, productivism and anti-humanism, and yet, paradoxically, had many of the character-istics of a religion. By the 1930s this historiography had become a *lieu commun* in Catholic circles, a theme with variations. A more important subject of debate was the nature of the desired *nouvelle chrétienté*.

Already in his 1922 work *Antimoderne*, Maritain was categorical that 'new' meant much more than 'another'. For him Rome's 1926 condemnation of *Action française's nationalisme intégral* was also the rejection of nostalgia for what Henri-Irénée Marrou called 'la pseudo-chrétienté du XVIIe siècle'.[26] As *Humanisme intégral* explained, there was no question of any return to the 'sacral' Christendom of the Middle Ages, which served in Maritain's thought as no more than an analogue for the *nouvelle chrétienté* he was seeking: *la primauté du spirituel* implied the indirect power of the Church over temporal affairs and a political pluralism based on the distinction of the lay-person's action 'en tant que chrétien' (as a member of the Mystical Body of Christ) and 'en chrétien' (as a member of the earthly City). And, as Berdyaev had written in 1927, 'aucun simulacre d'État chrétien n'aboutira à des réalisations authentiques'.[27] Although in the 1930s the promoters of a new Christian civilisation used what one might call a 'vocabulary in re-' ('reconquête', 'refaire chrétiens nos frères') inherited from the previous decade, they were in the first instance reacting against *passéiste* notions of Christendom and in general against the religious and social conservatism of what Maritain called 'le monde chrétien'. This 'monde clos' (in Bergson's term) was moralistic, *sulpicien*, pietistic and therefore individualistic. It was 'Jansenist', or even 'Manichean', in its mistrust of the body. Rejecting the possibility of a *nouvelle chrétienté* based on the alliance of Church and a rechristianised *peuple*, it connived at the privatisa-tion of religious belief, and thus at the *libéral* 'separatism' it claimed to oppose.

One phrase summed up the shortcomings of that type of Catholicism: 'un déficit d'incarnation'.[28] In the second half of the 1920s and in the 1930s 'tout un vocabulaire de l'incarnation',[29] if not yet a full incarnational theology, justified 'une attitude d'incarnation des chrétiens dans la société moderne par un recours à l'Incarnation du Christ', and found expression in the theology of the Mystical Body of Christ, in liturgy, in Christian humanist philosophies, in literature and in the endeavour to 'créer des institutions chrétiennes, ou infléchir les institutions existantes dans le sens du christianisme'.[30] The JOC, seen as the evangelisation of the working class by the working class, was the most dynamic of these Christian institutions. Refusing to accept the present divorce between 'un tout laïc' and 'un tout chrétien', the new Christian civilisation would express 'le caractère totalitaire de la foi' and therefore the totality of human potential.[31] It would be the incarnation of a true humanism.

Clearly this new civilisation would be viable only if, as Maritain had said in his 1922 work, it was both *antimoderne* and *ultramoderne*. Catholicism would have to show that its stability was that of 'un principe transcendant de vie spirituelle qui permet toutes les adaptations nécessaires, mais selon une même idée directrice'.[32] Or, as the Christian Democrat Étienne Borne put it, '[le] retour à l'intégrité de la doctrine est la condition de la plus neuve et de la plus éclatante modernité'.[33] The social and the intellectual *reconquête* of the modern world could be accomplished only if, guided by the principles of the Church's social doctrine (which did not purport to provide a technical programme for economic, political and social action), Catholics were ready to 'adapter [leurs] méthodes d'apostolat aux conditions nouvelles de la vie'.[34] The JOC was just such an adaptation, involving in intention the bold incorporation of all that was of value in a social class which was, through its Socialist and later Communist allegiance, traditionally hostile to the Church.

On the intellectual plane, also, the Church had to take into account the fact that, as Fr. Bernadot, the founder of *La Vie intellectuelle*, saw, the modern industrialised world represented 'un changement total de civilisation'.[35] This civilisation was shaped by economic forces and the rise of the masses, but also by nineteenth- and twentieth-century philosophies of history, of which Marxism was of course one. It was in this context that the Church had to demonstrate that Catholic doctrine 'assume et complète toutes les justes pensées de l'homme', for it was not true that 'l'âge moderne n'aurait connu, hors de l'Église, qu'erreur et décadence'.[36] Such was the task Henri de Lubac set himself in his *Catholicisme*, 'la meilleure défense et illustration théologique de la nouvelle chrétienté',[37] and that *La Vie intellectuelle* had been engaged on since its foundation in 1928. A similarly bold attitude to modernity was evident in Maritain's *Humanisme intégral*, which was the most influential expression of the ideal of a *nouvelle chrétienté* and, along with Fr. Chenu's historicised form of Thomism, moulded *La Vie intellectuelle*'s response to Marxism. In Maritain's work, Thomism is presented as the only philosophy capable of preserving, or 'saving' the truths contained in modern philosophies (including Marxism), for 'le monde moderne a cherché des choses bonnes par de mauvais chemins'.[38] In the same way the review *Esprit*, which, like Paul Vignaux, came to have a far broader view of the hoped-for new civilisation than Maritain, elaborated an eclectic personalism which had for Emmanuel Mounier a dual function: to assimilate aspects of non-Marxist thought and to adapt Catholic thinking to the needs of the new age.

Overall, therefore, many factors enabled *catholicisme intégral* to respond positively to the intellectual challenge of modernity: the vibrant pluralism of Catholic philosophy (which we can only hint at in this chapter) and the vigour of Catholic theology in the 1930s; a social doctrine susceptible of different interpretations (usually, it is true, corporatist); the many links between Catholic thinkers such as Chenu and *Action catholique* (especially JOC) militants; and the fact that, as Étienne Fouilloux points out, most 'théologiens en veston' (lay theologians like Étienne Gilson and Henri-Irénée Marrou) were teachers in the public sector and therefore predisposed to reconcile religious culture and secular culture.[39] This positive response, which saw adaptation as the means to a hoped-for rechristianisation of society, can with difficulty be seen as implying any broad 'opening' to the modern world. Nevertheless, if one cannot discern any 'ouverture compréhensive et nuancée en direction du marxisme',[40] whether Communist or Socialist, one can trace the ways in which the ideal of a *nouvelle chrétienté* brought about a far more nuanced attitude to Communist Marxism than might be inferred from many Catholic responses to the *main tendue*.

Communist Marxism as ontology, system, project and strategy was to be rejected absolutely. Any *non-conformiste* could agree with Étienne Gilson that 'le marxisme bolcheviste est une doctrine inhumaine, parce que son essence est de mettre la personne au service d'une classe, et de sacrifier les droits de l'individu à une conception matérialiste de l'état'.[41] Any Christian could see Communist Marxism as a virulently atheist 'primauté du matériel'.[42] However, for many Catholics the Russian experiment in social engineering had added significance. Indeed, Berdyaev's 1927 book, subtitled *Réflexions sur les destinées de la Russie et de l'Europe*, had placed Russia at the centre of the debate on the nature of a *nouvelle chrétienté*, while, nine years later, Maritain described Soviet anthropocentric humanism as 'la position athéiste pure', diametrically opposed to Christian faith.[43]

For thinkers such as Maritain, Gilson and Mounier it was axiomatic that the unity of a culture was determined in the first place by its metaphysical unity: a 'civilisation saine' was a 'civilisation métaphysique'.[44] Whereas Russia was not the *libéral* State without a metaphysic,[45] and was doomed basically for that reason. As Marrou wrote, 'pour la première fois depuis l'écroulement de la chrétienté médiévale, nous assistons à un effort pour redonner à la culture la vie et la santé en la subordonnant à une doctrine'.[46] Communism was both project and incarnation (or Incarnation) calling upon enthusiasm and self-sacrifice, qualities of fully incarnated men and women. Drawing on the young Marx's 1844 *Economic and Philosophical Manuscripts*, Lefebvre presented Marxism in the 1936 *La Conscience mystifiée* as the humanism of *l'homme total*, a new Renaissance Man who created himself freely in a fraternal society from which all forms of alienation, including religion, had disappeared. This was a direct challenge to the Church's claim to be a spiritual force which could 'transfigurer la vie totale'[47] and was answered as such by de Lubac in his *Catholicisme*: 'Pas plus qu'en se soumettant à Dieu ou qu'en s'unissant à Dieu, l'homme, en s'intégrant au grand Corps spirituel dont il doit être membre, ne se perd ou ne se dissout. Il se trouve au contraire, il se libère, et s'affermit dans l'être.'[48] For, by replacing a theocentric humanism by an anthropocentric 'humanisme séparé de l'Incarnation', Communism aimed to 'substituer à l'universalité du corps mystique du Christ son propre universalisme terrestre'.[49] Whereas, from different perspectives but through a common stress upon personal *engagement*, thinkers like Maritain (following Berdyaev) and Mounier were, they claimed, able to integrate the Renaissance discovery of individual freedom into their ideal of a new civilisation, Soviet Communism was not; it was in their eyes a return to the intolerant theocracy of the Middle Ages. But Communism was a 'théocratie à l'envers', even a 'satanocratie', ruled by a pseudo-Church with a pseudo-theology.[50] Soviet totalitarianism was therefore a bogus form of modernity, a *contrefaçon* and intensification of the worst aspects of the *passéiste* Christendoms dear to the conservative Catholic opponents of the ideal of a *nouvelle chrétienté*; and Communist Man, whether the 'New Man' of Bolshevik propaganda, or the 'total', 'de-alienated' Man of the young Marx as presented by Lefebvre, was not the Pauline New Man but the Old Adam, 'l'homme naturel, esclave de la nécessité'.[51]

However, if Communist Marxism was the ideology of a false

modernity, it also provided a powerful critique of the false modernity of *libéralisme*. As such it stimulated and challenged aspects of Catholic social doctrine's critique of capitalism. This was less paradoxical than it might appear: Marxism was after all in Catholic eyes a product of nineteenth-century *libéralisme*; indeed, as the Marx scholar Georges Lichtheim was to say, Marxism was the 'critical self-consciousness'[52] of the nineteenth-century bourgeois epoch. Marxism held up a mirror to modern Western society, providing an illuminating analysis of what *La Vie intellectuelle* called the 'transformations sociales inévitables qui devaient suivre l'évolution de l'économie moderne'.[53] Indeed, as Maritain wrote, 'combien de choses … seraient différentes si … c'était un disciple de saint Thomas qui avait écrit sur le Capital un livre aussi décisif que celui de Marx mais fondé sur des principes vrais',[54] for Marxism had pre-empted Catholic theoretical as well as organisational opposition to capitalism. The Christian critic's task was to operate a theoretical 'reconquête', to put what was true in Marxism – important aspects of its critique of capitalist exploitation – in the service of Social Catholicism. *Humanisme intégral* attempted this task, distinguishing between the justice of much of the Marxist account of the capitalist mode of production and the erroneous conclusions (such as the theory of surplus value) drawn from this account. At this time, *Action catholique* militants were being encouraged to effect what René Rémond calls 'une révolution copernicienne'[55] in their social thinking: the replacement of a normative method by a method of 'enquête', one of 'Voir, Juger, Agir'. Ancel's writing on Communist Marxism reflect this approach. For him, Marxism was to be rejected as system and strategy ('Juger' and 'Agir'). But, as a method which had 'groupé un certain nombre de faits indiscutables', Marxism had 'mis nettement en lumière certains facteurs de l'évolution historique que l'on aurait grand tort de laisser de côté' (for example, the major part played by economic factors in most great revolutions and class struggles).[56]

From a somewhat different perspective Paul Vignaux saw Marxism as essentially an economic doctrine which had 'plus ou moins pénétré un moment d'histoire en trouvant une dialectique du nouveau monde industriel'. As such it posed questions that no 'anticapitalisme conséquent' could ignore and was a stimulus to Catholic social thought in spite of its unacceptable metaphysical presuppositions.[57] From a different perspective again, Marcel Moré saw Marxism as an indispensable tool to reveal the painful reality concealed beneath *libéral* economic categories. The task was to 'reprendre les analyses marxistes pour en dégager le gros œuvre durable des partis pris philosophiques'.[58] Moré carried out this task in the Popular Front period with growing discernment, abandoning an initial, sometimes uncritical, acceptance of Marxist theses (such as 'the State is the instrument of the dominant class') which was the result of a visceral Catholic anti-capitalism.[59] For him, as for Maritain and many other Catholics, Marxist 'cynisme' unmasked the sham of a purely 'formal' democracy and demystified the self-interested *libéral* justifications of capitalism with their superficial rationalism and ideology of progress and social harmony. It was only too true that in the nineteenth century 'la vie spirituelle n'était guère qu'un épiphénomène, une adaptation idéologique aux choses d'en bas'.[60] And in modern *libéral* society spiritual life was very much a 'reflection' (to use the Marxist–Leninist term) of material life. On the philosophical level, too, Marxism's thoroughgoing historicised anthropology unmasked the illusion not only of bourgeois idealism but also of a humanism which, like *libéral* values in general, lived on borrowed capital. Without God there was, as Berdyaev and Paul-Louis Landsberg argued, no Man, no human essence.

However, Marxism provided more than a critique of the abuses of *libéral* capitalism and of the obfuscations of *libéral* ideology. In the eyes of many Catholics it provided also a critique of modern society as such. Nothing perhaps reveals more clearly the *intransigeant* origins of the *nouvelle chrétienté* ideal than the tendency of Catholic writers to read the works of Marx, and especially of the young Marx, as a spiritual protest against the dehumanising effects of the Industrial Revolution. Moré, whose articles in *Esprit* pioneered the pre-war Catholic discovery of the young Marx and whose thought was dominated by the *fin de siècle* millenarian enemy of the modern world, Léon Bloy, saw Marx as essentially the prophetic denouncer of the evil social effects of the machine age. Marxism was an indispensable tool to analyse the disorders, conflicts and fragmentation of a Godless world: it was, as Mounier said, a penetrating analysis of the alienation of Modern Man. As such it could be used as much against the Communist East as against the capitalist West. Laymen like Moré and Churchmen like Fessard could use Marx against the Marxists, they could turn against Communist Marxism and its incarnation, the Soviet Union, the very early writings that Communists were adducing to prove the humanist soul of both.

With some satisfaction they condemned Marxism–Leninism as a materialist, dogmatic 'deviation' of the young Marx's thought, and denounced Communist Russia as a tyranny unfaithful, so Fessard argued, to the young Marx's aspirations towards an End of History which was *ipso facto* the end of alienation.

If many Catholics were able to see the Marxism of Marx as *antimoderne*, this was fundamentally because there were, as Moré pointed out, profound analogies between the Pauline view of the world after the Fall of Man and the Marxist dialectic of history, as well as between Pascal's view of the contradictions of Man and the Marxist view of the contradictions of society. Above all, there was an analogy between the Biblical and Marxist options for the poor. The reason for this resemblance was, in Maritain's view, not far to seek: the 'intuition' of alienation, or dehumanisation, was 'prégnante de valeurs judéo-chrétiennes',[61] a fact which was readily understandable given the Protestant theological matrix of Marx's thought. In other words, it was as a Christian 'heresy' that Marxism needed to be 'saved' from its own distortions. Marxism was therefore much more than an enemy weapon which could be turned against another enemy, *libéralisme*, and against itself. It was a mode of thought which echoed imperfectly the incarnational themes which were central to the ideal of a *nouvelle chrétienté*. To the extent that it was such an echo, Marxism provided a confirmation of Christian values which had been lost sight of in the pietistic Catholicism of the nineteenth and early twentieth centuries, but which were now being recovered by a return to Christian sources. Since Marxism reminded Catholic thought of its riches, just as it reminded Catholics of their social duties, it was a stimulus to Catholics to be 'catholiques d'abord', to 'purify' both their faith and their works.

Many promotors of the ideal of a *nouvelle chrétienté* therefore responded positively to Marx's thought in so far as it was a 'vision optimiste du monde',[62] which, like Bergsonianism and other modern philosophies but unlike *sulpicien* Catholicism, accorded importance to the temporal and the historical; and in so far as it was – unlike bourgeois idealism and bogus, otherworldly spiritualities – a unity of theory and practice which aimed to transform both the material world (which it valued) and Man (real, social Man, not the isolated individual of bourgeois subjectivism and Catholic pietism). Moré for one welcomed the philosophy of interaction between Man and nature sketched in the 'practical–critical' *Theses on Feuerbach*[63] while, from a perspective at once more philosophical and practical, Vignaux welcomed the young Marx's 'foi en l'homme' and his 'appel en la raison' to improve the lot of the working class.[64] Although far less impressed by Marx's humanism than either Moré or Vignaux, Maritain welcomed in Marx the stress on the importance of the temporal (which Maritain saw as an 'infravalent' end in its own right rather than merely a means to an end) and on the dignity of matter (over which spirit has primacy in Maritain's philosophy). Above all, perhaps, Maritain welcomed the belief of Marx and of the whole Socialist tradition in the 'mission' of the working class, the class which was to provide the 'sociological base' of the *nouvelle chrétienté* Maritain desired. Maritain criticised sharply what he called the 'secessionist', pseudo-eschatological aspects of Marx's understanding of this 'mission', but resolutely refused in both the pre-war and post-war periods to allow Marxism the monopoly of the word. As for the Jesuit Jean Daniélou, who was with Henri de Lubac and Henri-Irénée Marrou one of the architects of the renewal of patristics in France, his two articles on Marx's thought are structured around what he saw as the central themes of Marx's thought: progress and community. These themes echoed the progress and the unity that were for the Greek Fathers the two essential aspirations of human nature. Daniélou felt that, as a philosophy of Man's self-creation through labour, Marxism could help Christianity regain a positive view of history. Indeed, Daniélou saw the eleventh *Thesis on Feuerbach* as inaugurating the new epoch, the *nouvelle chrétienté*, he desired, one in which the New Man, 'un homme ouvrier',[65] would affirm a philosophy of action, of mastery over nature through technology. For, *pace* Moré, it was the Church's duty to, in Bruno de Solage's words, 'faire servir la machine à l'extension du règne de Jésus-Christ'.[66] The Church could welcome too the sixth *Thesis on Feuerbach*'s communitarian conception of Man, which provided such a powerful critique of religious individualism. For his part, more sensitive to the anti-personalist and, of course, atheistic implications of Marx's view of Man as an *ensemble* of social relations, de Lubac nevertheless appreciated the contribution that Marxism and modern social sciences in general had made to the understanding 'de l'ampleur et de la profondeur du lien social'.[67]

If, in conclusion, we consider why the richness of pre-war Catholic critiques of Communist Marxism has not always been appreciated by historians of ideas, we find some obvious, 'extrinsic' reasons, both political and intellectual, of the type discussed in the first half of this chapter. It is clear that the hiatus in the discovery of Marxism between 1938 and 1939 was followed by what historians insist was the *coupure* of the war. After the Liberation, the Catholic discovery of Communist Marxism was carried out in a very different socio-political and religious climate by a whole new generation of Catholics, some of whom – for example, the Jesuits Bigo and Calvez – had discovered Marx during the war years. Clearly, too, French intellectual life had moved on. Hegelianism, phenomenology and existentialism, which had begun to take root in France during the pre-war period, now provided the context for the discussion of Marx's humanism and economic analysis.

What is perhaps less obvious is that the importance of the Popular Front Catholic discovery and revision of Marxism–Leninism and of Marx's own thought, as well as the *aggiornamento* this discovery had represented for the Church, were obscured also by the fortunes of the very ideal which had inspired those Churchmen and laymen who effected both – that of a *nouvelle chrétienté*. For, the relevance of this ideal to the immediate post-war situation was contested by many Catholics: by 1950 it was seen as 'repressive' by Catholic radicals.[68] Even Étienne Borne, who had played a leading part in promoting the ideal of a *nouvelle chrétienté* in the 1930s, spoke somewhat ironically in the 1950s of his generation's ambition to lay 'les pierres d'attente de la chrétienté de demain'.[69] No doubt what he called 'les mots désuets et vieillots de notre cher langage d'alors' helped to imprison the pre-war Catholic discovery of Communist Marxism in the dusty tomes of an 'avant-guerre si proche et pourtant si inimaginable à de plus récentes générations'.[70] And, of course, the discredit into which political theologies of Christendom have fallen since the 1950s has done nothing to make that vocabulary more accessible.

Nevertheless, in the 1930s the ideal of a *nouvelle chrétienté* was, as we have seen, 'une idée mobilisatrice et d'avant-garde' on the intellectual level as in the social and political domains.[71] And it was an ideal which bore fruit. As Yvon Tranvouez suggests, post-war Catholic *progressisme* owes much more intellectually to *La Vie intellectuelle* and to *Humanisme intégral* than to the 'Catholic Marxism' advocated in the pages of the marginal journal *Terre nouvelle*.[72] And, even if the idea of a Christian 'reconquest' of the modern world appeared increasingly dated, the incarnationalism that was at the heart of the ideal of a *nouvelle chrétienté,* and the latter's strategy of adaptation to modernity, were relevant to a post-war intellectual situation which saw, alongside a strong eschatological current, the elaboration of a 'théologie des réalités terrestres' and, alongside an onslaught on Communist anti-humanism, a dialogue between Christian humanisms and Marxist humanism.

At the same time, one may suggest that it was as a critique of false modernities rather than as the project of a true modernity, that the *nouvelle chrétienté* ideal had the most long-lasting effects. In spite of Maritain's efforts to present this project as a 'concrete historical ideal', it was, after all, basically not a programme or an 'orthodoxy',[73] but a spiritual aspiration ultimately dependent for its success on God's grace. What is more, this critique stood the test of time much better as a critique of Communist theory and practice than as a critique of *libéralisme,* whose values – and longevity! – it greatly underestimated. The war-time evolution of Maritain's political thought towards a more positive evaluation of Liberal Democracy is significant in this respect. In the post-war period the critique of Communist Marxism (which was usually but the first manifestation of a lifetime interest in the subject on the part of some influential thinkers, priests and laymen) was carried further. One may trace to the pre-war period both the widespread post-war Catholic tendency (weakened by Louis Althusser's anti-humanist reading of Marx) to see Marxism as a pseudo-religion, a system of values, a *Weltanschauung,* and the post-war Catholic endeavour to learn from what was in intention a rigorous analysis of the contradictions of Capitalism; the Dominican Fr. L.J. Lebret's association *Économie et Humanisme* played a distinguished part in this enterprise. Though political, social and economic conditions had changed, the main problem facing the Church twenty years after the war was still that of 'coming to terms with the modern world: a world of rapid technological progress, industrialisation and technocratic planning'[74] – in a word, that of being both *antimoderne* and *ultramoderne.*

NOTES

1. Denis Maugenest, *La Foi chrétienne à l'épreuve du marxisme* (Paris: Le Centurion, 1978), p. 15.

2. R.P. Delaye, *Une Enquête sur le communisme* (Paris: Action populaire, 1937), p. 146.

3. Étienne Fouilloux, 'Traditions et expériences françaises', in *Histoire du Christianisme des origines à nos jours*, 12 vols (Paris: Desclée–Fayard, 1990), XII, 451–522.

4. Jean-Marie Mayeur, *L'Histoire religieuse de la France, 19e–20e siècle. Problèmes et méthodes* (Paris: Beauchesne, 1975), p. 156.

5. René Rémond, preface to E. Terrenoire, *Un Combat d'avant-garde. Francisque Gay et 'La Vie Catholique'* (Paris: Bloud et Gay–Cerf, 1976).

6. M. Scherer, 'Sur un débat clos', *La Vie intellectuelle*, April–May 1937, 186–94.

7. Julian Jackson, *The Popular Front in France: Defending Democracy, 1934–38* (Cambridge: Cambridge University Press, 1988), pp. 259–64.

8. Serge Berstein and Jean-Jacques Becker, *Histoire de l'anti-communisme en France*, 2 vols (Paris: Orban, 1987), I, 386–87.

9. René Rémond, 'Les Catholiques et le Front populaire (1936–1937)', *Archives de sociologie des religions*, 2 (1960), 63–69.

10. Michael Kelly, *Modern French Marxism* (Oxford: Blackwell, 1982), p. 26, p. 47.

11. J.-V. Ducattillon, 'Doctrine communiste et doctrine catholique', in *Le Communisme et les chrétiens*, ed. François Mauriac et al. (Paris: Plon, 1937), pp. 5–151.

12. Ducattillon, 'Doctrine communiste et doctrine catholique'; Alfred Ancel, *Dogme et morale communistes. Les Communistes nous tendent la main. Que faire?* (Paris: FNC, 1937).

13. Emmanuel Mounier, *Esprit*, 56 (1937), 306–7.

14. Described in David Curtis, *The French Popular Front and the Catholic Discovery of Marx: From Refutation to Revision* (Hull: Hull University Press, 1997).

15. See Michael Kelly, *Hegel in France* (Birmingham: Birmingham University Press, 1992).

16. Georges Friedmann, *La Crise du progrès. Esquisse d'histoire des idées, 1895–1935* (Paris: Gallimard, 1935), pp. 158–61.

17. Henri de Lubac, *Catholicisme. Les Aspects sociaux du dogme* (Paris: Cerf, 1938), p. 263.

18. 'La Philosophie du Communisme', *Archives de philosophie*, XV (1939).

19. Gaston Fessard, *La Main tendue. Le Dialogue catholique-communiste est-il possible?* (Paris: Grasset, 1937).

20. Moré's articles on 'Les années d'apprentissage de Karl Marx' appeared in *Esprit* from April to October 1935.

21. D. McLellan, *Marxism and Religion. A Description and Assessment of the Marxist Critique of Christianity* (London: Macmillan, 1980), p. 136.

22. De Lubac, *Catholicisme*; J. Daniélou, 'La foi en l'homme chez Marx', *Chronique sociale de France*, 3 (1938), 163–71; 4 (1938), 275–82.

23. René Rémond, 'L'Évolution du catholicisme français depuis cent ans', *Documentation Catholique*, 74 (1977), 671–75.

24. Jean-Marie Mayeur, *Catholicisme social et démocratie chrétienne. Principes romains, expériences françaises* (Paris: Cerf, 1986), p. 18.

25. Ibid., p. 267.

26. Henri-Irénée Marrou, *Fondements d'une culture chrétienne* (Paris: Bloud et Gay, 1934), pp. 121–22.

27. Nikolai Berdyaev, *Un nouveau Moyen âge* (Paris: Plon, 1927), p. 284.

28. Yves Congar, 'Une conclusion théologique à l'enquête sur les raisons actuelles de l'incroyance', *La Vie intellectuelle*, July–September 1935, 214–49.

29. Yvon Tranvouez, 'Entre Rome et le peuple', in *Histoire des catholiques en France du XVe siècle à nos jours*, ed. François Lebrun (Toulouse: Privat, 1980), pp. 413–43.

30. Bernard Besret, *Incarnation ou eschatologie. Contribution à l'histoire du vocabulaire religieux contemporain, 1935–1955* (Paris: Cerf, 1964), pp. 50–65.

31. Congar, 'Une conclusion théologique'.

32. R.P. B. de Solages, *Le Christianisme dans la vie publique* (Paris: Spes, 1937), p. 26.

33. Étienne Borne cited in J. Prévotat, 'Théologiens laïcs des années trente', *Les Quatre Fleuves*, 17 (1983), 49–69.

34. De Solages, *Le Christianisme dans la vie publique*, p. 139.

35. Georges Hourdin, *Dieu en liberté* (Paris: Stock, 1973), pp. 148–49.

36. De Lubac, *Catholicisme*, p. 222, p. 229, p. 250.

37. Étienne Fouilloux, 'Courants de pensée, piété, apostolat: le catholicisme', in *Histoire du Christianisme*, XII, 116–39.

38. Jacques Maritain, *Le Crépuscule de la civilisation* (Paris: Les Nouvelles Lettres, 1939), p. 7.

39. Fouilloux, 'Courants de pensée'.

40. Maugenest, *La Foi chrétienne*, p. 16.

41. Étienne Gilson, *Pour un ordre catholique* (Paris: Desclée de Brouwer, 1934), p. 55.

42. Ibid.

43. Jacques Maritain, *Humanisme intégral. Problèmes temporels et spirituels d'une nouvelle chrétienté* (Paris: Aubier, 1936), p. 42.

44. Marrou, *Fondements d'une culture chrétienne*, pp. 82–83.

45. Gilson, *Pour un ordre catholique*, p. 44, p. 52.

46. Henri-Irénée Marrou, *Crise de notre temps et réflexion chrétienne de 1930 à 1975* (Paris: Beauchesne, 1978), p. 64.

47. Berdyaev, *Un nouveau Moyen âge*, p. 149.

48. De Lubac, *Catholicisme*, p. 257.

49. Jacques Maritain, *Religion et culture* (Paris: Desclée de Brouwer, 1930), p. 35; *Le Crépuscule de la civilisation*, p. 12.

50. Berdyaev, *Un nouveau Moyen âge*, p. 152; p. 268.

51. Ibid., p. 265, p. 21.

52. Georges Lichtheim, *Marxism in Modern France* (New York/London: Columbia University Press, 1966), p. 197.

53. H.D. Gardeil, 'Le matérialisme dialectique', *La Vie intellectuelle*, February–March 1938, 406–20.

96 Catholicism, Politics and Society

54. Maritain, *Religion et culture*, p. 50.

55. René Rémond, 'Les transformations sous les derniers pontificats (1924–1958)', in *Histoire du Catholicisme en France*, 3 vols, ed. André Latreille (Paris: Spes – Éditions ouvrières, 1962), III, 573–685.

56. Ancel, *Dogme et morale communistes*, pp. 28–30.

57. Paul Vignaux, review of Fessard's *La Main tendue*, *Politique*, 10 (1937), 749–52.

58. Emmanuel Mounier, 'Notre humanisme', *Esprit*, 37 (1935), 5.

59. For Mounier's initially uncritical acceptance of the Marxist critique of Capitalism, see Michael Kelly, *Pioneer of the Catholic Revival. The Ideas and Influence of Emmanuel Mounier* (London: Sheed & Ward, 1979), pp. 35–36.

60. Berdyaev, *Un nouveau Moyen âge*, p. 270.

61. Maritain, *Humanisme intégral*, p. 55, n. 3.

62. Daniélou, 'La foi en l'homme chez Marx', p. 170.

63. Moré, 'Les années d'apprentissage de Karl Marx'.

64. Paul Vignaux, 'Retour à Marx', *Politique*, 11 (1935), 900–14.

65. Daniélou, 'La foi en l'homme chez Marx', p. 165.

66. De Solages, *Le Christianisme dans la vie publique*, p. 139.

67. De Lubac, *Catholicisme*, p. 275.

68. Yvon Tranvouez, *Catholiques d'abord. Approches du mouvement catholique en France. XIXe–XXe siècle* (Paris: Éditions ouvrières, 1988), p. 130.

69. Étienne Borne, 'Souvenirs de l'autre temps', *La Vie intellectuelle*, August–September 1956, 97–108.

70. Ibid.

71. Tranvouez, *Catholiques d'abord*.

72. Ibid., p. 174.

73. Jean Grenier, *Essai sur l'esprit d'orthodoxie* (Paris: Gallimard, 1938).

74. Lichtheim, *Marxism in Modern France*, p. 110.

5

Ralliés and résistants: Catholics in Vichy France, 1940–44[1]

Nicholas Atkin

In June 1940 French Catholics were in ambivalent mood. While there was dismay at the way in which Hitler had laid waste the allied armies, there was also hope for the future. Marshal Pétain's government promised a return to traditional values. In the event, Vichy proved a disappointment, and opened up divisions within the Church that had been eclipsed at the moment of defeat. As has been observed, in the 1920s and 1930s a 'relaxed tension' in Church–State relations 'loosened the tight discipline' that was forged during the anti-clerical phase of the Third Republic when committed Catholics had rallied to the defence of religious liberties.[2] Accordingly, conservatives in the hierarchy became concerned that they were 'losing control over the disparate enthusiasms' of the lower clergy and laity.[3] Under the Occupation, ironically a time when Pétain called for restraint, there was worry that this indiscipline would get out of hand. Although most Catholics obeyed their bishops, a minority of rank-and-file adherents made their opposition to both Vichy and Nazism plain. Ultimately, these 'resisters' redeemed the actions of their superiors who had hoped to profit from national humiliation by establishing a Third Ralliement.[4]

In summer 1940, the power of the Catholic Church remained firm. As Hall argues, whereas the State bureaucracy crumbled before the German advance, clerical institutions survived largely 'intact'. Despite the division of France into two, the hierarchy continued to function. On 28 August 1940 the *Assemblée des cardinaux et archevêques* (ACA) re-convened at Paris, although admittedly it was only members of the northern episcopate who were able to attend.[5] The international links of the Church also remained in place, evidenced by the interest which the Vatican took in the destiny of France. As well as accrediting Valerio Valeri as the Papal Nuncio to Vichy, on 29 June 1940

Pius XII addressed French bishops outlining his hopes for their country's revival.[6] Nor had the educational structures of the Church been dislodged by Guderian's Panzers. In 1940 almost a million children attended Catholic primary schools, roughly one-fifth of the school population; in the secondary sector, Catholic institutions taught a third of all pupils. Many of these children graduated to the powerful Catholic youth organisations which fell under the aegis of the *Action catholique de la jeunesse française* (ACJF). The function of these bodies was, of course, to halt the tide of secularisation that was felt to have submerged France during the 1930s. It was in this decade that Gabriel Le Bras conducted his pioneering sociological studies highlighting a fall in religious observance.[7] Defeat halted that decline. As Halls has suggested, prayers, pilgrimages and processions were back in fashion. Throughout the Occupation, the statue of Notre-Dame de Boulogne travelled from village to village, often pausing before the local war memorial, where onlookers called for the return of prisoners of war.[8]

Given the powerful position which Catholicism occupied in 1940 and the totality of Germany's victory, it is small wonder that a disorientated public looked to Church leaders for an explanation of defeat. Like other commentators, few prelates mentioned military impreparedness but focused instead on moral decadence. No-one was sure of the origins of this decay but many blamed the secular culture of the Third Republic.[9] In the pages of *La Croix*, the official newspaper of the Church, there was discussion whether defeat was God's way of punishing France for past transgressions.[10] Even members of the Catholic Left, who in the 1930s had 'horrified' traditionalists by their criticisms 'of capitalism and the laissez-faire State', joined in this chorus of recriminations.[11]

In addition to explaining defeat, Church representatives were called upon to articulate a response to the new political order at Vichy. Although in 1939 Daladier had effected some improvement in Church–State relations,[12] this brief interlude did not prevent a majority of prelates from embracing the Pétainist regime. Abandoning the reserve which the Church had hitherto exercised in its relations with civil authority, some bishops even declared that Vichy was the 'pouvoir légitime', a claim echoed by the ACA meeting in August 1940.[13] Given the appeal of Pétainism and the widespread belief that there was no alternative to the Armistice, most rank-and-file Catholics followed the lead of the episcopate. Yet other elements within the Church were more measured in their response. Although evidence remains impressionistic, it seems that younger clergy, especially those who had not fallen under Pétain's spell during the First World War, were less enamoured by the regime.[14] Among the religious orders, the Dominicans and Jesuits, long accustomed to thinking for themselves, likewise adopted a cautious position. As Père Dillard, the eminent Jesuit remarked, the Vichy enterprise was 'a magnificent adventure to be resisted'.[15]

In summer 1940, 'such wavering between acceptance and rejection of the new regime was characteristic of the more politically minded members' of the Church.[16] Among Catholic intellectuals, Emmanuel Mounier, founder of the journal *Esprit*, was troubled by the authoritarian nature of Pétain's powers; yet, at the same time, he was excited by the promise of the *révolution nationale*, concluding that the best way of tempering Vichy's absolutist leanings was by working within the system.[17] Among youth organisations, the *Jeunesse agricole chrétienne* (JAC) was clearly attracted by Pétain's 'retour à la terre' philosophy, yet both the *Jeunesse étudiante chrétienne* (JEC) and the *Jeunesse ouvrière chrétienne* (JOC) were already apprehensive about the possibility of Vichy establishing 'une jeunesse unique'. Christian Democrats, represented by the pre-war parties the *Parti démocrate populaire* (PDP) and *Jeune république* (JR), were also worried by the new political environment. Admittedly, on 10 July a majority of their deputies voted for Pétain as *chef de l'État français*. In their view, the marshal needed such control if he was to build a society based on Christian principles. Yet a handful of Christian Democrats, notably the PDP leader Champetier de Ribes, recognised that Vichy was an affront to liberal values and refused to accept the Armistice. Having voted against Pétain on 10 July,[18] it is no surprise that Champetier de Ribes would gravitate towards the Resistance. Among Social Catholics there were similar divisions, reflecting the tensions that had long existed between those who favoured a paternalistic approach to economic problems and those who sought to create a 'democratic, non-elitist society'.[19] Whereas Père Desbuquois, head of the social welfare body *Action populaire*, argued that an authoritarian State was needed to advance a programme of Christian reform, Jules Zirnhald, in charge of the *Confédération française des travailleurs chrétiens* (CFTC), feared that the *révolution nationale* might go too far in rescinding the trade union legislation of the Third Republic. Such disagreements would bedevil Social Catholics throughout the Occupation.[20]

As will be seen, subsequent developments in the war forced Church members to redefine their position towards Vichy and led a small number to join the Resistance. By contrast, as Halls has stated, the attitudes of the ACA failed to evolve. Until 1944, the assembly remained rooted to the statement it devised in July 1941: 'Nous voulons que, sans inféodation, soit pratiqué un loyalisme sincère et complet envers le pouvoir établi.'[21] Admittedly Vichy was no longer the 'pouvoir légitime', merely the 'pouvoir établi'; this was a distinction the ACA had first made in January 1941, aware that it was at risk of compromising itself with civil power. Yet, overall, the hierarchy had failed to break completely with the regime. When in February 1944 it drafted another declaration, it balanced criticism of the Laval government with praise for Pétain and condemnation of allied bombing.[22]

How do we explain the hierarchy's enduring support for Vichy? First, it should be remembered that it was customary for the Church to recognise a *de facto* government, and that Catholic leaders were not alone in acknowledging Vichy. The regime was accepted by virtually everyone, save the Free French and the British. The Vatican's endorsement carried particular weight with the bishops. In 1941 Pius XII even gave his blessing to Pétain's *Principes de la communauté*, an exposition of *révolution nationale* beliefs, although he did urge the author to have greater respect for individual liberties.[23] By 1942 the Curia was troubled by the persecution of Jews in France but its failure to condemn Vichy outright meant that French prelates were hesitant to voice their own criticisms. Second, the episcopate regarded Vichy as a bulwark of stability. As Halls has acknowledged, although the Church had survived defeat more or less intact, there remained a 'fear' of upheavals ahead: 'a fear of the Germans'; a fear of the Paris collaborators; a fear of de Gaulle; a fear of allied intentions; and a fear of Communism and possible civil war.[24] With the approach of an allied invasion, several members of the ACA, nourished on a pre-war diet of anti-Bolshevism, came to view Vichy as the only alternative to a Left-wing coup. Third, clerical adherence to Pétain's government sprang from an enthusiasm for the values of *travail, famille, patrie*. Even when the fizz ran out of the *révolution nationale*, there was hope that the marshal might grant Catholics further concessions.

This faith in the 'homme providentiel' forms a fourth factor explaining the hierarchy's continuing support for Vichy. Indeed, the extent of episcopal loyalty to Pétain ensured that the Church, alongside the veterans' organisation the *Légion française des combattants*, served as one of the key pillars propping up the cult of marshalship.[25] Several aspects of the Pétain myth attracted the bishops. Apart from the commitment to the values of *travail, famille, patrie*, it was not overlooked that Pétain had been a pious child and was a product of Catholic education. His military record, in particular the compassion he had displayed towards the *poilu*, also had appeal. No fewer than fifty-one of France's 'ninety-six prelates had served in the First World War'.[26] Only a small number of sceptics among the laity dared point out the *chef de l'État* was not an especially fervent believer and was married, through a civil ceremony, to a divorcee.[27] To regularise this state of affairs, in 1941 Suhard arranged for Pétain to be married by proxy in a secret religious service conducted in Paris. Ultimately, the episcopate's *maréchaliste* loyalties proved a liability: bishops were hesitant to speak out lest they offended Vichy's leader.

Although Catholics in 1940 granted a warm welcome to Pétain and Vichy, they greeted the Germans with reserve. Despite the French Church's pre-war obsession with Communism, it was not oblivious to the dangers of Nazism. At hand, it possessed the papal encyclical *Mit brennender Sorge* of March 1937 reproaching National-Socialist dogma, as well as numerous reports on events in Germany.[28] In 1939 the hierarchy was disappointed by Pius XII's position of neutrality; yet, in the propaganda battle, this proved less of a problem than anticipated. Drawing on their undisputed patriotism, French bishops described the conflict as a 'just war'.[29] Thereafter, both the higher and lower clergy retained a healthy suspicion of the occupier. Not surprisingly, this opposition was most marked in those areas where the German presence was strongest. In the *zone annexée* of Nord-Pas-de-Calais an anglophile priesthood, recalling the events of 1914–18, was out of step with Dutoit, the collaborationist bishop of Arras.[30] In the unoccupied zone, opposition to the Germans was also apparent. Rémond, bishop of Nice, observed that clerics in Alpes-Maritimes were pro-Vichy but against 'toute idée de collaboration'.[31]

Catholics had good reason to fear the Germans who were suspicious of the institutional power of Catholicism and the influence it exerted on public opinion. In 1940 'close surveillance of the bishops was ordered'.[32] Thereafter, as Halls observes, religious affairs came under the watchful eye of the occupying authorities: the Wehrmacht which, initially at least, respected the rights of churchgoers; the embassy at Paris, under the control of Otto Abetz, the ambassador, who was anxious to counter the influence of clericalism at Vichy; and the SS which was hostile to any institution that might rejuvenate French nationalism.[33] Together, these bodies subjected Catholics, especially their youth movements, to harassment. As the war dragged on, harassment became persecution. Priests suspected of orchestrating resistance, including Dillard, were deported to Dachau. Members of the hierarchy were treated little differently. In 1944 Théas (Montauban), Piguet (Clermont), and Rodié (Agen), among others, were dispatched to various transit and concentration camps. Overall, however, Catholics escaped the fate of their fellow Christians in the annexed territories of Alsace and Lorraine where the SS had little hesitation in openly persecuting both Catholics and Protestants.[34]

In view of German hostility to religion, it is perhaps surprising that any Catholics should have favoured collaboration. Such support might seem even more curious given that a majority of the Paris collaborators were secular in attitude. Pro-German newspapers such as L'Appel and Au Pilori kept a close watch on the Church's activities, accusing Catholic schools of being the mouthpieces of the BBC.[35] Nevertheless, a handful of Catholics did come out in favour of the New Order. Prominent lay collaborators included Marcel Bucard, founder of the Franciste, and Alphonse de Châteaubriant, the Catholic writer, who in September 1940 established the cultural body, Groupe Collaboration. Leading clerical collaborators were Canon Polimann, former deputy of the Meuse, and Cardinal Baudrillart, the elderly rector of the Institut catholique in Paris. An ardent Germanophobe during the First World War, in 1940 Baudrillart believed that Nazism offered the only real obstacle to Bolshevism. A curious group of clerical collaborators also gravitated to Bordeaux, transforming the town into the centre of the Catholic press for the occupied zone. Why Bordeaux? The answer lies in the leniency displayed by the bishop, Mgr Feltin; the relocation of the Paris-based La Croix to Limoges; and the willingness of La Liberté du Sud-Ouest, the influential regional Catholic daily, to loan out its presses, to such militants as abbé Bergey and Paul Lesourd.[36] Inevitably, some Catholics gravitated to the Légion des volontaires français contre le bolchevisme (LVF) and the Milice, notably Paul Touvier, a former member of the ACJF, who became a prominent milicien in the Rhône.[37] It has been alleged that after 1944 Touvier was able to evade justice through the assistance of fundamentalist religious orders and officials from within the Archbishop of Lyon's palace, an indication perhaps that not all Catholics had relinquished their collaborationist sympathies. Overall, however, such sympathies were never widespread. Those few Catholics who rallied to the German cause were driven by a variety of political and theological motives, often a fear of Communism. What they possessed in common was a political naiveté.

Neither the LVF nor the *Milice* were forthrightly condemned by the Church hierarchy, an indication that members of the ACA remained anxious to curry favour with Vichy. In 1940, this desire was more blatant. Although a number of clerics warned against profiting from national humiliation, the Church was quick to articulate an agenda of its own.[38] In August the ACA raised a number of issues with Vichy. As well as demanding rights for *enseignement libre*, the assembly called for a regularisation of the legal situation of religious orders, and insisted that the CFTC should be allowed to continue its activities (earlier a law of 18 August had banned employers' and workers' confederations, an early indication of Vichy's authoritarian tendencies).[39] This may be why the ACA was keen to celebrate the proselytising mission of Catholic youth organisations, a warning to the government not to establish a *jeunesse unique*. Finally, the ACA may have raised the possibility of a concordat.[40] Overall, it had taken the episcopate two months to put together an ambitious programme, the ultimate purpose of which was nothing less than the re-conversion of France to Catholicism.

This agenda was given generous consideration by early Vichy cabinets.[41] Apart from Pétain himself, who strongly valued clerical support, these ministries contained a number of prominent Catholics: Raphaël Alibert, the *Action française* sympathiser who served at Justice; Jacques Chevalier, a philosophy professor from Grenoble, who briefly took charge of Education; and Xavier Vallat, a First World War *mutilé* who headed Veterans' Affairs. In 1941 Vallat became Vichy's first commissioner of Jewish Affairs, yet it was not lost on Berlin that this xenophobe hated Germans as much as he did Jews, and in 1942 he was replaced by Louis Darquier de Pellepoix. Nonetheless, the influence of Catholics at Vichy, even during the opening months of the Occupation, should not be exaggerated. It was always tempered by the presence of moderate believers such as Paul Baudouin, Minister of Foreign Affairs until October 1940. It is also significant that Catholics occupied lesser posts – for example, Georges Lamirand at Youth Affairs and General de La Porte du Theil in control of the *chantiers de la jeunesse*. As the war continued, the numbers of Catholics in government decreased. On 13 December the Church was relieved when Pétain dismissed his most powerful minister, the anti-clerical Pierre Laval. Yet Laval's place was soon taken by another anti-clerical, Admiral Darlan. He had little time for the traditionalists in Pétain's cabinet, describing them as 'beardless altar boys'.[42] His preference was for young technocrats who sought to use 'the temporary submissiveness of their stunned countrymen to reinvigorate France and make it a respected partner in Hitler's Europe'.[43] By the time of Laval's return in April 1942, there were few prominent Catholics at Vichy other than those in Pétain's immediate entourage. The exception is Philippe Henriot, who in 1943 became Secretary of State for Information and Propaganda. The voice of Radio Vichy, Henriot experienced little difficulty in reconciling his Catholic beliefs with those of Fascism.[44]

Given declining clerical influence at Vichy, it is no surprise that Catholics made the greatest gains in 1940–41. In educational affairs, the *manuels scolaires* of the *école publique* were purged of their republican bias; Left-wing schoolteachers were sacked; and the catechism was briefly restored onto the State-school timetable.[45] By a law of 2 November 1941 State aid was granted to private elementary schools, albeit on a temporary basis. In youth affairs, Catholics were conspicuous in the new organisations created by Vichy. The *Compagnons de France*, designed to give the young unemployed a taste for hard work, was founded by the Catholic Scout leader, Henri Dhavernas. Another Catholic Scout, Père Forestier, was chaplain-general of the compulsory *chantiers de la jeunesse*. Catholics were also prominent in Vichy's leadership schools especially that at Uriage fronted by Pierre Dunoyer de Segonzac.[46] Here, in the foothills of the Alps, an elite of civil servants and intellectuals, destined to become the *chefs* of the *État français*, received lectures from Mounier, Jean Lacroix and Bruno de Solages.

In administrative affairs Catholics were well represented on the *Conseil national*, designed to form a new constitution, and benefited from the shake-up of local government. In its attempts to destroy the political Left, Vichy filled the town halls of provincial France with Pétainist disciples, who possessed strong clericalist sympathies.[47] In the affairs of the religious orders, Vichy lifted the teaching ban on monks and nuns, granted legal recognition to the Chartreux and revised the law on associations of 1901.[48] In family matters, Catholics were heartened by an extension to Daladier's *code de la famille*, a tightening-up of the abortion and divorce laws and the restrictions placed on women's employment. In the economic domain, Social Catholics welcomed Pétain's corporatist rhetoric, and looked forward to Vichy's *charte du travail*. Published in October 1941, this drew heavily on the doctrines of Leo XIII, Pius XI and La Tour du Pin. Nonetheless, Jocistes and representatives of the CFTC, still smarting from the law of 18 August 1940 and troubled by Darlan's technocrats, remained convinced that Vichy was planning a *syndicat unique*. In June 1943, this worry led a majority of CFTC supporters to boycott the *charte*, a move which went against the advice of the bishops and which highlighted further the divisions among Social Catholics.[49]

One important gain remained beyond the reach of the Church: a definitive religious settlement for France. Before the war, concordats in Poland (1925) and Italy (1929) had conceded a number of privileges to Catholicism.[50] In 1942 Franco negotiated an agreement for Spain. Accordingly it was no surprise that the French Church should have considered a similar option. Prominent Vichyites, such as Léon Bérard, Pétain's ambassador to the Vatican, were also keen on the idea; Bérard, in turn, played a key role in the tripartite discussions that took place between Vichy, Rome and the bishops.[51] Ultimately, no-one took the plunge. For its part, Vichy wanted a say in such things as episcopal appointments. As to the bishops, they sought to keep State interference to a minimum. The real stumbling block was the Vatican. It retained fears of the Gallican tendencies of the French Church, and by 1943 understood that Vichy was a temporary regime. Thus discussions petered out, although it was probably not until the 1960s that the hierarchy in France relinquished dreams of a concordat.

What should not be overlooked is that, alongside the gains of the *révolution nationale*, Catholics were building on initiatives, first undertaken in the 1930s, to counter the spread of dechristianisation. While heartened by the revival of religious practice in 1940, concerns about the spiritual health of France persisted. It was in the course of the Occupation that abbé Godin, a little-known priest from Paris, highlighted the need to re-convert the working-class districts of the capital.[52] To this end, the *Ligue ouvrière chrétienne* (LOC), established in 1935 by the JOC, became the LOC–MPF (*Ligue ouvrière chrétienne–Mouvement populaire des familles*) extending its 'clientele' to include 'all working-class families'.[53] In the countryside, Père Epagneul founded the *Frères missionaires des campagnes*. Complementing these moves were plans to improve catechismal teaching. In 1941 the ACA created a *Commission nationale de catéchisme* which was instrumental in revising the national catechism, thought to be overly detailed and unassimilable.[54] Ultimately, these efforts failed to halt the long-term decline in religious observance and boost numbers in the priest-hood.[55] Nonetheless, the Occupation years were a productive time for Catholic theologians in their attempts to come to terms with the challenges posed by a secular society.

Hopes for a spiritual revival may provide a further explanation as to why the hierarchy was reluctant to break with Vichy. It will be recalled that in 1941 the ACA had described Vichy as the 'pouvoir établi', but still pledged a 'loyalisme sincère et complet' towards the regime. Most of the faithful heeded this advice, yet for a small number of politically and socially progressive Catholics the Church had not done enough to distance itself from an increasingly discredited government. Outside of France, the entry of the Soviet Union and the USA into the war cast doubts on the policy of collaboration that Pétain had announced at Montoire. Within France, the Darlan Direc-torate was clearly no friend of religion, threatening both a *syndicat unique* and a *jeunesse unique*.[56] Although these projects remained pipe-dreams, they signalled Vichy's growing authoritarianism. In 1942 this tendency came to the fore when the Laval government participated in the Final Solution and agreed to deport French labour to Germany. These two events, more than any other issue, revealed the deep divisions among Catholics.

The origins and course of Vichy's racial persecution have been amply documented and need not be rehearsed here.[57] The Catholic response is also well known, especially the vacillations of the hier-archy which compare unfavourably with the tough line generally adopted by Protestant leaders.[58] When the ACA met in August 1940 it did not even mention Vichy's recent laws revising naturalisations.[59] The following year, it merely urged the government to have 'respect for the human person'.[60] In subsequent meetings, the issue of Jews rarely surfaced. Individual prelates were also reticent. The silence of Liénart (Lille), a long-standing critic of racism, was especially odd although it should be noted that he had to operate under close German supervision and did assist individual Jews.[61] For his part, Suhard (Paris) made discreet protests to both Pétain and Abetz. It is, however, Gerlier (Lyon), who, say Marrus and Paxton, 'best epitomises the hesitations' of the episcopate. In 1941 this ardent *maréchaliste* registered several complaints about the treatment of Jews, and in 1942 helped Jews escape round-ups in the Lyon area,[62] encouraging priests and nuns to do the same. Undoubtedly he deserves praise for these actions. Yet, as the chief prelate residing in the unoccupied zone and as *primat des Gaules*, the spiritual leader of the French Church, he was in an ideal position to condemn racial persecution outright. No such statements were delivered. When on 6 September 1942 he chose to make a public protest, he still urged Catholics to pledge allegiance to Vichy. As has been observed: 'Ambiguity and indecisiveness, coupled with a modicum of blindness and prejudice, appear to characterise his comportment.'[63] In this situation, it was left to others, notably Saliège, the independent-minded Archbishop of Toulouse, to make a stand. On 23 August 1942 he became the first bishop to speak out against the treatment of Jews. A week later his condemnation was echoed by Théas at Montauban. Even so, 'fewer than half the prelates of the unoccupied zone made public statements from the pulpit; and not one in the occupied zone'.[64]

How do we explain this reticence? As suggested, part of the answer lies with the episcopate's devotion to Pétain and the ambivalent attitude of the Vatican. Whether the papacy approved of Vichy's early anti-Semitic legislation, as Bérard claimed, remains debatable;[65] yet it was not until summer 1942 that Valerio Valeri urged French bishops to make their protests known. Nonetheless, given the initiatives in resisting racial persecution displayed by the Dutch and Danish bishops, it is clear that members of the ACA could have done more. That they did not owes something to the peculiar situation in the France of summer 1940. As has been observed, in the atmosphere of *reconquista* 'Jews were easily forgotten'.[66] Nor was the episcopate free of prejudice. Although few bishops were blatantly racist, during the 1930s several were troubled by the influx of refugees from Eastern Europe. Would these newcomers constitute a nation apart? It was this fear of unassimilable elements that in August 1940 led ACA representatives in the unoccupied zone to accept that Vichy's discriminatory measures were necessary for the 'common good', and admit there was a 'Jewish problem'.[67] Perhaps if the ACA had understood the fate awaiting Jews, it would have taken a tougher stand. Until the second *statut des juifs* (June 1941), it took reassurance that Vichy legislation did not affect either the property or the person of Jews. Even when the round-ups were under way, there is doubt whether the bishops appreciated the full horror of racial persecution. By the time the Church woke up to the tragedy, it was almost too late to act.

The hesitancy of the bishops clearly discouraged other Catholics from making a stand. When in June 1941 four professors from the Catholic University of Lyon drafted a declaration against the second *statut des juifs*, their efforts were stymied by the ecclesiastical authorities.[68] However, it must also be acknowledged that Catholics, like public opinion at large, were not unduly troubled by Vichy's initial anti-Jewish measures. This legislation was seen as being within the spirit of the law and was deemed necessary for the success of the *révolution nationale*. It naturally complemented the moves which Vichy was taking against the other forces of the 'anti France': freemasons and Communists. Indeed, elements of the lower clergy took an active part in denouncing such 'subversives'.[69] Catholics may also have persuaded themselves that Jews were suffering no more than anyone else, although it was difficult to maintain this view in the Occupied zone where the German-led persecution caused disquiet.

In 1942, when the *grandes rafles* began in earnest, it was no longer possible for consciences to remain immune. April and May saw the first convoys of foreign Jews leave Drancy for Auschwitz. In response *Témoignage chrétien*, the most influential Catholic Resistance publication, called on Christians to denounce racism. Words were matched by deeds. In the diocese of Lyon, Père Chaillet's ecumenical group *Amitié chrétienne* worked in conjunction with CIMADE,[70] the Protestant relief agency, dispersing Jewish children among religious houses. The fate of such children remained a matter of concern; and, during the final two years of the Occupation, lay Catholics, Jécistes and lower clergy, supported by such prelates as Saliège, Théas, Rémond and Gerlier, worked hard to shield Jews. It was an effective campaign that angered the collaborationist press as well as the SS and Vichy's *Commissariat général aux questions juives* (CGQJ).

It will be remembered that the other key issue troubling Catholic opinion in 1942–43 was the deportation of labour to Germany, the *service du travail obligatoire* (STO). Here, again, rank-and-file Catholics were more forthright in their criticisms than were the bishops. The dilemmas raised by the STO were rehearsed by *Témoignage chrétien* in July 1943.[71] Taking heart from recent declarations by Dutch and Danish bishops as well as the opposition voiced by Protestant leaders in France, *Témoignage chrétien* concluded that the STO should be resisted. Not only did conscription break international law, it went against the Christian conscience. Similar conclusions were reached by Catholic youth leaders. Meeting in March 1943, the *conseil fédéral* of the ACJF opposed the STO as did the movement's official mouth-piece, the *Cahiers de notre jeunesse*.[72] In the event, it was difficult for Jocistes and Jécistes to avoid being called up. Although some took to the *maquis*, a majority complied with the law. Maybe Berlin regretted having recruited such workers; Catholic deportees, especially those belonging to Church youth movements, proved a constant nuisance to the Nazi authorities.[73]

The hierarchy's ambivalence towards the STO is seen most clearly in the case of Liénart. As Halls suggests, whereas Gerlier was the obvious prelate to speak on racial affairs, Liénart was the 'natural' commentator on forced labour. Based in the industrial heartlands of northern France, from where many young people were being deported, he had close ties with the Catholic working class. Aware of his pastoral responsibilities, on 15 March 1943, records Halls, he addressed a large, and predominantly youthful, audience at Roubaix. The text of his message is not known, but was interpreted in collaborationist circles as a call to obey the law.[74] This prompted him to make another speech six days later at Lille. Here, he appeared to come out on the side of compliance but acknowledged that it was not a sin to refuse the STO. The ultimate decision, he suggested, had to be resolved by human conscience, a message echoed by the ACA meeting the next month. Thus, for the first time, the hierarchy had advised, albeit obliquely, disobedience to Vichy law.

For the laity, however, the bishops had counselled only spiritual resistance, especially as they were keen to disavow the 'théologiens sans mandat' writing in *Témoignage chrétien*. Nor did the prelates speak with one voice. Some such as Dutoit preached obedience; others, notably Saliège and Rémond, made their opposition plain. Most adopted an ambivalent line. Nonetheless, as the war continued, there was a toughening of attitude. The call-up of women, authorised in February 1944, forced the ACA to protest to Pétain. Germany's refusal to allow chaplains to accompany deportees also raised concern. To provide for the spiritual health of the workforce, Suhard approved the despatch of clandestine priests. Nearly three hundred clerics, disguised as workers, left for Germany, the beginnings of the *Mission de France* and the worker-priest movement. In the event, deportation did not provide an opportunity for the re-christianisation of the workforce, yet it taught Catholic activists that they had more 'in common' with their fellows, Christians and non-Christians, than they had previously imagined,[75] an attitude that was important for the reconstruction of France in 1945.

Together, the persecution of Jews and deportation of workers opened fissures within the Church, and forced the hierarchy to question Vichy wisdom. Yet the factors that had driven the ACA to support Vichy in 1940, especially the loyalty to Pétain and fear of disorder, remained as binding as ever, hence the declaration of February 1944 in which the assembly balanced criticism of the Laval government with praise for Pétain and denunciations of allied bombing and the Resistance.[76] Some incautious prelates even described American and British air-raids as acts of 'terrorism'. Yet this term was most commonly deployed to denounce the Resistance which was perceived by several prelates as a Communist-led conspiracy. Only a handful of bishops, notably Théas, Saliège, Maisonobe (Belley) and Terrier (Bayonne), lent support to resistance networks. Members of the minor clergy and laity were more forthcoming. A feeling of patriotism, a disenchantment with Pétain, a desire to avoid the STO, a distaste for racism and a sense of Christian justice, among other factors, drove Catholics to resist. Admittedly, their numbers were small, but by 1944 they dominated several underground organisations. Who, then, were these *résistants*, and what activities did they engage in?

Early Catholic resisters were largely 'drawn from the traditional Right' and the Christian Democrat parties.[77] As Halls suggests, perhaps the first Catholic in metropolitan France to defy Pétain was Edmund Michelet, a former 'royalist turned Christian Democrat'. In the summer of 1940 he transformed the *Nouvelles équipes françaises* (NEF), the study circles founded by the Christian Democrat newspaper *L'Aube*, into a resistance network. Former PDP members, Georges Bidault and François de Menthon, were also responsible in November 1940 for the publication of the clandestine newspaper, *Liberté*. In 1941 de Menthon, along with Henri Frenay, an army officer, launched a new publication, *Combat*, which soon became a military-style organisation. Although never exclusively Catholic, *Combat* was one of the key resistance groups in the unoccupied zone. A Catholic presence may also be identified in the other principal movements in both the occupied and non-occupied zones. In the *zone annexée*, militants from the CFTC were prominent in the strikes of 1941 which crippled the coalfields of northern France.[78] In 1943 the Catholic contribution to resistance was rewarded by representation on the co-ordinating committees of both the *Mouvements unis de la résistance* (MUR) and the *Conseil national de la résistance* (CNR).

As well as Christian Democrats and trade unionists, Catholic resisters were drawn from the ranks of the young. In 1943 activists in the ACJF created the *Jeunes chrétiens combattants* (JCC) designed to co-ordinate protest among the Church's youth bodies. Among the lower clergy, regular orders were especially prominent. As male congregations were responsible to Rome rather than to their local bishop, they enjoyed greater autonomy in their internal affairs than did their secular colleagues,[79] although it should not be overlooked that several female religious orders used their convents to hide wanted persons and conceal weapons. It cannot be denied, however, that most resisters from the regulars were drawn from the independent-minded Dominicans and Jesuits. In December 1940 the Jesuit periodical *Études* reappeared as *Temps présent*; its willingness to question Vichy authority guaranteed its suppression eight months later. The influential *Témoignage chrétien* was also the brainchild of two Jesuit priests, Pères Chaillet and Fessard.[80] Published every two months, it achieved a circulation of fifty thousand and had particular appeal to Catholic intellectuals, another group making up the Catholic resistance. In France, their number included the writers Paul Claudel and François Mauriac; overseas Georges Bernanos in Brazil and Jacques Maritain in New York both lent their support to De Gaulle. As Halls suggests, whether Mounier should be counted among these intellectual dissidents is contested by historians.[81] Mounier's early enthusiasm for the *révolution nationale* has undermined his resistance credentials.

Involvement in the Resistance had a significant impact on French Catholicism. To begin with, it contributed to the short-lived reconc.- liation between Catholics and Communists in 1944–45. Admittedly before 1939 the two groups had not been irreconcilable. Some Jocistes had even taken out a party card.[82] Yet most pre-war Catholics had seen little chance of a rapprochement with the Left, and were bewildered by the intrigues within the Communist party that followed the Nazi–Soviet pact. It is now known that this agreement did not prevent Communists from entering resistance on an individual basis, but it was not until the launching in June 1941 of Operation Barbarossa that there emerged a Communist-led Resistance movement, the *Front national*. Perhaps it was a desire to counter the influence of this organisation – the strongest in metropolitan France – that led some Catholics to resist. Yet it should also be noted that the *Front national* sought to include all shades of opinion into its ranks. While this 'open-door' policy had more success in the industrial north than in the rural south, it still managed to forge a respect between Catholics and Communists, a trust which was important in the rebuilding of post-war France.

Catholic participation in resistance also contributed to the re-emergence of Christian Democracy. It was in January 1944 that Bidault and a number of like-minded Catholics established the *Mouvement républicain populaire* (MRP), a unitary Christian Democratic party dedicated to the creation of a new society founded on spiritual values. The party went on to play a key role in the coalition politics of the Fourth Republic. It was 'represented in all but four of the twenty-six governments' of that regime, and provided France with three prime ministers;[83] not since the 1870s had Catholics enjoyed such a share of ministerial portfolios. No doubt the MRP's popularity stemmed from its resistance credentials and desire to build a New Jerusalem. Yet it also benefited from the distance it kept from the bishops and Rome. Given their low standing in the *après-guerre*, neither the ACA nor the Vatican dared intervene in MRP business. Accordingly Bidault's creation escaped the fate of pre-war Catholic parties which had often been perceived as being little more than 'the mouthpieces of the episcopate'.[84]

This commitment to liberal democracy thus eased the transition to peace-time government, and helped effect a reconciliation between the Church and de Gaulle. In 1940–41 only a handful of Catholics had followed the recalcitrant general to London, among them Maurice Schumann, a former editor of *L'Aube*, René Pleven, the jurist and former head of the ACJF and Thierry d'Argenlieu, the Carmelite who devised the Cross of Lorraine. A committed Catholic, de Gaulle himself remarked, 'The synagogue sends me more than the cathedral.'[85] This was hardly surprising. The general's association with the British, held responsible for the bombing of Mers el-Kébir, as well as his defiance of Pétain, the 'homme providentiel', perturbed many Catholics. However, subsequent events in the war strengthened his appeal, and by 1942–43 it was rumoured that large sections of the lower clergy were pro-Gaullist. For his part, de Gaulle welcomed this support but did not forget the way in which the bishops had sided with Vichy. In August 1944, he made his disgust apparent by informing Suhard, who had recently officiated at the funeral mass for Henriot, that the cardinal's presence was not welcome at the service of thanksgiving for the Liberation to be held at Notre-Dame.[86]

It is now known that the general sought sanctions for those clergy who had behaved questionably during the Occupation. Yet these penalties were not as severe as those contemplated by Bidault. As head of the CNR, in June 1944 this ardent Christian Democrat drew up 'blacklists' of bishops whose resignations could be justified.[87] As Halls has stated, the most prominent names included those of Feltin, who had tolerated collaborationist activities in Bordeaux, and Suhard, who was reproached for the way in which he had allowed ACA declarations to be manipulated by the Germans. Some twenty other prelates were also cited. Additionally, Bidault composed a 'white' list of those who were to be promoted: Saliège, for example, was recommended as a cardinal. It was understood, however, that such a wide-ranging *épuration* of the episcopate might upset Catholic opinion and ignite religious arguments at a time when France needed to build for the future. It was further recognised that any resignations would ultimately be a matter for the Vatican, which was likely to temporise. The papacy, which did not establish full diplomatic relations with the new French government until late 1944, was indeed slow to react. It was only after months of delicate negotiations that the resignations of Auvity, Dutoit, Beausart (Paris) and Du Bois de la Villerabel (Aix) were announced. Dutoit had, in any case, been forced to flee his diocese at the Liberation. While three Apostolic Vicars overseas stood down, no cardinals or archbishops were removed. In October 1945 there followed a number of promotions: Saliège, Petit de Julleville (Rouen) and Roques (Rennes), received the purple. Overall, it was a moderate shake-out, in keeping with purges elsewhere in France. Undoubtedly, this *épuration* would have been more extensive had it not been for the actions of those rank-and-file Catholics who defied Vichy and the Nazis.

In many ways, the hierarchy deserved the opprobrium it received in 1944–45. Admittedly only a small number of prelates were collaborationists. The courageous stand of Saliège, Rémond, Théas and Terrier should also be remembered. Yet, for the most part, leading clerics, especially the cardinals, played an ambivalent role. Their desire for revenge on the Third Republic, their admiration for Pétain, their concerns for the spiritual health of France, their fear of

Catholicism, Politics and Society

the Germans, their mistrust of De Gaulle and the allies, their worries about civil disorder, their deference to the Vatican and their constant search for State concessions, prevented them from giving a firm lead to the faithful. Even the ACA's declarations on racial persecution and deportation were hedged with caveats. Nonetheless, such moderate criticism had been too much for Darlan and Laval, and ensured the Occupation did not witness a Third Ralliement. If such a reconciliation had emerged, it would in any case have been sabotaged by the Germans. As it was, it was left to the Provisional Government to revoke the few concessions granted to the Church.

Not surprisingly, then, in 1944 Church leaders had lost something of their authority. By this stage, historians suggest, Catholics were accustomed to making decisions on their own. Although only a minority defied their superiors by engaging in resistance, it was clear that the episcopate had failed in its attempts, first begun in the 1930s, to keep a tight leash on the activities of its flock. No doubt the more conservative prelates regretted this development, yet in other respects they owed a great debt to those rank-and-file adherents who had questioned ecclesiastical authority. It was thanks to the actions of these independent-minded Catholics that France in 1944 did not witness a massive 'anti-clerical outburst' similar to those of 1830, 1871 and the 1880s when the Church had paid dearly 'for its complicity with the Restoration, Second Empire and MacMahon's Moral Order'.[88] At the Liberation, the Church could have faced a massive loss of influence. Instead, in ways neither Vichy nor the episcopate had intended, the Occupation guaranteed that Catholicism would continue to play a key role in the political and social life of modern France.

NOTES

1. The author wishes to thank Professor James F. McMillan of Edinburgh University for comments on an earlier version of this chapter.
2. Maurice Larkin, *Religion, Politics and Preferment in France since 1890. La Belle Époque and its Legacy* (Cambridge: Cambridge University Press, 1995), p. 175.
3. Ibid.
4. W.D. Halls, 'Catholicism under Vichy: A Study in Diversity and Ambiguity', in *Vichy France and the Resistance: Culture and Ideology*, eds Roderick Kedward and Roger Austin (London: Croom Helm, 1985), p. 133.

5. On the ACA see André Deroo, *L'Épiscopat français dans la mêlée de son temps, 1930–1955* (Paris: La Bonne Presse, 1955), p. 12.

6. Letter of Pius XII to the French bishops, 29 June 1940, quoted in Mgr Émile Guerry, *L'Église catholique en France sous l'occupation* (Paris: Flammarion, 1946), p. 17.

7. See especially his 'Statistique et histoire religieuse: pour un examen détaillé et pour une explication historique de l'état de catholicisme dans les diverses régions de France', *Revue d'histoire de l'Église de France*, xvii (1931), 425–49.

8. René Bédarida, 'Églises et chrétiens', in *La France des années noires*, 2 vols, eds Jean-Pierre Azéma and François Bédarida (Paris: Seuil, 1993), II, 126.

9. Nicholas Atkin, *Church and Schools in Vichy France, 1940–1944* (New York: Garland Publishing, 1991), pp. 11–12.

10. Bédarida, 'Églises et chrétiens', p. 107.

11. Robert Paxton, *Vichy France: Old Guard and New Order, 1940–1944* (New York: Alfred A. Knopf, 1972), p. 149.

12. Jean-Marie Mayeur, 'La Politique religieuse', in *Édouard Daladier: chef du gouvernement, avril 1938–septembre 1939* (Paris: Presse de la Fondation nationale des sciences politiques, 1977), pp. 243–54.

13. W.D. Halls, *Politics, Society and Christianity in Vichy France* (Oxford: Berg, 1995), p. 46. This book provides the best overview of Catholic attitudes during the Occupation, and the present chapter is deeply indebted to its findings.

14. Étienne Fouilloux, 'Le Clergé', in *Le Régime de Vichy et les Français*, eds Jean-Pierre Azéma and François Bédarida (Paris: Fayard, 1992), p. 467.

15. Dillard quoted in Halls, *Politics, Society and Christianity*, p. 49.

16. Ibid., p. 51.

17. Among the vast literature on Mounier, see John Hellman, *Emmanuel Mounier and the New Catholic Left, 1930–1950* (Toronto: University of Toronto Press, 1981); R. William Rauch, *Politics and Belief in Contemporary France. Emmanuel Mounier and Christian Democracy* (The Hague: Nijhoff, 1972); and Michel Winock, *Histoire Politique de la revue 'Esprit' 1930–1950* (Paris: Seuil, 1975).

18. Jean-Claude Delbreil, *Centrisme et démocratie chrétienne en France: Le Parti Démocrate Populaire des origines au MRP, 1919–1944* (Paris: Publications de la Sorbonne, 1990), p. 414.

19. Halls, *Politics, Society and Christianity*, p. 242.

20. Ibid., pp. 241–68.

21. ACA declaration of 24 July 1941 quoted in *La Vie catholique. Documents et actes de la hiérarchie catholique, années 1940–1941* (Paris: La Bonne Presse, 1942), p. 65.

22. ACA declaration of 17 February 1944, discussed in Halls, *Politics, Society and Christianity*, pp. 82–83.

23. Gérard Cholvy and Yves-Marie Hilaire, *Histoire religieuse de la France contemporaine*, 3 vols (Toulouse: Privat, 1985–88), III (1988), 78.

24. Halls, *Politics, Society and Christianity*, p. 83.

25. See Jean-Pierre Cointet, 'L'Église catholique et le gouvernement de Vichy. Église et Légion', in *Églises et chrétiens dans la IIe guerre mondiale. La France. Actes du colloque tenu à Lyon du 27 au 30 janvier 1978 publiés sous la direction de Xavier de Montclos* (Lyon: Presses Universitaires de Lyon, 1982), pp. 435–41 and Yves

Durand, *La France dans la Deuxième Guerre mondiale, 1939–1945* (Paris: Armand Colin, 1989), pp. 73–74.

26. Halls, 'Catholicism under Vichy', p. 140.

27. Halls, *Politics, Society and Christianity*, p. 53.

28. See Alain Fleury, *'La Croix' et l'Allemagne, 1930–1940* (Paris: Cerf, 1986) and Christian Ponson et al., 'L'Information sur le nazisme dans la presse catholique entre 1933 et 1938', in *Actes: Lyon*, pp. 17–32.

29. Halls, *Politics, Society and Christianity*, pp. 32–34.

30. Fouilloux, 'Le Clergé', p. 465.

31. Rémond, quoted in ibid., p. 467.

32. Halls, *Politics, Society and Christianity*, p. 177.

33. See W.D. Halls, 'French Christians and the German Occupation', in *Collaboration in France. Politics and Culture during the Nazi Occupation 1940–1944*, eds Gerhard Hirschfeld and Patrick Marsh (Oxford: Berg, 1989), p. 75 and Hans Umbeit, 'Les Services d'occupation allemande et les églises chrétiennes en France', in 'Églises et chrétiens pendant la seconde guerre mondiale dans le Nord-Pas-de-Calais', ed. Yves-Marie Hilaire, *Revue du Nord*, 237–38 (1978), 301.

34. Pierre Barral, 'Le Clergé lorrain sous l'occupation', in *Actes: Lyon*, pp. 91–100 and François-Georges Dreyfus, 'Les Églises en Alsace annexée de fait', in ibid., pp. 127–28.

35. Archives Nationales (AN) 2 AG 128 SP60 A, press cuttings from *L'Appel*, 1 July 1943 and *Au Pilori*, 17 February 1944.

36. On Bordeaux, see Claude Lévy, 'La Presse collaborationiste de Paris et de Bordeaux et l'Église de France', in *Actes: Lyon*, pp. 443–50.

37. On Touvier, see Henry Rousso, *The Vichy Syndrome. History and Memory in France since 1944* (Cambridge, Mass.: Harvard University Press, 1991), pp. 116–26 and Eric Conan and Henry Rousso, *Vichy, un passé qui ne passe pas* (Paris: Fayard, 1994).

38. Jacques Duquesne, *Les Catholiques français sous l'occupation* (Paris: Grasset, 1966), p. 41.

39. Halls, *Politics, Society and Christianity*, p. 54.

40. François Delpech, 'Le Projet de concordat de l'été 1940', in *Actes: Lyon*, pp. 185–88.

41. Atkin, *Church and Schools*, p. 18.

42. Darlan quoted in Richard Kuisel, *Capitalism and the State in Modern France* (Cambridge: Cambridge University Press, 1982), p. 132.

43. Ibid.

44. See Roderick Kedward, 'The Vichy of the other Philippe', in *Collaboration in France*, eds Hirschfeld and Marsh, pp. 32–46.

45. On these changes, see Atkin, *Church and Schools*, passim.

46. Among the many studies on Uriage see Bernard Comte, *Une Utopie combattante. L'École des Cadres d'Uriage, 1940–1942* (Paris: Fayard, 1991) and John Hellman, *The Knight-Monks of Vichy France: Uriage, 1940–1945* (Montreal: McGill-Queen's, 1993).

47. See Yves Durand, 'Les Notables', in *Le Régime de Vichy et les Français*, eds Azéma and Bédarida, pp. 371–81 and Roderick Kedward, *Occupied France. Collaboration and Resistance, 1940–1944* (Oxford: Blackwell, 1985), p. 23.

48. On this legislation, see Atkin, *Church and Schools*, pp. 107–30.

49. René Bédarida, 'La Hiérarchie catholique', in *Le Régime de Vichy et les Français*, eds Azéma and Bédarida, p. 453; Halls, *Politics, Society and Christianity*, p. 250; and M. Launay, 'Le Syndicalisme chrétien et la Charte du Travail', in *Actes: Lyon*, pp. 189–209.

50. Atkin, *Church and Schools*, p. 33.

51. On these discussions, see ibid., pp. 33–36; Delpech, 'Le Project de concordat'; and W.D. Halls, 'Church and State: Prelates, Theologians and the Vichy Regime', in *Religion, Society and Politics in France since 1789*, eds Frank Tallet and Nicholas Atkin (London: The Hambledon Press, 1991), pp. 167–88.

52. Henri Godin and Yvan Daniel, *La France, pays de mission?* (Lyon: Éditions de l'Abeille, 1943).

53. Halls, *Politics, Society and Christianity*, pp. 259–60.

54. On catechismal reform, see Atkin, *Church and Schools*, pp. 41–60.

55. Cholvy and Hilaire, *Histoire religieuse de la France contemporaine*, III, 167–220.

56. On the *jeunesse unique*, see Alain Michel, *La JEC face au nazisme et à Vichy* (Lille: Presses Universitaires de Lille, 1988).

57. See especially Michael Marrus and Robert Paxton, *Vichy France and the Jews* (New York: Basic Books, 1981).

58. See François Delpech, 'Les Églises et la persécution raciale', in *Actes: Lyon*, pp. 257–80.

59. François Delpech, 'L'Épiscopat et la persécution des juifs et des étrangers d'après les procès-verbaux de l'ACA et les dossiers Guerry', in *Actes: Lyon*, pp. 281–92.

60. Halls, *Politics, Society and Christianity*, p. 99, p. 106.

61. Ibid., p. 122.

62. Halls, 'Catholicism under Vichy', pp. 141–42.

63. Ibid., p. 142.

64. Marrus and Paxton, *Vichy France and the Jews*, p. 273.

65. Ibid., pp. 200–01.

66. Ibid., p. 198.

67. Halls, *Politics, Christianity and Society*, p. 99.

68. François Delpech, 'La Persécution des juifs et l'Amitié Chrétienne', in *Églises et chrétiens dans la IIe guerre mondiale. La région Rhône-Alpes. Actes du colloque tenu à Grenoble du 7 au 9 octobre 1976 publiés sous la direction de Xavier de Montclos* (Lyon: Presses Universitaires de Lyon, 1978), p. 159.

69. See Roger Austin, 'Political Surveillance and Ideological Control in Vichy France: A Study of Teachers in the Midi', in *Vichy France and the Resistance*, eds Kedward and Austin, pp. 13–35.

70. See Madeleine Barot, 'La CIMADE et les camps d'internement de la zone sud, 1940–1944', in *Actes: Lyon*, pp. 293–303.

71. See Halls, *Politics, Society and Christianity*, p. 316.

72. Ibid., p. 323.

73. Émile Poulat, 'Les Catholiques français en Allemagne'. in *Actes: Lyon*, pp. 373–81.

74. See Halls, *Politics, Society and Christianity*, pp. 312–13.

75. Ibid., p. 333.

76. On bombing see ibid., pp. 165–75.

77. Ibid., p. 199.

78. Darryl Holter, *The Battle for Coal. Miners and the Politics of Nationalisation in France, 1940–1950* (DeKalb: Northern Illinois University Press, 1992), pp. 40–59.

79. Atkin, *Catholics and Schools*, p. 128.

80. See René Bédarida, *Les Armes de l'esprit: Témoignage Chrétien, 1941–1943* (Paris: Éditions ouvrières, 1977).

81. Halls, *Politics, Society and Christianity*, p. 214.

82. See Michael Kelly, 'Catholics and Communism in Liberation France, 1944–47', in *Religion, Society and Politics in France*, eds Tallet and Atkin, pp. 187–202 and Jean Verlhac, 'La Jeune génération catholique en 1944 et le parti communiste', in *Actes: Lyon*, pp. 501–05.

83. Larkin, *Religion, Politics and Preferment*, p. 185.

84. Ibid.

85. De Gaulle quoted in ibid., p. 176.

86. Charles de Gaulle, *Mémoires de guerre*, 3 vols (Paris: Plon, 1954–59), II (1956), 314.

87. See André Latreille, *De Gaulle, la libération et l'Église catholique* (Paris: Cerf, 1978) and Halls, *Politics, Christianity and Society*, pp. 361–81.

88. Larkin, *Religion, Politics and Preferment*, p. 174.

6

Les formes politiques de la démocratie chrétienne en France au vingtième siècle

Jean-Claude Delbreil

LES ORIGINES AVANT 1914

Si l'on peut faire remonter le premier emploi du terme de 'démocratie chrétienne' en France à un discours prononcé en 1791 par l'évêque constitutionnel de Lyon, La Mourette, qui se référait aux 'principes lumineux de la démocratie chrétienne', c'est à partir de 1848 qu'est apparu un premier mouvement d'inspiration démocrate-chrétienne autour du Journal *L'Ère nouvelle*. Lamennais avec *L'Avenir* en 1830 n'avait jamais employé cette expression. Mais l'émergence de cette 'démocratie chrétienne' doit être resituée au milieu d'autres courants qui avaient également surgi au dix-neuvième siècle, et notamment ceux du catholicisme libéral d'une part et du catholicisme social d'autre part. Le 'libéralisme catholique' au début du dix-neuvième siècle s'était divisé entre une tendance qui s'était durcie dans un sens conservateur sur le plan social et une autre qui avait accepté la démocratie politique et sociale. Quant au catholicisme social, avec ses racines à trouver dans 'l'intransigeantisme catholique' qui s'opposait lui aussi au libéralisme, il s'était de même divisé. Il avait commencé à s'orienter pour une partie du moins vers une acceptation des formes 'démocratiques' de la vie politique et sociale.

C'est dans ce contexte idéologique complexe que se sont affirmées à la fin du dix-neuvième siècle, en France comme dans d'autres pays, les premières formes 'archaïques' de la démocratie chrétienne. Ce fut notamment ici le cas avec la 'seconde démocratie chrétienne' des années 1890, et la création en 1896 d'un *Parti démocratique chrétien*, assez éphémère, qui résultait d'une fédération de groupes locaux, d'ouvriers chrétiens et de certains groupes intellectuels. Cette première organisation sur le terrain politique prétendait répondre au problème du rôle nécessaire des chrétiens dans la vie politique elle-même. La démocratie chrétienne pouvait désormais intervenir comme une des idéologies en concurrence dans le jeu démocratique. Il y avait la conception d'un 'peuple chrétien' plus ou moins organisé et préexistant, la véritable démocratie en ce sens ne pouvant être 'que chrétienne'. L'historiographie récente a mis l'accent sur les origines à trouver de ce courant dans le vieux fonds de 'l'intransigeantisme catholique', qui refusait un certain libéralisme. Mais ces complexités ont été encore accentuées par les interventions pontificales au début du vingtième siècle qui visaient à limiter l'emploi de l'appellation de 'démocratie chrétienne' à une certaine forme de catholicisme social. Ceci aboutissait à une certaine dépolitisation de cette notion qui ne pourra d'ailleurs pas être entièrement acceptée. Mais les partis de cette inspiration, jusqu'en 1945, ne pourront pas adopter la dénomination de 'démocrates chrétiens'. En France, ils la refuseront pratiquement jusqu'à nos jours, sauf pour quelques exceptions sporadiques, en préférant par exemple, dans l'entre-deux-guerres, sur le plan international, l'expression de 'partis démocrates d'inspiration chrétienne'.

L'évolution avait été encore compliquée par l'apparition d'un autre mouvement, celui du *Sillon* autour de Marc Sangnier, à partir de 1894. Celui-ci avait eu des relations complexes avec la démocratie chrétienne au sens strict du terme et avait essayé d'élaborer la doctrine de la 'démocratie sillonniste'.[1] Le *Sillon* avait connu de nombreuses scissions, en abordant de plus en plus le domaine politique, jusqu'à la condamnation pontificale de 1910, par laquelle il avait été recommandé de fonder des 'sillons catholiques' par diocèses. Mais le *Sillon,* autant et plus peut-être que la 'seconde démocratie chrétienne' avait contribué à former toute une génération, en particulier par l'intermédiaire de ses 'cercles d'études' et par une implantation locale importante dans de nombreuses régions. Il avait dessiné une géographie des forces disponibles autour de groupes dynamiques et par une implantation dans la presse. Le *Sillon* que l'on peut malgré tout intégrer dans l'esprit d'une 'démocratie chrétienne' au sens large avait de plus marqué une étape vers la laïcisation et la décléricalisa-tion, vers une acceptation plus franche de la démocratie parlement-aire. Après la condamnation de 1910, Marc Sangnier avait créé en 1912 un nouveau mouvement qui se situait uniquement sur le terrain politique, la *Ligue de la Jeune république*. Mais il n'avait pas réussi à y entraîner toutes les anciennes troupes du *Sillon,* et uniquement une 'gauche'. Quant à certains éléments venus à la fois du *Sillon,* d'une partie du catholicisme social s'orientant vers l'acceptation des formes démocratiques, ils avaient commencé à constituer avant 1914 des fédérations de 'républicains démocrates' (comme en région parisienne et dans le Finistère), à la recherche d'une nouvelle formule politique plus modérée, et s'orientant vers une entente possible avec certains catholiques sociaux et libéraux. En effet, le catholicisme social lui-même avait évolué depuis l'encyclique *Rerum novarum* de 1891 et connu des évolutions 'démocratiques' qui faciliteront des rapprochements avec les démocrates chrétiens. L'évolution avait été significative pour un mouvement comme l'*Association catholique de la jeunesse française* (ACJF). Elle avait défini une action 'sociale', puis 'civique', pouvant être considérée comme un prélude à une action politique dans laquelle beaucoup allaient par la suite s'engager. Quant au catholicisme libéral, certains de ses éléments s'étaient dirigés vers la création en 1902 d'un parti politique, l'*Action libérale populaire*, qui doit être également resituée dans le cadre du 'Ralliement' des catholiques à la République et à la démocratie. Cette *Action libérale* avait fourni l'exemple d'un parti formé essentiellement de catholiques, certains pouvant apparaître prêts à se rallier à une 'démocratie chrétienne modérée'.

LA SITUATION AUX LENDEMAINS DE LA PREMIÈRE GUERRE MONDIALE

Dans cette conjoncture, on assiste dès les lendemains immédiats de la Première Guerre mondiale à de nouveaux rassemblements. Ils conduisent en 1924 à la création du premier véritable parti organisé et plus ou moins durable d'inspiration démocrate-chrétienne en France, le *Parti démocrate populaire* (PDP), mais à côté d'autres forces de moindre importance comme la *Jeune république* (JR). Après la condamnation du *Sillon,* la création de la JR et des *Fédérations de républicains démocrates,* il y avait déjà une dispersion des forces au niveau politique, au moment où se produit après la guerre ce que l'on a appelé le 'second ralliement' des catholiques à la République. Au début de la Grande Guerre, la 'démocratie chrétienne' semblait être parvenue à un certain échec. Mais des germes de renouveau avaient commencé à surgir pendant la guerre elle-même. Des contacts avaient été pris dans le sens d'un rapprochement des groupes, autour d'un

organe comme *L'Ame française* (avec Ernest Pezet) qui, à partir de
1917, avait mis en relation des hommes venus à la fois du *Sillon*, de la
démocratie chrétienne et du catholicisme social. Aux lendemains du
conflit, beaucoup pensent à Marc Sangnier pour diriger et coordonner
un vaste rassemblement des démocrates chrétiens de diverses
obédiences et de certains catholiques sociaux et libéraux acceptant le
fait démocratique. Mais Sangnier se dérobe à ces invites au printemps 1919, craignant sans doute un rassemblement trop orienté à
droite. Pourtant les élections de novembre 1919 marquent un certain
succès de ces tendances sur le plan politique et une victoire de
'l'apaisement' sur le terrain des luttes religieuses dans le cadre du
Bloc National. Mais les élus d'inspiration démocrate-chrétienne ou
catholique sociale se dispersent entre plusieurs groupes. En 1920, un
compromis est néanmoins trouvé avec la création d'une *Ligue
nationale de la démocratie* (LND), entre la *Jeune république* et les
Fédérations de républicain démocrates. Mais c'est une fédération très
lâche où les divergences ne tardent pas à apparaître, aussi bien sur les
problèmes intérieurs et sociaux que sur les problèmes internationaux
et de l'attitude face à l'Allemagne. Après une vie difficile, on
débouche sur une rupture en 1922, la LND subsistant de façon
formelle. Mais, du côté des 'républicains démocrates', on pensait
désormais à une autre formule d'union, excluant la *Jeune république*,
en direction de certains leaders des mouvements d'inspiration
catholique sociale, comme l'ACJF, mais aussi la *Confédération
française des travailleurs chrétiens* (CFTC), créée en 1919, les *Semaines
sociales*, etc. En 1922 est mis en place, avec des leaders à la fois
démocrates-chrétiens et catholiques sociaux, le *Bureau d'action
civique* (BAC) qui est pendant deux ans la matrice de la formation du
PDP. Des 'cartels sociaux' sont installés avec des catholiques sociaux
et des syndicalistes chrétiens, et il est demandé aux 'groupements du
même esprit' d'adhérer au BAC. Une action politique est dès lors
clairement envisagée, en attendant le résultat des élections législatives du printemps 1924, qui doivent permettre la création de ce
'parti nouveau'. Ces élections qui marquent la victoire du Cartel des
gauches sont cependant une déception relative puisque l'on ne
parvient à constituer qu'un groupe de treize députés à la Chambre,
élus surtout en Bretagne et en Alsace-Lorraine. Mais, sur ces bases
assez faibles et grâce à une volonté clairement affirmée, on va pouvoir
passer malgré tout à la création d'un nouveau parti en novembre
1924, le *Parti démocrate populaire*.

LE *PARTI DÉMOCRATE POPULAIRE*

Le PDP peut donc être considéré comme le premier véritable parti d'inspiration démocrate-chrétienne en France, sans en avoir l'appellation et en dehors de toute référence confessionnelle directe.[2] Il s'inscrit dans un faisceau de traditions complexes et tout un héritage des organisations qu'il a rassemblées dans sa période de gestation en 1919–24. En simplifiant, il rassemble en 1924, en vue d'un effort politique une 'aile gauche' du catholicisme social, acceptant une évolution 'démocratique' sur le plan politique et social et une aile droite de la démocratie chrétienne qui refuse de suivre Marc Sangnier et la *Jeune république*. La 'revendication d'héritage' du PDP, notamment chez un de ses principaux doctrinaires, Robert Cornilleau, s'oriente plutôt vers la 'seconde démocratie chrétienne' des années 1890 que vers le *Sillon*, et même vers un parti 'modéré' comme l'*Action libérale*. Le rassemblement opéré par le PDP en 1924 exclut une 'droite' du catholicisme social davantage liée à une 'droite catholique traditionnelle' et une 'gauche' de la démocratie chrétienne, très minoritaire. L'appellation de *Parti démocrate populaire* fait référence à la fois à une adhésion aux idées démocratiques et aux thèses du 'popularisme' développées par le *Parti populaire italien* (PPI) de Luigi Sturzo, créé en 1919.

Ce parti naît en tout cas dans une conjoncture politique difficile, et un peu tardivement dans le contexte politique de la première après-guerre. Une typologie de ses cadres dirigeants dans les années 1920 permet cependant de repérer les origines catholiques sociales, démocrates-chrétiennes et sillonnistes, mais aussi l'importance de l'ACJF, du syndicalisme chrétien, des Alsaciens Lorrains. Ce nouveau parti, petite force politique, prétend néanmoins s'organiser comme un parti moderne, sur le modèle des partis de gauche comme la *Section française de l'internationale ouvrière* (SFIO) en particulier, avec des organismes centraux assez développés (Congrès national, conseil national, commission exécutive, secrétariat général), mais aussi des organisations parallèles (*Association des journalistes démocrates*, *Fédération féminine*, *Jeunesses démocrates populaires*). Mais ces structures ont toujours correspondu à une force réelle assez limitée sur le plan des effectifs, toujours inférieurs à vingt mille (espoirs vite déçus) et sur le plan financier, avec des moyens toujours précaires, malgré quelques appuis. Une implantation du parti s'est réalisée par la mise en place d'un réseau presque complet de fédérations régionales, dont certaines sont parvenues à une puissance relative. Une phase plutôt favorable s'est déroulée jusqu'en 1932. L'implantation a retrouvé certaines des zones de force traditionnelles de la démocratie chrétienne. Le PDP a par ailleurs privilégié une action par la presse. A côté du journal du parti, l'hebdomadaire *Le Petit Démocrate,* qui ne parvint jamais à devenir quotidien, un réseau de presse régionale et locale, militante et sympathisante, s'est progressivement constitué. Le problème du soutien du quotidien *L'Ouest Éclair* et de son rôle dans le parti s'est posé en particulier dans l'Ouest, ainsi que plus tard du journal *L'Aube* dans les années 1930. Le PDP avait défini son programme en 1924: programme politique de révisionnisme modéré, programme social de synthèse, évolutionniste et réformiste, débouchant sur le thème de l'organisation professionnelle, avec intégration du syndicalisme. Le programme international se dirigeait vers les idées d'entente et de conciliation, l'ensemble dans une tonalité catholique centriste, situant ce parti au centre droit. Ce programme s'est inscrit de plus dans un 'environnement doctrinal' assez riche, nourri par des revues de réflexion, comme notamment la revue *Politique.* Celle-ci a en effet constitué un rassemblement intellectuel sur les marges du parti, sous l'influence de Sturzo et de son 'popularisme démocratique', et relayée par Marcel Prelot qui a tenté une œuvre de synthèse doctrinale. Mais on a aussi trouvé dans cette revue l'influence de la 'théorie de l'institution' de Maurice Hauriou, de même que dans l'autre revue dans l'orbite doctrinale du PDP, *Les Cahiers de la nouvelle journée,* du philosophe Paul Archambault. Celui-ci a développé les thèses du 'personnalisme démocratique', qu'il a opposées au 'personnalisme révolutionnaire' d'Emmanuel Mounier. D'autres influences ont encore joué comme celles de Maurice Blondel, Jacques Maritain, ou d'un des leaders du parti, Robert Cornilleau, journaliste et écrivain. Avec ce faisceau doctrinal complexe, on a tenté, en particulier à *Politique,* une synthèse qui pouvait conduire sur le plan économico-social à un 'pré-corporatisme' et sur le plan politique au thème de la réforme de l'État. Un programme dans ce sens est présenté au Congrès de 1929 et certaines dimensions se sont précisées sur des sujets comme la réforme administrative, celle du suffrage ou le régionalisme. La question des 'influences corporatistes' s'est posée encore davantage dans les années 1930, mais le parti n'est guère allé au delà des thèses classiques de 'l'organisation professionnelle'.

C'est alors en tout cas une petite élite de dirigeants qui conduit le parti, avec Auguste Champetier de Ribes, président depuis 1926,

Robert Cornilleau, directeur du *Petit Démocrate,* Raymond-Laurent, secrétaire général, Ernest Pezet, Louis-Alfred Pagès, Paul Simon, avant un renouvellement dans les années 1930 et l'arrivée d'une nouvelle génération (Georges Bidault, Pierre-Henri Teitgen, Robert Schuman, etc.).

Dans sa vie relativement courte jusqu'à la Seconde Guerre mondiale, le PDP a d'abord connu une phase d''affirmation relative' de 1924 à 1932. En 1924–28, il montre une opposition au Cartel des gauches, mais en écartant toute obstruction systématique, avant un appui critique à l'*Union nationale* de Poincaré en 1926–28. Il doit se classer au milieu des forces politiques existantes, par une opposition aux extrêmes droites et aux ligues, et en se démarquant des modérés de la *Fédération républicaine* et de la droite catholique. Il se trouve ainsi plus proche des modérés laïcs de l'*Alliance démocratique,* avec lesquels apparaît une convergence de fait sur de nombreux terrains, voire des radicaux. Il entame des contacts avec ce que l'on appelle les *Jeunes équipes* (*Jeunes radicaux,* groupe de Georges Valois), pendant que Robert Cornilleau adresse en direction des socialistes son *Pourquoi pas?* pour une éventuelle collaboration. Il s'oppose d'autre part nettement à l'*Action française* (AF), tout en évitant de se mêler aux remous de la condamnation de 1926. Ceci n'empêche pas l'AF de mener contre lui de violentes attaques. Il essaie également sur le plan religieux de se démarquer de la *Fédération nationale catholique* (FNC) et de clarifier sa position sur les questions religieuses et scolaires: volonté d'apaisement, refus de toute apparence de confessionnalisme, ce qui n'a pas exclu des problèmes de relation avec l'Épiscopat et le clergé. Il tente de renforcer ses positions aux élections de 1928 qui sont pour lui un succès relatif avec dix-huit élus. En 1928–32, il soutient d'une façon générale l'Union nationale et les gouvernements modérés et refuse de fait la 'concentration' qu'il préconise en théorie. Il devient un parti de gouvernement par son président-ministre, Champetier de Ribes. Mais les équivoques de la 'concentration républicaine' demeurent face aux radicaux, liées au problème de la laïcité; il propose un plan complet sur la question scolaire en 1930, s'inscrivant dans une nouvelle tactique des catholiques face aux lois laïques. Mais les élections de 1932 marquent pour lui un échec et le début d'un déclin relatif, à partir de positions déjà faibles. Malgré tout, en 1924–32, le PDP avait développé des attitudes aussi bien sur le terrain social qu'international qui l'avaient assez largement démarqué de la droite traditionnelle. Il avait précisé un programme social réformiste, en faveur notamment des assurances sociales et des allocations familiales, et joué un rôle pratique en liaison avec les catholiques sociaux. Il s'était intéressé de près aux problèmes ruraux, au développement du mouvement syndical et ouvrier, par des relations privilégiées avec la CFTC. Il avait mené avec elle des combats communs, mais avait eu aussi des relations avec la *Confédération française des professions*, patronale. Il est resté lié aux milieux du catholicisme social et à l'ACJF, dont l'apport sur le plan humain est resté important, même si ce furent toujours des relations de personnes et non des relations organiques. Il a également développé des positions originales sur le plan international, en relation avec les liens déjà établis du côté du *Secrétariat international des partis démocratiques d'inspiration chrétienne* (SIPDIC), créé en particulier avec les Italiens du PPI de Sturzo à partir de 1924–26. Des contacts ont été noués également avec les Allemands du Zentrum jusqu'en 1929, dans le sens d'une adhésion à la politique de Briand d'union européenne et de rapprochement franco-allemand, soutenue par le Vatican. Il s'est aussi intéressé de façon privilégiée aux problèmes de l'Europe centrale (Pezet) et il a dégagé face à l'Italie une position anti-fasciste originale chez les modérés français. Le PDP a alors connu une vie régionale assez active dans le cadre de fédérations départementales d'une grande diversité, certaines puissantes et avec des débouchés électoraux, d'autres assez faibles. La question s'est posée de ses relations avec le parti de l'*Union populaire républicaine d'Alsace* (UPRA) qui est toujours resté indépendante du PDP, l'émergence de l'autonomisme pouvant parfois placer celui-ci en position difficile.

La période 1932–40 a vu ensuite un déclin, mais aussi un début de changement en profondeur du parti. En 1932–36, l'amorce de ce déclin se constate dans la conjoncture du 'second Cartel des gauches' où se manifeste une réserve accrue du PDP. Mais il se montre également méfiant face à l'agitation de droite qui conduit au 6 février 1934, malgré certains clivages internes et s'il se rallie à la 'seconde union nationale'. Il refuse encore la 'concentration' en 1935 (offre de Sarraut), mais en étant toujours l'objet d'attaques de l'extrême-droite contre ce qu'elle appelle 'les rouges-chrétiens'. Il manifeste son hostilité à l'égard des Ligues et des mouvements autoritaires et entretient des contacts intellectuels avec de 'nouvelles jeunes équipes' qui témoignent de 'l'esprit des années trente'. Dans cette période surgissent aussi dans ce parti des clivages et oppositions accentués, avec à la fois le mécontentement d'une 'droite' et l'inquiétude d'une 'gauche'. Les *Jeunesses démocrates populaires* agissent comme un facteur de renouveau et de trouble en même temps, ainsi que les rapports avec *L'Aube* dès cette période. C'est un parti affaibli et divisé qui affronte les élections de 1936 qui sont pour lui une nouvelle étape de son tassement face à la victoire du *Front populaire*. En 1936–40, il manifeste une opposition calme au ministère Blum, une attitude complexe face aux ministères Chautemps et un soutien au ministère Daladier d'union nationale. Il devient un des constituants idéologiques de la 'France de Daladier' en 1938–40. Les relations avec les autres partis modérés s'améliorent, et un rapprochement s'opère avec les radicaux. Dans le cadre d'un nouveau changement de climat entre l'Église et l'État, Champetier de Ribes joue un rôle pour un 'règlement d'ensemble' des problèmes, interrompu par la guerre. Mais une crise du parti s'aggrave, avec des divisions accentuées par la conjoncture intérieure et extérieure, et l'on peut aussi soulever la question d'un renouvellement suffisant des cadres. Les relations avec *L'Aube* commencent à poser interrogation, de même qu'avec les *Nouvelles équipes françaises* (NEF). Le problème est évoqué d'un 'élargissement', dans une 'mouvance' du parti qui tend à se diversifier. Le PDP continue cependant à développer ses positions sur le terrain social et international. Il tente de définir des remèdes face à la crise économique et sociale. Il soutient les réformes sociales du *Front populaire*, malgré des réserves sur leur inspiration. Il refuse la 'tentation corporatiste', tout en maintenant les relations avec les catholiques sociaux. Les problèmes internationaux et la 'montée des périls' singularisent encore le parti, malgré le départ des Allemands du SIPDIC. Il s'oriente, depuis des positions 'briandistes' vers une fermeté dans ce domaine, où il se distingue à nouveau de la droite modérée, aussi bien face à l'Italie dans la guerre d'Ethiopie que face aux coups de force hitlériens en Europe. C'est un esprit 'anti-munichois' majoritaire qu'il manifeste aussi dans la 'drôle de guerre'. Il montre également sa lucidité face au jeu de l'Axe dans la guerre d'Espagne.

Le PDP a donc connu un impact limité dans la politique française de l'entre-deux-guerres, mais il a marqué l'apparition d'une tonalité idéologique nouvelle. Il a joué un rôle dans le système des partis, en contribuant à poser la question du centre, et pour l'amélioration du climat politico-religieux. Il a constitué une étape pour le rassemblement d'une tendance jusqu'ici surtout intellectuelle

et sociale, pour la première fois organisée sur le plan politique. Il a
obtenu des succès partiels, laissé une trace historique et un héritage.
Les succès du MRP de 1945 n'auraient pas été possibles sans les
efforts et les échecs de ce parti-pionnier qui avait dégagé la route.

LA *JEUNE RÉPUBLIQUE*

Le PDP n'a pas été dans l'entre-deux-guerres le seul représentant
des formes politiques de la démocratie chrétienne qui avait continué
à se caractériser par une assez fondamentale dispersion. Celle-ci
remontait à l'avant-guerre de 1914 et elle s'est perpétuée par la
permanence de ce que l'on peut appeler 'le frère ennemi' dans la
démocratie chrétienne du PDP, la *Jeune république* (JR) fondée par
Marc Sangnier. Cette JR s'était placée sur un terrain strictement non
confessionnel, avec un programme qui se prononçait 'pour une
république plus démocratique, plus hardiment réformatrice'. Là
encore, les origines sont à trouver dans la démocratie chrétienne et le
catholicisme social, mais dans leurs tendances de 'gauche' et
'avancées'. Une séparation avait commencé à se faire avec ceux qui
avaient suivi Sangnier à la JR, et son organe de presse *La Démocratie*.
Si Sangnier avait fait échouer le projet d'un vaste rassemblement en
1919, la JR avait fait élire cinq de ses membres à la Chambre en 1919
et elle avait accepté de participer en 1920–22 à la *Ligue nationale de la
démocratie*. Mais les options de ce petit parti démocrate-chrétien
étaient différentes de celles des républicains démocrates, dans un
sens nettement plus à gauche, sur le plan intérieur, politique, social,
international. Il se prononce ainsi en faveur d'une évolution du droit
de propriété, et d'une certaine dose de nationalisations. Il est plus
favorable que le PDP à une intervention de l'État dans la vie
économique et sociale, moins favorable à l'idéologie des 'corps intermédiaires' ou de 'l'organisation de la profession'. Il veut se tourner
vers le monde ouvrier et syndical et manifeste des réserves à l'égard
du syndicalisme chrétien, en souhaitant davantage l'entrée des
catholiques dans les autres organisations syndicales. Mais, tout en ne
se voulant pas non plus un parti confessionnel, la JR défend dans les
milieux de gauche les intérêts du catholicisme. Elle prétend se situer
politiquement à gauche, pour y témoigner, entretient des contacts
avec le parti radical et le parti socialiste lui-même, les milieux laïcs et
anticléricaux, afin de tenter d'apaiser la querelle religieuse, tout

comme le PDP essaie de 'travailler' la droite modérée pour la convertir à ses idées sociales.[3]

C'est sur le plan international que Marc Sangnier et la JR manifestent la plus grande originalité, dans le sens d'une adhésion précoce aux idées de rapprochement international et franco-allemand en particulier. Sangnier veut en effet promouvoir ce qu'il appelle 'l'internationalisme démocratique'. Il organise des 'congrès démocratiques internationaux', dès 1921, et notamment le congrès de Bierville de 1926, sur le thème de 'la Paix par la Jeunesse', dans le cadre du soutien à la politique de Briand de rapprochement franco-allemand. Mais les deux actions, du PDP et de la JR, sont restées séparées, celle-ci étant à nouveau en contact avec des milieux de gauche. Marc Sangnier crée aussi alors, sur le modèle allemand, les premières auberges de la jeunesse en France. Cette action suscite un temps de grands espoirs, mais elle va se heurter à la dégradation de la situation internationale à partir de 1930–32. La JR peut donc être considérée à cette époque sur tous les plans comme plus à gauche que le PDP mais elle est restée à un niveau constamment inférieur à son 'rival' dans la démocratie chrétienne, avec des effectifs autour de cinq mille membres. Sur le plan électoral, la JR n'a eu aucun élu en 1924, un en 1928 et 1932, deux lors des élections partielles en 1934 et 1935. Ses relations sont restées constamment mauvaises avec le PDP, trop lié pour Sangnier à la droite conservatrice, réactionnaire et nationaliste. Les démocrates populaires mettent en cause de leur côté certaines dérives trop à gauche. En effet la JR a eu elle aussi des contacts avec les *Jeunes équipes* radicalisantes et socialisantes. Mais en 1932, elle est affaiblie par le départ de Marc Sangnier qui abandonne le combat politique pour se consacrer uniquement à l'action en faveur de la paix. Il fonde un nouveau journal et un nouveau mouvement, *L'Éveil des peuples* qui tente d'œuvrer pour la paix dans les circonstances de plus en plus difficiles des années 1933–39. Les principaux leaders de la JR sont alors Georges Hoog, Maurice Lacroix, Louis Rolland, Guy Menant, Philippe Serre et Albert Blanchoin. Elle développe un programme social face à la crise, pouvant aller jusqu'à ce qu'elle appelle une 'économie dirigée'. Elle continue un dialogue avec la gauche laïque sur les problèmes religieux et scolaires pour modifier le climat dans ces domaines. Certains, comme Francisque Gay, directeur de la revue *La Vie catholique,* d'inspiration elle aussi démocrate-chrétienne, n'avaient pas renoncé à l'idée d'un 'rassemblement des forces démocratiques d'inspiration chrétienne'. Ce fut un des objets du lancement du quotidien *L'Aube* en 1932, qui allait fournir l'occasion d'une collaboration avec les démocrates populaires, mais non sans créer des problèmes. En effet les divergences continuent à se manifester entre les deux tendances, surtout après 1934 et l'élaboration progressive du *Rassemblement populaire*. Aux élections de 1936, la JR transformée en parti depuis janvier fait élire quatre de ses candidats, plus deux qui le rejoindront. Alors que le PDP est dans l'opposition, la JR soutient l'action du Front à la Chambre et dans le pays. Sur le plan international, depuis 1932, la JR et Sangnier conduisent des actions parallèles en faveur de la paix. La JR continue à être présente à des 'conférences démocratiques'. Mais des divergences apparaissent aussi sur ce terrain, une tendance restant fidèle à un certain pacifisme jusqu'à Munich. Toutefois une solidarité active est manifestée à l'égard de la république espagnole. La division des démocrates chrétiens persiste jusqu'à la fin de l'entre-deux-guerres, et elle est encore accentuée par l'existence d'autres petits mouvements, comme les partis régionaux: c'est le cas pour le parti de l'UPRA, créée en 1919 avec le soutien de syndicalistes chrétiens, du clergé et d'une presse locale puissante; un certain nombre de ses élus siègent au groupe démocrate-populaire à la Chambre. En Moselle était aussi apparu un autre parti, l'*Union républicaine de Lorraine* (URL), dont une tendance peut être considérée comme démocrate-chrétienne, avec un homme comme Robert Schuman en particulier. Par ailleurs, la *Ligue nationale de la démocratie* avait un temps subsisté après la rupture de 1932. Une tendance de la 'JR minorité' avait intégré le PDP, autour du *Démocrate de Paris*, mais elle le quitte bientôt en le trouvant trop à droite. Il y avait également de petits groupes qui conservaient l'espoir d'une entente possible entre les tendances séparées, comme celui du *Mouvement* qui s'efforce de servir d'agent de liaison, et affirme nécessaire que le PDP et la JR conservent des liens. Le regret est ici permanent de voir les deux forces s'ignorer. Mais un débat dans la revue *Le Mouvement* montre l'ampleur des oppositions maintenues, malgré les efforts de l'abbé Lugan jusqu'à sa mort en 1932. C'est alors sur un autre terrain qu'a commencé une nouvelle forme de contacts autour du journal *L'Aube,* lancé par Francisque Gay, dans le but d'"informer' et d'"unir' les catholiques au-delà de leurs tendances différentes: démocrates populaires, Jeunes Républicains, mais aussi éléments plus à droite. Gay est au centre d'un vaste réseau de relations dans le catholicisme politique et intellectuel, du PDP à la JR, des catholiques sociaux aux syndicalistes chrétiens. Dans *L'Aube,* doivent s'exprimer toutes les tendances séparées et le quotidien s'adressera sans distinction de parti ou de groupement à tous les démocrates d'inspiration chrétienne. En définitive, *L'Aube* a joué un rôle autonome dans la démocratie chrétienne, surtout à la fin de l'entre-deux-guerres avec l'éditorialiste Georges Bidault qui se distingue de plus en plus. Une *Association des amis de l'Aube* est mise sur pied, et c'est autour d'elle que naît l'idée d'un nouveau rassemblement aussi large que possible. Ceci conduit à la création en 1928 des NEF. Gay affirme que 'tout ce qui est conscient de ses origines populaires et chrétiennes' peut s'y retrouver. La NEF joue aussi un rôle pour la réémergence de la tendance démocrate-chrétienne et catholique sociale dans la politique française, face au déclin de partis déjà traditionnels. Elle a commencé à préparer des collaborations et un début de fusion qui se révélera davantage possible par la suite. En fait l'activité de la NEF se manifeste surtout à la fin de l'entre-deux-guerres par des conférences et un rôle de liaison. Celui-ci avait été également le fait d'autres organes et revues comme *Sept,* de 1934 à 1937, puis *Temps présent,* dans l'orbite des dominicains, avec les *Amis de Temps présent* qui rassemblent également des démocrates chrétiens de diverses obédiences. Gay avait joué un rôle fondamental dans le mouvement vers l'union des forces dispersées, avec son mémoire *Pour un rassemblement des forces démocratiques d'inspiration chrétienne.*

LA GUERRE ET SES CONSÉQUENCES

C'est dans ce contexte de divisions maintenues et de tendances confuses vers une union que l'on trouve les démocrates chrétiens français au moment de la Seconde Guerre mondiale, et d'abord de la défaite de 1940. Les quatre députés JR présents avaient voté contre les 'pleins pouvoirs' au Maréchal Pétain le 10 juillet 1940, de même que trois députés démocrates populaires. L'attitude de la famille démocrate-chrétienne de 1940 à 1944, allait très largement résulter des positions que l'on peut qualifier de 'pré-résistantes' qui avaient émergé de 1936 à 1940, notamment face aux accords de Munich. Pour la JR, malgré une certaine pente 'pacifiste' apparue chez certains avant 1940, cela allait être à l'origine d'une attitude majoritairement 'résistante'. Beaucoup de ses membres tiennent une place importante dans des mouvements comme *Franc-tireur, Combat, Libération* ou

Résistance. Quant aux démocrates populaires, plus nombreux, il y a eu, surtout au début, davantage de clivages face à un régime de Vichy qui prétendait combler certains des vœux des catholiques sociaux en général, sur le plan intérieur et sur le plan social. Pour une tendance au moins du PDP, il y a eu ainsi une 'tentation vichyste'. Une petite minorité est allée plus loin jusqu'en 1944, ce qui rendra nécessaire une 'épuration' du parti à la Libération. Mais, du côté de Vichy, on s'était plaint très vite d'une 'bouderie' des démocrates populaires à l'égard du régime, que l'on estimait incompréhensible. Car au contraire, on vit assez rapidement un grand nombre d'entre eux passer dans ce que l'on a pu appeler 'la première résistance' en 1940–42, dans des mouvements auxquels ils ont apporté leur tonalité, comme en particulier *Liberté* qui fusionne bientôt avec *Combat*, *Temps nouveau*, *Témoignage chrétien*. S'il s'est agi pour certains d'une résistance surtout 'intellectuelle', d'autres sont allés plus loin, notamment en jouant un rôle de premier plan dans les 'institutions officielles' de la résistance. C'est le cas dans le *Comité général d'études* (CGE) avec François de Menthon et Pierre-Henri Teitgen, qui publie des *Cahiers* pour la préparation de la France de la Libération. Quant au *Conseil national de la résistance* (CNR), il est bientôt présidé, après la disparition de Jean Moulin en 1943 par le démocrate populaire Georges Bidault. Ceci manifeste la reconnaissance de la démocratie chrétienne et du PDP comme un centre des tendances politiques françaises, autour duquel pourrait se réaliser la volonté d'unanimité de la Résistance. Cette promotion de Bidault est aussi celle de son parti et de sa tendance qui s'approche de la phase de la Libération en bénéficiant de positions très solides dans la 'France combattante', symbolisées aussi par Maurice Schumann, le porte-parole de la France libre, ancien de la JR. Dans ces conditions, c'est une nouvelle époque qui allait pouvoir s'ouvrir en 1944 pour la démocratie chrétienne française et pour ses forces politiques.

LA NAISSANCE ET LES DÉBUTS DU MRP

Dès la Libération, se crée en effet un nouveau parti d'inspiration démocrate-chrétienne, sous la forme du *Mouvement républicain populaire* (MRP) qui s'inscrit lui aussi dans cette tradition, mais sans référence confessionnelle. Il surgit en 1944, en obtenant d'emblée une audience sans commune mesure avec celle de son principal prédécesseur de l'entre-deux-guerres, le PDP. Comme ce dernier, il s'intègre dans le même faisceau de traditions complexes, de la démocratie chrétienne au catholicisme social et libéral. L'échec relatif du PDP avait préparé le terrain, organisé un premier rassemblement déjà en voie d'élargissement dans les années 1930. Si les démocrates chrétiens restaient divisés entre PDP et JR, le choc de la guerre et le rôle commun dans la Résistance rendent possible la création d'un nouveau parti en 1944. Le courant démocrate-chrétien se présente comme une des grandes tendances politiques de la France de la Libération. Cette situation rend possible l'élargissement souhaité par certains avant 1940, face à d'autres éventualités comme la reconstitution des forces anciennes ou un rassemblement plus vaste avec certains socialistes, sous la forme un temps envisagée d'un 'parti travailliste'. La transformation dans le sens d'un élargissement est soutenue en particulier par les éléments engagés dans la Résistance, et surtout les milieux autour de l'ACJF. La formation de ce parti nouveau avait été décidée par certains des principaux leaders démocrates-populaires engagés dans la Résistance, avec le soutien des 'anciens de l'ACJF' et d'un homme comme André Colin pour dépasser le 'vieux' PDP et lui substituer une autre formule. Cette 'coalition' avait déjà visé à mettre à l'écart l'essentiel des anciens dirigeants du PDP et des réunions dans ce sens ont lieu à Paris dès janvier 1944. C'est le 3 novembre 1944 que se tient un congrès du *Mouvement républicain de libération* (MRL), première forme du MRP, avant la formation du gouvernement, où l'on trouve trois démocrates populaires, Bidault, de Menthon et Teitgen. A ce moment, le PDP n'est toujours pas dissous, et il tente même, autour de certains de ses leaders, de tenir des réunions. Mais c'est une force politique divisée et en plein désarroi qui réunit sa commission exécutive le 29 octobre, une partie de ses membres ayant déjà rejoint le MRP. On a ici un exemple de substitution plus ou moins forcée d'une nouvelle force politique à une ancienne, par une sorte de fait accompli, le rôle équivoque tenu par certains de 1940 à 1944 ayant servi de prétexte. Le 25 et 26 novembre se réunit le congrès exécutif du nouveau MRP. Certains dirigeants du PDP y sont présents et d'autres refusent d'y participer. Maurice Schumann en est élu président et André Colin devient secrétaire général. Dans ces conditions, ce qui restait du PDP, la plupart de ses membres et dirigeants rejoignent le MRP, malgré une résistance dans certaines régions. Quant à la JR, le problème se pose pour elle, tout comme en 1919, d'une éventuelle fusion avec les autres démocrates chrétiens dans le nouveau parti. Son comité national la rejette une nouvelle fois, si une minorité avec Schumann l'accepte. Un certain nombre de jeunes républicains passent aussi à l'*Union démocratique et socialiste de la résistance* (UDSR). La JR signe un pacte d'unité d'action avec cette dernière et la SFIO aux élections d'octobre 1945 où elle obtient cinq élus. Au congrès d'octobre 1945, Marc Sangnier accepte pour sa part de devenir le président d'honneur du MRP, ce qui est pour lui la consécration de toute son action antérieure et le symbole de la réconciliation de la majorité des démocrates chrétiens. En effet la JR va rester, à côté du MRP un mouvement marginal, incarnant, surtout après 1947, une gauche dissidente et indépendante. Elle soutiendra Mendès-France en 1954, une moitié de ses membres ralliant le *Parti socialiste unifié* (PSU) en 1960, et Mitterrand en 1965. Jusqu'à sa disparition au début des années quatre-vingts, elle veut rester fidèle à un 'socialisme personnaliste', qui refuserait aussi bien l'individualisme que l'étatisme. La JR allait nettement plus à gauche que le MRP et elle a contribué à préparer dans certaines régions une rupture non seulement avec la droite mais avec le centre pour une fraction du catholicisme français.

Quant au nouveau MRP, il se veut donc être un 'mouvement' organisé sur la base de fédérations départementales. Sa direction théorique appartient au congrès national qui se réunit annuellement, et dans l'intervalle, à un conseil national. Pour l'organisation, on a affaire à un parti de structure mixte, où le principe fédératif coexiste avec des organes centraux pouvant être mis au service d'un 'parti de masse'. Une commission exécutive permanente nomme à sa tête un président. Le congrès constitutif élabore d'emblée un *Manifeste* où toute référence confessionnelle est évitée. Le terme de 'révolution' apparaît à diverses reprises, mais au service de la 'personne humaine'. A côté de Maurice Schumann, premier président du parti, il y a parmi les principaux dirigeants un certain nombre d'anciens démocrates populaires comme Georges Bidault, François de Menthon, Pierre-Henri Teitgen, Robert Bichet, aux côtés de Paul Bacon, André Colin. Sur trente membres de la première commission exécutive, vingt et un avaient appartenu au PDP et deux à la JR, avec notamment des représentants de la 'deuxième génération' du PDP. Le nouveau parti est par ailleurs confronté rapidement au redémarrage de la vie politique nationale et un programme est publié à l'occasion du référendum et des élections d'octobre 1945. Le 'double oui' préconisé par De Gaulle et le MRP l'emporte, pendant que celui-ci devient le second parti de France avec cent cinquante et un élus, derrière le Parti communiste français (PCF). Ici avaient joué à la fois l'affaiblissement de la droite traditionnelle et l'absence de parti gaulliste pour expliquer un résultat qui en fait une des principales forces politiques de la France de l'après-guerre. Une partie de l'électorat modéré soutient les démocrates chrétiens, combattus avant la guerre, comme rempart anti-communiste. De plus le MRP peut alors apparaître, sinon comme le parti gaulliste, du moins comme 'le parti de la fidélité'. Il est un des partisans de la nouvelle constitution, après le départ de De Gaulle en janvier 1946, qui marque la rupture entre le 'parti de la résistance catholique' et le 'chef catholique de la résistance'. S'il combat le premier projet, repoussé le 5 mars 1946, il contribue à élaborer le second, après l'élection de la seconde Constituante le 2 juin, où il devient le premier parti de France avec 28% des suffrages et cent cinquante-neuf sièges. Le second projet est adopté le 13 octobre, malgré un 'oui tiède' du MRP. La cassure s'accentue avec De Gaulle qui s'était prononcé pour le 'non'. Le MRP apparaît de plus en plus comme un des nouveaux partis de la Quatrième République, dès l'époque du Tripartisme en 1946–47, aux côtés du PCF et de la SFIO. Il surgit comme un élément neuf dans le système politique, et perturbe les clivages traditionnels.

IDÉOLOGIE, PROGRAMME ET RÔLE POLITIQUE

Le MRP occupe un espace laissé libre au centre-droit par l'effacement de la droite traditionnelle, même si sa volonté initiale était plus ou moins de se situer au centre-gauche, notamment sur le plan social. Mais un décalage va assez vite apparaître entre les dirigeants du parti et un électorat venu de la droite traditionnelle, ce qui allait marquer la difficulté de 'faire une politique de gauche avec un électorat de droite'. Ceci n'empêche pas le parti de développer un programme qui prétend s'appuyer sur les principes fondamentaux de la démocratie chrétienne, et aussi sur l'idée de la 'personne'. Il doit s'agir en particulier d''approfondir' la démocratie, là encore sur la base de 'communautés intermédiaires', qui seraient tout d'abord la famille avec une politique 'familialiste', mais aussi la profession organisée et le syndicalisme libre. A la Libération, le MRP présente un programme économique et social que l'on peut estimer être assez à gauche, en faveur d'un certain nombre de nationalisations et d'une 'politique de progrès'. Il appuie aussi bien les lois sur la sécurité sociale que les débuts de la planification. Ce programme initial de l'après-guerre immédiat allait être ensuite constamment précisé et affiné, en particulier dans les congrès du Parti.[4]

Le MRP a assez vite commencé à évoluer, notamment sous l'influence de la nouvelle conjoncture politique, à partir de la rupture du 'tripartisme' avec les communistes en 1947. C'est alors l'élaboration de la formule dite de la 'troisième force' face aux deux oppositions naissantes au régime de la Quatrième République, les communistes à gauche et le nouveau *Rassemblement du peuple français* (RPF) gaulliste à droite. Le MRP devient un de ses constituants principaux, et un des soutiens naissants, aux côtés d'une droite traditionnelle de retour, qui se réorganise autour du *Centre national des indépendants* (CNI), des socialistes SFIO et des radicaux. Il dirige au gouvernement cette formule politique à plusieurs reprises, ainsi avec le ministère Robert Schuman en 1947–48, celui de Georges Bidault en 1949–50. Il est présent dans tous les gouvernements, avec ses leaders Bidault et Schuman aux Affaires Étrangères. Cependant une première rupture se produit avec la SFIO en 1950 (ministère Bidault), ce qui témoigne de la fragilité de cette 'troisième force'. Les élections de 1951 marquent ensuite le premier recul électoral assez net du parti et aussi en fait une certaine régularisation. Malgré le système des 'apparentements' entre les listes de la troisième force face aux oppositions communistes et gauchistes, le MRP régresse assez fortement, en ne conservant plus que quatre-vingt-quatre sièges avec 13,4% des voix. La concurrence des deux autres partis de droite, RPF et CNI, avait joué pour l'expliquer, une partie de l'électorat de droite qui avait voté MRP en 1945 ayant reflué vers ces deux partis. Malgré tout, la troisième force qui va en gros se perpétuer jusqu'en 1952 avait incarné un temps les espoirs du MRP d'une forme de coalition 'centriste', de 'concentration' comme pour le PDP avant 1940. Mais la résurgence de la question scolaire et du problème de l'aide à l'enseignement libre (loi Barangé) avaient également joué un rôle.

Dans la législature 1951–56, le déclin amorcé du MRP continue. Il ne dirige pas les gouvernements, s'il participe à la plupart, sauf au gouvernement Mendès-France en 1954. Les élections législatives de janvier 1956 marquent une nouvelle étape de son tassement. Il n'obtient plus que soixante-quatorze sièges, en dépit d'une stabilité en voix. Le déclin électoral se confirme politiquement sous le ministère socialiste de Guy Mollet, qu'il soutient cependant, sans participation. Après la chute de Mollet, il ne participe pas non plus au gouvernement radical de Bourgès-Maunoury, s'il est représenté dans le gouvernement radical plus à droite de Félix Gaillard. L'histoire du MRP se confond alors avec la crise finale de la Quatrième République et se rallie difficilement à la 'solution De Gaulle'.

Le MRP avait été, de façon incontestable, l'un des principaux partis de gouvernement et un des piliers de ce régime éphémère. Il avait occupé pendant ces années à lui seul cent soixante-dix postes ministériels sur huit cent neuf, mais avec trente-quatre ministères seulement. Il s'était largement identifié avec ce régime et il ne tardera pas d'ailleurs à payer le prix, après sa chute, d'un certain discrédit le frappant dans l'opinion. Toutefois son rôle historique dans cette période n'avait pas été négligeable. Il avait contribué, avec d'autres forces politiques certes, à assurer le redressement difficile de la France de l'après-guerre sur tous les terrains politiques, économiques, sociaux et extérieurs. Au milieu de ces difficultés, il avait réussi à conserver une certaine homogénéité interne, en dépit de tiraille-ments provenant en particulier d'une gauche 'ouvriériste' du parti (et de certains courants de la CFTC) qui n'a pas tardé à trouver excessives ses évolutions vers le centre-droit. En effet, assez rapidement, au-delà de son programme initial et des vastes ambitions de la Libération, il a adopté peu à peu un programme plus 'centriste' qui associait un réformisme social à une politique économique qualifiée de 'raisonnable' contre les tendances gauchisantes et socialisantes. Des divisions internes se sont aussi de plus en plus aggravées. Face au ministère Mendès-France, si une majorité lui a été hostile, une minorité l'a soutenu. Dans les années 1950, aussi bien la conjoncture politique que les pesanteurs sociologiques ont joué pour un parti qui a alors accentué ses caractères de 'parti modéré', mais à gauche de la droite traditionnelle, et donc assez nettement au centre-droit. Malgré ces évolutions, il est resté un 'parti de militants', sur la base de fédérations départementales actives, avec une géographie qui a souvent repris les traits principaux de l'implantation de la démocratie chrétienne et notamment du MRP. Ses effectifs en ont fait, au départ du moins, ce que l'on peut appeler un 'parti de masse', avec deux cent cinquante mille adhérents en 1927, mais avant un déclin rapide de plus en plus accentué: quarante mille adhérents seulement en 1957.

L'ACTION SOCIALE ET INTERNATIONALE

Au début de son histoire, le MRP avait réalisé une carte électorale assez diversifiée géographiquement, à la fois dans les régions catholiques traditionnelles, mais aussi dans d'autres, de tempérament plus 'à gauche' et plus 'radical'. Cependant, il s'est peu à peu contracté dans les années 1950 dans des fiefs sociologiques liés surtout à la pratique religieuse. Un électorat de droite plus 'laïc' lui a préféré le RPF ou le CNI. De plus le MRP a été abandonné par une partie de son électorat ouvrier et populaire. S'il s'est toujours voulu, comme ses prédécesseurs, un parti 'laïc', il n'en était pas moins constitué en majorité dans ses cadres de catholiques notoires et sa doctrine restait d'inspiration chrétienne, ce que d'ailleurs il admettait. Le problème ne pouvait que continuer à se poser de ses relations avec l'Église, la hiérarchie et les mouvements d'action catholique. Il s'agissait toujours, comme pour le PDP avant lui, de continuer la réconciliation des catholiques avec la République et la démocratie, mais également d'établir, conformément aux principes de la démocratie chrétienne une société à la fois pluraliste et communautaire, contre l'individualisme conservateur d'une part, le collectivisme d'inspiration marxiste d'autre part. Le MRP a également défendu vigoureusement des positions en faveur de la liberté de l'enseignement. Sur le terrain syndical, ses sympathies à l'égard du syndicalisme chrétien et de la CFTC ont été incontestables et réciproques. Ses relations avec un certain monde sociologique catholique se sont accentuées dans les années cinquante, par exemple du fait de l'importance de jeunes dirigeants issus de la *Jeunesse agricole chrétienne* (JAC). Ceci témoignait de la place du monde rural dans son implantation sociologique et son électorat. Celui-ci a été d'autre part plus féminin que la moyenne, à côté d'une implantation croissante dans les classes moyennes et en régression dans les classes ouvrières et populaires.

Ce parti, que certains ont pu qualifier de 'perturbation provisoire dans la vie politique et idéologique française' a en outre joué un rôle considérable dans une autre direction, celle des problèmes extérieurs, et principalement des problèmes européens et de la construction européenne, dont il est devenu très vite un des soutiens principaux.[5] Cependant, et en dépit d'une tradition internationaliste qui remontait à l'entre-deux-guerres, ce n'est pas immédiatement après 1945 qu'il est devenu 'le parti de l'Europe'. Après la guerre, les tendances nationalistes et anti-allemandes y subsistaient fortement. Mais assez tôt aussi des contacts internationaux avaient été renoués autour des partis démocrates chrétiens de l'après-guerre, et notamment ceux d'Allemagne et d'Italie. Ils ont conduit d'abord à la création des *Nouvelles équipes internationales* (NEI), auxquelles toutefois, le MRP a refusé de se lier en tant que parti. La peur de l'appartenance à une 'Internationale catholique' avait joué. C'est surtout à partir de 1950 et de la déclaration de Robert Schuman sur le 'Pool charbon-acier' que l'idée d'union européenne prend son essor dans un parti où apparaissent ceux que l'on a appelés 'les ultras de l'Europe'. Les NEI jouent alors un rôle dans la création du *Mouvement européen* et pour les rencontres au plus haut niveau entre les responsables politiques démocrates-chrétiens. A l'époque de la Guerre Froide, le MRP se prononce en faveur du pacte atlantique et ses principaux leaders adhérent à l'idée d'une Europe plus ou moins 'fédérale', fondée particulièrement sur la réconciliation franco-allemande. Après le soutien accordé à la *Communauté européenne du charbon et de l'acier* issue du plan Schuman, c'est celui accordé au projet de *Communauté européenne de défense* (CED). On vérifie ici l'affirmation dans cette 'bataille de la CED' en 1952–54 d'une véritable 'passion européenne' du parti face à ses adversaires qui sont en particulier les communistes et les gaullistes. Après son échec devant le parlement français le 30 août 1954 ('le crime du 30 août' pour le MRP), qui marque la rupture définitive avec Mendès-France, l'évolution vers une 'relance européenne' est cependant appréciée favorablement, jusqu'à l'élaboration du marché commun et des traités de Rome en mars 1957. En revanche, le retour de De Gaulle aux affaires en 1958 est accueilli avec une certaine appréhension pour la construction européenne. Cette adhésion enthousiaste à l'idée européenne avait été l'occasion de critiques contre ce que certains de ses adversaires avaient appelé 'l'Europe vaticane', qui avait semblé être symbolisée un temps par Robert Schuman en France, De Gasperi en Italie et Adenauer en Allemagne. Mais celle-ci n'a jamais vraiment existé en tant que telle. Sur les problèmes coloniaux, le MRP avait été un des promoteurs de 'l'Union Française', évolution de l'ancien empire colonial. Il a défendu cette Union avec certains de ses ministres responsables, lors de la guerre d'Indochine, mais aussi dans un sens favorable aux changements jugés nécessaires pour l'Afrique Noire. Pour l'Afrique du Nord et notamment l'Algérie, il a soutenu une politique de développement avec la loi Cadre et une attitude jugée 'libérale' par la droite et l'extrême droite nationaliste, avec cependant des divisions internes.

LES DÉBUTS DE LA CINQUIÈME RÉPUBLIQUE: FIN ET MUTATION DU MRP

Le MRP s'était rallié à de Gaulle en 1958, mais les débuts de la Cinquième République marquent ensuite la phase finale de son déclin. Il se prononce pour le 'oui' à la nouvelle constitution au référendum de septembre. Mais après l'élection de novembre, il n'a que cinquante-sept élus, étant victime du scrutin majoritaire, malgré un certain maintien en voix. La régionalisation de son implantation s'accentue. Néanmoins il participe au gouvernement de Michel Debré de janvier 1959. Il compose alors un 'flanc gauche' de la majorité en approuvant les évolutions de la politique algérienne de de Gaulle, mais il émet des réserves sur une politique économique et sociale jugée trop conservatrice, sur le caractère 'présidentiel' des institutions, et surtout sur la politique européenne et son 'freinage' par de Gaulle. Il accepte de participer au gouvernement de Georges Pompidou d'avril 1962, mais ses cinq ministres démissionnent un mois plus tard après la conférence de presse du 15 mai où de Gaulle qualifie l'Europe de 'volapük intégré'. La rupture est bientôt consommée sur le projet d'élection du président au suffrage universel. Le MRP s'agrège au 'cartel des non' sur cette question et il se retrouve dans le camp des vaincus au référendum. Aux élections de novembre 1962, c'est l'achèvement du déclin du parti qui n'a plus que trente-six élus.

Face à cette situation, l'idée d'une transformation était dans l'air depuis le congrès de Dijon en 1962, et la création d'un groupe républicain populaire et du centre démocratique à la Chambre. Le congrès de 1963 à La Baule se prononce en faveur d'un rassemblement de l'ensemble des démocrates. L'espoir apparaît un temps de créer une fédération démocrate-socialiste, allant des républicains populaires aux socialistes. Mais le projet de 'grande fédération' autour de Gaston Defferre tourne court, le MRP craignant de devenir une 'force d'appoint'. Il est de plus en plus victime à la fois du scrutin majoritaire et du rapprochement à gauche entre socialistes et communistes. Il ne tient plus de congrès à partir de 1964 et n'a plus qu'un semblant d'existence. En octobre 1965, Jean Lecanuet, devenu président, annonce sa candidature aux élections présidentielles de décembre, comme démocrate social et européen, et il obtient 15,8% des suffrages. Il lance l'idée entre les deux tours d'un *Centre démocrate* dont il publie un manifeste fondateur le 7 janvier. Il est constitué officiellement le 2 février et tient une première convention à Lyon en avril. Son comité directeur comprend certains leaders du MRP, à côté d'indépendants et de radicaux. Les organes nationaux au MRP continuent à fonctionner jusqu'aux élections de mars 1967, mais il demande à ses adhérents de s'inscrire au *Centre démocrate*. Celui-ci n'a pas recueilli tout l'héritage et le personnel du MRP, et il s'est orienté vers d'autres tendances, pendant que d'anciens républicains populaires se dirigent vers des formations gaullistes ou intégrées à la majorité présidentielle (*Centre progrès et démocratie moderne* à partir de 1967). Une minorité de gauche va vers le PSU, la SFIO, ou des mouvements comme *Objectif socialiste* (Robert Buron). Une *Amicale des anciens du MRP* subsiste jusqu'à nos jours, et une influence diffuse de la tendance qu'il a incarnée continue à se manifester, au delà des partis qui sont plus ou moins dans sa filiation comme le *Centre démocratique et social* (CDS) créé en 1976, dans le cadre d'une certaine dispersion actuelle de l'héritage politique de la démocratie chrétienne.

NOTES

1. A ce sujet, voir Jeanne Caron, *Le Sillon et la Démocratie chrétienne* (Paris: Plon, 1966); Madeleine Barthélemy-Madaule, *Marc Sangnier 1873–1950* (Paris: Seuil, 1993).

2. A ce sujet, voir Jean-Claude Delbreil, *Centrisme et Démocratie chrétienne en France. Le Parti démocrate populaire des origines au MRP* (Paris: Publications de la Sorbonne, 1990).

3. A ce sujet, voir Claudine Guerrier, *La Jeune république de 1912 à 1945* (thèse, Paris-II, 1978).

4. A ce sujet, voir Robert Bichet, *La Démocratie chrétienne en France. Le Mouvement républicain populaire* (Besançon: Jacques et Demontrond, 1980); François Callot, *Un parti catholique de la démocratie chrétienne en France: le MRP* (Paris: Rivière, 1978).

5. A ce sujet, voir Philippe Chenaux, *Une Europe vaticane?* (Bruxelles: Ciaco, 1990).

7

Catholicism and the Left in twentieth-century France

Michael Kelly

Catholicism in France shifted significantly to the Left over the twentieth century.[1] The evidence for this view is overwhelming, at least in terms of where Catholic priests and laity cast their votes, which public policies they may support or criticise and which intellectual traditions they draw their ideas from. But as a generalisation, this conceals as much as it reveals. The period between the banning of the *Sillon* (1910) and the removal from office of Mgr Gaillot (1995) saw fundamental changes in the religious and political landscapes. Both French Catholicism and the French Left became more diverse entities, and relations between them appear correspondingly more complex. By the close of the century, Catholicism itself had largely ceased to be a focus for conflict in French politics, even if the ghosts of earlier dissentions occasionally wandered across the front pages.[2] However, the interrelation between religious and political issues did not cease to appear close or contentious. Before tracing the changing relation between Catholics and the Left over the course of the century, in political, social and intellectual terms, it is therefore important to analyse briefly how each of the two protagonists can be understood.

FRENCH CATHOLICISM

Even in relation to 1900, the notion of 'Catholicism' embraces a diversity of meanings, although both its representatives and its critics were at different times and for different reasons keen to convey the impression of a homogeneous and monolithic entity.[3] A first distinction may be made between clergy and laity.

Priests and members of religious orders, by virtue of their

profession, belong to a formal organisational structure, based on a hierarchy of spiritual authority, whose chain of command leads ultimately to Rome. But far from being a seamless garment, the institutional Church comprises many levels and sectors, whose relations were frequently complex and almost always subject to negotiation. Even authoritative declarations emanating from Rome, for example in the form of papal encyclicals or decrees of Vatican Congregations, are usually the result of often protracted negotiations, and certainly give rise to lengthy processes of interpretation. Between Rome and the French Cardinals and Archbishops, the relationship has been a delicately negotiated one. France, as the *fille aînée* of the Church, has exercised considerable influence in the Vatican as well as more widely in the Catholic world, and intermittently asserts its Gallican inclinations. Further down the hierarchy, diocesan Bishops and the Superiors of religious orders resist encroachments on their areas of authority. And strong-minded individuals or groups among the lowest echelons of the clergy can often exercise a considerable margin of independent initiative.

For most of the century, negotiations within the Church structures were conducted away from the glare of publicity, and when dissentions became public, they were typically expressed in a highly coded form, using the language of fraternity and submission to appropriate authority, which tended to buttress the impression of a monolithic structure and mask the underlying complexity. After the Second Vatican Council, a greater openness and even a modicum of democracy emerged, which encouraged both a greater frankness about existing divergences and a greater willingness to contemplate adding further ones. Protests from below and rebukes from above more readily enter the public domain.

In the lay world, where the same spread of divergences is also present, their complexity is compounded by both personal and organisational variations. The personal religious commitment of individuals ranges from the most devoutly practising to the most residually 'sociological' of Catholics, and in any individual's life its effect may vary sharply according to different areas of activity (work, home, leisure, public life, etc.). Similarly, the identification of particular bodies as 'Catholic' may range from those which can be seen as a direct arm of the Church's activities, like the Catholic Action movements, to those which are merely seen as having an ethos broadly sympathetic to Catholics, like certain newspapers or political parties. This diversity has contributed to the considerable uncertainty around the difficult demarcation line between the spiritual and the temporal, the religious and the political.

THE FRENCH LEFT

The Left in France is often described as a family, albeit an ill-tempered and unruly one.[4] From its beginnings, it has been more than a group of political movements, and comprises an entire culture. As Emmanuel Mounier suggested, writing in 1932: 'La justice est à gauche avec Picasso, les fonctionnaires, M. Homais, l'hygiène sociale, le féminisme, la liberté et la psychologie expéri-mentale. La liste est ouverte, complexe, paradoxale.'[5] The French Left has a history, going back to the Revolution of 1789, and a set of values, traditions and affinities which cannot easily be mapped against a definable programme or party. In 1900, the Left's historical values included a hostility to religion, which stretched from the Republican separation of Churches and State through to the most virulent forms of anti-clericalism and militant atheism. But the Left also professed a strong ethical imperative which broadened over the century to embrace a strand of spiritual values.

The most obvious divergences within the Left are those expressed by the different political parties: notably the Socialists and Commun-ists, but also the more moderate groupings of liberals, democrats and republicans, and the more radical anarchists, trotskyists and others. They have interacted often with bitter enmity and less frequently in alliance or coalition with each other, their stances and their influence fluctuating markedly over time and space. With them stand an array of political and social groupings with differing relations to particular parties: these include the trade unions, the campaigning organisa-tions (for peace, human or civil rights, women, the environment, minorities, etc.), interest or affinity groups (war veterans, charities, health and education associations, freemasons, etc.), international friendship and solidarity groups, political clubs and the formal or informal networks grouped around reviews and newspapers. Among these dense organisational thickets are the powerhouses of politics, generating ideas and pressures which in due course find their way into the parties of the Left.

The Left is therefore a relative rather than an absolute concept, despite intermittent attempts to anchor it to a particular line, ideology or individual, and despite repeated attempts to achieve broad Left unity on different occasions (1905, 1934, 1944, 1972, 1981). Conceptually, there is no single principle or 'slate' which identifies the Left, not even the Republican motto of *liberté, égalité, fraternité*. While most on the Left might in the abstract warm to *liberté*, for example, it is unlikely that each would feel equally positive about liberalisation in all the particular instances of divorce law, the economy, the education system, broadcasting and international trade. Adapting the insight of Benedict Anderson, it may be true of the Left that it is an 'imagined community',[6] whose continued existence requires the preparedness of its members to believe in it and to embody that belief in their discourse and practice, part of whose function is to symbolise that community. However, the ideological construction also rests on a socio-economic base, whose major component is the wage and salary-earning population, but also extends into the liberal professions especially, as Mounier suggests, those most closely bound to the public sector. Though it would be wrong to assume an exact correspondence between social class and political affiliation, the Left has had its strongest roots in the working class and its most vigorous campaigns have been in support of increased employment and improved working conditions.

The complexity of the Left arises in part from the sphere of production, the world of work with the dramatic changes it increasingly undergoes, and the conflicting interests between different groups of workers. But its also arises from the fact that these economic issues, however complex and pressing, cannot be entirely separated from the wider range of political issues which parties and governments must address. Historically, the most divisive issues have arisen in the sphere of national identity, concerning the development of the French nation and the French State as a whole, its constitution and its changing relations with its neighbours and with the wider international context. These appear dramatically in times of war, but are also evident in the economic, political and even cultural tensions which may be experienced metaphorically as wars (trade wars, cold war, defence of the French language, etc.). However, divisions increasingly also stem from the sphere of social reproduction: the expanding world of family, health, education, personal relations and social and cultural activities. The growing politicisation of these issues is directly related to the growing role of the State in them, not only in setting parameters in the form of institutions, laws and regulations, but also in providing or promoting a growing range of services which have come to be viewed together as the Welfare State.

BEFORE 1929

The twentieth century began with bitter conflict between the Catholic Church and the French State, fuelled by the polarisations of the Dreyfus Case, and symbolised by the Separation of Churches and State in 1905.[7] The presence of the Socialist Alexandre Millerand in Waldeck-Rousseau's moderate Republican government served to exacerbate its anti-clericalism, especially in respect of education, and the intransigent Pope Pius X (1903–14) not only multiplied denunciations but also seized the opportunity to reinforce his direct authority over the French Church. Any suggestion of a relationship between Catholicism and the Left is anachronistic in the first quarter of the century. It was the ultra-conservative governments of the early 1920s, based on the 'Chambre bleu horizon',[8] that worked to restore relations between the Church and State. They were opposed on the one hand by the Left which wanted no dealings with a Church synonymous in their view with wealth and property, and on the other hand by the French bishops who wanted no truck with the Republic, whose principles (democracy and secularism, not to mention Socialism) had been resoundingly anathematised in papal encyclicals. In this the bishops were more intransigent than the diplomatically oriented Pope Benedict XV (1914–22).

The ancestors of Catholic involvement on the Left in the early part of the century were Charles Péguy and Marc Sangnier. Péguy, an active Socialist and Dreyfusard, was one of a series of intellectual converts to Catholicism in the early years of the century. He deplored the way Jaurès abandoned the pure 'mystique' of the Dreyfus campaign for the dirty 'politique' of parliamentary electioneering, and in his review *Les Cahiers de la quinzaine*, founded in 1900, he combined his utopian Socialism with Catholic mysticism, Bergsonian vitalism and patriotic fervour.[9] Killed in the early stages of the war, Péguy's unorthodox and ambiguous ideas attracted both Left- and Right-wing Catholic intellectuals in the 1930s and 1940s. Sangnier, a charismatic leader, founded the *Sillon* in 1894, as both a review and a movement of Catholic renewal, which espoused a democratic and socially aware form of Christianity.[10] Keen to extend his Christian mission into Republican and even anti-clerical circles, Sangnier was gradually drawn into a more direct political involvement, and stood unsuccessfully for parliamentary election. As he attempted to distance his organisation from institutional Catholicism, Sangnier provoked growing alarm among Church authorities, culminating in an official letter from Pius X in 1910, condemning the *Sillon* for evading proper authority and preferring secular political ideas to Catholic doctrine. This immediately put an end to the movement, which submitted unreservedly. Shortly afterwards, Sangnier founded a purely secular movement, the *Ligue de la Jeune république*, which played a marginal political role in the inter-war period, but lacked the scope and potency which the combination of spiritual and political fervour had given the *Sillon*. Although this episode was taken up as a founding narrative in the mythology of the Christian Democratic parties, its wider significance was to provide an early bridge between Catholic militants and an involvement in wider social and political issues.

For most commentators, the key moment in changing the political complexion of French Catholicism was the announcement at the end of December 1926 by the Holy Office (formerly the Inquisition, now the Congregation for the Doctrine of the Faith), that the review *Action française* was placed on the *Index* of books which Catholics were forbidden to read.[11] Led by Charles Maurras, *Action française* (AF) was the principal far-Right anti-Republican movement. Though not explicitly a Catholic organisation, it professed an 'integral' Catholicism, and drew almost all of its support from Catholics, including many French clergy right up to the highest levels. Formally accused of subordinating religion to politics, it responded with virulent polemic and a provocative 'Non possumus', probably inspired by high-ranking Vatican dissidents. This had the effect of triggering an extensive purge in which its sympathisers among the French clergy were systematically removed from positions of influence, especially in education, training and youth work. The result was to divert the Catholic mainstream away from its traditional political affiliations on the Right to begin exploring Centre and Left orientations, a process accelerated by the younger generation of Catholics who henceforth had much less exposure to the *intégriste* orthodoxy. This last point assumed particular significance since, at about the same time, the official Catholic youth organisation,

Action catholique de la jeunesse française (ACJF), began to establish specialised sections which undertook with some success to train a future *cadre* of well-informed and self-confident Catholic leaders in a wide range of social groups. The resulting organisations, the *Jeunesse ouvrière chrétienne* (JOC), the *Jeunesse agricole chrétienne* (JAC) and the *Jeunesse étudiante chrétienne* (JEC), brought the new Catholic elite into public life largely outside the influence of *Action française*, and open as never before to democratic and Socialist ideas.[12]

Taken together, the condemnations of *Sillon* and *Action française* defined the political spectrum of Catholicism at the time, from the powerful nationalist Right to a small Christian Democratic current evolving gradually towards the Left. The condemnations also set the parameters for relations between Catholics and politics. Church leaders must abstain from endorsing political parties, and parties must not claim a monopoly of Catholic virtues. In practice, this arm's-length policy proved mainly to be a blow to the nationalist Right in France.[13] What followed was a period of questioning, especially among Catholic intellectuals. One of the most prominent erstwhile supporters of *Action française*, Jacques Maritain, used his neo-Thomist philosophy to draw important distinctions, which quickly made him a *maître à penser* for the Christian Democrats. Drawing a careful division of functions between politics and faith, he opposed the AF slogan 'politique d'abord' with his own 'primauté du spirituel', which theoretically affirmed the primacy of Catholic values in political or social action.[14] In practice, it gave Catholics like himself a protected space where they could withdraw from traditional Right-wing politics, and subject its exponents to critical analysis. Hence, the emergence of a Catholic Left was paradoxically dependent on a measure of withdrawal from politics, a constitutive premise of commitment, which had far-reaching consequences.

Maritain drew a distinction between two forms of Catholic political activity. On the one hand, action *en tant que catholique* involved individuals acting as a direct consequence of their Christian doctrine. Maritain argued that it could best be expressed as very long-term principles rather than specific tactical objectives, especially since they were in a sense invoking the responsibility of the Church, and were therefore accountable to episcopal authority. Action *en catholique*, however, involved Catholics acting essentially on their personal responsibility in public life, albeit their judgements would be informed in this as in all things by their faith. Maritain's distinctions were subtle and prone to ambiguous interpretation, but they enabled Catholic lay people to claim a margin of independence both from their own clergy and from the Catholic Right, within which to explore new social and political options.

THE 1930S AND THE WAR

The aftermath of the 1929 Wall Street Crash and the menacing rise of Fascism in Europe posed urgent economic and political problems, which traditional Catholic teaching found difficult to address. To a large extent, Maritain's analysis laid the theoretical basis for the gradual development of Catholic involvement in Left-wing politics during the 1930s, uncoupling Catholicism from specific endorsements and taking the long view. Its practical implications were more sharply outlined by his protégé Emmanuel Mounier, who founded and directed the intellectual review *Esprit* from 1932. The manifesto of the first issue was entitled 'Refaire la Renaissance', handsomely confirming Maritain's emphasis on the very long term. Mounier's programme was to dissociate the spiritual from the reactionary, and to confront the deep-seated disorders of the world, 'le désordre établi', with a revolution at the level of a civilisation that would be both moral and political, personalist and communitarian. His approach carried strong echoes of Péguy's dictum that 'Tout commence en mystique et finit en politique', even though he was prepared to see politics as more than the degraded residue of human aspirations. As he put it:

> Il n'y a aucune proportion entre la totalité de notre œuvre et ses coordonnées proprement politiques. Le politique peut être urgent, il est subordonné. Le dernier point que nous visons, ce n'est pas le bonheur, le confort, la prospérité de la cité, mais l'épanouissement spirituel de l'homme.[15]

Finding some virtues in the Marxist diagnosis of the crisis, Mounier presented an ostensibly disengaged view of politics which treated Right and Left with equal scepticism. This was in much the same mould initially as the 'ni droite ni gauche' position long argued by centrists of various persuasions, but given fresh impetus by the 'non-conformist' movement *Ordre nouveau* and its related publications. In its early days, *Esprit* was associated with an embryonic political movement, *La Troisième Force*, led by Georges Izard and André

Déléage, which sought to find a middle way between capitalism and Communism. After the February 1934 riots, the movement merged with Gaston Bergery's *Front commun contre le fascisme* and eventually the *Rassemblement populaire*, watched at a distance by Mounier. As the polarisation of the mid-1930s eroded the scope for a centrist position between Right and Left, Mounier and his review declared openly for the Left. However, it was a reluctant move, not because of their opposition to the programme of the *Front populaire*, but rather because it entailed a contraction of their broader project of reorienting French civilisation, which was predicated on the ability to maintain communications between a spectrum of political forces, drawing all of them towards a recognition of values more fundamental than politics. In his later writings, Mounier called this the 'prophetic' pole of commitment, as opposed to the political pole.

During the formative period leading to the election of the Popular Front government, the main channels for Catholic Left-wing political activity were a small number of groupings with quite diverse political, social, cultural or intellectual aspirations, and located outside the main parties.[16] Two of them were directly involved in electoral politics: the residual *Troisième force* current within the *Front commun* and the *Jeune république* (JR), which had emerged from the *Sillon*. *Jeune république* in particular acted as a minority Left wing of the Christian Democratic movement. Unlike its larger companion the *Parti démocrate populaire* (PDP), it supported the Popular Front, and gained four parliamentary seats in 1936. The other Left Catholic groupings were centred on intellectual reviews. Mounier's *Esprit* was the most influential, but the most assertively political was the tiny group of 'progressistes' around the controversial review *Terre nouvelle*, best-known for its audacious logo of the hammer and sickle super-imposed over the Cross. In the teeth of official disapproval, these progressives attempted a synthesis of Marxism and Christianity which would allow them to give full expression both to their faith and to their revolutionary commitment.

Each of the groupings had their own objectives and consti-tuencies, but these were not sharply delineated, and there was considerable overlapping and shifting of membership. What they all shared was a strong commitment to moral and spiritual imperatives, and conversely a sharp awareness of the dangers of official dis-approval by the Church, whether from the French bishops or from

Rome. The Catholic hierarchy was still overwhelmingly conservative in its political persuasions and repeatedly recalled its long record of condemning members who strayed into liberal or socialist paths. The danger was a real one, as *Terre nouvelle* found when it was banned in 1936. And the non-aligned Dominican review *Sept* suffered the same fate in 1937 after printing an interview with Léon Blum. The more cautious *Esprit* narrowly escaped the *Index* in 1936, but only after a robust lobbying campaign behind the scenes with the Archbishop of Paris, and in the corridors of the Vatican.

One of the most important developments of the period was the Communist decision to woo Catholics.[17] The *Parti communiste français* (PCF) had traditionally been fiercely anti-religious, but in 1934 had begun to moderate its position, dropping the 'clenched fist' approach to Catholics. A few days before the elections of April 1936, the party's General Secretary, Maurice Thorez, went on national radio to declare his policy of national unity, including an unprecedented appeal to Catholics: 'Nous te tendons la main, catholique, ouvrier, employé, artisan, paysan, nous qui sommes des laïques, parce que tu es notre frère, et que tu es comme nous accablé par les mêmes soucis.'[18] Though it raised many hackles among Communists, the policy was applied with remarkable vigour, bringing an abrupt and permanent end to Communist attacks and harassment against the Church, Catholics and their organisations. Some of its effect spilled over into socialist and centrist ('radical') movements, though these retained (and still do retain) strongly anti-religious elements. On the Catholic side, Thorez's appeal found an echo in a small number of intellectuals, such as Robert Honnert, who welcomed the opportunity to explore common ground.[19] More typically, the *main tendue* caused alarm among the clergy, several of whom wrote pungent rebuttals.[20] Pius XI was motivated to intervene with a categorical denunciation of atheistic Communism in the encyclical *Divini redemptoris* (28 March 1937).[21] Warning that Communists had not abandoned their war against God, the Pope forbade Catholics to co-operate with them in any circumstances. The Catholic intelligentsia immediately bowed to this instruction, though their own reactions to the *main tendue* were more characterised by embarrassment and exasperation. On the one hand, Thorez had aimed his words directly at the Catholic working class, by-passing their lay or clerical spokespeople. And on the other, he offered a purely political rapprochement, ignoring ideological differences: the precise opposite of the

Maritain–Mounier approach. In electoral terms, the *main tendue* itself had little immediate effect, but it introduced a new factor into the relationship between Catholics and the Left, which was initially something of a *dialogue de sourds*, but gradually came to be the root of significant long-term ideological developments.

A first taste of an incipient realignment may be seen in the response of French Catholics to the Spanish Civil War. Franco's efforts to represent his rebellion as a crusade on behalf of the Church found a widespread echo in traditional circles, but for others they painfully recalled AF's strategy of hijacking religion in support of a Right-wing political agenda. Serious reservations were expressed not only by the supporters of the Popular Front, but also by prominent Catholic writers of a more traditional cast, including the novelists François Mauriac and Georges Bernanos. But undoubtedly, it was the experience of war that produced the most far-reaching changes in Catholic political attitudes.

In many respects, the period from the Fall of France to the Liberation was a triumph for the most traditionalist forms of Catholicism. Marshal Pétain and his Vichy regime were enthusiastically supported by the Church leaders, who could scarcely imagine a more favourable environment for their own values and aspirations, and who enjoyed an assertive re-clericalisation of the State education system and strong support for Catholic institutions.[22] Though few of the higher clergy advocated active collaboration with the Nazi project of European domination, there were equally few who did not warn sternly against breaches of duty to the Vichy authorities. A small number of bishops voiced muted protests at the persecution of Jews, but many regularly denounced the bandits and traitors who joined the Resistance. However, the apparent triumph of Catholic values sharply exacerbated the underlying divisions, not only between Left and Right, but also between the hierarchy and the lower clergy and laity. Many lay Catholics and priests were drawn into resistance against the instructions of their bishops, whether by their understanding of their patriotic duty, or by rejection of the oppressions and persecutions carried out by the occupying and collaborating forces. While the majority were drawn from Christian Democratic and Left-leaning circles, the Catholic opposition also attracted figures from the nationalist Right, including most prominently de Gaulle himself. As the war progressed, the programme of labour conscription to work in Germany (*service du travail obligatoire*, or STO) increasingly drove young men of all persuasions into the *maquis* and other forms of clandestine activity, and the turn of public opinion left the hierarchy increasingly isolated. At the same time, the experience of both the internal and external resistance brought a degree of contact and co-operation between Catholics and their erstwhile Left-wing opponents, encapsulated in Aragon's celebration of 'Celui que croyait au ciel/Celui qui n'y croyait pas', the believer and non-believer united in a common cause.[23] The bonds of trust and solidarity created in the resistance provided a framework for the close post-war relations between Catholics and the Left.

THE FOURTH REPUBLIC

The Liberation brought to the surface the shifts which had been taking place for the previous decade. The traditional Right was all but silenced, discredited by its implication in collaboration, while the Catholic bishops had invested much of their authority in supporting Pétain, and were now constrained to a measure of humility. The Director of the moderate *Chronique sociale de France*, Joseph Folliet, noted the consequences:

> Il faut, objectivement, comme un historien, reconnaître que l'équivoque de Vichy a empoisonné la vie de l'Église autant que celle de la nation, creusant deux fossés que l'alluvion du temps n'a pas comblés encore, l'un entre les masses françaises et certains troupes catholiques de tendances conservatrices, l'autre entre les élites chrétiennes et une notable partie de l'hiérarchie.[24]

The alienation of the Catholic elites, especially the intellectual elite, was perceived to be potentially disastrous and, with few other options available, the bishops' strategy was to put their support behind those Catholics who had emerged with good records of resistance. Most of them were leading young activists who had been formed in the wake of the *Sillon* and the Catholic youth movements. Politically, the main beneficiaries were the Christian Democrats of the newly formed *Mouvement républicain populaire* (MRP), but the situation also gave a new prominence to the intellectuals around *Esprit* and former Resistance papers like *Combat* and *Témoignage chrétien*, most of whom were closer to the Socialists than to the Christian Democrats.

With few exceptions, there was a general recognition of the urgent requirement for national unanimity and reconstruction, shared across the political spectrum, and expressed in the composition of the

Provisional Government. The Left now energetically espoused a national agenda, especially the Communists, who under the slogan of 'la Renaissance française' placed the battle for production above the class struggle.[25] And even the more anti-clerical Socialists refrained from excessive recriminations against the Church's war-time activities. Conversely, the Catholics now espoused a social agenda, and through the MRP supported the creation of a welfare state which had been outlined in the charter of the *Conseil national de la résistance* (CNR). And while the bishops did not warmly welcome the involvement of priests and laity in Communist-led organisations, such as the *Front national* Resistance movement, they did refrain from open condemnation. For a time, at least, many of the barriers between Catholics and the Left were lowered. Large numbers of Catholics joined the Socialist Party or the array of Left-leaning groupings which had arisen from the Resistance, among them young men like François Mitterrand and Jacques Delors.[26]

More surprisingly, a significant number of young Catholic activists, workers and intellectuals, were attracted to the *Parti communiste français* (PCF). The poet Loÿs Masson was a highly public example, combining a robust and unorthodox Catholic faith with an equally energetic and unconventional Communist fervour. The phenomenon was sufficiently widespread to prompt *Esprit* to publish an enquiry into it in early 1946.[27] It focused on young intellectuals in Paris and on whether and why they were intending to join the PCF. The choice of questions, respondents and responses was evidently designed to strengthen the reticence of those who were tempted but wavering. Nonetheless it revealed that roughly a quarter of the sixty respondents questioned, all aged between twenty and thirty, had already joined, with as many again seriously considering it. The strong and cohesive PCF group in the *École normale supérieure* (ENS), France's prestigious training ground for its intellectual elite, maintained close links with the Catholic group.[28] Two of the better-known intellectuals of this generation to move from the Catholic student movement to the PCF were Maurice Caveing, who later played a leading role in Catholic–Communist dialogue, and Louis Althusser, whose theory of ideology became a major element in Marxist analyses of religion. Left-leaning lay people wrote discouraging the phenomenon,[29] or calling for Communism to be transcended,[30] and a succession of clergy warned against what they variously called the temptation or the seduction of Communism.[31] The Jesuit Gaston

Fessard went further and declared that: 'Aujourd'hui, un an après la libération, il nous faut signaler le nouveau péril qui, sous le couvert de la Résistance, menace la France, le *Communisme*.'[32]

Certainly, the question of what relations were possible with Communists became a central preoccupation, as Jean Lacroix noted: 'Le problème politique français, et même mondial, est commandé par l'attitude communiste et par l'attitude envers les communistes.'[33] Some Catholics, hesitating to join the PCF, nonetheless formed a group of 'progressistes', close to the Communists and reminiscent of the pre-war *Terre nouvelle*. The Communists for their part were keen to attract Catholic recruits, and Thorez confirmed the policy of non-aggression: 'Nous sommes partisans de la liberté de conscience. Ce n'est pas un nouveauté. Quant à moi, comme Engels, j'ai toujours considéré que déclarer la guerre à la religion était une bêtise.'[34]

The flow of Catholics into Communist organisations was slowed in the late 1940s by the onset of the Cold War, but there were many examples of common causes where Catholics and Communists found themselves in at least *de facto* political alliance. This occurred on the economic front, in the struggle against the severe hardships in living conditions and the widespread waves of industrial action; on the cultural front, in the struggle against imported American films and comics;[35] and on the moral front, in campaigns against prostitution and even contraception. In early 1948, several non-Communist groupings came together to attempt to form a new Left movement, which hoped to exercise a critical influence on the Communists and Socialists. As well as Catholic personalists, it included existentialists of Sartre's *Temps modernes* current, and Left Socialists like Georges Altman and David Rousset.[36] Catholic intellectuals such as Emmanuel Mounier, Paul Fraisse and Jean-Marie Domenach tried to inject both spiritual values and realism into the resulting *Rassemblement démocratique révolutionnaire* (RDR), but it failed to find a large-scale base of support or to make an impact on the major parties, and fell apart among dissentions after a little over a year of existence.[37]

The rapprochement between Catholics and Communists remained largely at the level of common interests rather than the meeting of minds, and a halt to co-operation, which proved temporary, was called by the Vatican in a decree of the Holy Office in July 1949, which recalled the terms of *Divini redemptoris* and forbade Catholics to read or co-operate with Communist propaganda. At the same time, the French Cardinals, in endorsing the decree, were at pains to deny that it should be seen as an anti-Communist crusade or as taking sides for capitalism.[38] The Vatican's intervention emphasised the Cold War isolation of Communists, but also had the effect of redirecting the energies of Catholics into Left-wing causes which were not dependent on Communist participation. Some were motivated to explore the political organisations of the non-Communist Left, including revolutionary groupings within the Socialist current. Some were challenged to demonstrate the depth of their commitment to the emancipation of workers and the alleviation of poverty by joining action groups and campaigning organisations. And some were prompted to express their solidarity with oppressed peoples in the Third World, especially in France's tottering colonial Empire. None of these courses was without risk, but all held ample scope for the leadership skills and the generous spirit of self-sacrifice which now circulated so widely in Catholic circles. Moreover, many of the initiatives came to pose far-reaching questions to the Church which contributed to the intellectual and institutional upheavals of the 1960s.

Long-term intellectual shifts already launched in the 1930s were given new impetus in the post-war period. The review *Esprit* and Mounier's personalist philosophy exercised a powerful influence, and even those who did not approve of Mounier's dialogue with Communists were nonetheless drawn to his flexible framework for balancing the calls of individual, social and spiritual development.[39] Its new openness allowed Catholics to explore the intellectual resources of the Left, notably Marxism, but also Proudhon and the libertarian socialist tradition. Simone Weil's posthumously published writing emphasised an austere ethic of personal and social emancipation.[40]

The participation of Catholics in the construction of a hegemonic humanist synthesis at the Liberation emphasised the convergence with secular modes of thought. This point is well illustrated by an important study, *Le Drame de l'humanisme athée*,[41] by the leading Jesuit theologian Henri de Lubac. Written during the war, it broadly argued that humanism, whether stemming from Feuerbach, Nietzsche or Comte, was essentially atheistic. Published after the Liberation, it was widely taken to be an attack on these atheistic forms of humanism in favour of a non-atheistic Christian humanism. The idea that humanism could be separated from atheism was strongly canvassed by Maritain and the Thomists,[42] and grudgingly conceded by de Lubac.[43] It was further developed by theologians such as Jean

Daniélou and Marie-Dominique Chenu to suggest that there might be forms of Marxism which could be separated from their atheistic origins.[44] Though the Holy Office's decree of 1949 attempted to limit this exploration, the essential step had already been taken in enabling Catholic intellectuals to explore horizons beyond the limited scope of papal encyclicals. In this perspective even the modestly forward-looking social encyclicals *Rerum novarum* (1891) and *Quadragesimo anno* (1931) lacked the critical concepts to analyse the rapidly changing post-war world.

The Church's intellectual shortcomings were mirrored by its social and economic shortcomings, which became seriously apparent in the harsh conditions of the 1940s. On the one hand, it was clear that the vast majority of the French working class had no contact with the Church. Being substantially dechristianised, or pagan, it could be regarded somewhat shockingly as a mission-field, as the abbés Godin and Daniel put it.[45] The Church's response, first in Paris during the war, then nationally, was to launch the missionary movement of worker-priests, whose mission was to re-christianise the proletariat and whose method was to become workers themselves, fully sharing the proletarian condition in the same way as some of them had shared the conditions of prisoners in German camps. The major outcome of the initiative was to reveal how little the Church understood of working-class life and the hardships it involved. The shock was reflected in Gilbert Cesbron's sentimental novel on the subject, *Les Saints vont en enfer* (1952). Responding to the appalling conditions they met, many of the priests felt bound to participate in the workers' efforts to improve their life, and became active in social and industrial action, and in trade unions. Some priests, including the theologian Maurice Montuclard, joined the PCF, which was playing the leading role in working-class organisation, and became increasingly persuaded, like Chenu, that Christians had much to learn from Marxist ideas. The worker-priest movement came under growing pressure from more conservative quarters, who pointed especially at its policy of 'humanising before evangelising'. In January 1954 Pope Pius XII intervened directly to put an end to it. Strikingly, a large number of priests refused to submit, and chose to maintain their commitment even at the cost of their priesthood.[46] The episode became a symbol of the new 'option for the poor' which added a new element of spiritual fervour to the Left as well as a new strand of social militancy to Catholicism. The worker-priest concept was eventually reinstated in 1965. One of the most immediate consequences of the 1954 crisis was the success of the charitable campaign on behalf of the homeless, launched in the same month by the abbé Pierre (Henri Groues), a former MRP deputy and founder of the Emmäus community. His initiative was given wide media coverage, with the bearded abbé appearing as an Old Testament prophet,[47] a phenomenon which was repeated some forty years later, when the priest, then in his eighties, led a group of *exclus* to occupy an unused block of government offices in the rue du Dragon in Paris.

The emancipatory aspiration became an important aspect of Catholic action in the mission-fields of Africa, Asia and Latin America. The traditional work of spreading the Gospel was now seen as inseparable from that of improving the living conditions of people in what was now termed the Third World. Growing numbers of Catholics, priests and laity, volunteered for service in developing countries, and were supported by movements at home, both in parishes and in quasi-political associations, and extensively covered by Catholic journals. The struggle against exploitation and oppression took on a particular significance as France's crisis of decolonisation deepened. In marked contrast to the MRP's colonialist hard-line, the journals of the Catholic Left, notably *Esprit*, *Témoignage chrétien* and *La Quinzaine* maintained a constant campaign of criticism against government policies and military activities in South-East Asia and in Africa.

As the Algerian crisis intensified in the mid-1950s, deep divisions emerged between Right and Left Catholics.[48] In the teeth of often physical threats, which extended to the bombing of their homes and offices, Left-wing intellectuals, including many well-known Catholics, campaigned against government policies, especially the use of military repression and torture, and argued for the right of Algeria to self-determination and therefore national independence.[49] Anti-war protests were also launched by the Catholic youth and student movements, including the Scouts, and by the newly emergent Catholic movements for peace and reconciliation. The sharp divisions revealed by the crisis recalled those of the occupation years between colla-boration and resistance.[50] This time the Catholic hierarchy proved less compliant with the wishes of the government and the military leadership, and particularly resisted the call to a Holy War from people such as the MRP leader Georges Bidault, who was urging 'la lutte de la Croix contre le Croissant'.[51] The Church was, however, as divided as the nation, and while the cardinals and archbishops formally denounced the use of torture as 'des moyens intrinsèquement mauvais' in 1957, there were marked differences of approach between Cardinal Feltin, who urged his chaplains to support the army in its difficult duties, and Cardinals Liénart and Gerlier who emphasised the duty of Christians to heed their conscience. And attempting to keep the Church out of politics, the bishops also took the risk of a confrontation which threw the Catholic youth movements into crisis in 1957.[52]

THE 1960S AND 1970S

Despite the initial wave of popular support for General de Gaulle and his new Republic, the 1960s and 1970s developed the political division of France along bipolar Left and Right lines. The twenty years of government by the Gaullist and neo-Gaullist majority was achieved at the expense of consolidating a Left opposition which regularly polled almost half the votes. The centrist MRP dwindled to a shadow of its former strength before dissolving into a series of small Christian Democratic groupings. The sometimes sharp divisions between Catholics at all levels over issues of national policy were a reflection of the general national divisions, and signalled the incorporation of the Church into the political life of the country as a whole, rather than as the partisan force which it had once been. This evolution was accelerated by the wind of change which blew through the Church with Pope John XXIII, elected just a month after the establishment of the Fifth Republic.

The process of *aggiornamento* undertaken by the Second Vatican Council was powerfully influenced by theologians like Jean Daniélou, Henri de Lubac and others who had helped to lead French Catholics out of the Right-wing ghetto in the 1930s and 1940s. Every aspect of Catholic life and teaching was subjected to close scrutiny, debate and review. Though it may arguably have been launched as an attempt to stem the tide of modernity and reverse the Church's disastrous loss of influence,[53] the result of Vatican II was to open up Catholic thinking to an unprecedented degree. It radically reappraised its approaches to its own practices (liturgy, scripture, priesthood, religious life), its relations with other belief-systems (Christian denominations, non-

Christian religions, non-believers) and its attitude to the modern world (particularly urgent social, economic and political issues).[54] Although the Church proclaimed its doctrinal continuity, the new tone was one of acknowledgement of past insufficiencies, willingness to listen to others and respect for human dignity even in its past or present adversaries. The spirit of dialogue and openness was one which encouraged the closer meeting of minds on the French Left.

An early sign of the change was the transformation of the small Catholic trade union, the *Confédération française des travailleurs chrétiens* (CFTC), traditionally the least militant wing of the French labour movement, and closely associated with the MRP. The union split in 1964, with the majority choosing to become a secular and more assertive movement under the title *Confédération française démocratique du travail* (CFDT). Developing links with the Socialists of the *Section française de l'internationale ouvrière* (SFIO) and the *Parti social unifié* (PSU) the CFDT became the cornerstone of the reinvigorated 'second Left', looking to the Proudhonist and syndicalist tradition as an alternative to Marxism. It was generally more sympathetic to the student movement in 1968, pressed demands for worker participation in company management and encouraged the 'green' and decentralising thinking of the 1970s.

The social upheavals of May 1968 combined with Vatican II to create a sense of intellectual crisis and a turning point.[55] It accelerated the movement of Catholics into the Socialist Party, with prominent former MRP figures such as Georges Hourdin and Robert Buron.[56] But it also propelled others into an exploration of more radical options outside the parliamentary Left and the established Church, which both appeared as relics of a former age.[57] The effect of the new types of Catholic thinking on social issues was to inflect the profile of the French Left. The rhetoric and at times the practice of Catholic militants frequently outflanked the parliamentary Left, which by contrast often appeared cautious and bureaucratic. The willingness of Catholics to undertake *prophetic* interventions, aimed at *bearing witness*, differentiated them from the characteristic Communist and Socialist concerns with *political* interventions aimed at securing *material change*. In this respect they had much in common with the *gauchistes* of the post-1968 far Left, and many Catholic activists found themselves on the radical fringes of the Socialist Party and in the *Parti socialiste unifié*.

The two main Left parties were largely marginalised in the events of May 1968, but were spurred into intensifying their search for a united strategy to wrest power from the Right-wing majority, now strengthened by the conservative backlash against the May events. The Communists made a strong bid to reassure and attract potential Catholic supporters, relaunching the *main tendue* at their 1970 party congress, followed by a highly publicised interview with the PCF leader Georges Marchais in the conservative Catholic newspaper *La Croix* later in the year.[58] This was followed by numerous initiatives aimed at underlining the non-atheistic nature of Marxism, its compatibility with Christianity, and shared concerns with social progress in France, peace and disarmament, and international co-operation and solidarity. For the Socialists, there was a good deal less to prove, since it had leaders like François Mitterrand and Jacques Delors with good Catholic pedigrees, and a long tradition of leading Protestant figures from André Philip to Michel Rocard. The Common Programme agreed in 1972 between the reconstituted *Parti socialiste* (PS) and the PCF provided a broad platform, like the Popular Front before it, to which a number of Left and Centre groupings were attracted, including Catholic ones, such as the middle-class *Vie nouvelle* community movement. At this stage, the Catholic elites had probably moved more to the Left than the majority of the *fidèles*, and it was noted that in the 1973 parliamentary elections 34% of priests voted for Left-wing parties, as against 25% of their flock.[59]

Among Communist intellectuals, the new Catholic openness was grasped initially by the PCF's philosophical spokesman, Roger Garaudy. As part of the slow process of de-Stalinisation, Garaudy had been seeking an alternative basis for Marxism to replace the narrow dogma of Stalinism. Returning to the notion of Marxism as a form of humanism (and indeed the highest form of humanism),[60] he embarked on a dialogue with all the currents of thought which recognised themselves as humanist.[61] Garaudy particularly fostered relations with Left-wing Catholics such as Jean Lacroix, philosophy columnist of *Le Monde* and a member of the *Esprit* group, and with the philosophical supporters of Pierre Teilhard de Chardin, whose posthumous writings attracted an enthusiastic following in the mid-1960s. *Esprit*'s political philosophy and Teilhard's reconciliation of faith and the natural sciences were strong currents in the thinking of Vatican II. Garaudy's ambition was to reach a humanist synthesis, and he played an active role in encouraging dialogue between

Catholics and Communists in particular. His own development eventually brought him into conflict with the PCF, from which he was expelled in 1970, and closer to the Church, which he subsequently joined, before finally converting to Islam. But despite jibes that this was a conversation between Christians who no longer believed in God and Marxists who no longer believed in class struggle, the dialogue initiated by Garaudy was maintained after his departure by the PCF, who saw it as a logical extension of the *main tendue*.[62]

Garaudy's attempt to synthesise Marxism and Christianity was on the one hand easier to achieve in the 1960s and on the other had a more limited impact than it might have had earlier. In effect it became part of a flourishing sub-culture of alternative world-views in the 1970s.[63] This was in part because of important shifts in the intellectual culture of both Marxism and Catholicism. On the Marxist side, the PCF abandoned the notion of an 'official' philosophy,[64] opening the way to a pluralist approach to ideological relations, and therefore in due course the abandonment of its traditional espousal of atheism.[65] This latter step, which surprised many Marxists and Catholics, was articulated by Lucien Sève, who built on Althusser's distinction between ideology and knowledge, to argue that while Marxism had the scientific aspiration to achieve knowledge, atheism was merely ideological and therefore not essential to the Marxist project.[66] The Communist acceptance of ideological pluralism also confirmed what had long been evident, that the Communists no longer held a monopoly of Marxism, which had on the contrary become part of the general background of French intellectual life.

On the Catholic side, a similar evolution had taken place, with an increasing pluralism of approaches especially to social issues. The tradition of papal encyclicals, especially since *Rerum novarum,* had become constituted as 'Catholic social doctrine', but in the wake of Vatican II, and the withdrawal from political partisanship, its dogmatic force was distinctly attenuated. The culminating document, *Gaudium et spes* (December 1965), largely drawn up by Parisian theologians,[67] avoided the term 'social doctrine' in favour of 'social teachings', and concluded on a very inclusive note, emphasising the eagerness for dialogue, leading to truth and the need to work together with others to build up the world in a spirit of peace.[68] The stress on learning from others and working together with them was not easily reconciled with a claim to have all the answers, and traditional 'social doctrine' was increasingly criticised as an ideology which had now served its usefulness and should be abandoned.[69] Though not all theologians were as radical as le père Chenu, there was a widespread feeling that 'social doctrine' was of a piece with the political conservatism which had so long been dominant in Catholic circles.[70] It no longer appeared as a challenging or persuasive social theory, and the Left Catholics looked increasingly to varieties of Marxism as their intellectual point of reference.

Freed from the monopoly of Communism, Marx began to appear as the latest of the great Hebrew prophets. His call to revolution struck the same eschatological note as the final chapters of the book of Revelation where the new Jerusalem descends from the heavens and God on His throne proclaims: 'Behold, I make all things new' (Revelation 21.5), a passage frequently quoted after 1968.[71] The long process of encounter with Marxism reached a culmination in the early 1970s, with the emergence of a Christian–Marxist movement, confident that it could incorporate the principal lessons of Marxism into a pastoral theology based on Scripture. The consequences were studied nervously by the bishops,[72] and the appeal of Marxism was analysed by Jacques Ellul, a forthright critic of 'Christian Marxist ideology', as arising from four factors: the awareness of social injustice, the importance of the poor, the 'credibility gap' between Christian theory and practice and the Christian rediscovery of the material world.[73] The interpellation of Marxism called Christians back to the fundamentals of their faith, he argued, and sparked not only new materialist readings of the Gospels but also new theologies of Service, of the Poor and of Liberation. He might have added that the Christian interpreters also transformed the landscape of French Marxism. Some of the most serious historical analysis of Marx and Marxism had been undertaken by Jesuit scholars such as Jean-Yves Calvez and Pierre Bigo in the 1950s and continued by others.[74] As this work gathered momentum through the 1960s and during the 1970s, Catholic writers came to be some of the most active proselytisers on behalf of Marxism.[75]

Parallel to the adoption of Marxism, and related to it, two currents of thought gained ground in the 1970s: Liberation Theology, and neo-Hegelianism. Both were influential internationally and had strong bodies of support in France. Liberation Theology sprang from the confluence of Vatican II, Marxism, neo-anarchist communitarianism (Paulo Freire and Ivan Ilich) and the challenge of poverty. It was resoundingly launched at the Latin American bishops' conference at Medellin (Colombia) in 1968, which declared its 'preferential option for the poor'. The new synthesis inspired both the old missionary and new Third Worldist currents within French Catholicism, giving an explicit social dimension to the former and a theological foundation to the latter.[76] It became one of the most dynamic and contentious movements within the Church throughout the 1970s and 1980s, and provided a strong impetus to the social work of Catholics in addressing poverty and injustice at home. Its emphasis on grass-roots activism and the formation of 'basic communities' chimed well with the libertarian spirit of May 1968, and offered an attractive alternative to the flagging Catholic Action movements.

Neo-Hegelianism similarly owed much to Vatican II and the influence of Marxism, but also drew on the Christology of the German Protestant Karl Barth, with its socially oriented analysis of incarnation.[77] Developed by a group of Louvain theologians in the 1950s, it was refined by the German Swiss theologian Hans Küng, whose master-work on the incarnation of God drew on Hegelian philosophy. It opened access to Hegel's sophisticated analyses of the State and civil society, and offered a kind of Left-Hegelian alternative to Catholic 'social doctrine'.[78]

The French hierarchy was careful not to endorse any particular social analysis or political option, to stress the need for pluralism and to point out that politics was not the whole of human reality. However, a specially convened assembly of the French bishops in 1972 did recognise that the world was entering a new era, called on Catholics to be 'active citizens', and concluded: 'Comment ne pas lire cette évolution comme une interpellation de notre Dieu qui, au commencement, a confié la terre à nous tous, les hommes, pour que nous nous efforcions, sa grâce aidant, d'en faire un lieu de justice et de fraternité.'[79] The call for justice and fraternity was suitably general, but was widely taken as being coded support for the social and political programmes which were more likely to found to the Left of Centre. And before long the theme of man's stewardship of the earth was extended to embrace the new emergence of environmental issues in French politics. Perhaps more significant was the recognition that the withdrawal from politics initiated nearly fifty years earlier had served its purpose, and that re-emphasising it now could only appear as a conservative strategy, quite at odds with the main post-conciliar momentum towards engagement in the modern world.

The Leftward movement of Catholics during the 1960s and 1970s was not a one-way traffic. The 'supplément d'âme', the extra touch of spirituality, which they brought to the Left, reinforced the growing recognition of the importance of values and culture in the socialist project, a point made forcefully in the newly rediscovered writings of Gramsci, with their attention to the role of ideology in the struggle for social hegemony. This was a cornerstone of the 'Eurocommunist' development of the late 1970s. Catholic presence on the Left also meant an attenuation of the Left's former militant secularism. Anti-clerical elements could still be found, especially in the PS, in the CERES faction (*Centre d'études de recherche et d'éducation socialiste*) and among the teaching movements close to the party, but nonetheless the influence and institutions of the Church largely ceased to be a political issue.

In so far as religious issues persisted on the political agenda, they were largely focused on the sphere of reproduction, both social (family, marriage and divorce) and biological (contraception, abortion and fertility). The Common Programme envisaged liberalisation of the laws on divorce, contraception and abortion, in direct contradiction of Catholic teaching, especially as set out in Pope Paul VI's encyclical *Humanae vitae* of 1968. However, these issues failed to become polarised between Right and Left, for several reasons: first, French Catholics increasingly regarded them as matters of private morality, and did not welcome or follow the Church's intervention; second, some on the Left, especially the Communists, had a record of resistance to 'bourgeois' liberalisation of morality; and third, the liberalisations which did occur in the 1960s and 1970s were achieved by Right-wing governments, most notably the legalisation of abortion, which was steered into law by Simone Veil in 1974, even if she required Left-wing support to achieve it.

RECENT YEARS

The victory of François Mitterrand in the presidential elections of 1981 was widely hailed as a victory of the Left, and his first government reflected the breadth of the Left coalition which had contributed to his election. However, it came more than three years after the collapse of the Common Programme in a welter of bitter recriminations between Socialists and Communists, and the rankling differences were only hastily patched up in between electoral rounds. The result, a narrow majority for Mitterrand, appeared as another confirmation of the bipolarity of French politics, but it was in many respects anachronistic, and the two *septennats* which followed were characterised by the fragmentation of both Left and Right, in a movement which echoed the more general fragmentation of economic, social and cultural life in what has come to be called the post-modern condition.[80]

During the 1980s, the PCF entered a sharp decline in both votes and influence. Its electorate slumped from over 20% to less than 10%, with some evidence that Jean-Marie Le Pen's extreme-Right *Front national* was a beneficiary. It was divided by a series of unsuccessful attempts to reform, renovate or refound the party. The attraction of Marxism waned under the post-modernist assaults on Master Narratives, and largely evaporated after the spectacular collapse of the Soviet Union and its satellites at the end of the decade. The *Parti socialiste* for its part found the Mitterrand experience a mixed blessing, sharing the vicissitudes of the President's popularity without being able to resist his drift towards the Centre, or towards a monarchical style which tended to replace politics with patronage. After a succession of splits and dissentions, Michel Rocard's perception of his party in 1995 as 'un champ de ruines' was widely shared, and reflected the wider loss of identity on the Left.[81] Parallel to the disillusionment with existing parties, many potential activists committed their energies to a variety of political movements and campaigns which had emerged in the 1970s and did not sit easily with the earlier class-based party alignments. The women's movements, 'green' movements, the regional and autonomist movements, the gay and lesbian movements, the anti-racist movements and others presented a 'rainbow' effect which in each case might bring together people from a range of political and religious persuasions. Though arguably the centre of gravity of the new movements tended to be Left rather than Right, there was no easy synthesis which brought them together either in theory or practice, despite the efforts of individuals like Pierre Juquin and Brice Lalonde.

A similar process of fragmentation was also in train within the Catholic Church. The election of Pope John Paul II in 1978 marked a sharp restoration of conservative values at the head of the Church. He reversed the momentum of reform in the life of the Church, considering that Vatican II had gone far enough towards liberalisation and democratisation. His reassertion of authority was not accepted with the submissiveness it might have met seventy years before, and prominent French Catholics were quick to affirm their independence. Georges Montaron, writing in *Témoignage chrétien*, spoke for many when he declared: 'Nous n'avons jamais reçu la parole du pape ou celle des évêques comme des ordres ... Nous ne sommes pas une armée, ni même un parti, et le pape n'est ni premier général, ni premier secrétaire.'[82] The rebuff contained a scarcely veiled allusion to the Pope's native Poland, where the Communist Party's rule depended on military support. It highlighted the widely held perception that, more than his Italian predecessors, John Paul II was a man with a strongly partisan agenda, informed by the political and social conservatism of Polish Catholicism. As his papacy developed, he undertook a series of interventions against prominent groups and figures on the Catholic Left, including sympathisers with Marxism, Liberation Theology, or neo-Hegelianism. And he systematically made key appointments from those who shared his views – preferring, for example, to choose his bishops from religious orders rather than from parish clergy, who might be judged too close to lay concerns.

Within France, perhaps the most contentious example of papal intervention was the revocation of Mgr Jacques Gaillot, Bishop of Évreux, in January 1995. Gaillot exemplified the 'modern', perhaps more accurately 'post-modern', face of the Church, campaigning on behalf of *les exclus*: the poor, the unemployed, the homeless, immigrants, asylum-seekers, prisoners, AIDS sufferers and others, with a particular openness to non-believers and those of other faiths.[83] Though he was not charged with any breach of doctrine or morals, his high media profile and his sharp criticism of government policies made him a controversial and symbolic figure. He was removed from his diocese with the support of the conservative Cardinal-Archbishop of Paris, Mgr Lustiger, in an action which was widely commented on as revealing deep divisions within the Church and a fierce struggle between traditional and modern conceptions of Catholic faith.[84] But for all the clamour, the affair revealed the depleted state of the Catholic Left.

Over two decades, John Paul's papacy largely replaced the supporters of Vatican II with conservative figures in the hierarchy. Left Catholics have increasingly been driven into defensive positions of internal or external opposition. Some have become focused on the internal struggle against papal conservatism: defending the rights of priests and laity against Vatican authoritarianism, advocating the ordination of married men and of women, or opposing the restoration of pre-conciliar piety centred on the cult of the Virgin Mary. Others have abandoned the institutional Church, seeking new forms of religious expression, and thereby contributing to the long-term decline of French Catholicism.[85] The fragmented and decentred character of contemporary Catholicism in France may be illustrated by the fact that in the 1984 controversy over the State funding of private (Catholic) schools, the Left Catholics did not support the massive and mainly Right-wing protests which led to a government climb-down. Some, including Mgr Gaillot, publicly defended the government. The fragmentation is also noticeable in the continuing decline of formal Catholic observance, set against the rise of more diffuse forms of religiosity, shown among other things by a renewed fashion for spirituality, a spreading mosaic of non-Christian religions in France and a growing number of small sects.[86]

The recent history of relations between Catholics and the Left is therefore no longer that of 'les deux grandes maisons d'en face'. Both houses are now substantially depleted, both have many mansions, and there is no clear boundary between them. Priests have long stood for election, often on Left-wing tickets.[87] Catholics have routinely appeared in Left-wing governments: Michel Rocard's government of 1988 contained three trained theologians.[88] Priests have been vocal opponents of political conservatism in matters such as government policy on housing or nationality, while non-believers have been staunch advocates of theological modernism in matters such as Vatican pronouncements on collegiality and priestly celibacy. Both the Left and Catholicism in France contain a diverse spectrum of political and religious positions, and are in that sense 'a broad Church', even if in their different ways embattled and diminished. The efforts of Pope John Paul to reduce this diversity among his flock have if anything been counter-productive, while President Mitterrand visibly relished the scope for manoeuvre and manipulation which pluralism provided.

Recent intellectual developments have mirrored the splintering of the religious and political fields. While some joined Mitterrand's entourage, especially in the promotion of French culture in its various forms, many Left-wing intellectuals balked at the prospect and, disarmed in their commitment, returned to their studies. Third World activists were often similarly dismayed by the performance of erstwhile liberation movements once they had achieved power. And even those who had been fierce critics of 'existing Socialism' could not find great cause for celebration in the restoration of capitalism in former Communist countries. Several Left-leaning intellectuals have turned to religious and spiritual preoccupations. Those attracted back to Catholicism have included Julia Kristeva, Philippe Sollers, Jean-Luc Nancy and, as it posthumously emerged, Louis Althusser. However, their beliefs have been characteristically heterodox, and owe more to the Jewish spirituality of Emmanuel Levinas or even Jacques Derrida than to the best-selling homilies of John Paul II.

The failures of successive Socialist and Gaullist governments to alleviate the major social ills has provided the most fertile ground on which Catholic and Left-wing sensibilities can unite. Rising unemployment, housing crises, ghettoisation of ethnic minorities, drugs, crime and violence have given rise to a plethora of movements and campaigns, and given new life to established ones, such as the abbé Pierre's campaign for shelter for the homeless. But to a large extent these responses have been fragmentary, without organisational or theoretical synthesis. The portmanteau concept of 'exclusion' has been widely adopted to characterise the problems but affords little analytical purchase on the problems. The wave of public sector strikes in the first year of Jacques Chirac's presidency provoked an initial refocusing of social demands and brought a number of Left intellectuals once more into a common cause, at the same time as a limited revival of interest in Marxist ideas emerged.[89] Whether these are isolated incidents or whether they augur a significant change in the fragmentation of the political and religious fields in France is not yet clear. The challenge to their participants, and especially the intellectuals, is no longer to work out a viable relationship between Catholics and Socialism or Communism, or even between religion and politics, but rather to define a role and identity either for Catholicism or for the Left in the post-modern world. In that sense, their fate remains inextricably linked.

NOTES

1. See Georges Suffert, *Les Catholiques et la gauche* (Paris: Maspéro, 1960); Mary Theresa Moser, *The Evolution of the Option for the Poor in France 1880–1965* (New York: University Press of America, 1985).

2. See René Rémond, 'La culture politique des catholiques aujourd'hui', *Vingtième siècle*, 44 (1994), 58–64. The ghosts would include changes in the funding of private (mainly Catholic) schools, for example.

3. See Christian Cannuyer, *Les Catholiques français* (Paris: Brepolis, 1992); Gérard Cholvy and Yves-Marie Hilaire, *Histoire religieuse de la France contemporaine*, 3 vols (Toulouse: Privat, 1985–88); Valérie Hanotel, *Les Cathos* (Paris: Plon, 1995).

4. See Tony Judt, *Marxism and the French Left* (Oxford: Clarendon Press, 1986), p. 22.

5. Emmanuel Mounier, *Œuvres complètes*, 5 vols (Paris: Seuil, 1961), I, 139. M. Homais refers to the self-aggrandising pharmacist in Flaubert's novel *Madame Bovary*.

6. Benedict Anderson, *Imagined Communities. Reflections on the Origin and Spread of Nationalism*, 2nd edn (London: Verso, 1991).

7. See Adrien Dansette, *Histoire religieuse de la France contemporaine* (Paris: Flammarion, 1951).

8. The reference is to the colour of uniforms of French army officers, who were elected to the National Assembly in large numbers after the First World War.

9. See Eric Cahm, *Péguy et le nationalisme français* (Paris: Seuil, 1972).

10. See Jeanne Caron, *Le Sillon et la démocratie chrétienne 1894–1910* (Paris: Plon, 1966); Jean de Fabrègues, *Le Sillon de Marc Sangnier, un tournant majeur du mouvement social catholique* (Paris: Perrin, 1964).

11. See Adrien Dansette, *Destin du catholicisme français, 1926–1956* (Paris: Flammarion, 1957).

12. See William Bosworth, *Catholicism and Crisis in Modern France* (Princeton: Princeton University Press, 1962).

13. See Michel Darbon, *Le Conflit entre la droite et la gauche dans le catholicisme français, 1930–1953* (Toulouse: Privat, 1953).

14. Jacques Maritain, *La Primauté du spirituel* (Paris: Plon, 1927).

15. Emmanuel Mounier, 'Refaire la Renaissance', in *Œuvres complètes*, I, 141.

16. See Paul Christophe, *1936: Les Catholiques et le Front populaire* (Paris: Éditions ouvrières, 1986).

17. See Francis J. Murphy, *Communists and Catholics in France 1936–1939. The Politics of the Outstretched Hand* (Gainesville: University of Florida Press, 1989), and the useful collection of documents in René Rémond, *Les Catholiques, le communisme et les crises 1929–1939* (Paris: Armand Colin, 1960), rev. as *Les Catholiques dans la France des années 30* (Paris: Éditions Cana, 1979).

18. Maurice Thorez, 'Pour une France, libre, forte et heureuse' (discours prononcé le 17 avril 1936 au micro de Radio-Paris), in *Œuvres choisies*, 3 vols (Paris: Éditions sociales, 1965–67), I (1965), 309–21 (p. 320).

19. Robert Honnert, *Catholicisme et communisme* (Paris: Éditions sociales internationales, 1937).

20. See Gaston Fessard, *Le Dialogue catholique-communiste est-il possible? La Main*

tendue (Paris: Grasset, 1937); Le P. Coulet, *Communisme et catholicisme. Le message communiste* (Paris: Spes, 1938); Marc Scherer, *Communistes et catholiques* (Paris: Cerf, 1936).

21. Pius XI, *Divini redemptoris* (abridged) in *The Social Teachings of the Church*, ed. Anne Freemantle (New York: Mentor–Omega, 1963), pp. 95–103.

22. W.D. Halls, *Politics, Society and Christianity in Vichy France* (Oxford: Berg, 1995) gives a detailed account of the period. See also the earlier Jacques Duquesne, *Les Catholiques français sous l'occupation* (Paris: Grasset, 1966); and the official Catholic account offered by Mgr Émile Guerry, *L'Église catholique en France sous l'Occupation* (Paris: Flammarion, 1947).

23. Published in Louis Aragon, *La Diane française* (Paris: Seghers, 1944), and frequently anthologised.

24. Joseph Folliet, *Les Chrétiens au carrefour* (Lyon: Éditions de la Chronique sociale de France, 1947), p. 26.

25. See Michael Kelly, 'Revolution, Renaissance, Redressement: Representations of Historical Change in Postwar France', in *Reconstructing the past: Representations of the Fascist Era in Postwar European Culture*, eds Graham Bartram, Maurice Slawinski and David Steel (Keele: Keele University Press, 1996), pp. 32–48.

26. See *A Biographical Dictionary of French Political Leaders since 1870*, eds David Bell, Douglas Johnson and Peter Morris (Hemel Hempstead: Harvester Wheatsheaf, 1990).

27. Emmanuel Mounier, 'Ceux qui en étaient et ceux qui n'en étaient pas. Enquête sur le communisme et les jeunes', *Esprit*, 119 (1946), 191–260.

28. Jean-François Sirinelli, 'Les Normaliens de la rue d'Ulm après 1945: une génération communiste?', *Revue d'histoire moderne et contemporaine*, 4 (1986), 569–88.

29. Louis Salleron, *Un Jeune Catholique devient communiste, malgré les cordiaux avertissements de Louis Salleron* (Paris: La Jeune Parque, 1949).

30. Jean Lacroix, 'Dépassement du communisme', *Esprit*, 12 (1944), 56–64.

31. See Jean Daniélou, 'Tentation du communisme', *Études*, 4 (1946), 116–17; Gaston Fessard, 'A propos des rapports entre communistes et catholiques', *Chronique sociale de France*, LIV (1945), 192–98; Émile Rideau, *Séduction communiste et réflexion chrétienne* (Paris: Éditions de la Proue, 1947).

32. Gaston Fessard, *France, prends garde de perdre ta liberté* (Paris: Éditions du Témoignage chrétien, 1945), p. 1. The title is a reference to Fessard's well-known Resistance pamphlet, *France, prends garde de perdre ton âme*.

33. Jean Lacroix, 'Dépassement du communisme', p. 56.

34. In Michel P. Hamelot, 'M. Maurice Thorez nous précise la position du Parti communiste', *Temps présent*, 2 (1945), 1; reprinted as 'Union française et démocratique', in Maurice Thorez, *Œuvres choisies*, II (1966), 302–7.

35. Michael Kelly, 'Catholic Cultural Policy from 1944 to 1950: *bande dessinée* and Cinema', in *France and the Mass Media*, eds Brian Rigby and Nicholas Hewitt (London: Macmillan, 1991), pp. 20–36.

36. See Jean-Paul Sartre, David Rousset and Gérard Rosenthal, *Entretiens sur la politique* (Paris: Gallimard, 1949). The episode is summarised in Michel-Antoine Burnier, *Les Existentialistes et la politique* (Paris: Gallimard, 1966), pp. 63–75.

37. See Michel Winock, *'Esprit'. Des intellectuels dans la cité 1930–1950*, édn rev. et aug. (Paris: Seuil, 1996), pp. 321–25.

38. See 'The Hierarchy's Response', in *The Social Teachings of the Church*, ed. Anne Freemantle (New York: Mentor–Omega, 1963), pp. 103–07. The text is misleadingly presented as a response to the earlier encyclical.

39. See Michael Kelly, *Pioneer of the Catholic Revival. The Ideas and Influence of Emmanuel Mounier* (London: Sheed & Ward, 1979).

40. Simone Weil, *L'Enracinement. Prélude à une déclaration envers l'être humain* (Paris: Gallimard, 1949).

41. Henri de Lubac, *Le Drame de l'humanisme athée* (Paris: Spes, 1944).

42. See Jacques Maritain, *Humanisme intégral. Problèmes temporels et spirituels d'une nouvelle chrétienté*, nouvelle edn (Paris: Aubier, 1968); Louis Gardet, 'Principes d'une politique humaniste', *La Revue thomiste*, September–December 1946, 613–23.

43. Henri de Lubac, 'L'idée chrétien de l'Homme et la recherche d'un homme nouveau', *Études*, October–November 1947, 1–25, 145–69.

44. See Jean Daniélou, 'La vie intellectuelle en France: communisme, existentialisme, christianisme', *Études*, September 1945, 241–54; Marie-Dominque Chenu, 'L'homo œconomicus et le chrétien: réflexions d'un théologien à propos du marxisme', *Économie et humanisme*, 19 (1945).

45. Henri Godin and Yves Daniel, *La France, pays de mission?* (Paris: Éditions de l'Abeille, 1943).

46. See Roger Mehl, *Le Catholicisme français dans la société actuelle* (Paris: Le Centurion, 1977), pp. 81–95.

47. See the well-known essay 'Iconographie de l'abbé Pierre', in Roland Barthes, *Mythologies* (Paris: Seuil, 1957), based on coverage in *Paris Match*, 13–20 February 1954.

48. See Pierre Houart, *L'Attitude de l'Église dans la guerre d'Algérie* (Bruxelles: Le Livre africain, 1960).

49. See Suffert, *Les Catholiques et la gauche*.

50. See Philip Dine, 'The Inescapable Allusion: The Occupation and the Resistance in French Fiction and Film of the Algerian War', in *The Liberation of France. Image and Event*, eds Roderick Kedward and Nancy Wood (Oxford: Berg, 1995), pp. 269–82.

51. Houart, *L'Attitude de l'Église dans la guerre d'Algérie*, p. 37.

52. See Mehl, *Le Catholicisme français*, pp. 95–104.

53. This view is argued by Henri Mendras and Alistair Cole, *Social Change in Modern France. Towards a Cultural Anthropology of the Fifth Republic* (Cambridge: Cambridge University Press–Éditions de la Maison des Sciences de l'Homme, 1991), p. 68.

54. See *Vatican Council II. The Conciliar and Post Conciliar Documents*, ed. Austin Flannery (Leominster: Fowler Wright, 1975).

55. See Jean Lacroix, *La Crise intellectuelle du catholicisme français* (Paris: Fayard, 1970).

56. See Georges Hourdin, *Catholiques et socialistes* (Paris: Grasset, 1973).

57. See 'Réinventer l'Église', a special number of *Esprit*, November 1971.

58. 'Une interview de Georges Marchais à *La Croix*', in Roland Leroy, Antoine Casanova and André Moine, *Les Marxistes et l'évolution du monde catholique* (Paris: Éditions sociales, 1972), pp. 176–90. The interview was published in *La Croix*, 19 November 1970.

59. Mehl, *Le Catholicisme français*, pp. 170–71.

60. Roger Garaudy, *Humanisme marxiste, cinq essais polémiques* (Paris: Éditions sociales, 1957).

61. See especially Roger Garaudy, *Perspectives de l'homme* (Paris: Presses Universitaires de France, 1959).

62. Among many examples, see Georges Marchais, *Les Communistes s'adressent aux chrétiens de France* (Paris: Éditions de *l'Humanité*, 1976).

63. Its most concerted expression was in Roger Garaudy, *L'Alternative* (Paris: Robert Laffont, 1972).

64. See 'Résolution: Sur les problèmes idéologiques et culturels', *Cahiers du communisme*, 5–6 (1966), 265–80. This was the result of an important meeting of the PCF Central Committee held at Argenteuil, 11–13 March 1966.

65. For a detailed discussion, see Michael Kelly, 'Marxism and Faith', in *Beliefs and Identity in Modern France*, ed. Martyn Cornick (Loughborough: ASMCF–ERC, 1990), pp. 179–93.

66. The argument is developed at length in Lucien Sève, *Une introduction à la philosophie marxiste* (Paris: Éditions sociales, 1981).

67. The main editor was Mgr Pierre Haubtmann (Rector of the Catholic Institute, Paris), assisted by Fathers J.-Y. Calvez, L.-J. Lebret, and D. Dubarle. See Jean-Yves Calvez, 'L'Enseignement social de l'Église en France après Vatican II', in *Le Mouvement social catholique en France au XXe siècle*, ed. Denis Maugenest (Paris: Cerf, 1990), pp. 167–88.

68. Translated as 'Pastoral Constitution of the Church in the Modern World', in *Vatican Council II*, ed. Flannery, pp. 903–1001 (p. 1000).

69. See Marie-Dominique Chenu, *La Doctrine sociale de l'Eglise comme idéologie* (Paris: Cerf, 1979).

70. See Jean-Yves Calvez, P. de Charentenay, René Rémond, and C. Théobald, *Cent ans après 'Rerum novarum' (1891). La Tradition sociale du catholicisme français* (Paris: Médiasèvres, 1991).

71. See for example J. Leca, F. Houtart, J.L.L. Aranguren and M.-D. Chenu, *Société injuste et révolution* (Paris: Seuil, 1970).

72. See *La Foi chrétienne à l'épreuve du marxisme. Textes de l'épiscopat*, ed. Denis Maugenest (Paris: Le Centurion, 1978).

73. Jacques Ellul, *L'Idéologie marxiste chrétienne* (Paris: Le Centurion, 1979), esp. pp. 5–18.

74. See Pierre Bigo, *Marxisme et humanisme* (Paris: Presses Universitaires de France, 1954); Jean-Yves Calvez, *La Pensée de Karl Marx* (Paris: Seuil, 1956); Henri Niel, *Karl Marx* (Paris: Desclée de Brouwer, 1971).

75. See for example Jean Guichard, *Le Marxisme. Théorie de la pratique révolutionnaire*, 4th edn (Lyon: Chronique sociale de France, 1976); P.D. Dognin, *Initiation à Karl Marx* (Paris: Cerf, 1970).

76. See *Théologies de la libération. Documents et débats*, eds Bruno Chenu and Bernard Lauret (Paris: Cerf–Le Centurion, 1985).

77. See *Bilan de la théologie du XXe siècle*, eds Robert Vander Gucht and Herbert Vorgrimmler, 2 vols (Paris/Tournai: Casterman, 1970).

78. See the discussion in Michael Kelly, *Hegel in France* (Birmingham: Modern Languages Publications, 1992), pp. 55–63.

79. Assemblée plénière de l'Épiscopat français, *Pour une pratique chrétienne de la politique (20 octobre 1972, Lourdes)* (Paris: Le Centurion, 1972), p. 64.

80. See Jean-François Lyotard, *La Condition postmoderne* (Paris: Minuit, 1979).

81. See Serge Berstein, 'Les Deux Septennats de François Mitterrand: esquisse d'un bilan', *Modern and Contemporary France*, ns 4 (1996), 3–14.

82. Georges Montaron, 'Les Chrétiens face à l'avortement', *Témoignage chrétien*, 8 January 1979, quoted in *Les Idées en France 1945–1988*, eds Anne Simonin and Hélène Clastres (Paris: Gallimard, 1989), p. 352.

83. See Jacques Gaillot and Catherine Guignon, *Monseigneur des autres* (Paris: Seuil, 1993).

84. See Christian Makarian, 'Cathos contre cathos', *Le Point*, 21 January 1995, pp. 52–58; Luc Ferry, 'Le péché mortel de modernité', *Le Point*, 21 January 1995, pp. 58–59; François Devinat, 'Retour de balancier pour l'Épiscopat français', *Libération*, 23 January 1995, p. 6.

85. See Claude Askolovitch and Pierre-Henri Allain, 'A gauche: plutôt le capitalisme que Jean-Paul II', *L'Événement du jeudi*, 1–7 June 1995, p. 65.

86. See Jacques Duquesne, 'Dieu: les nouveaux croyants', *Le Point*, 15 May 1993, pp. 44–52.

87. See René Rémond, 'L'Évolution du comportement des prêtres en matière politique', in *Politique et foi* (Strasbourg: CERDIC, 1972), pp. 80–100 (p. 88).

88. See Henri Tincq, 'Une Église de docteurs et de mystiques', *Le Monde*, 6 October 1988, pp. 16–17. The three are Roger Fauroux (Minister for Industry), Catherine Trautmann and Philippe Essig.

89. For example, the International Marx Conference and the Engels Centenary Conference both held in Paris in 1995 attracted substantial audiences.

8

Accueillir l'étranger: immigration, integration and the French Catholic Church

Kay Chadwick

In 1990, Mgr Jacques Delaporte, Archbishop of Cambrai, the then president of the *Commission épiscopale française 'Justice et Paix'* and formerly head of the *Commission épiscopale des migrations*, called on behalf of the Church for the full integration of immigrants into French society on the grounds that 'l'intégration est sans doute, en effet, la solution la plus conforme au respect des Droits de l'homme auquel un chrétien ne peut pas déroger'.[1] This direct link between integration and human rights is significant in terms of the Church's response to the immigration question in France. For if, as has been argued, the publication of the 1789 *Déclaration des droits de l'homme et du citoyen* marks France out in the eyes of the world as the birthplace of human rights, then the Catholic Church was a late convert to the cause. Indeed, while Republican texts and constitutions have continually upheld and restated the principle of human rights since 1789, the Church only finally officially adopted a human rights stance after the Second World War with its approval of the December 1948 universal Declaration of Human Rights. The Church's evolution since that time is such that a human rights policy is now publicly voiced at all levels of the institution from ordinary priests to the Pope himself: for example, during his visit to Reims in September 1996 to celebrate the baptism of Clovis, King of the Franks, in 496 AD, John Paul II defined the Republican values of *liberté, égalité, fraternité* as 'valeurs chrétiennes'; and, during the *Journées mondiales de la jeunesse catholique* held in France in August 1997, the Pope saluted France as 'le pays des droits de l'homme', declaring that 'là où les hommes sont condamnés à vivre dans la misère, les droits de l'homme sont violés: s'unir pour les faire respecter est un devoir sacré'.[2]

In immediate post-war France, however, there were few services provided by the State, the Church or any other body which were dedicated to the reception and integration of immigrants. The government's *Office national d'immigration* had been created in 1945 in order to manage the post-war influx of European immigrant workers on which France had set her sights, but which failed to materialise, with immigration instead dominated at this time by workers from Algeria. The French Catholic Church, too, had created new structures, setting up the *Commission épiscopale des migrations* and its associate organisation the *Service national de la pastorale des migrants* in 1946, but these agencies offered little practical assistance to immigrants and were slow to move to concrete action. What little support was offered by the Catholic Church at this time was directed principally at Catholic immigrants and largely provided by representatives of their church of origin, while immigrants of non-Catholic origin (mainly North African Muslims) were, more often than not, left to their own devices. However, since the 1960s, the French Catholic Church's involvement in the immigration issue has evolved and intensified alongside the changing nature of immigration: as family immigration has overtaken and largely replaced the immigration of workers, and as the Islamic dimension of immigration has become especially significant, so the resultant definitive settlement (or *sédentarisation*) of different peoples has placed increasing demands on the social and economic structures of France as a *terre d'accueil*. The Church has attempted to respond to this evolution by developing and broadening its activity in the domain of immigration, and now regularly addresses issues which affect all immigrants, Catholic and non-Catholic alike. In 1990s France, there are few, if any, aspects of the immigration question on which the Church fails to pronounce: the heated debate on the restrictive immigration and nationality legislation drafted by the Right-wing *Rassemblement pour la République* administration (headed by Premier Édouard Balladur) in the summer of 1993 was largely sustained by Church intervention on behalf of France's immigrants;[3] moreover, the much-publicised *affaire des sans-papiers* during the summer of 1996 once again focused on the Church as a player on the immigration stage, when over three hundred Africans, *en situation irrégulière* and threatened with expulsion from France, took refuge in two Catholic churches in Paris, on each occasion being removed by force by the French authorities.[4] With these points in mind, it is the purpose of this chapter to analyse the motivating factors behind the evolution of the French Catholic Church's response to the immigration question and to assess what this reveals not only about its own and French society's view of its role and status in late-twentieth-century France, but also about the Church's relationship with both the secular State and France's second religion, namely Islam.

The fundamental principle on which the Church has based its immigration message is that of *l'accueil dû à l'étranger*, repeatedly underlined in the Bible[5] and, in the contemporary context, reactualised during the Second Vatican Council (1962–65). *Gaudium et spes* (7 December 1965) outlined the Church's response to all forms of discrimination, clearly including immigrants in its argument that:

> Toute forme de discrimination touchant les droits fondamentaux de la personne, qu'elle soit sociale ou culturelle, qu'elle soit fondée sur le sexe, la race, la couleur de la peau, la condition sociale, la langue ou la religion, doit être dépassée et éliminée, comme contraire au dessein de Dieu ... Au surplus, en dépit de légitimes différences entre les hommes, l'égale dignité des personnes exige que l'on parvienne à des conditions de vie justes et plus humaines ... Que les institutions privées ou publiques s'efforcent de se mettre au service de la dignité et de la destinée humaines.[6]

Focusing specifically on immigration, Mgr Delaporte commented that such documents as *Gaudium et spes* emphasise that 'pour le christianisme, tous les hommes sont enfants de Dieu; ils constituent donc une même famille humaine', which explains why 'l'Église appelle constamment à dépasser les nationalismes pour construire une fraternité universelle, une véritable communauté des nations'.[7] Difference, therefore, is legitimate and should prove no obstacle to the aim of integration, and alternative theories of immigration are to be rejected: *assimilation* is unsatisfactory since 'elle vise à gommer toutes les différences; assimiler c'est rendre semblable à soi, c'est exiger des étrangers qu'ils abandonnent leurs valeurs pour se fondre dans un moule uniforme', while *insertion* results in nothing more than 'la juxtaposition de deux entités qui ne s'interpénètrent pas, [qui] vivent les unes à côté des autres sans qu'il n'en résulte aucune dynamique particulière'.[8] Advocacy of integration as opposed to any other theory of immigration is common in documents published by the French Catholic Church. And, over the years, the Church has not simply limited itself to the repetition of theoretical statements or biblical and encyclical references, but has increasingly tried to contextualise its message by taking a stand on relevant issues according to the demands of the contemporary social and political environment.

The nature of immigration into France must be borne in mind in any consideration of the French Catholic Church's response to the immigration issue. As indicated, the Church has no difficulty with difference within its overall rhetoric of integration and human rights, which represents a basic reference point for the Church's treatment of all immigrants. Its assumption and expansion of that role since the Second World War have been so successful that there are few, if any, who would argue that the Church operates outside its religious remit in pronouncing moral judgements in the sphere of human rights, while Mgr Joseph Duval, as president of the *conférence des évêques de France*, emphasised at the time of the 1993 immigration legislation that 'que l'Église se fasse le porte-parole des plus pauvres, dont font partie les immigrés, est dans son devoir'.[9] In practice, however, the Church does deal differently with immigrants according to their religious and cultural specificity, subdividing them into Christian and non-Christian groups. Moreover, although many distinct migrant groups in France can be identified by religion (for example, Catholic, Protestant, Jewish, Buddhist and Muslim groups, among others), it is clear from Church documents that by 'Christian' the institution principally means Catholic immigrants (and primarily those from Spain, Italy and Portugal), while by 'non-Christian' it principally means Muslim immigrants (and primarily those from North Africa).[10] This focus on Catholic and Muslim immigrants can be easily sourced in the fact that they represent the two most numerous immigrant groups in France. But the distinction between Christian and non-Christian immigrants should be further explained, since it reveals much about the Church's interpretation of the immigration issue and of its role therein. In many respects, this subdivision is perfectly logical, simply because the French Catholic Church has a network of structures ready and available to facilitate the integration of Catholic immigrants, and its response to such immigrants clearly emphasises religious similarity, as will be seen. But this does not mean to say that the Church simply 'abandons' non-Christian immigrants. On the contrary, the Church believes that it should work to ensure and protect the prospect of integration for all immigrants alike since 'c'est ensemble qu'il faut les intégrer'.[11] In the case of non-Christian immigrants, religious difference may mean that there exists no obvious common ground, but humanitarian concerns set in a context of equality are seen to outweigh religious difference in the quest for integration, with the Church demanding that:

Que l'on sorte d'un discours trop axé sur la question de l'identité ou du religieux et que l'on tienne compte de tout ce qui favorise ou au contraire freine l'intégration: le travail, l'école, le logement, la vie sociale ... Ensuite que l'on veille à assurer l'égalité des droits. S'il n'y a pas égalité des droits il n'y aura pas intégration. (ibid.)

On one level, this statement simply represents ample proof of the Church's humanitarian role in the modern world. On another level, however, it also indicates the Church's willingness to lend its voice to the debate on the social problems of the day, and therefore stands as evidence of the Church taking on a role made possible by the *laïcisation* (or secularisation) of France established by the 1905 *loi de séparation des Églises et de l'État*. The State's refusal to recognise or subsidise any and all religions after 1905 may in the short term have restricted Church activity in the name of the secularisation of public life, but, in the longer term, the result of the 1905 law has been effectively to grant the Church social and political independence from the State and therefore precisely to free the Church to pass moral judgements in such areas as it sees fit. The French Catholic Church's involvement in the immigration debate stands as one illustration of its wider evolution in twentieth-century France. From an institution which viewed *laïcité* (or secularism) in negative and restrictive terms, the Church has come to see positive value therein which can be defended and exploited not only in terms of its own role and status in France, but also in terms of its response to France's other representative religions. The Church's acceptance of *laïcité* suggests that it has come to terms with the construction of France as a modern pluralist society and, in so doing, it is intent on preserving a role for itself therein, one expression of which is its moral voice in the immigration debate. Moreover, as this chapter will later argue, its ability to operate successfully within the secular State both prompts and (in its eyes) permits the Church to demand similar respect for *laïcité* from all other representative religions. That the Church should plead for *laïcité* would have been unthinkable at the beginning of the twentieth century. That it does so now, on the grounds that *laïcité* is a means to integration, suggests that the Church has evolved to use the secular principle both to safeguard its own status and as a means of handling other religions, in particular, Islam.

THE CHURCH AND CATHOLIC IMMIGRANTS: THE FIGHT AGAINST *DÉSAGRÉGATION RELIGIEUSE*

Before the Second World War, immigrants in France were princi-pally Catholic and European. The 1931 population census indicates that 2.45 out of France's then 2.71 million foreigners were European – many of whom could be directly identified as Catholic, since the census counted 808,038 Italians, 351,864 Spaniards, 507,811 Poles and 48,963 Portuguese resident in France. Italian and Polish immi-gration fell consistently in the post-war period to reach a low in the early 1980s of 333,740 Italians and 64,820 Poles, whereas the number of Spanish and especially Portuguese immigrants increased significantly until, by 1968, France numbered some 530,285 Spanish and 550,121 Portuguese immigrants. Although Spanish immigration fell back after this date to 321,440 by the early 1980s, by the same date Portuguese immigration had reached a high of almost 800,000.[12]

Pastorally speaking, these Catholic immigrants initially remained dependent on their church of origin. Church attitudes to Catholic immigrants had long been generally positive, as witnessed by the creation in Paris between 1920 and 1922 of an *administration diocésaine de l'immigration* which encouraged the foundation of new *missions* (outposts of foreign Catholic churches in France).[13] But the French Catholic Church did not have appropriate or sufficient manpower to provide grass-roots spiritual support to foreign Catholics, and so this was mainly left to priests sent from abroad and attached to their respective *mission*. This situation was formalised throughout the Roman Catholic Church in 1952 through the papal text *Exsul familia*, which stated that each church of origin was responsible for sending missionary priests to any appropriate reception country in order to cater for the spiritual needs of their migrant *coreligionnaires*. In France, what this meant in practice was that hundreds of thousands of migrant Catholics depended for their religious framework on just a small number of representatives from their native land: for example, in mid-1960s France there were just ten priests from Portugal and eighty from Spain, without doubt insufficient numbers for the task. The situation began to change in 1969 following the publication of the papal text *Pastoralis migratorum cura*, which stated that each appropriate reception church was henceforward to assume joint pastoral responsibility for Catholic migrants with the church of origin. The concrete effect of this text in France was the subsequent expansion of the work of the *Commission épiscopale des migrations*, which, since 1969, has had a double function: first, to act as the Church's mouthpiece on immigration issues; second, and in conjunction with the church of origin, to organise and co-ordinate the work of France's twenty or so *missions*, each of which represents a specific national group. While some *missions* have long operated in France (the longest-established is the Polish *mission*, created in 1836), others are of more recent origin (such as the Portuguese *mission*, founded and developed in the 1960s). All, however, remained relatively isolated in their task until their effective takeover by the *Commission épiscopale des migrations* from 1969.[14] In more recent years, the *missions* have had to face increasing difficulties in the recruitment of priests and other workers. Each church of origin now spends less and less time and effort in the pastoral care of their migrants in Europe, often because they are experiencing a general *crise de vocations* at home and do not have spare workers to send abroad (as is particularly the case in Portugal), but also because the long-standing and often permanent nature of immigration seems to demand less support on the part of the church of origin.

As Catholic immigration into France has sedentarised, so the French Catholic Church has tried to increase and improve its links with the churches of origin, seeing this as a concrete way of responding to its duties and responsibilities as a church of reception. Its motivation in this is not only its desire to facilitate integration but also a recognition of the potential for what is termed *désagrégation religieuse* (or a loss of religious focus and practice) as a consequence of the uprooting entailed in the migration process, whether this be migration within France (for example, the rural exodus of French people towards towns and cities[15]) or, as concerns us here, the migration of peoples across borders into France. The Catholic Church as a whole is concerned that the transplantation of a migrant can lead to a loss of contact with religion if that migrant remains isolated in the host country or region, which could, if it remained unchecked, result in dechristianisation. Efforts have been made in France (as elsewhere) to combat that possibility through the provision of a religious framework which aims fully to involve migrant Catholics. In respect of Catholics from other countries, the French Catholic Church has been active in promoting the role of the *missions* in the local French Catholic community and in developing links between migrant and French Catholic communities. The role and status of these *missions* is detailed in a document entitled *Au service de la catholicité de l'Église*,[16] published by the French episcopate in 1987. This sets out the Church's preferred policy of integration which emphasises co-operation, understanding and dialogue between all Catholics in France, but which still takes account of an immigrant's cultural specificity, thereby stressing the common factor between all members of the universal Catholic Church while, at the same time, accepting individual cultural and national heritage (the loss of which could entail a break with one's roots) but avoiding the creation of national quasi-ghettos within local Catholic churches. The concretisation of this policy has taken many varied forms. In particular, attempts have been made to encourage immigrant *laïcs* (lay members) to take on a more active role in the French church, either as catechism teachers or by involvement in Catholic action and aid groups such as *Le Secours catholique*; the Church also promotes what is termed *un travail inter-aumôneries ethniques*, whereby *missions* of similar origin (for example, all the Latin groups) meet in order to discuss particular issues of collective interest, such as the reception of seasonal workers or of students from their respective countries. Moreover, shared pastoral publications on such issues as the catechism, marriage preparation and childcare are now common, as is the publication of joint pastoral letters written with churches from other countries and intended for migrants from those countries. But perhaps the most public manifestation of this approach lies in the form of shared religious practice: given that 'catholic' means 'universal', individual churches are encouraged not to hold separate celebrations of mass in different languages according to the typology of their congregation, but to include all members in one common act of worship. One of the best examples of such practice occurred in Cambrai in January 1985, when Catholics living in France but all from different national backgrounds joined in a televised celebration of mass, a service broadcast live across France.

Much has been done, therefore, although clearly not all parishes have achieved the integration of their cross-section of immigrant Catholics. Very often, parishes will remain too French, unaware that other Catholics are not always at ease or fully involved in the life of their church. Language, in particular, can prove to be a significant barrier. At the Second Vatican Council, the document *Sacrosanctum concilium* (4 December 1963) permitted the use of the vernacular instead of Latin in church services, thereby facilitating understanding for French Catholics in France, but not necessarily for foreign Catholics whose abilities in the French language were often limited and who at least recognised the structures and elements of the Latin mass. Although mass in the vernacular has often been interpreted as a positive sign of modernisation in the Catholic Church, for some it has served as a means of further exclusion in churches where Latin is not at least occasionally maintained, although this effect weakens as later generations are born and socialised in France and as French becomes a familiar, if not first language. But exclusion through language means that some foreign Catholics remain incomplete participants in their local French church. This, in turn, can be symptomatic of their experience of French social structures in general where progress towards integration has been made, but where continuing difficulties remain ill-perceived by the host community. The French Catholic Church does not, at least, claim complete success in the integration of foreign Catholics; indeed, it seems only too aware of the need for continuing vigilance in this domain, announcing to foreign Catholics in 1987 that 'l'Église qui est en France se doit de vérifier périodiquement sa responsabilité pastorale à l'égard des migrants catholiques et la façon dont les communautés s'ouvrent à eux'.[17] It has also openly acknowledged its own often less than perfect role in the integration process, calling on foreign Catholics to take their due place in the French Church 'car vous en êtes membres à part entière' while admitting that 'le témoignage de votre présence nous est essentiel, mais nous l'avons trop souvent oublié'.[18]

THE CHURCH AND MUSLIM IMMIGRANTS: INTEGRATING THE OTHER

One of the most striking features of post-1945 immigration into France has been the significant growth in the number of Muslims, the great majority of whom are North African (or *maghrébin*).[19] Most of these are of Algerian origin (not surprisingly so, given France's colonial past), and their impact has been such that, by 1982, they had outstripped the Portuguese as the most populous immigrant group in France.[20] This shift in immigrant typology in France corresponded with a shift in the nature of immigration. Following the halt called to non-EEC immigration in 1974, the movement of peoples into France evolved from an *immigration de travail* of primarily young, single male workers to an *immigration de peuplement*, characterised by the movement and settlement of women and children in particular, within what was termed *regroupement familial.*[21] Settlement and generational expansion have meant that there are now around four million Muslims living in France,[22] of whom approaching a million possess French nationality.[23] The category of French Muslim (that is, a Muslim who is or has become French as opposed to one living in France without being French) is a relatively recent phenomenon. However, it is no less significant for all that in terms of its import for a definition of modern French national identity, especially as this population group will expand as the third and subsequent generations are born French.[24] The days when being French meant being white, Catholic and European are long gone.

French Catholic Church activity in support of Muslim immigrants dates back to the 1960s, although initially it was limited in both range and impact. Around 1960, for example, a few priests and lay workers in major cities held literacy classes and offered basic humanitarian aid; and, towards the end of the 1960s, priests could be found working alongside such immigrant defence associations as the *Association de solidarité avec les travailleurs immigrés* or the *Groupe d'information et de soutien aux travailleurs immigrés.*[25] But it was the rise in family immigration and settlement from the mid-1970s which activated the Church's increased involvement on behalf of Muslim immigrants, influenced in this respect by its commitment to the defence of the family unit as the desirable social structure and, by extension, to the fight against the family's potential destabilisation by social and economic difficulties. With Muslim immigration henceforward a permanent feature of the French economy, many families soon became both psychologically and materially unable to envisage life anywhere but France. The Church believed that France should respond positively to this evolution and recognise the place of Muslim immigrants within the nation. To this end, exclusion was identified as the enemy and integration as the goal, the whole couched in a discourse rich in human rights.

Since the mid-1970s, the French Catholic Church has been concerned to voice an appropriate humanitarian message on immigration as required by its interpretation of the prevailing social, political, economic and cultural context. In so doing, it has operated within a nation which promotes social unity but which is faced with the demands of a multi-cultural population, and it has had to take account of the various developments and occurrences both within and outside France which have politicised the debate on immigration, but without delegitimising its humanitarian stance through what could be construed as political action. Such developments include, for example, the problems created by severe economic crisis, and especially public reaction to immigrants and 'non-standard' French during periods of high and rising unemployment; the difficulties associated with social crisis, particularly as experienced in those suburban areas where immigrant families are often concentrated to the extent of 'ghettoisation'; the rise and impact of Jean-Marie Le Pen's *Front national* (launched in 1972) and the outlet thereby created for the expression of xenophobic opinion in France; the movement of peoples into France precipitated by war and conflict elsewhere and the resultant demands for refugee status; and also the long-standing problem of illegal immigration (*les clandestins*) and of immigrants who are either *en situation irrégulière* or *sans papiers*, especially significant in the post-Maastricht debate on immigration into Europe and on rights of residence and citizenship across the Union. Within France, governments of both Left and Right have responded to these developments with a barrage of legislation and proposals on immigration, nationality and citizenship which have become increasingly restrictive as the years have passed.

In the communication of its message on immigration, the French Catholic Church has acted consistently over the years on the premise of *l'accueil dû à l'étranger*. In 1973, for example, when Tunisian and Moroccan immigrants undertook hunger strikes in protest at their standard of living, Catholic communities in Toulouse, Grenoble and Marseilles opened their churches to them in support of their protest;[26] in 1977 Mgr Saint-Gaudens, then president of the *Commission épiscopale des migrations*, expressed the Church's disapproval of the *mesures Storélu*, drafted by Giscard d'Estaing's current administration, which suspended the practice of family regroupment;[27] and, in 1979, the restrictive proposals of the same administration's *loi Bonnet* on immigrant entry and residence rights prompted the creation of an ecumenical think-tank on immigration matters in which the French Catholic Church was involved alongside other Christian and non-Christian representatives.[28] Since the late 1970s France's principal religious groups have increasingly combined forces on matters relating to immigrant rights. Just prior to the French presidential election of 1981, and therefore at a time when their action would attract significant public and political notice, a Catholic priest, a Protestant priest and a young Algerian immigrant went on hunger strike in Lyon with the aim of focusing attention on the difficulties experienced by young Muslim immigrants in particular at school and at work. And further joint action came in late 1983 when religious representatives united with youth groups in what was known as the *marche pour l'égalité et contre le racisme*, an event which marked a real move towards rapprochement between the nation's religious *responsables*, resulting in the publication of a common declaration which praised youth solidarity across national boundaries.[29] Then, in November 1985, France's religious groups combined forces for the first time with humanitarian organisations such as the *Ligue des droits de l'homme* and the *Ligue internationale contre le racisme et l'antisémitisme* (LICRA) in an *appel commun à la fraternité* which called for the tolerance of difference and support for the disadvantaged.[30]

The advent of the Socialists to power in 1981 heralded a series of measures designed to improve the lot of France's immigrants. The French Catholic Church generally appreciated such efforts and speaks of the first Socialist *cinquennat* as a time when 'le climat s'est relativement détendu'.[31] In particular, the Church welcomed the regularisation of the status of some 100,000 *clandestins* between 1981 and 1983, although it expressed concern about the conditions suffered by the remaining *clandestins* on the grounds that 'un clandestin reste un homme qui a les droits, même si on lui conteste celui d'être là'.[32] But, as the decade progressed and increased economic difficulties began to bite, resulting in rising unemployment, attitudes towards immigrants hardened in some quarters. As the National Assembly prepared to debate the immigration issue in May 1985, the far Right-wing *Front national* repeated its call for the compulsory deportation of France's immigrant population and for national preference in the allocation of jobs, in a rather crude and propaganda-laden attempt to 'solve' the unemployment problem at one fell swoop.[33] The Church's contribution to the debate was to publish what has become a key document on immigration, entitled *Au-delà des différences: les chances d'un avenir commun*, which dealt in particular with the threat posed by racism and those ideologies which inspire its expression and which is described by the Church as 'l'axe de notre travail pour un vivre ensemble dans une société démocratique'.[34] Where the *Front national* rejected difference, the Church upheld its argument that 'les différences fondées sur l'origine, la religion, ne peuvent constituer un obstacle majeur à l'intégration dans un ensemble national', restating the legitimacy of the immigrant presence in France and calling for tolerance of and respect for difference 'conformément au principe même de la laïcité'.[35]

Laïcité is a theme which recurs frequently in any consideration of the immigration question in France, and a principle to which the French Catholic Church has made consistent reference over the years within its discourse on the integration of Muslim immigrants, as illustrated by the ongoing debate on nationality and residence. This debate has been especially acute since the 1986 National Assembly elections, following which the newly formed Right-wing administration headed by Premier Jacques Chirac proposed a series of restrictive measures on nationality and residence, drafted by Charles Pasqua as *ministre de l'Intérieur*. The most contentious proposal involved a major reform of the *code de la nationalité* which would require young people born in France to foreign parents (otherwise called second-generation immigrants, or *beurs*) to request French nationality at the age of 18, rather than be granted this automatically on the basis of what is termed the *droit du sol* (the right to nationality by virtue of birth in France). Negative public reaction to this proposal was echoed within the French Catholic Church, on the grounds that it would create a harmful distinction between young people in France and that it was therefore divisive and discriminatory: Mgr Coffy, Archbishop of Marseilles, described the proposal as 'incertain et dangereux', adding that it was 'en retard d'une déclaration des droits de l'homme et du citoyen' and that 'elle interrompt le processus d'intégration',[36] while Mgr Gaillot, Bishop of Evreux, denounced the 'selection' process these proposals entailed, arguing that 'une nation ne choisit pas ses enfants; elle doit reconnaître ceux qu'elle a engendrés'.[37] Opinion was such in 1986 that the government was forced to shelve its proposals, making this one of the most significant failures of the two-year administration. As far as the Church was concerned, its message to the government was that it was prepared to speak out on matters of social and political concern and that it believed that it had a right and a duty to do so both on humanitarian grounds and on the basis of *laïcité*. That the Church should so clearly uphold the principle of *laïcité* in 1986 illustrates just how far its interpretation of its own role and of its relationship with the State had evolved in comparison with the situation which prevailed at the time of the 1905 *loi de séparation des Églises et de l'État*.

This conclusion can be reinforced by an analysis of the Church's subsequent involvement in the nationality and residence issue. Following its overwhelming victory in the 1993 National Assembly elections, the Right revitalised its 1986 proposals on nationality, entry and residence rights with the expectation that these would be swiftly passed through parliament given the government's significant political majority. Between 1986 and 1993, public opinion on the immigration issue had hardened in response to increasing unemployment (still often blamed on immigrants) and a series of violent incidents in localities heavily populated by immigrants, and the sympathetic voices of 1986 were therefore fewer in 1993. But for the French Catholic Church the argument remained the same: the integration process was once more under threat, as it explained to France's immigrants in a *message de solidarité*, 'en ces jours où de nouvelles dispositions légales peuvent donner l'impression que l'on vous désigne comme la cause de tout ce qui ne va pas dans notre pays'.[38] On this occasion the Church was accused by Charles Pasqua (reappointed *ministre de l'Intérieur* in 1993) of contravening *laïcité* by meddling in politics through its apparent condemnation of governmental policy, although Church leaders quickly refuted this charge and argued that their sole motivation was humanitarianism. Pasqua's sharp reminder that the Church should not interfere in politics on the grounds that 'il n'y a pas de confusion en France entre les Églises et l'État, nous sommes dans un État démocratique et laïque'[39] suggests that he saw political intention where none existed and basically overreacted. That the situation was quickly diffused, thereby avoiding the rekindling of a hostile debate on Church–State relations, is largely because public opinion rejected the charges laid at the Church's door, itself indicative of a general acceptance in 1990s France that the role, right and duty of the Church is precisely to comment on issues of a moral and humanitarian nature and that it was therefore acting within the boundaries set by *laïcité*.

The pressure brought to bear in 1993 by the Church and other institutions acting in defence of human rights forced the government to redraft some of the more contentious legislation relating in particular to family regroupment, although the reform of the *code de la nationalité* and the curtailment to the automatic acquisition of French nationality at 18 remained in force. As a result of this legislation, access to the ten-year residence permit brought in by the Socialists in 1984 was restricted: foreigners who had been in France for years and who were clearly in the process of integration were turned into illegal immigrants, while foreign parents of children born in France became vulnerable to deportation. One well-publicised illustration of this legislation in practice occurred during 1996 in what was known as the *affaire des sans-papiers*. In March 1996, and in fear of deportation, more than three hundred African immigrants *en situation irrégulière* in Paris took refuge in the Catholic *église Saint-Ambroise* in order to draw attention to their demand for legal permits. Four days later, they were forcibly removed from the church by the French riot police at the request of the French episcopate. This request seems surprising, given the Church's previous support for immigrants. However, on this occasion, the Church clearly felt that the very real plight of the Africans had been hijacked by certain interest groups who intended to extract political mileage from the situation through an attack on the government, and so it decided to disassociate itself from what Mgr Lustiger, Archbishop of Paris, denounced as 'stratégie politique'.[40] The Church failed to avoid political involvement, however, since it suited the government to capitalise on this pronouncement: reference to humanitarianism was lost beneath political gamesmanship as Lustiger's words were appropriated by the *ministre de l'Intérieur*, and as public opinion thereby associated Church and government, a link which earned the institution a fair degree of criticism. Public reaction to the Church's arguably misguided response to the situation, coupled with the behaviour of the police, served to rally numerous associations, political and pressure groups to the Africans' cause.[41] The *sans-papiers* moved on to a second Catholic church, the *église Saint-Bernard*, at the end of June 1996, where ten of their number began a hunger strike further to focus public attention on their situation, while their support groups all signed an appeal to President Chirac, calling on him to compel the government to negotiate in just fashion with the Africans for the allocation of legal permits.[42] But, in late August, Premier Alain Juppé ordered that the church be cleared: arrests and detentions resulted, followed by deportation for some, regularisation for a minority and stalemate for the majority. The *affaire des sans-papiers* dogged the Juppé administration to its end in May 1997. Aware of the potentially explosive nature of this affair, the newly elected Socialist government quickly announced that it intended to address the question of citizenship and residence,[43] and some aspects of the restrictive 1993 nationality and immigration legislation were subsequently reworked in late 1997.[44] However, those who demanded widespread regularisation for France's *sans-papiers* have been disappointed, since only 70,000 of the 145,000 requests made have been approved, as many have been rejected and just a few cases remain on file. By April 1998 six Catholic churches around Paris and Le Havre were still occupied by *sans-papiers* and their supporters, some on hunger strike, and Church representatives were still calling for 'la plus large régularisation possible'.[45] But, in July 1998, Premier Lionel Jospin warned campaigners not to use hunger strikes as a pressure tactic and announced categorically that 'on régularise de bonne foi tous ceux qui peuvent l'être, [mais] notre politique n'est pas de régulariser tous les sans-papiers'.[46] Despite this statement, the affair is by no means settled. The campaign for regularisation will continue, and government promises to deal humanely with those refused regularisation will be closely monitored by humanitarian and immigrant defence groups. A small spark of discontent is all that will be needed to re-ignite the whole affair.

The French Catholic Church's exploitation of *laïcité* to justify its right to speak out on immigration matters (among others) means not only that it has become an important and influential advocate of the secular principle, but also that *laïcité* is therefore inextricably linked with the Church's evolved definition of its own role and status in France. If respect for *laïcité* moulds the Church's relationship with the secular State, it also characterises its response to France's other representative religions – in this context, particularly Islam. The Church's ability to operate successfully within the secular State underpins its call for Islam to adopt a similar respect for *laïcité*, this as a means to integration. For the Church, the acquisition of nationality cannot alone stand as the determinant of integration, referencing in its argument the many Muslims who possess French nationality but who are often no better integrated than their non-French Muslim colleagues since they are still perceived as foreign. The chances for full integration, it argues, rest heavily on an evolution of attitude, not only on the part of the 'standard' French towards Muslims but also on the part of Muslims themselves, especially as regards their Islamic faith. If *laïcité* accepts all religions but publicly recognises none, then no religion can or should expect different, even special treatment from the State. And, the Church argues, if it can adapt itself to operate within the secular State, then so can (and should) Islam, effectively bringing it into line with Catholicism in terms of the status of the faith and its operation within the State. To that end, the French Catholic Church is therefore interested in the adaptation of Islam to a French context, calling for what amounts to the *laïcisation* of Islam to match its own accommodation to the secular State realised over the course of the twentieth century.

The Church's own *laïcisation* is most clearly illustrated by an analysis of its evolution in the domain of education, where, according to the December 1959 *loi Debré*, those private (mainly Catholic) schools under voluntary financial contract to the State must in return – among other requirements – respect pupils' individual freedom of conscience within the mainstream curriculum, effectively meaning that such schools may not impose religious instruction on their pupils although religion may form a part of extra-curricular activities.[47] The question of the *laïcisation* of Islam also focuses most publicly on the realm of education, as seen in the two *affaires du foulard* which dominated the social and political agenda in France in late 1989 and again over the 1994–95 school year. The original affair involved three Muslim schoolgirls who were excluded from their State *collège* in Creil, north of Paris, since they had insisted on wearing their religious headscarves in what amounted to a secular environment. This affair revealed two definitions of *laïcité*: on the one hand, a hard-line interpretation which rested on religious neutrality and social homogeneity and which, in the pursuit of integration, demanded no difference of attitude or behaviour on the part of State school pupils; and, on the other hand, a modern definition which permitted the headscarf on the grounds that *laïcité* had evolved to mean *le droit à la différence* and which therefore viewed integration in terms of co-existence. At the time, this second definition prevailed, lent significant support by such parties as *SOS-Racisme* and other immigrant defence groups, as well as by the French Catholic Church which advised a 'position mesurée',[48] no doubt at least partly as a result of the Pope's recent reminder on World Peace Day (4 October 1989) of the right of religious minorities to express their faith while respecting the demands of national unity.[49]

By the time of the second affair, however, the social and political atmosphere had changed and tolerance seemed no longer to be the watchword. In September 1994, estimates suggested that some seven hundred Muslim girls were now demanding the right to wear their headscarves at school, many of whom referenced the outcome of the earlier affair as their justification. This significant rise in the number of headscarf cases fuelled fears of an attempted *islamisation* of France through what many chose to interpret as a systematic attack by fundamentalist Muslims on the education system as the cornerstone of the French Republic. On this second occasion, a hard-line interpretation of *laïcité* prevailed, concretised in the form of a circular published on 20 September 1994 by the education minister François Bayrou, a member of the Right-wing majority elected to government in March 1993. The so-called *circulaire sur les signes religieux* banned what Bayrou called religious 'signes ostentatoires' from State schools on the grounds that these represented difference and separation in direct contravention of what he termed 'une certaine idée de la citoyenneté, une idée française de la nation et de la République', based on the declared goals of inclusion, unity and equality.[50] Somewhat ironically, however, the circular proved to be discriminatory since it targeted only 'signes ostentatoires' (in this context clearly the Muslim headscarf) and not what were termed 'signes discrets' (such as the cross worn by many Catholics or the Jewish skullcap). Girls who refused to comply, either of their own volition or under pressure from their families, were subsequently excluded from the classroom and either confined to less sensitive areas of the establishment (such as the school library) or told to stay at home and placed on the distance learning programme.[51] Calls for an actual law prohibiting all religious symbols at school followed, supported by some (including *SOS-Racisme*) who had defended the right to wear the headscarf in 1989 but who now argued that the appearance of any such symbol at school represented evidence not only of 'une offensive généralisée contre la laïcité'[52] but also – given the increased number of headscarf cases – of 'un islamisme conquérant et organisé', of religious proselytism in operation.[53] Tolerance of the headscarf, it was feared, would lay the education system open to attack from 'des noyaux intégristes [qui utilisent] le foulard comme drapeau',[54] with the ultimate target identified as the Republic itself. That such a situation had arisen was, it was claimed, a direct result of the failure of the State's integration policy.

The reaction of the French Catholic Church at the time suggests that it exploited this second headscarf controversy and Bayrou's resultant circular in order once more both to stake out its own ground and to publicise its interpretation of the status of Islam in France. *Laïcité* again marked its discourse. Much as the State had warned the Church in 1993 not to intervene in political matters on the grounds of the separation of Churches and State, the Church (through Mgr Lustiger as spokesman) now warned the State in return that it had no authority to deal with the headscarf controversy 'sur le plan religieux, celui notamment des prescriptions de l'islam', and that it could intervene politically only if the affair concerned public order – that is, if the headscarf were thought to represent 'un instrument de provocation en vue de favoriser une politique de tension'.[55] This exploitation of *laïcité* to defend religious status had previously been employed by the Church, although never before seemingly on behalf of Islam. But this apparent defence of Islam's religious status and of its right to express its religious requirements carries a subtext, since it can and must also be read as a restatement of the Catholic Church's own rights and status in matters of religious expression, as permitted by a modern, tolerant definition of *laïcité*. The Church's intervention, therefore, can be understood more in terms of a defence of *laïcité* than a defence of Islam. Church education representatives argued that the Church's own adaptation to secular circumstances spared it as a target of Bayrou's circular on religious symbols at school since 'l'enseignement catholique a abandonné le prosélytisme religieux'.[56] But this, they maintained, did not mean that they were prepared to accept any other form of religious proselytism. Mgr Lustiger himself was categorical, arguing that 'il ne faut pas accepter de dérogation à la laïcité'.[57] Just as the Church has evolved to accept *laïcité* over the course of the twentieth century, so Islam must be granted the time to 's'incorporer à notre histoire nationale et à notre culture', a process which, according to Lustiger, will be 'une affaire de deux générations, une affaire de trente ans'.[58]

Although the long-term outcome of Lustiger's prediction remains to be seen, there are recent signs of compromise on the headscarf issue on the part of some leading Muslim representatives, which stand as evidence of evolution towards a reformed, French-style Islam. In a meeting with Jean-Pierre Chevènement (*ministre de l'Intérieur*) in Cairo in April 1998, Mohammad Sayed Tantaoui, Egypt's principal imam, announced that 'les musulmans ont le devoir de se conformer aux lois du pays où ils vivent' and that the French State is within its rights to judge the headscarf contrary to national tradition and interest, adding that its use is a secondary concern and that 'le plus important pour notre religion est qu'une musulmane porte une tenue décente'.[59] And in France, a book by Soheib Bencheikh (chief mufti in Marseilles) argues that it is education rather than the headscarf which today preserves the dignity of Muslim girls and guarantees them a future,[60] while Bruno Étienne, founder of the *Institut des études supérieures islamiques* (opened in 1998), maintains that 'aujourd'hui la quasi-majorité des jeunes imams sont favorables à l'intégration républicaine'.[61] It is Islam's recognition of and adaptation to *laïcité* which will stand as evidence of its integration in France, which will give it common ground, status and interests with France's other representative religions and which will facilitate the transformation of the 'other' into an accepted constituent part of modern multicultural French national identity. In its dealings with the French State and in its acceptance of *laïcité*, the French Catholic Church has forged a path down which Islam must follow.

NOTES

1. Mgr Jacques Delaporte, *Immigration: le cœur et la raison* (Paris: Desclée de Brouwer, 1990), p. 26.

2. See Henri Tincq, 'La France des droits de l'homme et la France des saints', *Le Monde*, 22 August 1997, p. 6. These words were originally spoken on 17 October 1987 by Père Joseph Wresinski, founder of the association *Aide à toute détresse Quart-monde*. They have been engraved on a plaque to mark his memory at the Trocadéro in Paris, unveiled by John Paul II on 21 August 1997 (ibid.).

3. See Kay Chadwick, 'The French Catholic Church and the 1993 French Immigration Laws: Rekindling *la guerre laïque*?', *French Studies Bulletin*, 55 (1995), 1–3.

4. *Le Monde*, 27 August 1996, p. 1, p. 5.

5. See, for example, Matthew 25: 38–40; Hebrews 13: 1.

6. *Gaudium et spes*, 1965, 29 (2–4), in *Le Discours social de l'Église catholique*, ed. Denis Maugenest (Paris: Centurion, 1985), p. 399.

7. Delaporte, *Immigration*, p. 40.

8. Ibid., p. 26. The three immigration theories of *intégration*, *assimilation* and *insertion* are detailed and discussed in Michel Hannoun, *L'Homme est l'espérance de l'homme* (Paris: Documentation française, 1987).

9. Mgr Joseph Duval, in *Le Monde*, 27 May 1993, p. 4.

10. *L'Église catholique en France: documents pour la presse* (Paris: Secrétariat général de l'Épiscopat, 1986), p. 122.

11. Delaporte, *Immigration*, p. 51.

12. Jacqueline Costa-Lascoux, *De l'immigré au citoyen* (Paris: Documentation française, 1989), p. 19.

13. Gérard Cholvy and Yves-Marie Hilaire, *Histoire religieuse de la France contemporaine*, 3 vols (Toulouse: Privat, 1985-88), II (1986), 352.

14. For details of the history and work of the *missions*, see ibid., II, 352–54.

15. For a discussion of the causal relationship between the rural exodus within France and *désagrégation religieuse*, see Danièle Hervieu-Léger, 'Socio-religious Change in France: Trends in French Catholicism', in *Contemporary France. A Review in Interdisciplinary studies*, eds Jolyon Howorth and George Ross (London: Frances Pinter, 1987), pp. 111–29; and 'The Case of French Catholicism', in *The Postwar Generation and Establishment Religions*, eds Wade C. Roof, Jackson Carroll and David Roozen (Colorado: Westview Press, 1995), pp. 151–69.

16. *Au service de la catholicité de l'Église* (Paris: Documents de l'Épiscopat, 1987).

17. Ibid., p. 45.

18. *Des Évêques s'adressent aux immigrés qui sont en France* (Paris: Commission épiscopale des migrations, 1983).

19. The term 'North African' is taken to include Algerians, Moroccans and Tunisians.

20. Costa-Lascoux, *De l'immigré au citoyen*, p. 19. Algeria was a French colony from 1830 until it was granted independence in 1962.

21. So significant was this shift towards the *sédentarisation* of immigrant families that by the mid-1980s over 70% of non-EEC foreigners living in France had been there for at least ten years.

22. Brian Fitzpatrick, 'Immigrants', in *France Today*, ed. John Flower (London: Hodder & Stoughton, 1997), pp. 115–42 (p. 134).

23. John Flower, 'Religion', in ibid., pp. 167–88 (p. 172).

24. Second-generation immigrants born in France currently become French at 18. Their descendants (the third and subsequent generations) will be French at birth since they will be born to French parents.

25. Delaporte, *Immigration*, p. 35.

26. Ibid., p. 38.

27. *Documentation catholique*, 1728, 16 October 1977. The ban on family regroupment was lifted in 1978.

28. *Documentation catholique*, 1766, 17 June 1979.

29. *Documentation catholique*, 1886, 17 December 1983.

30. The full text of the *appel* can be consulted in, for example, *Le Matin*, 14 November 1985, p. 6.

31. Delaporte, *Immigration*, p. 42.

32. Ibid., p. 43.

33. A common slogan of the *Front national* at this time was 'Trois millions de chômeurs, c'est trois millions d'immigrés en trop'. *Front national* employment policy rested on one aim: 'Réserver sur notre territoire national le travail en priorité aux fils et filles de France' (Jean-Marie Le Pen, *La France est de retour* (Paris: Carrère–Laffon, 1985), p. 51).

34. *L'Église catholique en France: documents pour la presse*, p. 123.

35. *Au-delà des différences: les chances d'un avenir commun* (Paris: Les Grands Textes de la Documentation catholique, 58, 10 May 1985).

36. Mgr Coffy, interviewed in *L'Est républicain*, 8 November 1986.

37. Mgr Gaillot, interviewed in the *Bulletin diocésain d'Evreux*, 11, 29 May 1987.

38. Mgr Joatton, president of the *Commission épiscopale des migrations*, published the *message de solidarité* on 20 May 1993. The full text is published in *Le Monde*, 24 May 1993, p. 1, p. 5.

39. Radio interview with Charles Pasqua, Europe 1, 24 May 1993, reproduced in *Le Monde*, 26 May 1993, p. 7.

40. *Le Monde*, 23 March 1996, p. 8.

41. The organisations involved included the political parties of the Left, four of France's biggest trade unions and various human rights groups such as the *Mouvement contre le racisme et pour l'amitié entre les peuples* (MRAP) and the *Commission nationale des droits de l'homme*.

42. Extracts from the appeal are published in *Le Monde*, 21 August 1996, p. 1, p. 5.

43. *Le Monde*, 11 June 1997, p. 1, p. 8.

44. *Le Monde*, 18 December 1997, p. 8.

45. *Le Monde*, 14 April 1998, p. 7.

46. *Le Monde*, 7 July 1998, p. 30.

47. For an analysis of the 'secularisation' of Catholic education in France, see Kay Chadwick, 'Education and Secular France: (Re)defining *laïcité*', *Modern and Contemporary France*, ns 5 (1997), 47–59.

48. Cardinal Decourtray, Archbishop of Lyon, *Le Quotidien de Paris*, 28–29 October 1989, p. 1.

49. The Pope's declaration was published in *La Croix*, 21 October 1989, p. 7.

50. The full text of Bayrou's circular is published in *Le Monde*, 21 September 1994, p. 5.

51. For details of sample exclusion cases, see *Le Monde*, 28 September 1994, 26 October 1994 and 27 October 1994. By September 1995, some eighty Muslim girls had been excluded from State education for wearing headscarves.

52. Fodé Sylla, president of *SOS-Racisme*, in *Le Monde*, 27 October 1994, p. 5.

53. Julien Dray, co-founder and trustee of *SOS-Racisme*, in ibid.

54. Ibid.

55. *Le Monde*, 2 November 1994, p. 6.

56. *Le Monde*, 6–7 November 1994, p. 8.

57. *Le Monde*, 2 November 1994, p. 6.

58. Ibid.

59. *Le Figaro*, 16 April 1998, p. 9.

60. Soheib Bencheikh, *Marianne et le prophète ou l'islam dans la France laïque* (Paris: Seuil, 1998).

61. *Le Figaro*, 16 April 1998, p. 9.

9

Yeast in the dough?
Catholic schooling in France, 1981–95

Nicholas Beattie

BACKGROUND INFORMATION

In 1992–93, there were 2,043,054 pupils in Catholic schools in France: 895,210 of them were in nursery and primary schools; 1,104,694 were in secondary schools (*collèges*, ages 11–15, and *lycées*, ages 15–18: the ages are indicative only because *redoublement*, or repeating of a year, is common in France); 43,150 were in agricultural schools and colleges.[1] Apart from indicating that Catholic schooling in France is a substantial enterprise, these figures have little meaning until they are compared with those from other parts of the system. As soon as such cross-sector comparisons are made, certain inferences can be drawn. First, that Catholic schools dominate the private sector where they constitute 95% of all schools other than State schools. Secondly, that Catholic primary schools educate 13.4% of the total school population in that age group. From the age of compulsion (six), the Catholic primary school caters for about 15% of the available child population, while Catholic pre-schooling absorbs only 12% (it should be remembered that in France virtually all children are in school from age three). This 3% gap between pre-school and primary phases reflects the Church's problem in finding resources to build facilities in new estates, for example, where young children are to be found in large numbers. Thirdly, that Catholic *collèges* cater for 20.01% of all pupils in school at that level. Fourthly, that Catholic *lycées* cater for 19.15% of all pupils in school at that level. Finally, that the proportion of pupils passing through the Catholic system is thus somewhat higher at secondary than at primary level.

In spatial terms, these pupils are not spread evenly round France. Metropolitan France is divided into twenty-six *académies*, or educational regions. Only 4.03% of primary children in the Strasbourg *académie* are in Catholic schools; in Nantes the figure is 37.63% and in Rennes 38.36%. At secondary level, Nantes (39.76%) and Rennes (42.93%) retain their pre-eminence as bastions of Catholic schooling, but Limoges (9.44%) is beaten to bottom place by Corsica (7.52%). Such figures reflect historical patterns. Two hundred years ago, the rural West (Nantes, Rennes) was the centre of popular resistance to the Revolution, and remains strongly Catholic;[2] Limousin (Limoges) was long a Socialist stronghold; Alsace (Strasbourg) has a substantial Protestant population, was incorporated into the German *Reich* from 1871 to 1918 and has inherited from that period a different (in French terms, pre-1905) legal basis for its schools.

If the present picture is compared with the recent past, Catholic schooling appears to be fairly stable. It catered for 18% of the national child population in 1960–61, 17% in 1993–94. However, it should be remembered that, in 1935, 47.7% of pupils at secondary level were in private schools,[3] so that – over the longer term – change has been substantial: the growth of State secondary provision has greatly eroded the pre-war position of the Catholic sector.

So far, these figures have presented Catholic schooling as though it were an island, sharply differentiated from public schooling. For a statistical snapshot, that separateness has to be maintained; but as soon as one considers the percentage inconsistencies between levels of schooling – as between, for example, pre-school and elementary school, or elementary school and *collège* – one realises that in the course of an educational career individual children may move frequently from public school to private or vice versa. In fact, in 1992–93, 258,000 pupils made such a move: 155,900 moved into Catholic schools from the State sector, and 102,000 made the reverse journey. It is calculated that in general about 30% of school-leavers have had some experience in both sectors.[4] One consequence of this movement between sectors is that a higher proportion of the adult population than is suggested by the simple attendance statistics has been touched by Catholic education at some point. Random polls suggest that the number of former pupils of the Catholic sector is about fourteen million. The English-speaking reader, familiar with the idea that 'private school' means a school for which parents pay fees at something approaching a business rate, may need to be reminded that the extensive mobility between sectors in France is made possible by the fact that fee levels are modest. A handbook of 1990, for example, cites annual average basic fees at 2,240 francs at primary level 2,800 francs at secondary level and 1,830 francs at nursery level.[5] Normally, different tariffs are available corresponding to different parental income levels. If one remembers that most of these schools are day schools, and that curriculum and examinations and 'quality control' are identical with those available in the State sector, it becomes clear that 'private school' is in reality more like a 'voluntary' school in England and Wales (that is, essentially a State school with certain derogations and possibilities) than it is like an 'independent' or 'private' school operating more or less as a business and heavily dependent on fees paid directly by parents. For completeness, it should be mentioned also that French higher education, like the school sector, contains a minority of Catholic institutions: five universities and a range of tertiary level institutes catering for approximately twenty thousand students.[6] These are sizeable and dynamic enough to warrant another chapter; but this one is restricted to Catholic schooling.

THE SEPARATENESS OF CATHOLIC SCHOOLING

Figures of the sort listed above are useful in giving a general preliminary idea of the system and in suggesting certain lines of thought. Inevitably, however, they reflect one of the weaknesses of some writing about Catholic education in France: the tendency to view it primarily as a distinct and separate entity which can be described and dissected rather as one might describe and dissect a strange insect in isolation from its environment.

Many writers overcome this problem by locating Catholic schooling in its political context. As we shall see, for some purposes it does make sense to see the Catholic system as an embattled minority defending itself against secular attacks or asserting its interests in a wide range of pressure-group strategies. Such studies, whether hostile, neutral or sympathetic, tend to highlight Catholicism as a more or less unitary, coherent and rational grouping and again focus on the sharpness of the boundary between Catholic schools and the secular world in which they must survive.

Rather few observers take at all seriously the schools themselves. In what ways are they different from their public counterparts? Ostensibly, the whole purpose of these schools is to be different, to provide choice – yet in France the central reality of their day-to-day

operations, curriculum and examinations is identical to that provided in public schools, and must be so if they are to receive from the
State the finance on which they depend. Apart from a few crucifixes
or holy statues in buildings, what, basically, is uniquely *Catholic*
about them? This question reminds us that many writers about
Catholic schools in France discuss them as though theology did not
exist. Yet if they wrote about *rites de passage* in New Guinea, such
writers would go to great trouble to describe sensitively what their
informants thought they were doing in organising their outwardly
strange ceremonies. Catholic schools in France claim to exist in
order to promote or extend a Catholic presence in French society. In
the images of the Gospels, they are supposed to be the light on the
lamp-stand, the salt in the food, the yeast in the dough. Are they?
That is the elusive question that this chapter will discuss. It is of
course a question that forces the questioner to move beyond statistics,
history and pressure-group politics – though all those elements will
have to be considered. It also produces a blurring or erasure of the
sharp boundary between 'Catholic schools' on the one hand and
'public schools' on the other. Finally, it requires the questioner to
look more objectively at the very wide spectrum of attitudes, opinions
and motivations present in French Catholicism in the 1990s.

CATHOLIC–SECULAR CONFRONTATION, 1981–84

Paradoxically, we have to begin to explore this question by looking at
a phase of Catholic activity when boundaries were apparently sharp
and attitudes clear and single-minded: the energetic and successful
defence of Catholic schools against the Socialist attempt to integrate
them into the national system (1981–84). This whole episode may be
seen as a deliberate reassertion of the old boundary, a deliberate self-
distancing of Church from State.

The facts are complex but must be rapidly compressed and
interpreted.[7] The Left, dominated by François Mitterrand's *Parti
socialiste* (PS), was elected to national power in May 1981. Since the
inauguration of the Fifth Republic in 1958, the Left had never held
national office, so the sense of euphoria was great: the moment had
come for a radical change to a system which many felt was 'rigged' in
favour of the Right. Part of the Common Programme of the Left was
the intention to create 'un grand service public et unifié de l'édu-

cation nationale'. Successive attempts by Alain Savary, the incoming education minister, to devise a viable plan to integrate public and private schools provoked massive opposition. The government found itself as 'piggy in the middle', vainly striving to elaborate practicable schemes for unification which, as soon as they became public, stiffened the resistance of the Catholics, or of the secularists, or of both. A fierce national debate was carried on sporadically over three years, punctuated by huge rallies and demonstrations. In July 1985, President Mitterrand withdrew support from Savary's latest proposals; Premier Pierre Mauroy resigned and the government fell. The outcome in terms of the Catholic schools issue was (neutrally) an acceptance of the status quo. From the viewpoint of radical secularists it represented a sell-out; or, from the viewpoint of many Catholics, a triumph.[8]

From some years' distance, the picture seems more *nuancé*. What did this protracted confrontation mean? Obviously, the debate could take place over such a long period, with contributions of different sorts from so many individual citizens, only because it drew upon a long previous history. This is well known and extensively documented. On both extremes, the rallying-cries were drawn from a conflict going back at least as far as the Revolution.[9]

This long history had produced networks and institutions on both sides which were well placed to organise and represent their respective viewpoints. On the Catholic side, for example, the central official organisation of the *Secrétariat général de l'enseignement catholique* was backed by UNAPEL *(Union nationale des associations de parents d'élèves)*, a parents' organisation representing 850,000 families.[10] On the secular side, the CNAL *(Comité national de l'action laïque)* grouped a number of organisations of which the most substantial was the Left-inclined primary teachers' union, the SNI *(Syndicat national des instituteurs)*.

As the confrontation rumbled on, several things became apparent. First, that each 'side' or 'camp' in a sense reflected the other; their styles were similar and so were the kind of problems they had to solve to stay 'in business' and sustain their political momentum. Secondly, that each 'side' covered a large range of opinion: on the Catholic side, from extreme Right-wingers and Latin-mass enthusiasts to 'lefty' Catholic Action zealots; on the secular side, from unreformed Stalinists to pacific *soixante-huitards vieillissants* (some of whom could be found, after a slight shift in ideology, in the Catholic ranks also!). Both 'sides' also incorporated large numbers of people who were usually indifferent to politics and could not readily be labelled. Thirdly, the Catholic leaderships [*sic*] quite soon realised that they had popular support to an extent they had hardly suspected. Understandably, Catholic confidence grew. Fourthly, from the standpoint of the Catholic leaderships, risks were soon identified. One was that the Catholic cause would be assimilated to Right-wing party politics. A second was that the more hot-headed elements in the Catholic ranks would push the Church into a position where negotiation or compromise with government would become impossible. A third was that the basic role of the hierarchy as the guarantor of the catholicity of Catholic schooling would be occluded or usurped by parents and by the schools themselves.[11]

That all these risks were largely avoided through three years of crisis inevitably had an impact on how Catholic schools came to conceive their role in the 1990s. First, one is conscious of a certain confidence and firmness – even serenity – in the way Catholic schooling now projects its identity. We are dealing with a system which in 1944 was seen by many as disgracefully complicit with the Vichy regime. Catholic schools withered on the vine for fifteen years after the Liberation, and had to be rescued from financial collapse by the *loi Debré* of 31 December 1959. Leclerc suggests that even as late as the early 1980s the French episcopate was often reluctant to take a stand on public issues because of an uneasy awareness that parts of the Church had too easily accommodated to Pétain.[12] Certainly the near-total isolation of Catholic schools from public schools (which meant that, for example, teachers in a Catholic school would very likely never even meet their counterparts in the public school next door) made it easy for the image of Catholic education to be seen as outdated and inappropriate to a modern democracy, with nothing of any educational interest to offer to the public sector. In 1990, by contrast, the Secretary-General of Catholic Education argued that thirty years of association amounted to the official recognition of Catholic private education, that this had a quite different position vis-à-vis the national system; and that it could no longer be regarded as a mere stop-gap or competitor but claimed full recognition as a partner.[13]

In this context, a number of interesting documents re-thinking the role of the school in general and of the Catholic school in particular have been published by the *Secrétariat général*. For example, *Donner du sens à l'école* reviews the aims of schooling.[14] It is based on a very wide consultation of dioceses, schools and families – including children who, imaginatively, were asked to respond to the invitation 'dessine-moi une école', and whose drawings were then analysed and exhibited. The style of these discussion documents is very different from the style of documents produced in both 'le monde anglo-saxon' and French public education. They make frequent use of words like 'épanouissement', 'humanité', 'vérité' and 'amour'.[15] Such phraseology may seem vague and over-rhetorical, but what it is actually about is similar to the more familiar terms of educational discourse in the UK, such as progression, differentiation, pastoral care, education for relationships, moral education and so on: a concern for whole learners and for their motivation and personal initiative. It is significant that Catholic education has the confidence to develop and use its own rhetoric, concepts and vocabulary.

Such national consultations are conducted within the framework of a national organisation co-ordinating and monitoring a basically diocesan system. The whole structure is described and codified in the *Statut de l'enseignement catholique*, agreed in 1991 and approved by the episcopate at the *Conférence des évêques de France* in 1992. The statute clearly reflects the task of Catholic education in working within the rules provided by the State. 'Servir la nation' is a key principle, and involves respecting 'la liberté religieuse et la liberté de conscience des élèves et de leurs familles'. The 'caractère propre' of Catholic education is to be developed through a *Projet éducatif*, a sort of mission-statement-cum-development plan to be worked out by and for each school. The aim is to make the school a 'communauté éducative', with the participation of teachers, parents, local clergy, non-teaching personnel and pupils. Thus the school serves the Church, too, by striving to 'éduquer la personnalité chrétienne'.

Whether all this apparatus and all these words are mere verbiage depends, of course, on the individual school and how it works. The only way to look sensibly at the Catholic school in France is to compare it constantly with its non-Catholic counterpart. It is only by making that comparison that the Anglo–Saxon reader can begin to sense what is unusual about Catholic schools in late-twentieth-century France, and what impact they may have had on their public counterparts.

THE 1959 ACT AND ITS CONSEQUENCES

Catholic schools operate essentially within the provisions of the *loi Debré* of 31 December 1959, and a scatter of subsequent legislation and interpretation through the courts.[16] Manifestly, this basic framework is more a pragmatic mechanism than a set of aims or ideals. The provisions of the *loi Debré* are a compromise, not a rallying-cry. They represent what a clever politician (Michel Debré), functioning in a period of massive institutional change (the inauguration of the Fifth Republic), and determined to use that moment to rescue Catholic education from bankruptcy, could 'sell' to a wide range of different interest groups. This pragmatism may make it difficult to discern the long-term significance of the Debré arrangements, which (apart from rescuing Catholic schools) were not necessarily very plain at the time.

One way to think about this is to contrast these arrangements with the traditional image and purpose of the Catholic school in France. Simone de Beauvoir, for example, describes her own Catholic education in the 1920s in the following terms:

> On ne peut imaginer enseignement plus sectaire que celui que je reçus. Manuels scolaires, livres, classes, conversations: tout convergeait. Jamais on ne me laissa entendre, fût-ce de loin, fût-ce en sourdine, un autre son de cloche. J'appris l'histoire aussi docilement que la géographie, sans soupçonner qu'elle pût davantage prêter à discussion. Toute petite, je m'émus au musée Grevin devant les martyrs livrés aux lions, devant la noble figure de Marie-Antoinette. Les empereurs qui avaient persécuté les chrétiens, les tricoteuses et les sans-culottes m'apparaissaient comme les plus odieuses incarnations du Mal. Le Bien, c'était l'Église et la France.[17]

De Beauvoir describes a school which is essentially unitary, separate, ghettoised, ideologically coherent, indoctrinating. This style of education is one which the Debré law fundamentally undermines, without consciously setting out so to do. It subverts the traditional, oppositional Catholic school by requiring schools, in exchange for State subsidy, to offer exactly the same curriculum as public schools and to accept pupils without selecting them for the religious or other beliefs of their parents. In the short term, no doubt, some schools preserved the old style, or aspects of it, well into the 1960s and 1970s; but over a generation the Debré rules had the effect of marginalising the directly religious and ideological aspect of Catholic schools. From the pupil's viewpoint, the one adopted by de Beauvoir, schools become less hermetically convergent; the specifically Catholic aspect becomes more 'value-added', more an optional extra or top-dressing.

The Debré law has another feature which is less often noted: namely, that the contracts which it inaugurated are not with the Church but with individual schools. The assumption was that those schools would sink or swim in competition with public schools, and the mechanism for survival would be parental choice. This sounds familiar from a contemporary perspective, but in 1959 the Right-wing 'market' rationale for 'choice' had not been developed – certainly not in France, with its deep-rooted tradition of a unitary, compulsory, centralised system run by *fonctionnaires* (tenured civil servants). The impact of choice on the internal organisation of Catholic schools was twofold. First, choice implies difference. Schools began to realise that they would attract pupils by having something different to offer (as will be discussed below), although we should note that schools being different, having distinctive 'school climates', is quite alien to the traditional French idea of a centrally defined, egalitarian system. Secondly, contracts with individual schools, and the consequential stress on choice and difference, imply a reinforced role for the head teacher. He or she becomes less of a low-level administrator, and more of a publicist, policy-maker and team-builder. This again is at odds with traditional French views of the State school head as *primus inter pares*: French heads are typically in position for a fixed period before reverting to classroom teaching. They act essentially as two-way channels for administrative com-munications between Paris or the local *académie* and the school. In this tradition, the head has no part to play in the selection of staff (who are selected for lifelong employment in national competitive examinations, or *concours*[18]) or in the assessment and career develop-ment of colleagues. The head, especially at primary level, is thus decidedly subordinate to inspectors.[19]

In Catholic schools, the traditional role of the head has been distinctly different from that of his/her State counterpart. Tradi-tionally, and especially at secondary level, the Catholic head was a religious one, with the hierarchical position, superiority and authority of one whose vocation was God-given. The decline in religious vocations over the last generation has radically secularised the staffing of Catholic schools: 51% of heads were lay people in 1974, 88% in 1992.[20] The head's guiding role remains central in the

Catholic school, but the increasing rarity of religious heads or teachers means that in the perception of parents and pupils it is now closer than it was to the public school head. Under different impulses, heads in both sectors become more similar.

Against this staffing background, it is possible to reassess the effect of the *loi Debré* a generation after its implementation. Its covert impact was to encourage and legitimise the autonomy of schools, as opposed to its overt purpose of getting State money into private schools. The Act propelled schools into a market long before the ideology and vocabulary of 'marketing education' came into existence. Inescapably, more and more parents found themselves making choices between State schools and Catholic ones. Research demonstrates that such choices are rarely made on purely religious grounds, but are frequently made on assumptions about the educational outcomes expected.[21] Parents argue that a particular school is more likely than its locally available State counterpart to secure for a particular child a place in a particular prestigious *grande école*, or will enable him/her to recuperate a poor examination result achieved in a State school, or to ensure that he/she will escape the disaster of being held back for a year – or, more simply, to provide a more disciplined and traditional school environment. The careful study published by Langouët and Léger in 1994 teases out trends over time in how families use the 'dual network' open to them.[22] Langouët and Léger argue that the importance of the private sector in France has been consistently underestimated, since 28% of any given generation of pupils experience both sectors at some stage in their schooling. More and more parents avail themselves of the choice available to them, which blurs and weakens the theoretically strict zoning procedures of the *carte scolaire*. The private sector is in consequence less socially exclusive than it was. More working-class parents are opting for private schools; at the same time, more *cadres supérieurs* are placing their children in State schools.

The choices described in this study take place in a system which necessarily propels the public sector into competition with the private. Whether that competition was deliberately planned or whether the rules of the competition are fair are additional issues. As early as 1982, Ballion was urging that the same liberties should be accorded to the public sector as were already enjoyed by their private counterparts.[23] Since those words were written, the State sector has moved to modify some of its habits and procedures in a more 'private' direction (see below). It has done so hesitatingly and not always coherently, and within the framework of a commitment to administrative decentralisation much broader than the educational sector alone.

Thus the way in which (private, Catholic) yeast works on (public, secular) dough is quite complex and elusive in respect of the structure of schooling and parental attitudes to this. The structural impact of the *loi Debré* has been multi-faceted: it has been unintended – a by-product of the Act rather than a conscious plan to modify State schools by providing competition for them; it has been delayed and long-term, with a marked increase (according to Langouët and Léger) from the mid-1980s, perhaps as a result of the huge publicity of 1981–84; it has not been driven by any explicit free-market or Hayekian ideology, which has only recently crept into French discussion of education policy;[24] it has been tempered by the strength of the central State in France, by the solidity and durability of the normative legislation and by the status of teachers as tenured *fonctionnaires*.

PRIVATE TO PUBLIC: THE COPYING HYPOTHESIS

The argument of the previous section suggests that the main impact on public education of the post-1959 renewal of Catholic education has been through the legitimation and strengthening of choice. Sooner or later, choice brings in its train shifts in the internal and external 'economy' of schools. Choice is the main active ingredient in the 'yeast' of Catholic schooling. Choice is primary and concrete changes which flow from choice are, I suggest, secondary in character. There are at least three rather obvious ways in which the minority Catholic sector appears to have directly affected the majority public sector. These are, first, the machinery of school government; secondly, the role of the head teacher; and, thirdly, the emergence of the school development plan, or *projet d'établissement*.

I have discussed French school government at length elsewhere,[25] and argued that the Catholic idea of *la communauté éducative* and its institutional expression in committees and elsewhere was in a sense available and ready for adaptation into the public sector after the crisis of 1968. More recently, a concerted campaign has been evident to train and retrain heads in the realities of formulating a school policy and seeking support for it from consumers – in practice, parents.[26] A central plank of such a policy is a *projet d'établissement* which every school is required to produce by the *loi d'orientation* of 1989.[27]

It is not the task of this chapter to discuss these developments in detail. I would suggest, however, that they may represent not so much a straight copying from private to public, as natural consequences (within the overall constraints of the French bureaucratic structure) of the introduction of choice – and hence, logically, of greater school autonomy and the possibility of distinctive 'school climates', 'managerial styles', and so on. The process of innovation may arise largely *within* the public sector, yet be influenced more by earlier generic decisions than by the ready availability of concrete alternative models. More research is needed. It is regrettable that it was rare to link the two systems in serious academic study until the mid-1980s.[28]

THE RENEWED SECULAR DEBATE

The 1981–84 confrontation probably had a direct impact on family choices simply by bringing into public consciousness an area of the education system customarily seen as separate and inaccessible. Another set of direct influences may be observed in the renewal of a national debate on *laïcité*. The secular basis of State education in France is deeply rooted in French history, especially in the Revolution and the nineteenth century, and is an extremely complex issue, philosophically, politically and educationally.[29]

A good starting-point for a fuller account of recent interactions between Catholic education and *laïcité* would be Vandermeersch's 1981 article 'Laïcité 1881–1981' (the author is a well-known Jesuit educationalist, writing in this case in the premier intellectual journal of the Jesuits, *Études*).[30] Vandermeersch describes the situation as he sees it immediately after the Socialist victory of May 1981. He describes a national system divided into secular and Catholic camps, each frozen in principled but abstract opposition to the other, and prevented by this paralysis from engaging seriously with fresh and urgent educational problems. Upon both parties he urges a profound attitude change, which can come about only by considering without *parti pris* the concrete needs of families, teachers and children (ibid.,

p. 339). He warns against the dangers of using ideological confrontation to avoid the more painful and demanding task of attempting concrete change in real schools and real classrooms (ibid., p. 340).

The 1981–84 confrontation seems to have brought about at least some of the 'unfreezing' which Vandermeersch called for. I have already commented on the greater confidence and serenity on the Catholic side, whose publicity and ideological self-justification in the 1990s are markedly less shrill and aggressive than in the Catholic ghetto evoked by Simone de Beauvoir in her account of growing up as 'une jeune fille rangée' in the 1920s. But on the secular side, lacking the external impetus which the Catholics had of the post-war crisis and the post-Debré reorganisation, the movement has been altogether more abrupt and more dramatic. It is as though the shock of discovering in the early 1980s that the forces of religion were still alive and well, and certainly not a political or intellectual pushover, compelled a serious review of the themes and conclusions of organised *laïcité*. By that I do not mean that secularists have turned to Catholicism, or come to doubt that they are in the van of progress. The *Ligue de l'enseignement*, the historic bastion of secularist thinking and activism, with deep roots in the teaching profession in the public sector,[31] responded to the 1984 settlement by starting to consider seriously the role of religion in society and in individuals' lives. A network of local discussion groups, the *cercles Diderot*, sprang up under the aegis of the *Ligue*. They focused on educational questions which previously had hardly surfaced, or been restricted to relatively peripheral areas of intellectual debate, inhabited largely by progressive Catholics like Vandermeersch.

The questions which then emerged across the media and in more specialist writing began to probe quite deeply into the basic assumptions of democracy and education in the late twentieth century. Was a curriculum which excluded all reference to religious influence or religious experience biased, partial, even undemocratic? Should State schools teach not religion or religious education, but the history of religions?[32] Was it part of the State school's remit to teach morality?[33] If the consensual morality incorporated into the curriculum by Jules Ferry in the 1880s now seemed outmoded, what might be put in its place? How should the secular school respond to Islam, in a society where many pupils are from Muslim families, and many others are from families of *colons* who fled from North Africa a generation ago, where militant forms of Islam are widely publicised and feared, and where thinking people are acutely aware of the travails of Algeria just across the Mediterranean?[34] Such questions are quite widely discussed and researched by educationalists in the UK, and there is a long-standing and extensive literature relating to religious and moral education, multi-cultural and anti-racist approaches to schooling, and reflected in established scholarly and professional journals such as the *Journal of Moral Education* and the *British Journal of Religious Education*. In France, on the other hand, the strength of the secularist paradigm, and perhaps also the half-conscious belief that French civilisation is in some sense norm-giving and self-evidently progressive, that 'France incarnates precisely that moral ideal that all nations should obey',[35] has tended to limit discussion of alternative social, cultural and ethical norms.

This is no longer the case. There is now a plethora of books and articles discussing such questions. There are still vigorous polemic defences of strict *laïcité* in the late-nineteenth-century style,[36] but most of the flood of new writing represents a determined attempt to rethink the status quo. Guy Coq, writing from a Protestant background, is a prolific contributor at all levels of debate. He argues that Christianity, having withdrawn from its traditional cultural dominance ('la chrétienté est devenue impossible'), must now seek 'une capacité de s'investir dans la culture humaine'.[37] In the same spirit, Baubérot argues that the successive compromises of the Napoleonic Concordat of 1801, and the separation of Churches and State in 1905, must now be replaced by a new 'pacte'.[38] This will take serious account of the fact that religion in various forms has survived in human consciousness and in the nation. Islam, as well as Catholicism, must be seen as a valid contributor. Such analyses evoke in breadth and depth all the themes sketched in this chapter on the narrower topic of Catholic schooling.

It would be simplistic to ascribe this change to the events of 1981–84 alone. During the 1970s, some were thinking along more open and pluralist lines, and some of the intellectual inheritance of the 1990s can be traced back to 1968 and beyond. It is plain also that the breaking of the traditional dual opposition of secular–Catholic by the more complex tripartism of secular–Catholic–Muslim has had a real impact on the way people feel and think about religion and religious passions in modern societies. To the Anglo-Saxon observer, it is also obvious that most of the current thinking in France, secular or Catholic, is characteristically Gallic in style: there is much stress on philosophical principles and little on classroom practice; there is an oddly tentative and abstract approach to moral education and little or no awareness of 'Anglo-Saxon' work on the components of moral choices and moral behaviour and how those might be related to teaching, little use even of Piaget's research. Even so, it seems beyond doubt that some sort of intellectual log-jam was cleared in the 1980s; and it is a reasonable inference that one of the major factors in breaking that log-jam was the (apparently mindless?) resistance of the Catholic schools system to their incorporation into the public sector.

This ferment on the secular side is reflected in the vast range of opinion on the Catholic side. The point has already been made, but it is worth repeating because the *image* of monolithic orthodoxy remains very strong. Its strength is partly a function of history, and is derived from an earlier period when Catholic schooling was the mechanism par excellence for promoting and protecting a unified and clearly articulated world-view. But the image is strong, too, because it corresponds to the needs of Catholic officialdom and the hierarchy (and ultimately to the needs of a conservative Pope) to demonstrate that the official machinery is in control, and that the message Catholic schools promote is unambiguous.

The reality, however, is different from the image. As in State schools, the extent to which a more or less democratic central authority can really control thoughts, motivations and classroom interactions is quite limited. The impact of schools on religious allegiances must be uncertain and unpredictable. The formal presentation of Catholic education reflects that uncertainty in its theology and vocabulary. A hundred years ago, the rhetoric was one of proclamation and certainty; now the talk is all of presence, freedom and service.

AN ALTERNATIVE APPROACH: THE *ÉQUIPES ENSEIGNANTES*

So far, this chapter has concentrated on the official, mainstream definition of the Catholic presence in education in a secular society. This is essentially institutional in character. Catholic values are sustained and promoted through a network of 'Catholic schools', a point which seems so self-evident as hardly to be worth remark. We now turn, however, to a sector of Catholic opinion which dissents from that definition. The number of people holding these distinctly different views is not large, but their opinions are sufficiently coherent and challenging to remind us of two important aspects of our topic which it is easy to overlook: the vast range of opinion within contemporary French Catholicism, and the contingent character of the impressive and durable apparatus of official Catholic schooling in late-twentieth-century France.

The group called, rather ambiguously, the *Équipes enseignantes* (teaching teams) has about three hundred and fifty paid-up members; 90% are teachers in all sectors of compulsory education. They have been in existence since the early 1940s, based in a house in Paris. They have extensive contacts with like-minded Catholics, especially educators, throughout the world, with a particular emphasis on the Third World. They issue a regular journal, *Partie prenante*, and have close links also with a specifically Third World-oriented Catholic group, *Dialogue et coopération*. They are decisively on the progressive wing of French Catholicism: the topics discussed in their journal and at meetings include worker-priests, increased lay participation, concern for the poor, a more reverent approach to the environment and disquiet about the traditional role of women in the Church. But the concern here is not to give an in-depth analysis of this group, but rather to summarise their views of the theme of this chapter. *Équipes enseignantes* agrees with the mainstream Catholic view that the 'dough' to be permeated and transformed is secular society, but it differs from the mainstream view in two ways. First, it sees the agents of change, the 'yeast', as being not institutions, but individuals: teacher members of the *Équipes* (the great majority) see their essential Christian duty as being to work in the public sector, not in a separate Catholic system. Secondly, the *Équipes* take a distinctly more positive view of *laïcité* than does mainstream Catholicism, and believes that the Church has much to learn from *laïcité* and from the pluralist world in which Christians live and work. A poem published as an editorial in the group's journal in 1987 draws a distinction between two types of faith: one an 'indoor', cosy, sheltered faith; the other an 'outdoor' faith, nourished by its struggle to survive in an apparently hostile environment, and trying to formulate 'une théologie de la laïcité'.[39] Beneath the poem is printed a brief prose summary of the movement's purpose: to be 'témoins à la laïcité dans l'Église, témoins à l'Église dans la laïcité'.[40] In such formulae, as in the poem, one senses the emotional charge behind the analysis. But there is also an intellectual substance. Most of this issue of *Partie prenante* is devoted to the 'théologie de la laïcité', which is seen as developing from Liberation Theology – almost a French, First World version of a view of the world which is most associated with Latin America and Asia.[41] The Christian should be beside the poor, the disinherited, the agnostic,[42] not bestowing charity and correct doctrine from above but living with, and learning from, individuals and society as they actually are. The 'théologie de la laïcité' number of the journal itself exemplifies this position by including an interview with the national secretary of the *Ligue de l'enseignement*.[43] A collection of anonymous testimonies allows members of the *Équipes* to spell out how a closed and militant Church ('hors de l'Église point de salut') produces a closed and militant *laïcité*, and vice versa, and how truth comes closer as individuals engage seriously and openly with people holding different views.[44] Another writer speaks of the 'still small voice of God' within the secular classroom – both on the days when things are going smoothly, but also on those days when the teacher struggles to control the children (ibid., p. 56).

Within such a perspective, *laïcité* comes to be seen not as an enemy to be fought by Catholics, but as 'la fille aînée de l'Église',[45] as a natural and proper product of Christian values and the Christian affirmation of the autonomy of the individual believer. In this perspective, 'ghetto Catholicism' becomes an aberration. An open, pluralist democracy is seen both as a proper environment for religious faith to flourish, and a logical product of that faith.

Such opinions are neither merely theoretical nor easily reached. The origins of the *Équipes* go back to the years of Occupation, Resistance and the mass murder of Jews and other 'undesirables'.[46] It was a period when young Christian teachers of a progressive inclination (the group was originally called *Jeunes enseignants*) readily found themselves out of sympathy with the episcopate, and motivated to band together in informal self-support groups on the margins of the official Church. After the Liberation, the *Équipes* profited from the national mood and the inclination, in some quarters at least, to break down old barriers and outmoded assumptions. The survival and stability of the movement over more than half a century shows that it meets real and continuing needs, and is driven not only by the desire to make intellectual sense of the outwardly contradictory position of Catholic teachers in secular schools, but by members' emotional needs as well.

In the publications of the *Équipes*, in their style as well as in their substance, the tension between intellect and emotion is apparent. It can be seen in the debate at the end of the 1980s on *l'affaire du foulard*: the exclusion from State schools, in the name of *laïcité*, of Muslim girls who insisted on retaining the headscarves required by their religion. The contributions from *équipiers* published in 1990 demonstrate an intelligent appreciation of the complexity of accommodating to a culturally and religiously plural society.[47] They show also the extent to which a large and visible Islamic presence in France, and its supposed links to *intégrisme* (militant and extremist versions of Islam), have fuelled passions which may be dangerous to both *laïcité* and democracy.

The *Équipes enseignantes* are not a large group, nor a prestigious one, but they take their 'yeast' function seriously. This can be seen both in their daily work as teachers in public schools and in the links they establish with non-Catholic associations and individuals. Their existence interestingly throws into contrast the more centralist, consensus-seeking style and theology of mainstream institutional Catholic education. The group shows that the style is by no means uncritically accepted by all Catholics; and that the theology which underlies and justifies the style is a social and intellectual compromise arrived at at a particular moment (post-Vatican II, post-1968) and in response to a particular constellation of forces (1959, 1981– 84). In that sense the Church does not differ from other human institutions.

A BALANCE-SHEET

It was stated earlier that official Catholic education – the central apparatus housed in the rue Saint-Jacques – has since 1959 (and with especial vigour since 1984) evolved its own language to describe, motivate and legitimise its own actions and those of the schools operating under its aegis. As in the case of the *Équipes enseignantes*, the language it uses incorporates an attitude to the world and, because these are in the last instance religious organisations, a theology.

To the Anglo–Saxon observer, much of the more or less ephemeral material – booklets, fliers, magazines – flowing from the rue Saint-Jacques may seem emptily rhetorical. It depends heavily on words or combinations of words which by constant repetition take on a specialised meaning of their own. 'Communauté éducative' is a good example. Both noun and adjective carry vague but positive connotations: 'communauté' implies togetherness, co-operation, localism; 'éducative' suggests the wider tasks of education beyond the merely cognitive, the development of whole persons, moral as well as intellectual growth.

A dossier prepared by Archbishop Panafieu of Aix-en-Provence on *L'Identité de l'enseignement catholique* sets out to define a number of key terms, including 'communauté éducative'.[48] There are stages in his account where a certain tension may be detected between, on the one hand, a manifest desire to aid 'les plus handicapés' – whose handicap may be social, affective or cultural – and, on the other hand, a view of the school as a 'micro-société', serving the wider society of the nation. The word 'terroir' is used, with its emotional evocation of the rural roots of Catholicism, even of its links with the political Right. 'Communauté' is a label which conveniently combines both support for individual members of the community and a wish to be involved in the collective, namely the State.

The tensions in such writing reflect in part the historical inheritance of French Catholicism. But they also represent a mind trying to engage productively with those tensions and represent them to ordinary intelligent Catholic parents and teachers who are presumably the intended readers. Perhaps the synthesis is not altogether successful, but the attempt seems honourable, even courageous. It certainly reflects a Church, and a school system, a very long way away from the school experienced by Simone de Beauvoir, and still present in the minds of many French people – including, no doubt, many Catholics. Other key terms described and discussed by Archbishop Panafieu include 'caractère propre'. What is specifically Catholic about a school? – quality, openness to the least favoured, openness to the whole nation, culture and faith, *laïcité* ('être présent dans le débat démocratique'), respect for conscience, service to the nation, and so on. Another similar text comes from Archbishop Coffy of Marseille.[49] For him, Catholic education is about 'comprendre'. To search for sense or meaning in one's life means desiring to 'vivre une réalité absente' (ibid., p. 4). The school should help the individual to do that, and in so doing it will begin to renew 'la pensée occidentale, dominée par des athéismes dogmatiques': Marx, Sartre and Camus are cited.

There is no space here to review these arguments in depth, or weigh their effectiveness and impact on the world of unbelievers. But

I want to close by alluding to this body of thinking and writing, because it seems to me that much of what is published about Catholic education in France is restricted to the institutional or political perspective. Even to dip quite superficially into the propaganda (as some would see it) emerging from the rue Saint-Jacques is to be reminded of a number of features of Catholic schooling in contemporary France which are often overlooked: its importance within the total educational provision of the Republic; its importance within French Catholicism (more individuals are in schools than at Sunday mass!); its range and eclecticism; its self-confidence; its distance from its ghetto image; its contribution to a rethinking of the traditional French school by revaluing what in English we label the 'pastoral' aspect of education; its role in focusing post-Vatican II theology in a form which is assimilable by ordinary people.[50]

Whether or not one approves of the particular historical compromise which Catholic schooling represents in late-twentieth-century France, it seems that as yeast it undoubtedly works on the surrounding dough. Its impact is frequently quirky and unpredictable, but it is alive!

NOTES

1. *Comité national de l'enseignement catholique*, 1993. This is the source of all the statistics in this section to which no other source is assigned.

2. Jean Penef, *Écoles publiques, écoles privées dans l'Ouest, 1880–1950* (Paris: L'Harmattan, 1987).

3. Gabriel Langouët and Alain Léger, *École publique ou école privée? Trajectoires et réussites scolaires* (Paris: Faber, 1994), p. 13, p. 26.

4. Bernard Toulemonde, 'Un grand service public ... pluraliste!', *Le Monde de l'éducation*, 226 (1995), 26–29.

5. Marie-Michèle Le Bret and Hervé Boulic, *Choisir une école catholique* (Paris: Centurion, 1990), pp. 46–48. 2,800 francs is roughly £300 at an exchange rate of 9.25 francs to the pound sterling.

6. Ibid., pp. 139–40, pp. 190–95.

7. Gérard Leclerc, *La Bataille de l'école, quinze siècles d'histoire, trois ans de combat* (Paris: Denoël, 1985); Antoine Prost, *Éducation, société et politiques* (Paris: Seuil, 1992).

8. Yves-Marie Labé, 'Privé: la rançon du succès', *Le Monde de l'éducation*, 119 (1985), 74–77.

9. Dominique Julia, *Les Trois Couleurs du tableau noir: la Révolution* (Paris: Éditions Belin, 1981).

10. Nicholas Beattie, *Professional Parents: Parent Participation in Four Western European Countries* (London: Falmer, 1985), pp. 34–35; Le Bret and Boulic, *Choisir une école catholique*, pp. 110–11.

11. Leclerc, *La Bataille de l'école.*

12. Ibid., p. 146.

13. Max Cloupet, 'Bâtir une forme originale d'école', supplement to *Enseignement catholique actualités*, 151 (1990), 2. The 1959 law inaugurated 'contracts of association' between individual Catholic schools and the State.

14. *Comité national de l'enseignement catholique*, 1994.

15. For example, ibid., p. 146.

16. Aline Coutrot, 'La loi scolaire de décembre 1959', *Revue française de science politique*, 13 (1963), 352–88; W.R. Fraser, *Education and Society in Modern France* (London: Routledge & Kegan Paul, 1963); Richard Teese, 'Private Schools in France: Evolution of a System', *Comparative Education Review*, 30 (1986), 247–59.

17. Simone de Beauvoir, *Mémoires d'une jeune fille rangée* (Paris: Gallimard, 1958), pp. 128–29.

18. Nicholas Beattie, 'Interview and *concours*: Teacher Assessment Procedures in England and Wales and France, and What They Mean', *Assessment in Education*, 3 (1996), 9–28.

19. Keith Sharpe, 'An Inspector Calls: An Analysis of Inspection Procedures in French Primary Education', *Compare*, 23 (1993), 263–75; Patricia Broadfoot and Marilyn Osborn, *Perceptions of Teaching: Primary School Teachers in England and France* (London: Cassell, 1993), pp. 39–40.

20. Toulemonde, 'Un grand service public ... pluraliste!', pp. 26–29. See also Bernard Panafieu et al., *L'Enseignement catholique en France, 1989–1990* (Paris: Enseignement Catholique Documents, 1989), p. 2.

21. Langouët and Léger, *École publique ou école privée?*, p. 140.

22. Ibid., p. 47.

23. Quoted in Leclerc, *La Bataille de l'école*, p. 158.

24. Robert Ballion, *Les Consommateurs d'école: stratégies éducatives des familles* (Paris: Stock, 1982) perhaps marks the start of this process.

25. Beattie, 'Interview and *concours*', pp. 27–63.

26. François-Régis Guillaume and Bruno Maresca, 'Les Chefs d'établissement et l'autonomie', *Éducation et formations*, 35 (1993), 43–51.

27. Jean-Pierre Obin and François Cros, *Projet d'établissement* (Paris: Hachette, 1991).

28. Lucie Tanguy, 'L'État et l'école: l'école privée en France', *Revue française de sociologie*, 13 (1972), 47–63, is an interesting exception to this generalisation.

29. Julia, *Les Trois Couleurs*; Christian Nique and Claude Lelièvre, *La République n'éduquera plus. La Fin du mythe Ferry* (Paris: Plon, 1993).

30. Edmond Vandermeersch, 'Laïcité 1881–1981', *Études*, 355 (1981), 325–40.

31. Katherine Auspitz, *The Radical Bourgeoisie. The Ligue de l'enseignement and the Origins of the Third Republic, 1866–1885* (Cambridge: Cambridge University Press, 1982).

32. Danièle Hervieu-Léger, *La Religion au lycée. Conférences au lycée Buffon, 1989–1990* (Paris: Cerf, 1990); Philippe Joutard, 'Enseigner l'histoire des religions', *Éducation et pédagogies*, 7 (1990), 80–87.

33. Louis Legrand, 'Enseigner la morale aujourd'hui?', *Revue française de pédagogie*, 97 (1991), 53–64.

34. Jacqueline Gautherin, 'La Laïcité: une idée neuve', *Revue française de pédagogie*, 97 (1991), 109–36.

35. Antoine Prost, *In the Wake of War: 'Les Anciens Combattants' and French Society* (Oxford: Berg, 1992), p. 90.

36. Denis Parigaux, *François Mitterrand: la divine comédie ou la laïcité trahie* (Saint-Maur: Fédération des cercles de défense laïque, 1993) presents a lively summary of the position argued by the *Fédération des cercles de défense laïque* and its journal *Laïcité*.

37. Guy Coq, *Démocratie, religion, éducation* (Paris: Mame, 1993), p. 214.

38. Jean Baubérot, *Vers un nouveau pacte laïque* (Paris: Seuil, 1990).

39. *Il y avait une foi* is a play on words: if *foi* ends in an *s*, the phrase means 'Once upon a time'.

40. Anon., *Partie prenante*, 4 (1987), 3.

41. Marie-Claude Beauvallet and Marie-Claire David, 'De la théologie de la libération à la théologie de la laïcité', *Partie prenante*, 4 (1987), 10–11.

42. Jean-François Six, 'Contact et dialogue avec l'agnostique', *Partie prenante*, 4 (1987), 32.

43. Michel Morineau, 'Laïcité 2000', *Partie prenante*, 4 (1987), 41–42.

44. Anon., 'Plantés en terre laïque', *Partie prenante*, 4 (1987), 54–60.

45. Georges Levesque, 'Laïcité, incroyance et foi', *Partie prenante*, 1 (1986), 14–17 (p. 15).

46. Hélène Prouët and Jacques Malandain, '1942–1992: 50 ans', *Partie prenante*, 3 (1992), 1–8.

47. Gabrielle Gaspard, 'La Laïcité et le voile', *Partie prenante*, 3 (1990), 8–10.

48. Bernard Panafieu, *Identité de l'enseignement catholique* (Paris: Secrétariat général de l'enseignement catholique, 1990).

49. Robert Coffy, *Réflexion théologique sur le sens* (Paris: Enseignement Catholique Documents, 1991).

50. Hans Küng, *On being a Christian* (Glasgow: Collins, 1978), pp. 598–601.

10

Les femmes catholiques: Entre Église et société

Evelyne Diébolt

INTRODUCTION

Les femmes, plus attirées que les hommes par un engagement dans l'Église, représentent en 1900 environ 70% des pratiquants.[1] Elles sont présentes sous la forme d'adhésions massives aux ligues féminines, à des associations, aux mouvements de jeunesse, au syndicalisme. Elles y tiennent un rôle de moins en moins subalterne, ont des sphères d'influence de plus en plus visibles,[2] même si, au début, leurs initiatives étaient énoncées ou reprises par des hommes. Lentement et irréversiblement au cours du vingtième siècle, les femmes catholiques ont pris de l'importance tant dans le fonctionnement des paroisses que dans la société civile.

Il y a lieu de réévaluer le jugement porté sur les associations chrétiennes qui longtemps n'ont été étudiées que par leurs sympathisants, délaissées par les historiens et négligées par les féministes, qui les classaient d'emblée dans le champ de la réaction. Une nouvelle approche d'origine anglo-saxonne parle de 'féminisme social' et souligne la portée qu'ont pu avoir ces regroupements.[3] Les femmes catholiques ont su mettre à profit les tâches que les hommes leur confiaient, et petit à petit elles sortent de la 'sphère privée'. Ce mouvement incontestable apporte des éléments de réponse à la question ouverte d'Émile Poulat, 'comment les femmes ont-elles su échapper à l'influence du clergé auquel on les disait particulièrement soumises?'[4]

C'est tout au long du vingtième siècle que, au sein de l'Église et dans la société française, les femmes catholiques voient s'accroître leur importance. Devenues petit à petit un maillon essentiel de la divulgation de la foi, elles font évoluer la condition des femmes françaises, en accompagnant parallèlement une certaine émancipation féminine. Elles s'émancipent personnellement à travers une prise de responsabilité sur le terrain, elles gagnent de l'assurance et prennent de l'importance.

LES FEMMES DANS L'ÉGLISE

Pratiquantes

Durant tout le vingtième siècle, les femmes sont plus pratiquantes que les hommes. Le dimorphisme sexuel de la pratique religieuse est plus accentué en 1900 qu'en 1950.[5] La pratique religieuse dominicale des Français(es) est relativement stable entre 1930 et 1960. Avec de très fortes inégalités régionales, on compte 30% de pratiquants sur l'ensemble de la population française qui se répartit de la façon suivante: deux tiers de femmes, un tiers d'hommes. L'effondrement de la pratique religieuse ne se manifeste que dans les quarante dernières années du vingtième siècle, des années 1960 à nos jours. Aujourd'hui la pratique religieuse se situe autour de 10%. Les femmes pratiquantes sont toujours deux fois plus nombreuses que les hommes.

Paroissiennes

Plusieurs aspects de la vie d'une paroisse étaient susceptibles d'être confiées aux femmes: l'accueil et la préparation aux sacrements, la direction des chants, l'accès à la gestion de la paroisse, une donnée importante depuis la séparation des Églises et de l'État en 1905. Ce n'est qu'à partir du concile en 1962 que les femmes s'occupent des lectures, du service de la messe, de l'animation des funérailles, du port de l'Eucharistie aux malades. L'évolution de la terminologie souligne l'élargissement des fonctions: d''aides aux prêtres' en 1946, elles deviennent des 'assistantes paroissiales' en 1960. On s'achemine vers l'animation d'*Assemblées dominicales en l'absence de prêtre* (ADAP). Dans certains diocèses, aux côtés des religieux elles se voient même confier des ensembles de paroisses. Mais les femmes sont aussi présentes dans les instances où se prennent les décisions dans la vie de l'Église: conseils pastoraux des paroisses, conseils diocésains, commissions nationales et synodes diocésains.[6] Quant aux sacrements, peuvent-elles les donner? Est-ce souhaitable? Comme s'interroge un historien des religions: 'Ordonner des femmes, est-ce partager un pouvoir? L'exercice d'une responsabilité dans l'Église est-il signe de promotion?' Georgette Blaquière dans *La Grâce d'être femme* (1981) considère que le ministère de la femme est vertical, qu'elle est prophète.[7] Et c'est la position des femmes attirées par le Renouveau charismatique qui prône le retour au diaconat féminin des cinq premiers siècles de l'Église. Un certain renouveau de la présence des femmes dans l'Église est donc en marche depuis un siècle, un renouveau dans la diffusion de la foi au quotidien, autant que dans l'approche de cette foi.

Catéchistes

Les lois de la République de 1881–82, en établissant un enseignement public gratuit et obligatoire, dissocient l'enseignement religieux de l'instruction primaire. L'instituteur ne fait donc plus fonction de catéchiste et la loi interdit aux prêtres de pénétrer dans les écoles publiques. C'est au prêtre, dans son église, de catéchiser. Et là, des femmes surveillent et encadrent, font revoir les leçons.[8] Dès 1882, deux jeunes filles, Mlle Sorin de Bonnes et Mlle Chanon, se portent volontaires pour rassembler des femmes disponibles et dévouées afin d'aider les prêtres à catéchiser les enfants. Mgr d'Hulst, recteur de l'Université catholique de Paris, les encourage et accepte la présidence de l'*Association de l'œuvre des catéchistes volontaires* (AOCV) (1886). Elles obtiendront une reconnaissance ecclésiastique lorsqu'en 1893 Léon XIII érigera cette œuvre en archiconfrérie. D'une offre de service facultative, qui répondait à un besoin conjoncturel, les femmes sont devenues indispensables: en 1905, Pie X demande la création dans chaque paroisse d'une AOCV. Et les femmes se mobilisent rapidement. En 1908, lors du premier congrès de l'association, les femmes catéchistes sont déjà vingt mille, elles s'occupent de cent mille enfants. En 1912, il existe dans toute la France soixante-treize confréries diocésaines.[9] Elles reçoivent une formation pour mieux enseigner le catéchisme, mais compétence et soumission ne font pas bon ménage, et une partie du clergé voit très vite le danger de les former.[10] Dès les années 1920–30, les femmes s'adaptent aux réalités rencontrées, puis prennent des initiatives, inventant des méthodes d'apprentissage. Entre 1960 et 1990 elles accèdent à la direction de la catéchèse. Leur présence à la tête des services diocésains de catéchèse est exponentielle: de quinze en

1982, elles sont trente en 1992. En 1984, quelques six cents catéchistes professionnelles rémunérées sont associées à la formation des
catéchistes à différents niveaux.[11]

En faisant de la catéchèse, les femmes se sont formées, et ont
retrouvé un rôle essentiel dans l'Église à l'image des Saintes femmes
de l'Évangile qui portèrent la bonne parole. Cette montée en présence
et en nombre, alliée à une prise de conscience, a pu leur donner plus
d'assurance. Les femmes ont donc progressivement transformé la
structure catéchètique dans laquelle elles agissaient, mais leur
rapport avec le clergé et l'Église reste ambigu.

Théologiennes

Avant 1947, dans les facultés de théologie, les femmes admises à
suivre les cours n'avaient pas le droit de passer les examens, ni
d'obtenir des diplômes correspondants. Les temps changent, en
1980, 40% des effectifs des cinq facultés de théologie françaises sont
des femmes, passant maîtrises ou doctorats. Dans le comité de
rédaction de la revue *Communio*, Jacqueline d'Ussel et Marguerite
Léna, agrégée de philosophie, religieuses de la communauté de
Saint-François-Xavier, se retrouvent aux côtés d'intellectuels et de
philosophes. Elles participent à la constitution d'une nouvelle génération de théologiens laïcs parmi lesquels les femmes sont présentes.
Les choses avancent-elles vers l'éclosion d'une pensée théologique
féminine? S'agit-il d'une reconnaissance de la spiritualité des femmes
et d'un début de vraie coexistence?

Religieuses

Après une hausse vigoureuse des effectifs jusqu'au milieu du dix-
neuvième siècle, la présence congréganiste féminine se stabilise, puis
subit un net déclin au début du vingtième siècle, lequel ne sera
jamais enrayé (vieillissement des congrégations religieuses, multiplication des départs, raréfaction des vocations). L'Église avait d'abord
été atteinte par des mesures législatives anticléricales. La loi de 1901
sur le droit d'association affaiblit déjà les grands ordres religieux.
Mais par ailleurs, cette loi permit à de nombreuses femmes catholiques de s'organiser et de se réunir. D'un effet négatif – peut-être
escompté – est résultée une formidable dynamique d'action pour les
femmes catholiques, comme nous allons le développer ci-dessous.[12]

La loi de 1904, supprimant le droit d'enseigner pour les congrégations, entraîne l'exil ou la sécularisation de ces ordres. Sur quatre cents congrégations féminines qui demandèrent le droit d'exercer, quatre-vingt-six seulement furent satisfaites. Quatre mille femmes se dispersèrent. Les religieuses françaises, en nombre important dans les missions,[13] évangélisant les pays d'outre-mer et diffusant la culture française, développent des échanges avec les cultures des pays où elles vivent, et qu'elles étudient. Elles écrivent des livres qui modifient parfois le sort des population locales, en infléchissant la législation de ces pays (en 1939, la loi Diouf et le décret Mandel qui permettent aux femmes africaines de se libérer du mari que l'on voulait leur imposer contre leur gré).

De cette présence française va résulter une réflexion, ponctuée par les interventions de Marie de l'Assomption (Marie Leroy-Ladurie) ou du père Jean Daniélou, lequel s'interroge en 1955, l'Occident a-t-il encore un devoir missionnaire? En 1969, la revue *Axes* verra le jour, centrée sur le thème Mission et Colonisation.[14] Les religieuses de terrain ont joué un rôle pilote dans l'approche des cultures d'outre-mer.

Militantes associatives

Il me semble nécessaire dans cette première partie où je souhaite mettre en avant le rôle fédérateur de l'Église pour les femmes de dresser une généalogie des multiples associations dont l'existence et les activités nous apparaissent aujourd'hui aller de soi mais qui, au début du vingtième siècle, étaient tout à fait novatrices. Citons d'abord des œuvres de piété aux effectifs souvent impressionnants: le *Revers*, la *Confrérie des mères chrétiennes*, l'*Apostolat de la prière*, la *Garde d'honneur du Sacré-Cœur* et deux ligues: la *Ligue des femmes françaises* (LFF) et la *Ligue patriotique des Françaises* (LPF) aux sensibilités politiques voisines (la première plus à droite que la seconde) qui eurent un rôle fédérateur majeur. La première fondée à Lyon en septembre 1901, dirigée par Mme Lestra, compte soixante-treize comités départementaux en mai 1902 et elle concentre ses efforts sur les œuvres à caractère religieux.[15] La deuxième née d'une scission d'avec la précédente, balaie un champ de compétences plus sociales. Dès 1914, elle compte 500.000 membres, implantées dans la plupart des diocèses. En 1933, fort d'un effectif de 1.500.000, elle devient la plus grande organisation de femmes de l'entre-deux-guerres. Sa capacité à recruter s'explique en partie par les dizainières (femmes qui ont la responsabilité de recruter puis de rester en contact permanent avec dix autres membres). Des jeunes femmes nobles composent la direction des deux ligues.[16] En 1933 Rome arbitre le différend entre ces deux ligues, en estimant qu'elles doivent fusionner en une ligue féminine d'Action catholique. Devenue en 1945 *Action catholique générale féminine* (ACGF), elle touche deux millions de femmes par son mensuel *L'Écho des Françaises*. Un tel colosse associatif décline dans les années soixante. En 1973, l'ACGF ne compte plus que 82.000 membres pour passer à 25.000 en 1988. Mais entre temps, ses objectifs, de paroissiaux qu'ils étaient au départ, sont devenus ceux d'un mouvement féminin, où les femmes s'engagent dans la vie civique et politique comme le montre la variété des débats au congrès de la Porte de Pantin, qui rassembla cinq mille femmes en 1978.[17]

Parmi d'autres associations nées elles aussi au début de ce siècle, citons, à l'initiative de Mme Henriette Brunhes,[18] la *Ligue sociale d'acheteurs* (LSA), et l'*Action sociale de la femme* (ASF) de Mme Chenu. Si elles rassemblaient moins de membres, elles surent trouver un créneau d'action où elles firent montre d'efficacité.[19] Dans ces mouvements les femmes se rassemblaient, échangeaient des idées et gagnaient en maturité, applicable à un champ de compétence de plus en plus vaste et qui ne néglige pas l'action sociale. Cette dernière constitue la préoccupation dominante d'un autre ensemble d'associations féminines.

Autour de 1900, les œuvres paroissiales deviennent des lieux où les catholiques se replient, en réaction aux attaques de la politique anticléricale du gouvernement de l'époque. C'est au sein de ces œuvres paroissiales – et parfois en marge – que naissent des associations d'action sociale, créées par des femmes d'une grande originalité. L'aspect novateur de leur regard est le garant d'une certaine dynamique, laquelle fait ensuite des émules dans les rangs d'associations plus classiques. Le quatorzième arrondissement de Paris joue un rôle central et exemplaire dans ce mouvement, avec l'abbé Soulange-Bodin qui réunit autour de lui de fortes personnalités masculines tant religieuses que laïques (l'abbé Viollet, de jeunes sillonnistes, des patrons sociaux) et des femmes catholiques pleines d'idées et d'énergie. En 1900, Léonie Chaptal crée de nombreuses associations sises rue Vercingétorix (*Assistance maternelle* et *Infantile de Plaisance*, la *Vie familiale*, la Maison-École d'infirmières ainsi qu'une société coopérative de consommation). Après 1920, seule la Maison-École survit, devenant le prototype de la formation des infirmières françaises et le berceau d'une association professionnelle, l'*Association nationale des infirmières diplômées de l'État français* (ANIDEF).[20] En janvier 1909, l'abbé Soulange-Bodin facilite l'installation d'Andrée Butillard et d'Aimée Novo au 38 de la rue Vercingétorix, qui souhaitent allier plusieurs types d'interventions sociales pour une meilleure efficacité. Andrée Butillard crée en 1911 l'*École normale sociale*, qui a une double vocation: former des syndicalistes et des assistantes sociales.[21] Entre 1919 et 1932, cette école forme surtout des syndicalistes, les premières syndiquées de la *Confédération française des travailleurs chrétiens* (CFTC),[22] avant de se transformer progressivement en école catholique de service social. En 1923, Andrée Butillard fonde aussi l'*Union des auxiliaires sociales* (UAS), association professionnelle pour les assistantes sociales.[23] Et en mars 1925, elle fonde l'*Union féminine civique et sociale* (UFCS) dont elle assure la présidence jusqu'à sa mort. C'est un lieu de formation pour les militantes catholiques qui joue un grand rôle après 1945 dans la formation des conseillères municipales et qui permet ainsi la présence de femmes catholiques dans des débats politiques.[24] L'UFCS se déconfessionalise en 1967.

Quant aux centres sociaux, ils ont vu le jour à côté des œuvres paroissiales, en y collaborant parfois. En 1894, 'l'œuvre de Popincourt', premier 'settlement' français, ouvert par Marie Gahéry, est directement inspirée des settlements anglais et américains. Trois ans plus tard, en 1897, mère Mercédes Le Fer de la Motte, religieuse de Saint Philippe de Néri, associe ses efforts à ceux de Gahéry. Mais très vite les deux femmes se séparent et Gahéry déménage pour continuer son œuvre – qui s'appelle l'*Union familiale*.[25] Quant à mère Mercédes Le Fer de la Motte, elle prend la tête du mouvement des maisons sociales (ou centres sociaux) jusqu'au jour où Marie-Jeanne Bassot, une de ses émules, se retrouve internée par ses parents, mécontents de son adhésion à ce mouvement. Un procès retentissant s'ouvre en mars–avril 1909 – Bassot attaque ses propres parents pour séquestration arbitraire! Ce procès provoque un scandale tel que les maisons sociales ferment et Mercédes Le Fer de la Motte se retire près de Douarnenez. Mais Marie-Jeanne Bassot, secondée par Mathilde Girault, loue en octobre 1909 une modeste maison ouvrière à Levallois-Perret, qui devient la Résidence sociale de Levallois-Perret, une nouvelle maison sociale.[26] Installée en quartier ouvrier, tous les aspects d'une vie familiale ouvrière sont considérés: activités intellectuelles et artistiques (cercle d'études, musique, théâtre, cinéma), enseignement ménager, jardin d'enfants, éducation physique, éducation sanitaire, apprentissage de la vie associative et coopérative de produits de consommation. Un tel déploiement de services fait école: en 1922 on compte cinquante-huit centres sociaux, en 1929 ils sont cent trente-deux. La crise de 1929 et la guerre mettent un frein à l'expansion de cette initiative, mais dans les années cinquante, avec le développement des banlieues, le nombre des centres sociaux explose à nouveau. Aujourd'hui un million de personnes les fréquentent en France. Les femmes catholiques ont créé des laboratoires de recherche sociale, cherchant, essayant, développant tous azimuts afin de parfaire l'efficacité de leur action sur le terrain.

Militantes des mouvements spécialisés

Dans les mouvements spécialisés, la naissance de la branche féminine est toujours postérieure à la création de l'organisation masculine. Peu d'études sur ces mouvements permettent de savoir si les cadres féminins étaient des copies des structures masculines, ou si les femmes disposaient de caractéristiques de fonctionnement qui leur étaient propres. Ces mouvements spécialisés se proposaient de ramener à Dieu le milieu social dans lequel ils s'implantaient. La *Jeunesse ouvrière chrétienne féminine* (JOCF) naît en 1928, la *Jeunesse étudiante chrétienne féminine* (JECF)[27] en 1929, la *Jeunesse agricole chrétienne féminine* (JACF) en 1933 puis la *Jeunesse indépendante chrétienne féminine* (JICF) en 1936. En 1937, le journal *Jeunesse ouvrière féminine* tire à 100.000 exemplaires.[28] En 1939, la JACF compte neuf cents sections, le journal *Jeunesse agricole féminine* tire à 86.000 exemplaires. La *Ligue ouvrière chrétienne* (LOC), née en 1935, est le premier mouvement d'action catholique à pratiquer la mixité mais les jeunes travailleuses se prennent en main et éprouvent vite le besoin de se retrouver entre elles. Le *Mouvement familial d'Action catholique ouvrière* est créé en 1935 par d'ancien(ne)s militant(e)s JOC/F, rejoints par d'autres de la LOC. Le *Mouvement populaire des familles* (MPF) milite en faveur d'un épanouissement de la femme en dehors de chez elle.[29] Déconfessionalisé en 1949, celui-ci donne naissance de façon plus ou moins directe à un grand nombre d'organisations diverses et bien connues: la *Confédération syndicale des familles* (CSF), la *Confédération syndicale du cadre de vie* (CSCV), *Culture et liberté*, et, pour parti, le *Parti socialiste unifié* (PSU). Le

MPF, devenu *Mouvement de libération du peuple* (MLP) en 1950, se divise dès 1951 et donne naissance au *Mouvement de libération ouvrière* (MLO). En 1957, le MLP se fond dans l'*Union de la gauche socialiste*. Entre les deux guerres, toutes ces organisations contribuèrent à la renaissance d'une 'élite' féminine catholique, issue d'horizons professionnels divers. Cette élite, pour se renouveler de façon efficace, avait besoin de se tourner vers la jeunesse.[30]

Animatrices de la jeunesse

Le catholicisme, en allant volontiers au-delà de la catéchèse, a développé l'encadrement des jeunes, déclinant sur une très large palette les sources de loisirs. Nous avons choisi d'en présenter quatre qui ont fait l'objet d'études approfondies et, pour certaines, récentes.

Les Noëllistes, nées en 1902 d'une revue de la Bonne Presse, préparaient les jeunes filles après leurs études à jouer un rôle futur dans leur paroisse. Ce mouvement comptait en 1921 200.000 adhérentes.[31] Les fédérations diocésaines aux noms pleins de poésie, *Edelweiss* ou *Fleurs d'Armor*, s'employaient à mettre en place un modèle de culture féminine, pétrie de valeurs tant religieuses que profanes.[32] Les patronages catholiques se multiplient également, sous la direction de Mme Duhamel, secrétaire générale de l'archiconfrérie des patronages. Les patronages de jeunes filles reliés à l'œuvre générale des patronages sont au nombre de 1.810 en 1914 et totalisent 137.000 membres. Mme Duhamel est par ailleurs à l'origine d'une grande aventure en mai 1923, la naissance d'un mouvement de jeunesse féminin et catholique: la *Fédération des Guides*.[33] Elle fut contactée en 1922 par deux protestantes, Marie Diémer et Renée de Montmort, propriétaire du château d'Argeronne en Normandie où cette dernière avait déjà accueilli des guides étrangères et des éclaireuses françaises (mouvement de jeunesse protestant). Les *Guides de France* furent dès l'origine un mouvement national mais agissant dans le cadre du diocèse placé sous l'autorité de l'évêque du lieu. Mme Duhamel n'a pas eu au-dessus d'elle un aumônier mais était en contact direct avec l'évêché, voire avec Rome. Mme Duhamel fait sa promesse de chef-guide, bénie par le cardinal Dubois. Elle participe en août 1923 au deuxième camp international d'Argeronne chez Renée de Montmort, où elle reçoit la caution de la protestante Lady Baden-Powell. En 1936, Mme de Kerraoul, nièce du maréchal Lyautey, est élue présidente et succède à Mme Duhamel. Le mouvement, dès ses débuts, fit la part belle aux évocations de la pure foi catholique. Cela se manifeste dans les pèlerinages, notamment dans les lieux marqués par la présence de Jeanne d'Arc, patronne des Guides. Marie Diémer, convertie au catholicisme en 1924, avait su adapter les rites initiatiques du scoutisme au guidisme. Les activités proposées à la jeune guide répondaient au besoin de mettre en place, par une didactique ludique, un système de valeurs correspondant à une image de la femme moderne, image faite d'enthousiasme, de générosité et d'action. Il était à l'époque tout à fait nouveau que l'on ne dissocie pas action et féminité. C'est tout naturellement que la jeune catholique, devenue adulte et ayant adhéré à des organisations d'encadrement de l'enfance ou de l'adolescence, rejoint les rangs d'associations catholiques. Soit de façon ponctuelle dans les paroisses, soit de façon permanente dans des associations, ligues ou mouvements. L'Église a été un lieu de rassemblement des femmes, leur offrant des structures d'accueil en fonction des différents âges. De là, les femmes catholiques s'investissent dans une vie sociale et publique.

LES FEMMES DANS LA CITÉ

L'éducation des femmes par elles-mêmes et pour elles-mêmes

Elles se sont formées, puis ont formé d'autres femmes, car, mieux conscientes de leurs besoins, elles étaient plus à même d'adapter seules leurs aspirations à de nouvelles méthodes d'éducation, à une ouverture sur le monde – celui de la culture notamment. Et les femmes se sont engagées sur des terrains très divers. Il y eut par exemple des conférences, des congrès, des enquêtes sociales, destinés à leur donner une culture, une opinion, un jugement sur des sujets d'actualité. Ce sont quelques-uns d'entre eux que nous nous proposons d'évoquer, toujours en montrant leur adaptabilité, une clef majeure de la fantastique ascension des femmes du vingtième siècle. Leur éducation put se faire dans les salons entre 1900 et 1920, car ensuite les salons sociaux disparaissent. Certains furent particulièrement significatifs. Citons celui de Mme Jeanne Chenu[34] qui, dès 1900, organise des conférences sociales pour les femmes du monde. C'est ici que va voir le jour l'association l'*Action sociale de la femme*.

Dans le salon de la baronne Piérard à Paris, se rencontraient mère Mercédes Le Fer de la Motte, Apolline de Gourlet, Lucie Felix-Faure Goyau, Marie Gahéry et de nombreux catholiques sociaux. C'est chez elle que le courant des Maisons sociales s'était constitué, avait mûri et pris de l'ampleur. Ou encore, les conférences de sensibilisation au guidisme: dès 1922, des réunions étaient organisées au Lyceum club,[35] à l'initiative de Renée de Montmort. Elles avaient lieu autour de Constance Marx, une instructrice venue d'Angleterre pour initier les Françaises à la pratique du scoutisme de Baden-Powell. Les congrès furent également un pôle de formation féminine. Les femmes étaient une partie assez notable de l'auditoire. Elles constituaient le public assidu des Semaines Sociales, nées en 1904 à Lyon pour enrichir et mettre au jour la réflexion sociale de l'Église. Évoquons encore, parmi un grand nombre de manifestations, les congrès de l'*Association Jeanne d'Arc*, les congrès nationaux de l'*Union des œuvres*, les congrès des associations professionnelles catholiques, etc. Très tôt, ces congrès sortent du cadre français: la *Fédération internationale des ligues de femmes catholiques*, fondée en 1910, organise des commissions parallèles au travail de la *Société des nations* (SDN). Les associations féminines catholiques françaises se regroupent alors par branche pour fonder des associations internationales. Éduquées, les femmes font preuve de compétence et participent à des commissions internationales, opérant des transferts de compétence entre femmes de différents pays. Les mouvements de jeunesse participent aussi activement à cette vie internationale.

Les femmes se forment en lisant. Des associations catholiques mettent des livres à leur disposition. Avant 1914, la LPF fait démarrer un important réseau de bibliothèques, nommées 'bibliothèques pour tous', particulièrement bien implantées dans les petites villes de province. Les 'bibliothèques pour tous' prendront leur indépendance en 1971, se sécularisent, et les vitrines de certaines d'entre elles ne proposent plus aujourd'hui de livres religieux. L'association l'*Action sociale de la femme* s'occupe dès 1903 d'une autre forme de lecture, le 'Livre Français', qui présente une sélection d'ouvrages. Enfin, il existe une vigoureuse et importante presse féminine catholique. De nombreuses revues de la Bonne Presse sont des publications de qualité, au tirage conséquent. Les femmes se forment également en faisant des enquêtes sociales, ce qui les amène à aiguiser leur propre jugement. Ensuite, elles élaborent des revendications pour les catégories sociales sur lesquelles ont porté leurs enquêtes. Par exemple, la *Ligue sociale d'acheteurs*, pendant l'année 1905–06, contribua à améliorer les conditions de travail des blanchisseuses, des demoiselles de magasins et des ouvriers coiffeurs. Cette éducation variée, orale, écrite, liée à la confrontation avec la réalité sociale, donne aux femmes confiance en elles. Cette confiance dispose certaines d'entre elles à participer à la vie politique.

Les femmes catholiques et la vie politique

Les femmes catholiques sont regroupées en ligues, associations, mouvements et soutiennent les efforts du parti conservateur et nationaliste, ainsi que le clergé maintes fois malmené par la majorité politique. Les militantes catholiques furent au départ les porte-parole d'intérêts masculins. Étonnant paradoxe, le courant du catholicisme à l'origine de ces mouvements féminins, provenait non pas du catholicisme libéral, ouvert à la modernité (le catholicisme libéral accepte en partie les institutions et les valeurs de la Révolution de 1789), mais du catholicisme intransigeant, hostile au monde moderne. Pour lui, il ne s'agissait donc pas simplement 'd'aller au peuple', mais de refaire une société chrétienne idéale: 'Le catholicisme s'est pensé, voulu et donné comme une solution intégrale et l'alternative radicale à la catastrophique irréligion des temps modernes.'[36] Le catholicisme social se différencie du catholicisme intransigeant après une période de longs conflits. Après 1920, ce sont les députés catholiques, influencés par les catholiques intransigeants, qui poussent aux votes de lois sociales et encouragent l'application de ces lois (lois de 1930 sur les assurances sociales et de 1932 sur les allocations familiales). En réalité, ces lois avaient également vu le jour dans la fertilité des recherches, des travaux, des enquêtes et des discussions des associations féminines.

Entre 1901 et 1907, les femmes n'hésitent pas à mener des actions publiques, s'opposant à la politique anticléricale du gouvernement. La *Ligue des femmes françaises* et la *Ligue patriotique des Françaises* avaient été fondées pour sensibiliser la femme catholique au problème de l'anticléricalisme du bloc des gauches, en 1901–02. On note quelques engagements féminins aux côtés des catholiques intransigeants: en 1901, la LFF collecte 630.000 signatures contre les expulsions des congrégations enseignantes. En 1902, place de la Concorde, la LPF manifeste et lance une souscription pour aider les religieuses. A l'occasion de l'inventaire des établissements publics du culte (paroisses, séminaires, évêchés), stipulé par la loi de 1905 de séparation des Églises et de l'État, les femmes prirent part aux affrontements qui s'ensuivirent. Après 1907, les femmes évoluent vers des actions plus sociales, et pour moins politisées, les femmes n'en deviennent pas moins actives. Écho de la tendance réformatrice du patronat catholique, la LPF se positionne sur un mot d'ordre comme 'servir en créant, en donnant son appui et en favorisant les organisations charitables et sociales qui, dans les classes ouvrières et chez les ruraux rassemblent les hommes, leur apprennent à s'aider les uns les autres, et par conséquent à s'aimer les uns les autres'.[37] Mais elle choisit d'agir maintenant dans le domaine de l'éducation sociale et de l'éducation populaire, avec la famille pour cœur de cible. Rien qu'en 1907, la LPF assure la création de dix écoles ménagères, dix-huit secrétariats du peuple, quatre-vingts bibliothèques et deux syndicats.

Ce n'est qu'en 1920 que les femmes réapparaissent sur la scène publique, et c'est pour demander le droit de vote. La déclaration du pape en faveur du vote des femmes date de 1919. Elle encourageait l'action suffragiste des chrétiennes, mais les femmes catholiques, maintenant légitimées, recueilleront une relativement faible audience. Même si d'une commission d'éducation sociale et civique de la femme fondée par l'association ASF était sortie, en 1920, l'*Union nationale pour le vote des femmes*, créée et dirigée par Mme Chotard.[38] Pourtant accorder le droit de vote aux femmes faisait d'autant plus peur à toutes les tendances politiques confondues, qu'elles représentaient plus de 50% du corps électoral. Le droit de vote féminin ne figurait dans aucun programme politique, même pas celui de la coalition électorale qui porta au pouvoir le socialiste Léon Blum en 1936. En 1945, Georges Bidault, leader du *Mouvement républicain populaire* (MRP) déclare 'avec les femmes, les évêques et le Saint-Esprit, nous aurons cent députés'. Effectivement, les voix des femmes aidèrent le MRP à obtenir cent cinquante et un députés, et ce sera d'ailleurs une femme catholique, Germaine Poinso-Chapuis, membre du MRP, qui devient la première femme française ministre en 1947 (ministre de la santé publique et de la population).

C'est donc par une formation dans les mouvements féminins catholiques que des femmes peuvent quelquefois briguer des postes de responsabilité politique. Parmi elles, citons plusieurs anciennes guides de France: Nicole Pasquier, déléguée nationale à la condition féminine en 1976; Monique Pelletier, ministre déléguée à la condition féminine en 1978, à la famille en 1980; enfin, Marie-Thérèse

Cheroutre, longtemps à la tête des guides de France, se voit appelée au *Conseil économique et social*. Les femmes, en même temps qu'elles sortent de la sphère privée, ont accès à la scène politique. D'abord avec le droit de vote, puis, et modestement, elles se sont vues confiées des postes de responsables, voire décisionnels dans des partis politiques et les conseils municipaux. Trop rares sont encore celles qui sont amenées à exercer des responsabilités aux plus hauts échelons de la vie politique. Mais à l'autre extrémité de cette échelle, du côté de la travailleuse, qu'en est-il de l'évolution de la femme catholique? Comment vit-elle le rapport entre son couple et l'Église?

Les femmes catholiques, la vie familiale et le monde du travail

Longtemps une volonté nataliste a freiné la reconnaissance du droit au travail des femmes. La morale catholique était en phase avec la politique gouvernementale. Ce faisant, les associations féminines catholiques approuvent sans réserve les mesures gouvernementales répressives contre l'avortement et la contraception (lois de 1920, 1923). En outre, sur la question de la maternité, ces associations comme les individus adhèrent totalement dans l'entre-deux-guerres à la position de l'Église réaffirmée dans l'encyclique *Casti connubii* (1931). Les rapports sexuels doivent être féconds à l'intérieur du couple marié, seuls les moyens dit naturels (en clair la continence périodique) sont autorisés.[39] Dans le premier tiers du vingtième siècle, ces incitations n'ont en rien enrayé la chute de la natalité en France. Ces mesures ont sans doute contribué au baby-boom (1943–54) plus accentué en France que dans les autres pays. Cependant l'Église en réaffirmant les interdits traditionnels dans l'encyclique *Humanae vitae* (1968) apparaît incapable de s'adapter à l'évolution des mœurs et s'est alors que se développe dans les années soixante un divorce entre les militants catholiques et les positions doctrinales de l'Église, divorce qui entraîne bien des défections.

Dans le même temps les associations s'informent et se préoccupent du travail féminin. C'est par un gros travail d'enquêtes sociales, de dossiers sur le travail féminin que les associations contribuent à faire évoluer la législation sur le travail des femmes (loi Astier sur la formation professionnelle des apprenties, contrats de travail établis à l'instar de ceux des hommes). En 1920, l'ASF demande des offices régionaux de placement, l'extension à toutes les professions du salaire minimum, l'assurance contre le chômage et la maladie. De sa fondation à 1939, l'UFCS se prononce en faveur de meilleures conditions de travail pour les femmes et ne demande dans un premier temps que l'application des lois existantes! Ensuite, elle demande que soit votée une loi qui garantisse à travail égal le salaire égal, la possibilité du travail à temps partiel, l'assurance maternité, l'inspection des travailleurs à la maison et la réglementation du travail de nuit. Considérant le syndicalisme comme un moyen de défendre les travailleuses, Andrée Butillard, une des pionnières du syndicalisme féminin catholique sait, en 1920, utiliser la loi sur le droit d'adhésion de la femme à un syndicat sans l'aval de son époux. Elle œuvra tout particulièrement à la naissance d'une fédération des syndicats féminins. Elle comprit la nécessité de rassembler tous les syndicats catholiques du pays, et c'est de cette initiative, féminine, qu'est née l'organisation mixte prélude à la constitution de la *Confédération française des travailleurs chrétiens* (CFTC).[40]

Ces associations ont suscité la protection de la travailleuse, législation qui ne l'incite pas à quitter son travail, une fois qu'elle devient mère. Réalisée en 1938, une enquête de l'UFCS a montré que 80% des femmes mariées étaient contraintes de travailler, vu la modicité des gains de leurs maris.[41] L'UFCS fut la principale organisation à s'engager pour le retour de la femme au foyer et l'adoption de mesures incitatives au retour au foyer.[42] Ces associations ont participé à la gestation de la loi du 22 août 1946, une loi qui apporte un soutien complémentaire aux familles nombreuses. Toute une série de mesures accompagnent les allocations: développement des services de protection maternelle et infantile, congé de grossesse porté à quatorze semaines, quotient familial pour les impôts, création en septembre 1948 de l'allocation logement, aide aux vacances familiales, réduction sur les transports pour les familles nombreuses. Ainsi, paradoxalement, la mère qui travaille se voit peu à peu protégée par une législation efficace ce qui ne l'incite pas à quitter son travail tout en étant incitée par des mesures financières à rester chez elle. Que décider? Quelle est la vie quotidienne et les revendications des mères au foyer des milieux populaires qui rejoignent les mouvements catholiques? Les femmes catholiques ne limitent pas leurs revendications à des réformes législatives et au syndicalisme mais tentent de réorganiser la société en faisant preuve d'un militantisme enthousiasme qui prolonge en les dépassant les traditions ouvrières.[43] S'élever contre les taudis et les garnis, prendre d'assaut les locaux vides, s'opposer à la police qui veut déloger les impécunieux, ce sont là des usages constants dans la vie ouvrière – et même des pratiques non spécifiquement féminines. En revanche, tenter d'aménager la vie d'un quartier, de subvenir pacifiquement à la fête des mères, d'instituer un service d'aides ménagères, d'envoyer des déléguées auprès des pouvoirs publics, ce sont là des comportements réellement novateurs. L'épouse pauvre n'a jamais été préservée des réalités sociales. La militante, de quelque origine sociale qu'elle soit, prend fait et cause contre la misère, et se bat aux côtés de la ménagère spoliée du minimum vital. C'est donc à partir de la réalité d'une situation d'injustice, analysée de façon empirique, que le droit des femmes a pu évoluer.

La militante n'avait pas toujours de parti pris, encore moins de formation préalable liée à son milieu d'origine, et c'est important pour comprendre les avancées des droits des femmes. A cet égard, on pourra se reporter à la vie d'une ouvrière de la JOC et à son itinéraire: Jeanne Aubert-Picard, première jociste de France. Sa carrière, réussie à bien des titres, la voit présidente générale du mouvement de 1928 à 1939. Elle entre alors à la LOC et participe à la création en zone sud des centres de jeunes chômeuses. En mai 1941, elle épouse François Picard, vice-président de la JOCF, dont elle a quatre enfants. Tous deux entrent au MPF. En 1942, Jeanne Aubert-Picard lance à Lyon les *Aides familiales du milieu populaire*. En 1953, elle est élue membre du conseil d'administration de l'*Union nationale des associations familiales* (UNAF) et membre du *Conseil économique et social* pour y représenter les familles. De 1958 à 1962, elle est en outre chargée de mission auprès du ministère du logement et de l'urbanisme pour y exprimer les désirs des mères de famille. De 1965 à 1974, date de sa retraite, elle est également présidente de l'*Union française des consommateurs* (UFC) et directrice de la revue *Que Choisir*.[44] Belle exemple de la variété des engagements catholiques et d'une promotion sociale par le milieu associatif.

Des femmes catholiques protestent contre le sort réservé à l'épouse-mère qui assume la survie de la famille quand le père n'assume plus ses responsabilités. Tout en ne remettant pas en cause la 'hiérarchie familiale', elles essayent d'obtenir du législateur des modifications du code civil pour affirmer le droit des épouses et des mères. En 1907, la femme dispose librement de son salaire. Réclamée de longue date par les associations féminines, la réforme du code civil de 1938 supprime l'incapacité civile de la femme mariée et la puissance maritale. Elle permet à celle-ci de tester, contracter, ouvrir un compte, poursuivre des études et passer un examen, demander un passeport, sans demander à son mari. Toutefois ce dernier reste le chef de famille, fixe comme tel le domicile conjugal, peut interdire à sa femme l'exercice d'un métier.[45] En France, la tutelle maritale ne disparaît qu'en 1965 et l'égalité des époux n'est complète qu'en 1985 avec la gestion commune du patrimoine conjoint. Une fois encore, il apparaît que c'est en réaction à des situations d'abus, liés à des observations de terrain – sur des femmes en situation de détresse – que les femmes sont montées au créneau, exigeant une évolution législative égalitaire.

Les mouvements féminins catholiques ont été un creuset où se sont élaborées des revendications qui ont abouti à l'adoption de mesures législatives. Des militantes y ont trouvé un lieu où s'exprimer et s'entraider. Elles ont indéniablement fait progresser les conditions de vie des Françaises.

Les femmes catholiques et le monde de la charité

L'exercice de la charité apparaît depuis des siècles comme un domaine d'action réservé en particulier aux femmes. Au vingtième siècle, des femmes catholiques font bouger ce monde. Certaines d'entre elles s'attachent à restructurer les instances de la charité. D'autres ouvrent un champ professionnel aux femmes.

A partir de 1920 le monde de la charité est traversé par des conflits qui dépassent le cadre français, et les femmes françaises vont devenir leaders et partie prenante dans ce débat international. Le débat est idéologique, théorisé, c'est une lutte entre le curatif (ou médico-social) et le préventif (social). Deux conceptions opposées de la charité se manifestent en France par trois courants. A leurs têtes, trois femmes catholiques qui, entre 1923 et 1924, mettent sur pied trois associations professionnelles.[46] Marie de Liron d'Airoles,[47] membre de la *Ligue patriotique des Françaises*, fondatrice de l'*Union catholique des services sanitaires et sociaux* (UCSS), recrute chez les infirmières et assistantes sociales. L'UCSS compte trois mille adhérentes en 1926, et quatorze mille en 1939, année où elle atteint son rayonnement maximum. Elle développe la conception professionnelle suivante: une bonne soignante doit posséder, avant tout, la vocation, la foi et la capacité d'obéissance, sa formation n'arrive qu'en second plan. Son personnel médico-social se devait de rester profession- nellement en retrait du médical, qui fournissait le cadre d'action – le catholicisme, lui, prenait à sa charge le cadre de pensée.[48] Avec le *Secrétariat catholique des œuvres privées sanitaires et sociales*, Marie de Liron d'Airoles fédère en 1930 l'ensemble des œuvres catholiques.[49] Enfin, elle décide de créer une organisation, le *Comité international d'études des associations catholiques d'infirmières*, qu'elle préside à partir de 1933. Autre fondatrice d'association professionnelle, Andrée Butillard crée au début de 1923 l'*Union des auxiliaires sociales* qui n'atteint jamais que quelques centaines de membres. Elle tend à regrouper les anciennes élèves de l'ENS ainsi que toutes les professionnelles qui s'orientent vers un service social dégagé de l'influence médicale. Son association n'affiche pas de tendance confessionnelle. Toutefois, elle participera en 1925 à la création de l'*Union catholique internationale de service social* (UCISS). La troisième, Léonie Chaptal, fonde en 1924 l'*Association nationale des infirmières diplômées d'État français* (ANIDEF). Une association neutre à laquelle adhèrent des protestantes, mais qui ne compte jamais plus des quatre mille membres de 1935. Elle est membre de l'*International Nurses' Council* (INC), fondée par des protestantes, dont elle devient la présidente en 1933.

Sur le plan international, un conflit se fait jour entre les tenants de la conception médico-sociale du service social et ceux de la conception 'sociale pure'. En 1925 pendant le Congrès de l'*Union internationale des ligues féminines catholiques* qui se tient à Rome, une quinzaine de déléguées, représentant les écoles sociales catholiques de douze pays, se sont réunies et créent l'UCISS, laquelle regroupe les écoles catholiques de service social, les associations d'auxiliaires sociales et des centres de formation sociale de tous pays. Sur la trentaine d'institutions adhérentes, deux sont françaises, l'ENS de Paris (Butillard) et l'École du sud-est de Lyon. De l'UCISS se diffuse et se développe une conception sociale de la charité.[50] *Caritas Catholica* – un organisme créé en 1924, et dont le but était de coordonner les organisations charitables – est investi par Mlle d'Airoles à partir de 1930. Elle dirige activement la section 'Formation à l'action charitable et sociale', et voit avec réprobation le développement de l'UCISS, cette association orientée vers le 'social pur'. Pour s'opposer à son influence, elle crée une autre association professionnelle internationale concernant le même public (infirmières et assistantes sociales): le *Comité international d'études des associations catholiques d'infirmières*. Ce comité, où la France est très influente, se réunit pour la première fois à Lourdes en 1933, en réponse au congrès prévu de l'INC, dont la présidente, Léonie Chaptal, est une autre catholique française. Une double réponse à l'UCISS et à l'INC. Les forces catholiques de l'UCSS l'emportent jusqu'en 1945.

La hiérarchie catholique était prise en étau entre ces deux courants de pensée. Elle oscilla de l'un à l'autre, sans jamais définitivement trancher la question jusqu'à la création de l'*Union nationale interfédérale des œuvres privées sanitaires et sociales* (UNIOPSS),[51] où les deux courants se sont retrouvés côte à côte dans une véritable institution œcuménique. L'UNIOPSS peut se positionner avec un poids conséquent face à l'État qui a mis sur pied en 1945 la sécurité sociale. Ce qui mit fin aux querelles? La peur des associations d'être absorbées par l'État, de n'être plus libres de faire la charité comme on l'entendait. Une génération de femmes est passée. Elles ne se retrouvent plus dans les cadres de l'UNIOPSS tels qu'ils apparaissent en 1947. Ce sont des hommes qui reprennent en main ce secteur associatif où les femmes deviennent les employées. Cependant, les femmes catholiques mettent sur pied des méthodes de travail, une gamme de professions nouvelles adaptées aux besoins du terrain.

Depuis le début du siècle, on assiste à une lente professionnalisation du monde de la charité. A la suite de la guerre de 1914, un certain nombre de diplômes d'État sont créés: diplôme d'infirmière et nombreux diplômes d'infirmière visiteuse. Léonie Chaptal crée immédiatement une association professionnelle: l'ANIDEF.[52] Les écoles (privées) reconnues par l'État délivrent des diplômes. En 1932, sous la pression des associations et de quelques personnalités, un diplôme d'État d'assistante sociale est aussi validé.[53] En 1933, un événement, funeste pour les associations, aurait pu faire vaciller sur ses bases un secteur d'activité où la bonne volonté tenait lieu de compétence: le projet de loi Fié rendant obligatoire l'obtention des diplômes d'État pour exercer les professions médico-sociales. La direction de l'UCSS, dès qu'elle eut connaissance du texte, contacta quelques députés dévoués à sa cause et la loi resta au stade de projet. Quant au diplôme d'assistante sociale tel qu'il existait, il n'a duré que six ans (1932–38), remplacé par un diplôme homonyme, mais dont l'esprit et le programme sont plus médicalisés. Moins sujet à caution que la polémique position des professions appartenant ou non au 'médico-social' (un débat qui a enflammé des générations de militantes), d'autres professions ont vu le jour peu à peu. En même temps que reconnues, sanctionnées par un diplôme, elles oscillèrent toujours au gré des reconnaissances publiques et des initiatives privées.

Citons le diplôme de professeur d'éducation ménagère (1934), ceux de bibliothécaire de lecture publique (1932), animateur socioculturel (1963), conseillers en économie sociale et familiale (1973), conseillères du travail (1945), éducateurs de l'éducation surveillée (1971), les jardinières d'enfants, aujourd'hui appelées éducatrices pour jeunes enfants (1973), puéricultrices (1947), travailleuses familiales (1949).

C'est le monde du travail qui s'ouvre aux femmes. Ce salariat apporte aux femmes une modification de leur statut social. Il est pour elles synonyme d'autonomie familiale et sociale. Le créneau professionnel qu'elles ont créé leur est bien adapté et leur procure un épanouissement professionnel et humain.

LA MIXITÉ EN QUESTION

Les associations féminines catholiques, les patronages, les mouvements de jeunesse pratiquent la non-mixité. Cette division anthropologique est très prégnante dans toute la société française: la séparation des sexes est une valeur partagée par les catholiques comme par les laïcs. Certains mouvements et associations ont bien voulu fusionner leurs branches féminines et masculines. Citons l'*Action catholique indépendante* (ACI) qui a fusionné en 1945 ou encore la JOCF et la JECF qui se sont fondues avec leur homologue masculin en un seul secrétariat en 1951. Qu'est-ce qui a inspiré à la femme catholique sa méfiance de la mixité? Un moyen d'action, un constat de terrain? La mixité, héritage logique d'une morale conservatrice, est pendant longtemps refusée. Les chrétiennes mettent l'accent sur la différence et la spécificité des sexes dans la vie privée et publique. Les femmes catholiques défendent l'égalité ontologique de l'homme et de la femme et veulent mettre en place un partenariat, ce qui ne se fait pas sans difficultés. Autour des années 1970, il existe un mouvement vers un regroupement des branches masculines et féminines des associations catholiques. Mais il bute sur le fait que les hommes ont du mal culturellement à vivre une codirection avec les femmes. Les femmes sont conscientes de ce que, si le principe de codirection n'est pas acquis dès le départ, elles vont se trouver reléguées, moins libres et peu influentes. Des fusions n'ont pas eu lieu, comme celle de la JICF qui se refuse à la mixité en 1979. L'ACGF (*Action catholique générale féminine*) au congrès de Pantin de 1978 écarte l'idée d'un rapprochement avec son homologue masculin.[54] Le guidisme, sur lequel nous possédons une étude approfondie, est un bon exemple pour constater cette tendance du refus d'un certain type de mixité. Si l'on parle de fusion en 1981 pour les *Scouts de France*, la seule perspective acceptable serait la création d'un grand mouvement des *Scouts et Guides de France*, avec responsabilité unique à tous les niveaux. Les *Guides de France* sont, elles, pour la création d'une union évolutive des deux associations fondées sur une identité guide et une identité scout, avec double responsabilité à chaque niveau. La motion de chaque association présentée aux assemblées générales a été rejetée par l'autre. Les *Scouts de France* ont ouvert leurs rangs à un recrutement féminin. Parallèlement, les *Guides de France* se définissent comme ayant la charge, en priorité, de l'éducation des filles, une mission où sont engagées de jeunes adultes, cheftaines et chefs, et des adultes hommes et femmes (dans une proportion de 25% pour ces derniers). Les *Guides de France* ont fait avancer les exigences d'inter-éducation. Cependant, en 1988 et 1989, pour tenter de dépasser les situations conflictuelles, les deux conseils d'administration ont créé un comité de recherches et de propositions. Aucun compromis n'a été trouvé, le dialogue continue.[55]

Les mouvements catholiques sont un des lieux de discussion et d'élaboration d'un nouveau positionnement des femmes vis-à-vis des hommes dans la société française.

CONCLUSION

Ainsi au vingtième siècle, l'importance des femmes s'est accrue dans l'Église, parallèlement à celle de leur rôle dans la société française. Mais à l'issue de cette présentation succincte des réalités du siècle, il me semble important de souligner que les femmes catholiques ne se sont pas engagées à l'origine par progressisme ou féminisme. Ces tendances sont apparues en épiphénomène greffé sur la logique – ou le bon sens – d'un travail sur la réalité sociale. Déterminées à obtenir des résultats pour faire reculer les injustices, conformément à l'enseignement du christianisme, les femmes ont poussé jusqu'au bout leurs enquêtes sociales et suivi leurs convictions. Dans ce processus elles se sont souvent trouvées dépassées par ce qu'elles faisaient, beaucoup d'entre elles n'ayant jamais désiré s'écarter des positions de l'Église. Cependant, sans toujours en prendre conscience, elles ont contribué à professionnaliser des activités charitables et ecclésiales, à promouvoir la participation des femmes à la vie de la cité et à faire avancer des réformes structurelles de la condition des Françaises. En revanche, les relations très ambiguës avec la hiérarchie religieuse obligèrent certaines militantes catholiques à douter de la possibilité dans un avenir proche d'un éventuel partage des respon-sabilités et à refuser une mixité qui serait perte d'autonomie et de pouvoir. Cependant, d'autres militantes se confrontent aux hommes tant dans l'Église que dans les associations. Elles tentent d'élaborer de nouvelles règles de partenariat entre les hommes et les femmes afin qu'il y ait une meilleure reconnaissance de la place de chacun. Ce dialogue stimulant modifie les relations hommes-femmes aussi bien dans le monde religieux que dans la société française. Toutefois, les positions du pape sur la contraception, de plus en plus éloignées des mœurs occidentales, sont loin de rallier à lui la majorité des femmes et des hommes catholiques. Si se manifestent de petits groupes de fervent(e)s militant(e)s anti-avortement, les positions officielles de l'Église sur tout ce qui touche à la sexualité et à la reproduction ont indéniablement contribué à détacher un grand nombre de croyant(e)s de la religion. Depuis 1960–65 de nombreuses femmes ont déserté les bancs de l'Église. La défection des femmes a une influence primordiale sur ce que certains appellent 'la crise du catholicisme contemporain', sans toutefois suffire à l'expliquer. Cette défection ne correspond-elle pas à une mutation du catholi-cisme qui se redéfinit sous nos yeux dans de nouveaux espaces et dans de nouvelles relations hommes-femmes?

NOTES

1. Ralph Gibson, 'Le Catholicisme et les femmes en France au XIXe siècle', *Revue d'histoire de l'Église de France*, LXXIX (1993), 63–93.

2. Evelyne Diébolt, *Women and Philanthropy in France*, working paper, Women and Philanthropy series (New York: Centre for the Study of Philanthropy, 1996).

3. Noémie Black, *Social Feminism* (Ithaca: Cornell University Press, 1989).

4. Émile Poulat, préface du livre de Sylvie Fayet-Scribe, *Associations féminines et catholicisme. De la charité à l'action sociale, XIXe–XXe siècle* (Paris: Éditions ouvrières, 1990), p. 8.

5. Claude Langlois, 'Toujours plus pratiquantes. La permanence du dimorph-isme sexuel dans le catholicisme français contemporain', *Femmes et sociétés*, 2 (1995), 229–60.

6. Marie Hébrard, *Les Femmes dans l'Église* (Paris: Le Centurion–Cerf, 1984); Elisabeth Behr-Sigel, *Le Ministère des femmes dans l'Église* (Paris: Cerf, 1987).

7. In Gérard Cholvy et Yves-Marie Hilaire, *Histoire religieuse de la France contemporaine*, 3 vols (Toulouse: Privat, 1985–88), III (1988), 395.

8. Geneviève Gabbois, 'Vous êtes presque la seule consolation de l'Église. La foi des femmes face à la déchristianisation de 1789 à 1880', dans Jean Delumeau, *La Religion de ma mère: le rôle des femmes dans la transmission de la foi* (Paris: Cerf, 1992), pp. 301–25.

9. Sylviane Grésillon, 'Catéchiste volontaire, une vocation féminine', dans Delumeau, *La Religion de ma mère*, pp. 327–42.

10. Ibid., p. 338.

11. Anne-Marie Aitken, 'La Catéchèse par les femmes dans la France d'aujourd'hui', dans Delumeau, *La Religion de ma mère*, pp. 363–71.

12. Evelyne Diébolt, *Les Associations face aux institutions. Les Femmes dans l'action sanitaire, sociale et culturelle, 1900–1965*, thèse de Doctorat ès Lettres et Sciences humaines, Université Paris VII, 1993.

13. Elisabeth Dufourcq, *Les Aventurières de Dieu* (Paris: Lattés, 1993).

14. Cholvy et Hilaire, *Histoire religieuse de la France contemporaine*, III, 278–82.

15. Anne Cova, *Femmes et catholicisme social: trois mouvements nationaux d'initiative lyonnaise. Cent ans de catholicisme social à Lyon et en Rhône-Alpes* (Paris: Éditions ouvrières, 1992), pp. 307–32.

16. Odile Sarti, *The Ligue patriotique des Françaises (1902–1933): A Feminine Response to the Secularisation of French Society* (New York: Garland Publishing, 1992); Anne-Marie Sohn, 'Les Femmes catholique et la vie publique: l'exemple de la *Ligue patriotique des Françaises*', in *Stratégie de femmes* (Paris: Tierce, 1984), pp. 97–120.

17. Gérard Dittgen, *De la Ligue à l'ACGF: histoire d'un mouvement de femmes*, 2 vols (Paris: ACGF, 1990).

18. Des notices biographiques des femmes catholiques mentionnées dans ce chapitre sont publiées dans Geneviève Poujol et Madeleine Romer, *Dictionnaire des militants de l'éducation populaire et de l'action culturelle* (Paris: L'Harmattan, 1996).

19. Fayet-Scribe, *Associations féminines et catholicisme*, pp. 93–102.

20. Evelyne Diébolt, 'Léonie Chaptal (1873–1937): pour une histoire des soins et des pratiques soignantes', *Cahier de l'AMIEC*, 10 (1988), 85–122; Evelyne Diébolt, 'Léonie Chaptal et ses œuvres dans Plaisance (1901–37)', dans *Les Associations face aux institutions*, thèse, Université Paris VII, 1993.

21. Henri Rollet, *Andrée Butillard et le féminisme chrétien* (Paris: Éditions Spes, 1960); Marguerite Perroy, *La Première Élève de l'École normale sociale, Madeleine Carsignol* (Paris: Éditions Spes, 1927); Marguerite Perroy, *Dans la lumière de Rerum Novarum, Georgette des Isnards* (Paris: Éditions Spes, 1933).

22. Marie-Louise Rochebillard, *Syndicat d'ouvrières lyonnaises* (Paris: V. Lecoffre, 1904); Marguerite Perroy, *Une ouvrière apôtre sociale, Maria Bardot* (Paris: Éditions Spes, 1931).

23. Evelyne Diébolt, '*Union des auxiliaires sociales* (UAS)', *Encyclopédie Catholicisme hier, aujourd'hui, demain* (Paris: Letouzey et Ané, 1997), pp. 487–89.

24. Amicale de l'UFCS, recherches sur l'UFCS à partir des archives du mouvement, texte dactylographié, novembre 1988. L'UFCS a, en 1939, 13.000 adhérentes.

25. Fayet-Scribe, *Associations féminines et catholicisme.*

26. Sylvie Fayet-Scribe, *La Résidence sociale de Levallois-Perret, la naissance des centres sociaux en France* (Paris: Éditions ouvrières, 1990).

27. Voir *Témoignages pour une histoire de la Jeunesse étudiante chrétienne féminine, 1930–65* (Paris: Les amis de la JECF, 1981).

28. Pierre Pierrard, Michel Launay, Rolande Trempé, *La JOC, Regards d'historiens* (Paris: Éditions ouvrières, 1984).

29. Geneviève Dermanjian, éd., 'LOC, MPF, MLP, MLO. Femmes, familles et actions ouvrières. Pratiques et responsabilité féminine dans les mouvements familiaux populaires (1935–58)', numéro spécial du *Cahiers du regroupement pour la recherche sur les mouvements familiaux,* 6 (1991).

30. Geneviève Poujol, *Des élites de société pour demain?* (Paris: Éditions ouvrières, 1996).

31. Georges Duhamelet, *Nouvelet et le mouvement noëliste* (Paris: Bonne Presse, 1937).

32. Jacqueline Roux, *Sous l'étendard de Jeanne. Les Fédérations diocésaines de jeunes filles, 1904–45: une ACJF féminine?* (Paris: Cerf, 1995).

33. Marie-Thérèse Cheroutre, en collaboration avec Gérard Cholvy, *Scoutisme féminin et promotion féminine, 1920–90* (Paris: Éditions des Guides de France, 1990); Marie-Thérèse Cheroutre et Gérard Cholvy, éds, *Le Scoutisme* (Paris: Cerf, 1994).

34. Comtesse de Keranslech-Kerneze, *Jeanne Chenu, 1861–1939* (Paris: Action sociale de la femme et le Livre français, 1940).

35. Le Lycéum club, association internationale de femmes s'intéressant à la littérature, aux arts, à la musique, aux sciences et aux œuvres humanitaires s'est fondé à Londres en 1903. Présidée par la duchesse d'Uzes, un club s'ouvre en 1906 à Paris. Dans l'entre-deux-guerres, le Lycéum club compte trente-deux filiales dans le monde et 20.000 membres.

36. Émile Poulat, *Catholicisme, démocratie et socialisme* (Paris: Casterman, 1977), p. 137.

37. *L'Écho de la Ligue patriotique des Françaises,* 1 (1903), 2.

38. Steven Hause and Anne Kenney, 'The Development of the Catholic Women's Suffrage Mouvement in France, 1896–1922', *The Catholic Historical Review,* 67 (1981), 11–30.

39. Martine Sevegrand, *Les Enfants du bon Dieu. Les Catholiques français et la procréation au XXe siècle* (Paris: Albin Michel, 1995).

40. En février 1919, à l'invitation des syndicats féminins de la rue de l'Abbaye, se rendent deux cents délégués. Les syndicats féminins proposent alors de constituer une fédération. Ainsi naît la CFTC.

41. Cette enquête, faite en 1930, porte sur 30.000 femmes. Voir Andrée Butillard, Joseph Danel, E. Baudouin, Henriette Brunhes, Mme Gaullet, *Le Travail de la mère hors du foyer et sa répercussion sur la natalité,* Commission catholique du quatorzième congrès de la natalité, Dijon, 22–23 septembre 1932 (Paris: Éditions mariage et famille, 1933).

42. Susan Pedersen, *Family, Dependance and the Origin of the Welfare State, Britain and France* (Cambridge: Cambridge University Press, 1993), pp. 224–91.

43. Dermanjian, 'LOC, MPF, MLP, MLO', p. 274.

44. En 1990, elle publie aux Éditions ouvrières *JOCF, qu'as-tu fait de nos vies? La*

Jeunesse ouvrière chrétienne féminine, sa vie, son action, 1928–1945, ouvrage rassemblant les témoignages de huit cents acteurs et observateurs.

45. Georges Duby et Michelle Perrot, éds, *Histoire des femmes* (Paris: Plon, 1992); Anne-Marie Sohn, *L'Entre-deux-guerres: les rôles féminins en France et en Angleterre* (Paris: Plon, 1992), p. 111.

46. Evelyne Diébolt, '80 ans d'associations professionnelles infirmières en France (1906–1984)', *Pénélope*, 11 (1984), 122–30.

47. Georges Duhamelet, *Marie de Liron d'Airoles* (Paris: Éditions de l'UCSS, 1945).

48. Evelyne Diébolt, 'Une association catholique: l'UCSS', dans 'Pour une histoire des soins et des pratiques soignantes', numéro spécial du *Cahier de l'AMIEC*, 10 (1988), 141–58; '*Union catholique des services de santé* (UCSS)', *Encyclopédie Catholicisme*, pp. 510–11.

49. Marie d'Airoles avec Jacques Guérin de Vaux et M. Poindron fonde une association loi 1901. Le but est d'assurer la liaison entre les œuvres ou les personnes catholiques qui consacrent leur temps, leurs efforts ou leurs ressources à l'hygiène et à la santé, et de constituer un centre d'études et de documentation.

50. La prédominance française est bien marquée à l'UCISS: au comité de patronage le R.P. Desbuquois, directeur de l'Action Populaire, et M. Duthoit, président des Semaines sociales de France. Mlle Novo, directrice de l'ENS fait partie du bureau.

51. Evelyne Diébolt, *Historique et dynamique d'une association interfédérale: l'UNIOPSS 1947–1987* (Paris: Fonds national de développement de la vie associative, 1988); 'L'UNIOPSS a 40 ans', numéro spécial d'*Union sociale*, 382 (1987); '*Union nationale interfédérale des œuvres et organismes privés sanitaires et sociaux* (UNIOPSS)', *Encylopédie Catholicisme*, pp. 513–14.

52. Evelyne Diébolt, 'Santé publique et personnel médico-social en France 1900–1930', dans *Actes du colloque 'Maladies, médecine et sociétés': approches historiques pour le présent*, 2 vols (Paris: L'Harmattan, 1993), II, 234–41.

53. Yvonne Kniebiehler, *Nous, les assistantes sociales. Naissance d'une profession* (Paris: Aubier, 1980).

54. Marie-Thérèse Cheroutre rappelle le commentaire suivant de l'ACGF au congrès de Pantin en 1978: 'L'ACGF comme telle a le devoir de ne pas oublier que la promotion de la femme n'est pas totalement accomplie ni dans le monde ni dans l'Église'. Dans ce même congrès, il est réaffirmé 'que les femmes prennent en main leur vie, n'exceptent pas que d'autres le fassent, l'organisent pour elles, sans qu'elles aient leur mot à dire' (Marie-Thérèse Cheroutre, 'Le Siècle d'or des militantes', *Notre Histoire*, 121 (1990), 37–39).

55. Voir Cheroutre et Cholvy, *Le Scoutisme*.

11

La sociologie religieuse du catholicisme français au vingtième siècle

Yves-Marie Hilaire

La sociologie religieuse du catholicisme français au vingtième siècle est assez bien connue grâce à l'utilisation des méthodes quantitatives prônée dès 1931 par Gabriel Le Bras. Une série d'enquêtes remarquables sont conduites sous l'impulsion de Fernand Boulard au milieu du siècle, puis des études historiques rétrospectives exploitent les chiffres contemporains dans les visites pastorales. Cependant lors de la crise de civilisation de 1968, la mode change: le militant politique et social intéresse beaucoup plus que le pratiquant religieux. Pendant vingt ans, les enquêtes rigoureuses disparaissent, les sondages sont censés les remplacer. Depuis quelques années, enquêtes et travaux précis ont repris et permettent de mieux éclairer certains problèmes.

Il convient donc d'évoquer d'abord l'œuvre des promoteurs de la sociologie religieuse historique. Puis nous prendrons en compte ses deux dimensions, l'espace avec la géosociologie et le temps avec la socio-histoire. Enfin, des aspects particuliers pourront être évoqués: celui de la déchristianisation ouvrière et celui de la crise récente très accusée en France.

LES PIONNIERS DE LA SOCIOLOGIE RELIGIEUSE HISTORIQUE

Influencée par l'observation des mutations sociales et culturelles, la sociologie religieuse, née en Allemagne avec Max Weber (1864–1920) et en France avec Émile Durkheim (1858–1917), s'est beaucoup développée sous l'impulsion de Gabriel Le Bras (1891–1970). La sociographie religieuse dont les méthodes ont été mises au point par Fernand Boulard (1898–1977) a connu son épanouissement dans le monde occidental pendant les Trente glorieuses (1945–73).

En 1931, lassé par les vaines querelles opposant les tenants des deux France, celle des Croisés, fervente et chevaleresque, et celle des Lumières, libertine et irréligieuse, Gabriel Le Bras, professeur de droit romain et de droit canon, lance une enquête sur la pratique religieuse concrète des populations françaises. Il fait observer avec humour que l'on 'recense les bœufs et les chevaux, mais qui songe à supputer le nombre des catholiques pratiquants dont la place est peut-être aussi appréciable sur notre sol?' Le Bras invite les lecteurs de la *Revue d'histoire de l'Église de France* (RHEF) à se transformer en enquêteurs bénévoles: il s'agit d'observer les pratiques des croyants, de compter les assistants à la messe et les pascalisants, de relever les manifestations de piété dans le cadre de chaque paroisse, de chaque archiprêtré, de chaque diocèse. Le Bras trouve un écho auprès de nombreux érudits ecclésiastiques, de quelques vicaires généraux désireux de prendre la mesure d'une éventuelle 'déchristianisation' et de quelques laïcs. Il publie régulièrement les réponses obtenues dans la RHEF, et vingt-cinq ans plus tard en 1956, les documents recueillis sont rassemblés dans deux volumes intitulés *Études de sociologie religieuse.*[1]

Les statistiques de pratique religieuse reposent principalement sur les chiffres contenus dans les comptes-rendus de visites pastorales effectuées par les évêques et les vicaires généraux ou de visites décanales effectuées par les doyens. Sous l'impulsion initiale de Gabriel Le Bras et sous la direction de M. Venard, D. Julia, J. Gadille et Ph. Lacoudre, cent cinquante chercheurs ont préparé le *Répertoire des visites pastorales de la France* publié entre 1977 et 1985.[2]

Une autre méthode plus récente mais moins précise pour évaluer les attitudes spirituelles provient des sondages qui se sont multipliés depuis une quarantaine d'années. Dans deux gros volumes intitulés *La Vie religieuse des Français à travers les sondages d'opinion (1944–1976)*,[3] Jacques Sutter a rassemblé tous les sondages intéressant les comportements religieux.

Au cours de ces enquêtes, Gabriel Le Bras se lie d'amitié avec un curé de campagne devenu aumônier national de la *Jeunesse agricole chrétienne*, puis de la section féminine, Fernand Boulard. Celui-ci, désireux de procurer des bases scientifiques à la réflexion pastorale, obtient l'aide des aumôniers jacistes pour ses recherches et publie en 1947 dans les *Cahiers du clergé rural* sa première carte religieuse de la France rurale; ses *Problèmes missionnaires de la France rurale* parus en 1945 décrivent l'état religieux des campagnes françaises.[4] Sollicité par des évêques qui redoutent une certaine déconsidération du clergé séculier, Boulard publie en 1950 une recherche socio-pastorale rigoureuse et neuve qu'il intitule *Essor ou déclin du clergé français*.[5] Si les interrogations suscitées par les écrits du Père Lhande, *Le Christ dans la banlieue*, *La Croix sur les fortifs*, *Le Dieu qui bouge* (1927–31)[6] avaient contribué à donner un écho aux premières enquêtes de Gabriel Le Bras, le retentissement du livre des abbés Godin et Daniel, *La France, pays de mission?* (1943)[7] accroit l'audience des recherches du chanoine Boulard. Chargé d'un enseignement à l'Institut catholique de Paris, Boulard souhaite mettre sa méthode d'enquête au service de ses élèves et de ses confrères et redige ses *Premiers itinéraires en sociologie religieuse* (1951)[8] qui connaissent un vif succès et sont traduits en quatre langues. Plus tard, lorsqu'il aura mené à bien la plupart de ses grandes enquêtes, Boulard, soucieux de répondre aux problèmes posés par la déchristianisation urbaine et ouvrière, tire des conclusions neuves faites sur les villes dans *Pratique religieuse urbaine et régions cultuelles*,[9] livre édité en collaboration avec Jean Rémy en 1968: les auteurs y donnent une carte religieuse de la France urbaine.

Entre-temps, de 1954 à 1968, Fernand Boulard a conduit une immense entreprise, les évêques français lui ayant confié les uns après les autres la direction d'enquêtes collectives diocésaines qui sont menées à partir de questionnaires distribués aux fidèles et remplis par eux, et dans lesquelles la recherche économique, démo-graphique, sociale et politique précède le plus souvent et complète la recherche religieuse. En 1968, ces enquêtes ont couvert presque toute la France et en 1971 trente publications diocésaines ont paru. Professeur à Paris, animateur de sessions nationales de réflexion et de prospectives pastorales, promoteur de la réorganisation des diocèses en zones et en secteurs pastoraux, expert au Concile de Vatican II, Fernand Boulard forme bientôt des disciples dans le monde entier. Il entretient d'étroits rapports avec les écoles espagnole et italienne et, à la fin de sa vie, il parcourt l'Amérique latine, notamment le Mexique.

Les années 1968–71 marquent un tournant. En 1968, Gérard Cholvy publie sa *Géographie religieuse de l'Hérault contemporain*[10] qui exploite une enquête Boulard d'assistance à la messe dominicale de 1962. Cette œuvre représente pour le préfacier Gabriel Le Bras 'le discours de la méthode par l'exemple' et la réalisation du programme qu'il s'était fixé trente ans auparavant, donc avant la naissance de l'auteur. L'œuvre sociographique française de Boulard s'arrête alors, parce que la crise de civilisation qui affecte particulièrement les années 1968–75 dévalorise pendant un temps une pratique dominicale et pascale qui d'ailleurs regresse très fortement. Une présentation statistique et graphique des résultats obtenus par les immenses enquêtes menées dans le domaine religieux sera faite dans l'*Atlas de la pratique religieuse des catholiques en France*,[11] paru en 1980 après la mort de Boulard.

Cependant, celui-ci n'a pas abandonné ses recherches dans la dernière décade de sa vie. Il lance en 1973 une nouvelle grande entreprise, *Matériaux pour l'histoire religieuse du peuple français*,[12] destiné à publier les statistiques religieuses des diocèses entre 1800 et 1968. Quatre volumes de statistiques accompagnés de notices et de cartes sont destinés à apporter un arrière-plan historique aux grandes enquêtes sociologiques des années 1954–68, à faire progresser l'histoire sérielle recommandée par Pierre Chaunu et à permettre de mieux comprendre l'évolution religieuse pendant un siècle et demi. Trois gros volumes ont paru respectivement en 1982, en 1987 et en 1992. Un autre est en préparation. L'*Histoire religieuse de la France contemporaine* de Cholvy et Hilaire (1985–88) présente les résultats de l'enquête effectuée pour réaliser les matériaux.[13]

Notons enfin deux autres apports méthodologiques: celui d'Alphonse Dupront, observateur attentif des gestes religieux et notamment des pèlerinages; et celui des historiens italiens, belges et allemands des mouvements catholiques sociaux ou politico-sociaux fort importants à l'époque contemporaine.

VIGUEUR DES CONTRASTES GÉOGRAPHIQUES

Gabriel Le Bras avait été frappé par la netteté des contrastes de géosociographie religieuse. Il donnait pour exemple le Maine partagé entre un Ouest très pratiquant et un Bassin Parisien central qui l'était fort peu. Le prospectus du tome II des *Matériaux pour l'histoire religieuse du peuple français* évoque le trajet Paris-Strasbourg: le voyageur qui le parcourt traverse successivement une Brie très fortement déchristianisée, une Champagne largement indifférente au dix-neuvième siècle, mais travaillée par d'actives minorités chrétiennes au vingtième siècle; une Lorraine de langue française attachée au catholicisme mais non cléricale, une Alsace fervente et pluriconfessionnelle. Aussi, chacun des trois volumes de l'*Histoire religieuse de la*

France contemporaine contient-il un chapitre qui tente de définir à trois moments différents, vers 1850, vers 1910 et vers 1950, les identités religieuses régionales de la France.

Ce paysage religieux différencié se retrouve en Europe. En effet, les nombreuses enquêtes effectuées en Europe occidentale entre 1950 et 1968, sous l'impulsion de Fernand Boulard et de ses disciples ou émules, l'espagnol Duocastella et l'italien Burgalassi, ont abouti à l'élaboration d'une carte européenne des assistants à la messe qui se situe vers 1960. Les contrastes régionaux sont accentuées et les ensembles territoriaux qui se dessinent chevauchent les frontières des états.

Limitons-nous ici à l'hexagone français et aux cartes dressées par Fernand Boulard en 1945–50 pour la France rurale et en 1968 pour la France urbaine. Trois grandes catégories apparaissent sur ces cartes: les zones pratiquantes, les zones à traditions chrétiennes et les zones déchristianisées.

Parmi les premières, trois ensembles se détachent: d'abord, le Massif armoricain appartenant au monde celtique. Puis des Hautes terres incluant le Pays basque, la majeure partie des Pyrénées, le Sud-Est du Massif central et les Alpes du Nord. Enfin, une partie de l'ancienne Lotharingie incluant la Moselle, l'Alsace, la Franche-Comté, la Savoie recoupe l'ensemble précédent. Jusqu'aux années 1960, les populations de ces régions fortement enracinées ont souvent une conscience très vive de leur identité régionale. Un solide encadrement pastoral entretient la ferveur et le particularisme. Les familles catholiques fécondes procurent à l'Église non seulement de nombreux prêtres, religieux et religieuses, mais aussi des missionnaires qui vont porter le christianisme outre-mer. Vers 1950, plus de 40% des prêtres ordonnés originaires des diocèses de Strasbourg, Lille, Vannes, Le Puy et Mende vont évangéliser d'autres diocèses ou partent en mission. La cellule familiale joue un rôle essentiel dans l'éducation de la foi et dans la transmission des valeurs chrétiennes: prière en famille, formation morale, attachement à la catéchèse, célébration de la première communion, participation des jeunes à la liturgie. Le prêtre est le plus souvent appelé pour les derniers sacrements, les missions paroissiales réveillent la ferveur à dates régulières tous les cinq ou dix ans, le peuple suit les processions traditionnelles, fréquente les pèlerinages ou les 'pardons'. Dans ces régions, le clergé respecté par les populations multiplie les œuvres d'éducation, de jeunesse, d'assistance et s'efforce de répondre aux problèmes sociaux. Des caisses de crédit agricole se sont développées, le syndicalisme agricole d'inspiration chrétienne tient une place importante. Dans le domaine politique, les populations de ces régions sont d'abord catholiques, elles votent volontiers pour les partis d'inspiration chrétienne.

Un deuxième ensemble de régions regroupe les pays à traditions chrétiennes où la pratique religieuse est minoritaire avec 15% à 45% d'habitants assistant à la messe chaque dimanche. Cet ensemble comprend les régions méditerranéennes, le Languedoc, la Provence, la Corse. Il se prolonge vers le Nord par l'Aquitaine, l'Auvergne, la vallée du Rhône, la Bourgogne, la Champagne, la Picardie, la Normandie orientale, le Maine et la Touraine. Dans ces régions diversement développées, les unes riches comme la Normandie, les autres plus pauvres comme les Alpes du Sud et la Corse, la pratique religieuse est partout minoritaire chez les hommes, mais elle reste parfois relativement élevée chez les femmes. Les rites de passage, baptême, première communion, mariage à l'Église, obsèques religieuses sont sollicités par presque toutes les familles. Si les derniers sacrements ne sont plus demandés que par une minorité, le culte des mores reste très important. La religion populaire, très vivante, a été christianisée à travers le culte des saints et le culte marial. Dans les pays méridionaux, la croyance reste fortement théocentrique: Dieu intervient dans la vie quotidienne et il est nécessaire de se concilier ses faveurs. Les populations sollicitent des bénédictions très variées et aiment les processions en l'honneur des saints ou de Marie, qui sont perçus comme des médiateurs entre Dieu et les hommes. Des associations locales ou des confréries de pénitents organisent les cérémonies traditionnelles dans des pays où l'encadrement pastoral est parfois assez faible et où l'anticléricalisme reste souvent vivace.

Les 'pays de mission', avec moins de 15% d'assistants à la messe, constituent un troisième ensemble de territoires qui comprend le Limousin, une partie des Charentes, du Berry et du Centre du Bassin Parisien. Dans ces pays, la pratique dominicale masculine est très faible et peut être presque nulle: la pratique féminine subsiste et sa mesure n'est pas négligeable puisque, dans les villes, elle reste le plus souvent supérieure à 15%. Les rites de passages sont abandonnés par une partie de la population: de nombreux enfants ne sont ni baptisés ni catéchisés, les mariages et les obsèques civils deviennent fréquents. Cette situation est généralement ancienne: ainsi, au milieu du dix-neuvième siècle, Mgr Dupanloup évoque 'ces malheureux diocèses qui avoisinent Paris'.[14] Vers 1900, l'anticléricalisme et la libre-pensée développent dans les quartiers populaires des villes et dans les campagnes des Charentes, du Limousin et de l'Yonne. Ainsi, des paysans du Limousin, des mineurs du Bassin houiller du Pas-de-Calais, des ouvriers d'Ivry-sur-Seine s'engagent par écrit à avoir un enterrement civil. Ils signent un formulaire qui permettra à leurs amis de résister à la pression éventuelle de la famille après leur décès pour assurer au signataire des obsèques civiles. Des religions de substitution apparaissent avec l'idéologie du progrès apportée par la République, le scientisme puis le socialisme, enfin le communisme. Étudiant le Limousin, Louis Pérouas intitule son livre *Refus d'une religion, religion d'un refus*.[15] Après la Seconde Guerre mondiale en France, un effort missionnaire a été effectué dans ces régions.

LES RYTHMES DE L'HISTOIRE RELIGIEUSE

Ici, il convient de remettre en question le schéma d'une déchristianisation perçue comme un phénomène linéaire, continu, irreversible. Tous les travaux effectués par les historiens depuis plus de trente ans révèlent les ambiguïtés de cette expression et soulignent qu'on ne peut dissocier cette déchristianisation des formes et des aspects d'une christianisation antérieure mais jamais complète. En nous limitant pour le moment à la période qui s'écoule entre 1800 et 1960, nous pouvons grâce à la géo-sociographie historique, tenter de suivre le mouvement de la vitalité religieuse. Si sur le long terme la déchristianisation semble l'emporter, quatre grandes périodes peuvent être distinguées entre 1800 et 1960 où alternent les phases critiques et déclinantes et les phases constructives et ascendantes.

La phase critique des Secondes Lumières (1800–35)

De 1800 à 1830–35, on se trouve dans une phase critique: celle des Secondes Lumières, marquée par le déisme et le moralisme que répandent les ouvrages de Voltaire et de Rousseau très lus sous la Restauration. Les prédicateurs eux-mêmes, troublés par le drame révolutionnaire, insistent sur un Dieu justicier, vengeur et redoutable. La restauration religieuse avec l'aide du pouvoir, tentée par les Bourbons, est un échec; le clergé reste divisé par les conséquences du schisme; la pratique, qui a repris inégalement, s'affaisse à nouveau dans plusieurs régions, notamment le Bassin Parisien et le Centre Ouest. Le discrédit de l'alliance du Trône et de l'Autel rend compte des manifestations anticléricales qui suivent la révolution de 1830.

La christianisation active de l'ère romantique (1835–80)

A partir de 1835, dans beaucoup de diocèses, les courbes de pratique religieuse deviennent stables (Soissons, Reims, Nancy) ou remontent (Orléans, Versailles, Nevers, Périgueux). Les églises, trop vite réparées sous le Premier Empire, s'avèrent délabrées ou trop petites; aussi, se met-on à construire, reconstruire ou agrandir un nombre considérable d'édifices cultuels: quatre cents dans le seul diocèse de Bordeaux sous l'épiscopat du cardinal Donnet (1836–82). On sauve alors nos cathédrales qui sont l'objet de grands travaux conduits par des fervents de l'art gothique. Si les modes intellectuelles sous l'influence de Chateaubriand, Montalembert, Viollet le Duc ont leur part dans cette renaissance, si le mouvement menaissien y prend une part importante, le renouveau est dû principalement à la prédication et à l'action du clergé séculier, des religieux et des religieuses, dont les effectifs globaux triplent entre 1830 et 1878, ce qui continue à expliquer l'essor de l'enseignement libre et des missions. En 1835, Lacordaire inaugure à Notre-Dame une prédication centrée sur le Christ et l'Église qui attire la jeunesse romantique. Une religiosité ultramontaine, christocentrique et mariale, beaucoup plus chaleureuse, se répand avec une pédagogie qui atteint les foules lors des missions et des neuvaines des pèlerinages par la parole et la diffusion d'images sculptées ou peintes: chemins de croix qui évoquent les souffrances du Christ, statues du Sacré-Cœur qui suggèrent l'amour infini de Dieu, autels du mois de Marie avec une statuette de la Vierge qui entretiennent dans les maisons un culte familial.[16] En quelques décades, on passe du 'Dieu terrible au Bon Dieu' de Gérard Cholvy en accord avec une sensibilité romantique séduite par la figure de Jésus.

Cependant, si l'influence du clergé est essentielle, comme l'a bien montré Ralph Gibson dans sa thèse sur le diocèse de Périgueux,[17] elle comporte un écueil, le cléricalisme, qui s'accuse sous le Second Empire et qui nourrit l'anticléricalisme au début de la Troisième République: 'le cléricalisme, voilà l'ennemi', répète Gambetta.

Nouvelle phase critique: des laïcisations à la séparation (1880–1905)

De la Séparation des Églises et de l'école réalisée par Jules Ferry à la Séparation des Églises et de l'État, en maintes régions, le conformisme change de sens et on assiste à une désaffection pour les offices dominicaux, messe et vêpres, et à un recul de la pratique pascale. Les courbes baissent fortement dans le Centre, le Berry, le Limousin où le détachement s'accélère, elles déclinent également dans la région de Paris, en Champagne, en Périgord. Le dimorphisme sexuel s'accentue. La pratique masculine tombe presque à zéro dans certains secteurs, chez les maraîchers de la banlieue parisienne ou les ruraux du Sud de l'Aisne. L'anticléricalisme extrême et la libre-pensée entrainent le rejet de la religion catholique dans certaines régions évoquées plus haut. Vers 1900–10, l'opposition géographique entre les deux France et le contraste entre les sexes sont à leur apogée. La religion se féminise, ce qui contribue à expliquer l'essor des cultes de Thérèse de Lisieux et de Jeanne d'Arc, et les pèlerinages mariaux, comme celui de Lourdes, qui restent populaires.[18] Les protestants, le plus souvent favorables à la Troisième République, se différencient nettement des catholiques qui tendent à former des contre-sociétés.

La phase de réveil et de militantisme du vingtième siècle (1905–60)

La Séparation provoque un choc qui amène les laïcs catholiques à mieux participer à la vie de l'Église, et l'union sacrée de la Première Guerre mondiale contribue à l'atténuation de la querelle religieuse en attendant que la Seconde Guerre mondiale à travers Vichy et la Résistance ne fasse rentrer en grand nombre les catholiques dans la vie politique. Les courbes de pratique religieuse traduisent cette histoire complexe dans laquelle le dynamisme des catholiques s'affirme.

On constate une érosion des très fortes valeurs de la pratique pascale, notamment en Bretagne et dans les Pays de Loire, où la pratique féminine n'est plus unanime.[19] L'Alsace et la Moselle, où la religion et le patriotisme local sont fortement associés conservent une pratique religieuse extrêmement élevée jusqu'au milieu du vingtième siècle avec des taux qui se situent au-dessus de 75%.

On observe une stabilité de nombreuses régions où la pratique religieuse se maintient à un niveau moyen: ainsi la Basse-Normandie. Enfin, la remontée des très faibles valeurs de la pratique masculine est sensible dans l'Ile de France, l'Orléanais, la Picardie, la Champagne, comme le montre le tableau suivant:

Table 1 Pascalisants – Hommes (dans les villes)

Diocèse	Date	Taux (%)	Date	Taux (%)
Reims	1923–26	10,0	1961	17,7
Châlons sur Marne	1924–25	4,8	1959	12,5
Troyes	1929–32	2,6	1960–62	9,0
Soissons	1922–27	5,4	1965	9,6
Orléans	1931–34	6,2	1955	8,9
Montpellier	1911	9,7	1962	11,4

Cette remontée de la pratique masculine est également sensible en Languedoc comme le montre l'exemple du diocèse de Montpellier et en Aquitaine, notamment dans le Lot et Garonne et les Landes: dans ce dernier département, elle passe de 12% en 1945 à 22% en 1964.[20]

La progression du militantisme catholique a des effets politiques; les députés du *Mouvement républicain populaire* (MRP) relaient les radicaux dans la Marne sous la Quatrième République. L'évolution des baptêmes et des enterrements religieux à Paris confirme cette orientation. Les villes ont des taux plus bas que les campagnes mais ne font pas exception. C'est le moment où l'on construit beaucoup d'églises, où l'on crée de nombreuses paroisses urbaines: cent églises construites dans le diocèse de Paris dans le cadre des chantiers du Cardinal Verdier (1929–40), cinquante dans le diocèse de Lyon de 1945 à 1965, trente dans celui de Grenoble pendant la même période, soixante-dix-sept dans celui de Nantes entre 1936 et 1966.

Le réveil intellectuel, illustré par les personnalités de Blondel, Maritain, Péguy, Claudel, Mauriac, Bernanos, et l'intériorisation plus profonde de la vie religieuse, marquée par les progrès de la communion fréquente, favorisent le réveil religieux. Enfin, cette période est celle de la montée de l'action catholique au sens large, sous ses différentes formes successives, entre 1905 et 1960: la première Action catholique, celle de Pie X, dominée d'abord par l'*Action catholique de la jeunesse française* (ACJF) et les ligues féminines, puis influencée par la *Fédération nationale catholique* (FNC) du général de

Castelnau en 1925; la deuxième Action catholique, celle de Pie XI, marquée en France et en Belgique par la spécialisation des mouvements selon les milieux sociaux à partir de 1927–31, après la naissance de la *Jeunesse ouvrière chrétienne féminine* (JOCF). L'influence du mouvement catholique est sensible au cours des années cinquante dans la Marne et les Ardennes où la presse de masse de la *Jeunesse agricole chrétienne* (JAC) atteint plus de 15% des jeunes et plus de 20% des femmes adhèrent à l'*Action catholique générale féminine* (ACGF). A l'autre extrémité de la France, dans les Landes, la remontée de la pratique masculine évoquée plus haut s'explique par la progression du nombre de militants et d'adhérents de la JAC.

De 1941 au début des années cinquante, les mouvements catholiques ont encadré et contribué à former plus de 20% des jeunes. En sens inverse, les crises des mouvements, après 1956, ouvrent une ère de difficultés sérieuses pour l'Église de France.

Protestantisme et judaïsme connaissent aussi leurs rythmes; le protestantisme français, divisé sous la Troisième République, a connu une remarquable renaissance religieuse et civique au cours des années trente du vingtième siècle, avec le barthisme, du nom du grand théologien suisse Karl Barth, qui l'a incité fortement à combattre le nazisme. Le judaïsme en France a oscillé entre la déjudaïsation, assez étendue au dix-neuvième siècle, et après l'affaire Dreyfus, au vingtième siècle, la recherche d'une identité et d'un ressourcement religieux.

UN DÉBAT: LE PROBLÈME DE LA DÉCHRISTIANISATION OUVRIÈRE

La 'déchristianisation' de la classe ouvrière, caractérisée par des taux de pratique oscillant entre 0 et 13% lors des enquêtes des années 1950, a donné lieu à de nombreuses discussions entre pasteurs, sociologues et historiens en France comme en Angleterre.[21] Le livre des abbés Godin et Daniel, *La France, pays de mission?* (1943), souvent cité sans le point d'interrogation que comporte son titre, a réveillé un débat qui s'est prolongé. En 1961, Sabino Acquaviva a intitulé un livre *L'Éclipse du sacré dans la société industrielle*,[22] considérant cette observation comme un fait scientifique dans une perspective néo-positiviste. Harvey Cox, après avoir publié en 1965 sa *Cité séculière*, annonçant un monde de plus en plus sécularisé, a été frappé par la renaissance du phénomène religieux, décrite dans son ouvrage *La Séduction de l'Esprit* (1973).

D'autre part en France, l'idéologie a influencé d'assez nombreux observateurs: pour ceux qui plaçaient un espoir messianique dans la classe ouvrière, l'homme de demain, c'était le militant ouvrier athée, membre de la *Confédération générale du travail* (CGT) et du *Parti communiste français* (PCF) que les prêtres ouvriers avaient rencontré dans les usines à la fin de l'ère stalinienne. Or, comme Gérard Cholvy l'a montré, la réalité est plus nuancée: 'La déchristianisation ouvrière a été majorée sous l'influence d'une triple surestimation et d'une triple sousestimation.'

En effet, il y a une surestimation; en premier lieu, du modèle du metallurgiste parisien, et, en deuxième lieu, de l'athéisme connu à travers les militants communistes du mouvement ouvrier qui, lui, ne s'identifie ni à la seule CGT, ni même au monde ouvrier. En revanche, il y a eu sous-estimation; d'abord de la diversité du monde ouvrier français en fonction des régions et des types d'activité; ensuite, de la religiosité ouvrière diffuse et diversifiée que les grandes enquêtes de pratique dominicale ne peuvent prendre en compte; et, enfin, du renouvellement du monde ouvrier par les migrations et par l'immigration, déjà importante au cours des années cinquante.

Le renouvellement du monde ouvrier est sensible une vingtaine d'années plus tard lorsque les musulmans réclament des salles de prière. En 1977, dans un sondage qui inclut les Français et ne concerne pas les étrangers qui travaillent en France, 17% des Français se déclarent 'sans religion'; or 25% des cadres supérieurs se rangent dans cette catégorie, mais seulement 16% des ouvriers.

LE DERNIER TIERS DU VINGTIÈME SIÈCLE

La chute de la pratique religieuse en France depuis quarante ans représente une crise de civilisation. La pratique religieuse dominicale qui se situait en France un peu au-dessus de 30% au cours des années cinquante, tombe aux alentours de 10% à la fin des années quatre-vingts. Les sondages nous permettent de l'évaluer. Ils révèlent que la chute est brutale entre 1961 et 1975, de 30% à 14%, plus lente depuis 1975. Cependant la courbe n'est pas régulière entre 1961 et 1975 et les sondages permettent d'affiner la recherche des explications. La première chute, de 30% à 25%, se produit entre

1961 et 1965, donc pendant le Concile de Vatican II (1962–65), puis un palier apparaît entre 1965 et 1968, suivi d'une deuxième chute, plus brutale, de 25% à 14%, entre 1969 et 1975, donc en pleine crise de civilisation.

La nouveauté des quarante dernières années réside dans le déclin des cérémonies de passage, celle des 'quatre temps de la vie', comme en témoignent les chiffres suivants:

Rapport	1958 (%)	1990 (%)
Baptêmes catholiques sur naissances	91	51
Mariages catholiques sur mariages civils	79	51

Les explications peuvent être nuancées selon les périodes puis se cumuler. Entre 1962 et 1965, la volonté d'*aggiornamento* (mise à jour) partagée par Jean XXIII et Paul VI, est interprétée comme une acceptation de la sécularisation par beaucoup de clercs et de laïcs: déconfessionalisation de la CFTC (1964) et de diverses associations, abandon des locaux d'œuvres paroissiaux, disparition des patronages, déclin de la presse de masse des mouvements.

Le légalisme ritualiste est dénoncé, la pratique est recommandée, mais non considérée comme obligatoire par les adultes et les enfants. Avec le prolongement de la scolarité obligatoire jusqu'à seize ans, les petits séminaires ferment. Les chorales sont touchées par la disparition du latin et par le déclin des structures paroissiales.

Le deuxième effondrement fait suite aux événements de mai 1968 et accompagne la crise de civilisation des années 1968–75. Cette crise se traduit par un refus des rites qui semblent imposés, par le déclin du sens du péché, par la surévaluation de l'engagement politique et syndical par rapport à l'évangélisation proprement dite.

L'Action catholique prétend au monopole de l'encadrement des laïcs mais entre en crise et ne cesse de décliner. L'autorité papale est contestée par une partie de la presse d'inspiration catholique après l'encyclique *Humanae vitae* (1968) qui est mal reçue. L'enseignement du catéchisme est remplacé par le parcours catéchétique qui part du vécu de l'enfant: la catéchèse commence à être moins fréquentée et les enfants sont beaucoup moins nombreux à la messe. Enfin des milliers de prêtres quittent le ministère.

Le déclin s'atténue à partir de 'l'année sainte', 1975, pour plusieurs raisons: abandon du quasi-monopole accordé à l'Action catholique, vitalité persistante de la religion populace, apparition du Renouveau charismatique – 'une chance pour l'Église' selon Paul VI – montée de nouveaux mouvements de jeunes et d'adultes accueillis d'abord par un petit nombre d'évêques, impulsion nouvelle donnée à l'Église par Jean-Paul II. Cependant, le tassement du nombre des pratiquants continue à cause de la prolongation de la crise de recrutement ecclésiastique (cent ordinations de prêtres séculiers par an entre 1977 et 1987, cent trente après 1988, contre plus de quatre cents avant 1968), phénomène qui affecte la France et le Bénélux et beaucoup moins les autres pays d'Europe où les vocations sont nettement plus nombreuses. Cette crise sacerdotale persistante oblige les évêques à regrouper les paroisses, ce qui décourage un certain nombre de pratiquants. Le diocèse de Paris fait exception avec quinze ordinations de prêtres séculiers par an au début des années 1990.

LA RÉPARTITION DE LA PRATIQUE RELIGIEUSE DANS LES ANNÉES 1990

Une étude du taux de catéchisation des enfants du cours moyen première année (CM1, âges 7–8) réalisée en 1993–94 (taux calculé sans prendre en compte les enfants musulmans et protestants) fait apparaître plusieurs faits: d'abord, une nette érosion de la catéchisation depuis vingt-cinq ans (seules les régions concordataires d'Alsace et de Moselle atteignent plus de 80%); puis, une répartition qui reproduit, dans ses grands traits, les conclusions de Boulard avec une remontée relative de la France du Centre et d'apparents déserts catéchétiques dans la banlieue et de la grande banlieue Est de Paris et dans certaines banlieues de quelques villes du Sud-est.

Cette relative stabilité géographique de la répartition de la pratique religieuse, à un niveau beaucoup plus bas qu'en 1960, est confirmée par les enquêtes locales: un travail très approfondi sur les catholiques en Basse-Normandie a été effectué dans les trois départements bas-normands et publié en 1992. Des enquêtes ont eu lieu dans divers diocèses comme Troyes ou Toulouse au cours de la periode 1985–1996. Des enquêtes locales dans le Nord-Pas-de-Calais permettent de dater la disparition de certains rites (derniers sacrements, célébration des vêpres) ou leur raréfaction (confirmation, voire profession de foi).

CONCLUSION

D'après les sondages, on peut évaluer à 70% le nombre des catholiques, à 20% celui des agnostiques, à 5% celui des musulmans, à 1,5% celui des protestants, 1% celui des juifs, 1% celui des membres des sectes, 0,5% celui des orthodoxes et 0,5% celui des bouddhistes. L'avenir est imprévisible. On peut simplement pronostiquer une accentuation du pluralisme religieux dans un pays où la très grande majorité de la population était catholique jusqu'aux années 1960, mais on peut aussi prévoir une multiplication des minorités ferventes catholiques comme en a témoigné l'accueil réservé en septembre 1996 au pape Jean-Paul II par plus d'un demi-million de personnes qui se sont déplacées pour le rencontrer.

NOTES

1. Gabriel Le Bras, *Études de sociologie religieuse* (Paris: Presses Universitaires de France, 1956).

2. Groupe de recherches coordonnés (GRECO) numéro 2, Histoire religieuse moderne et contemporaine, *Répertoire des visites pastorales de la France*, 6 vols (Paris: CNRS, 1977–85).

3. Jacques Sutter, *La Vie religieuse des Français à travers les sondages d'opinion (1944–1976)* (Paris: CNRS, 1984).

4. Fernand Boulard, *Problèmes missionnaires de la France rurale* (Paris: Cerf, 1945).

5. Fernand Boulard, *Essor ou déclin du clergé français* (Paris: Cerf, 1950).

6. Pierre Lhande, *Le Christ dans la banlieue* (Paris: Grasset, 1927); *Le Dieu qui bouge* (Paris: Grasset, 1930); *La Croix sur les fortifs* (Paris: Grasset, 1931).

7. Henri Godin et Yves Daniel, *La France, pays de mission?* (Lyon: Éditions de l'Abeille, 1943).

8. Fernand Boulard, *Premiers itinéraires en sociologie religieuse* (Paris: Éditions ouvrières, 1951).

9. Fernand Boulard et Jean Rémy, *Pratique religieuse urbaine et régions cultuelles* (Paris: Éditions ouvrières, 1968).

10. Gérard Cholvy, *Géographie religieuse de l'Hérault contemporain* (Paris: Presses Universitaires de France, 1968).

11. François Isambert et Jean-Pierre Terrenoire, *Atlas de la pratique religieuse des catholiques en France* (Paris: FNSP, 1980).

12. Fernand Boulard, Gérard Cholvy, Bernard Delpal, Jean Gadille, Yves-Marie Hilaire, *Matériaux pour l'histoire religieuse du peuple français*, 4 vols (Paris: EHESS, FNSP, CNRS, 1982–92). Vol. 1: Région parisienne, Haute-Normandie, Centre, Pays de la Loire, Centre-Ouest. Vol. 2: Bretagne, Basse-Normandie, Nord-Pas-de-Calais, Picardie, Champagne, Lorraine, Alsace. Vol. 3: Sud-Ouest, Sud du Massif

Central, Languedoc. Vol. 4: Bourgogne, Franche-Comté, Sud-Est, Corse (à paraître).

13. Gérard Cholvy et Yves-Marie Hilaire, *Histoire religieuse de la France contemporaine*, 3 vols (Toulouse: Privat, 1985–88). Voir aussi Gérard Cholvy, *La Religion en France de la fin du XVIIIe siècle à nos jours* (Paris: Hachette, 1991).

14. Christiane Marcilhacy, *Le Diocèse d'Orléans au milieu du XIXe siècle* (Paris: Sirey, 1964) et *Le Diocèse d'Orléans sous l'épiscopat de Mgr Dupanloup* (Paris: Plon, 1962).

15. Louis Perouas, *Refus d'une religion, religion d'un refus* (Paris: EHESS, 1985).

16. Yves-Marie Hilaire, *Une chrétienté au XIXe siècle? Le diocèse d'Arras de 1840 à 1914*, 2 vols (Lille: Presses Universitaires de Lille, 1977).

17. Ralph Gibson, *Le Diocèse de Périgueux au XIXe siècle* (thèse non publiée, Université de Lyon, 1980) et *A Social History of French Catholicism 1789–1914* (London: Routledge, 1989).

18. Nadine-Josette Chaline, *Des catholiques normands sous la Troisième République: crises, combats, renouveaux* (Le Coteau: Horvath, 1985).

19. Michel Lagrée, *Religion et culture en Bretagne 1850–1950* (thèse non publiée, Université de Rennes II, 1991).

20. Vincent Adoumié, 'Le Réveil religieux landais au XXe siècle', *Annales du Midi*, 3 (1996), 377–94.

21. Cholvy, *La Religion en France*, présente et résume le débat; voir aussi Hugh MacLeod, *Piety and Poverty: Working-class Religion in Berlin, London and New York 1870–1914* (New York/London: Holmes & Meier, 1996).

22. Sabino Acquaviva, *L'Éclipse du sacré dans la société industrielle* (Paris: Mame, 1967).

12

Secularisation and the (re)formulation of French Catholic identity

Colin Roberts

In his 1936 novel, *Journal d'un curé de campagne*, Georges Bernanos chose the setting of a rural parish to explore the crisis besetting French Catholic culture. The parish was the natural focus of identity. It was more than a geographical area: it had a history that reached back to the era of Christendom in which religion was woven into the social fabric, and shaped a whole culture. Moreover, French Catholicism from the Revolution until the First World War had a very clearly defined self-identity summed up in the word 'intransigence': namely, adherence to an interlocking set of anti-liberal political and religious principles. It is to this identity that a minority of French Catholics continue to cleave today. The majority, however, accept political pluralism, while remaining divided on how far liberal attitudes should be allowed to influence the content of religious belief itself.

That there is a crisis of identity in French Catholicism is apparent in the dispute over the criteria of identity. In Gabriel Le Bras's enquiry into French Catholicism in the 1930s the key determinant of belonging was attendance at liturgical worship, especially Mass.[1] Obeying the Church's moral teaching, especially in matters of sex, hearing Mass and receiving the sacraments still remain yardsticks of orthodoxy. Such formal criteria of belonging are challenged, however, by those who privilege a psycho–social approach to religious identity. Canonical definitions of incorporation are replaced by subjective expressions of faith which involve an element of indeterminacy. What does it mean to be a Christian, let alone a Catholic in contemporary French society, and where is the dividing line between the secular and the religious? Even the language of believers is becoming less religious. Where references to heaven, hell and the devil do occur, they are often to be found in plays and films, outside a liturgical context. They are no longer witnesses to Revelation but have become 'les ruines admirables d'une symbolique ouvrant à tous des possibilités d'invention et d'expression'.[2] The Church, of course, has magnificent monuments, but what use are they if they are empty of life, and what does the local or village church signify? In a country like France, with strong Catholic roots, the rich patrimony of Christian art and architecture is part of a collective memory, but it has ceased to symbolise the core of modern French culture.

THE BLURRING OF IDENTITY: THEOLOGIES OF SECULARISATION

While secular modernity dissolves all religious systems founded on the heteronomous authority of a tradition, it has allowed a new 'post-traditional' religious ethos to emerge, one that makes observance flow not from social custom but from personal commitment. Modernisers in the Church enunciate belief without reference to tradition, or if they refer to tradition they do not link it with belief. They call for 'la sortie de la religion', a form of 'religion-less' religion, one in which belief is deregulated and in which the authority of the priest is dissolved in that of the laity at large. The belief that secularisation means the retreat of Christianity is linked with a view of religion as bounded by time and space. The epoch of organised religion is identified with the era of Christendom. There is a structural link between memory and religion which has been fragmented and ultimately broken down by modernity. The sociologist of religion, Danièle Hervieu-Léger, claims that this has resulted in the collapse of 'l'imaginaire français et catholique de la continuité',[3] the erosion of the parish as the foundation of French religious life and the end of an ideal vision of a Catholic rural France.

Secular modernity has had the effect of creating a more metaphorical understanding of faith. Sociologists of religion like Jean Séguy suggest that metaphor is the only way to reconcile religious discourse with secular modernity, and that what is believed is less important than how faith is lived out; doctrinal theology has given way to religious humanism.[4] This is a reformulation of what modernist theologians like De Loisy in France and Tyrell in England were saying at the end of the last century.

In contemporary France, religion is less and less at the heart of the social matrix, and secular values and morality do not seek the sanction of the Church. In the eyes of those seeking to adapt faith to a secular age, the truth of Judaism and Christianity lies in the attempt to 'désenchanter la nature, l'histoire et les valeurs'.[5] They regard the seeds of secularisation as having been present from the very beginning in Judaism and Christianity, ushering in the modern world, creating political consciousness and helping to shape modern subjectivity; the monotheistic tradition helped to demythologise and desacralise nature, and recast faith as an ethical relation to the other. Those who share this theological outlook seek to express their religious commitment through political and social activism, which becomes the real, hidden language of faith, a point which John Ardagh makes when he observes that 'the Catholics of France have been turning from theology and ritual to social action'.[6] Clerical religion is seen as unfaithful to the Biblical tradition, and politics replaces metaphysics as the language of theology. For those who therefore seek a reconciliation between religion and modernity, secularisation is primarily a religious and theological rather than a sociological issue.

Since Vatican II, Catholic theology has shown a marked tendency to move away from a purely negative appraisal of secular culture, which is increasingly seen as the bearer of positive values. Modern secular culture fosters the emergence of a Christian community that no longer thinks in terms of Christendom. With the advent of a society whose technological nature seems to fall increasingly outside the Church's purview, Christians are free to adopt a more desacralised world view. For those Catholics who believe in dialogue with the world, this can be seen as a more mature form of Christianity. Much of modern theology has been concerned with freeing the believer of the need for external props of authority, and with stripping catechetics of the doctrinal accretions of centuries.

The traditional Catholic mind-set has been eroded by the values of secularisation. Gone is traditional Catholicism tied by an umbilical cord to the Right and steeped in religious triumphalism. Even the call to evangelise seems problematic, given that all truth is inscribed within limits. Michel de Certeau and Jean-Marie Domenach argue that religion has the capacity to be creative and fecund, allowing other truths to emerge. They call Christianity 'un phénomène limité'[7] in the history of humanity; it cannot absorb the whole of history, nor speak in the name of the entire world; its historical limitations flow from its association with Western culture.

Theologies of partial identity have exercised a subtle influence over the post-Vatican II Church, despite the opposition of traditionalists like Pope John Paul II, who is trying to curb some of the more radical formulations of Catholic belief. The fact that Catholicism is not incompatible with pluralism implies new ways of belonging to the Church. The modern believer no longer looks to the Church 'de le prendre en charge définitivement, mais lui demande seulement de l'inscrire dans une histoire, dans une mémoire'.[8] The Church no longer appears as a unified body, capable of integrating the totality of its members in a harmonious and hierarchically structured world. Authority in the Church has become more circumscribed, and believers identify with the institution to varying degrees: some might embrace the whole of Catholic discipline and dogma, others might view Church membership as no more than an affirmation of belonging to a Christian culture. For many contemporaries, traditional religious language has become pure folklore, signalling the end of 'un christianisme objectif'.[9]

In France, the events of May 1968 issued in a systematic denunciation of power, authority and social conformity. To many Catholics, the Church seemed out of step with the age, a conviction singularly reinforced by the papal condemnation of birth control in *Humanae vitae*, published the same year. Traditional Christian anthropology that underlay Catholic moral teaching seemed to lag behind changing attitudes to sex. Formerly orthodoxy and orthopraxy had characterised churchgoers. The condemnation of birth control represented a watershed, after which an increasing number of Catholics started to attach only a relative value to the teachings of the Church. This has been particularly true of young Catholics, of whom René Rémond observes that they have 'un comportement différentiel à l'égard de l'Église qui les conduit à une relativisation de sa parole qui risque de s'étendre à d'autres choses ... De proche en proche cela peut affecter non seulement les comportements moraux, mais le contenu de la foi'.[10]

The theologian Jean Rigal argues that the universal catechism promulgated in 1993 is too dogmatic and too insensitive to the hopes and aspirations of men and women in contemporary society.[11] He argues that Catholic evangelists in today's world need to take seriously respect for identities, and the modern believer's heightened sense of moral autonomy. The Church must respect the inviolability of the human conscience, the desire for happiness and quality of life, and sexual equality.

A measure of how far the values of secular society at large have been absorbed by significant numbers of priests and laity is to be seen in the increasing debate about democracy and dialogue within the Church. Many Catholics have reinvested their democratic ideals in the ecclesiastical institution itself, and believe that there will be a loss of credibility if the Pope calls for Catholics to defend liberty and human rights, but refuses to apply democracy to the Church itself. Democracy in the Church and openness to secular values have been championed within the French hierarchy by the outspoken voice of Jacques Gaillot, who paid the price by being removed from his post as Bishop of Evreux in 1995. At the time, the level of support for Gaillot in France was clearly indicated by the large demonstrations held in his favour, as well as by the thousands of messages of sympathy he received.

The extent to which secularisation has made inroads within the Church is illustrated by Yves Lambert's comparative snapshots of religious belief and practice in the Breton parish of Limerzel, in the early 1930s and the 1980s.[12] The advance of secular ideas and values is all the more stark in that Limerzel was not simply in the past a staunchly Catholic parish, but one which harboured Royalist sympathies up until the First World War. Indeed, at the time of the Revolution, it was associated with the insurgent Royalism of the *chouannerie*. In the early 1930s, Limerzel epitomised the old parochial culture of Catholic France. There were three priests and eight nuns, almost all the children were in Catholic schools and most parishioners attended Sunday Mass. Up until the 1950s, the religious life of the parish had a timeless quality which recalled the centuries of Christendom. Since then, however, it has witnessed a crisis of belief, a drop in vocations, dwindling church attendance and the replacement of orthodox belief with a new kind of transcendental humanism. This has been accompanied by both a decline in the Church's social influence and an increase in religious indifference and unbelief.

The secularisation of faith is also evidenced by the attempt to make the language of the liturgy resemble everyday speech through the use of French. There has been a move away from a vertical form of service that gives priority to the priest towards a more horizontal one that forges emotional bonds between worshippers. This theological thrust is linked with the search for base communities which have gathered on the margins of the parish structure while remaining within the Catholic fold. Such communities seek a liturgical symbolism that recalls daily life as much as possible, with the Eucharist, for example, resembling a meal around the table. Hervieu-Léger has taken the example of charismatic groups within French Catholicism to illustrate the rise of base communities which are attempting to give expression to a more prophetic Christianity. They have abandoned the traditional language of worship for 'speaking in tongues'. Their emphasis on emotion signals their rejection of the attempt to reconcile faith and reason. She argues that it is oversimplistic to regard the charismatics as returning to a primitive form of religious expression. Rather they manifest a religious sensibility that is finely attuned to secularisation, because they recognise that contemporary speech is indelibly secular and that the only form of religious expression possible is one that goes beyond language. Charismatic worship represents a 'recomposition du champ religieux: entre modernité et anti-modernité'.[13]

There are tens of thousands of members of charismatic groups and a thousand prayer groups in France.[14] At first, they were regarded with suspicion by the hierarchy, but have gradually been accepted. These new religious movements, Hervieu-Léger reminds us, call into question a major assumption of the sociology of religion: they do not attract those who are marginalised by modern society; their leaders and activists are drawn from the intellectual middle classes, managers and technicians, in other words, the very people who are the driving-force behind modernity. Members of charismatic movements emphasise the personal experience of the believer rather than formal assent to doctrine and tradition. They affirm the subjective experience of religion and the desire to find new ways of belonging to a community of faith, often outside the traditional parish structure. They stand for a conscious endeavour to give new impetus to religious faith, beyond the conceptual boundaries provided by the notion of Christendom. Their religious commitment represents a protest against modern secularism while simultaneously providing 'le moyen d'une adaptation distancié aux conditions de la vie dans le monde'.[15]

RE-AFFIRMING THE BOUNDARIES OF TRADITIONAL IDENTITY

Those who seek to distance themselves from traditional Catholic identity separate Christ from Christianity and claim that different religions represent parallel paths to God, even though all relate to the mystery of Christ. They accord only a relative value to what the Church has always regarded as its unique mission and status. Rigal goes so far as to claim that 'la plupart des théologiens catholiques partagent cette opinion'.[16] Jean-Marie Donegani believes that the Church has to oppose a minimum of resistance to the silent process of subjectivisation and to the 'porosité de l'identité catholique'.[17] He wonders how those Catholics brought up in the post-Conciliar Church, and especially those who were socialised in the 1960s, are going to get a sense of stability in the fragmented and changing Church of today.

As a reaction against the erosion of Catholic discipline and identity there has been a certain doctrinal hardening. The optimistic view of the world contained in the Conciliar document *Gaudium et spes* (1965) has given way to a new pessimism. The Church is seen by traditional Catholics as a beacon for humanity, lost in a sea of atheism and materialism. This has led to calls for a reaffirmation of traditional religious identity. John Paul II has adopted a conservative interpretation of Vatican II, talking in terms of a 'Christian reconquest' and of a 'second evangelisation of Europe': 'France, souviens-toi des promesses de ton baptême' was his rallying-cry on his first visit to France in 1980.

A return to certainties has marked the Pontificate of John Paul II. This is a reflection not just of the Pope's Polish roots but also of the the end of the euphoria of the 1960s, which in turn has led to a questioning of theologies of secularisation and cultural ecumenism. Catholic conservatives argue that the task of the Church is not to cultivate expressions of individual freedom, but to transmit a deposit of faith and to define the limits of institutional belonging. Rome has brought to book clergy who have promoted theologies of partial identity. The text *Redemptoris missio* (1990) talks of re-evangelising countries of long Christian tradition, where groups of baptised people have lost the sense of a living faith. John Paul II talks of 'new evangelisation' and calls for the Christian message to be imparted in all its fullness. He insists on the richness of Revelation in comparison to what we live already, and stresses the pertinence of the Christian faith in a fearful and rudderless age. The emphasis is on combating unbelief and on the message to be transmitted, rather than on those who are to receive it.

The priest in particular has suffered a crisis of identity. The movement *Échanges et dialogue*, created in November 1968, gave collective expression to the malaise surrounding celibacy and the increased role of the laity. The crisis of the priesthood goes to the heart of the crisis of Catholic identity. There are simply not enough priests to say Mass in parishes. In France, there are around one hundred diocesan priests ordained per year, whereas thirty years ago, in the country as a whole, there were more than a thousand ordinations per year.[18] Not since the Revolution has there been such a sustained collapse of vocations. After the war, half the missionaries, priests and religious orders were French. The crisis of the priesthood arose when the ministry lost a part of its sacramental meaning in the eyes of many Catholics. As long as he was cradled by a strong, mystical Christian culture, the priest was able to stand fast. But with the spread of secularisation outside and even within the Church, he found himself an anachronism. Hence the need felt by clergy to reclaim their own identity within the Church.

A reaction has set in against progressive priests who have eschewed clerical dress, celebrated a pared-down liturgy, and sought meaning to life in social praxis rather than in the sacramental life of the Church and in the eschatological Kingdom. There has been a revival of monasticism and of religious orders generally. The number of novices grew by 41% in the early 1980s.[19] Personal sanctification, rather than social evangelism, seems to be the main motive for new vocations. The Church is calling for a return to a simple, pious, unintellectual faith. Marian devotion, centred on Lourdes, and a strong emphasis on the leadership of the Pope are other indicators of traditional Catholic identity. The charismatic movement – potentially a disruptive force – has been brought into line by the Church, even though there are many traditionalists who fear a confusion between subjective emotional experience and divine revelation.

The crisis of self-confidence besetting laïcité has helped the emergence of a more assertive style of Catholicism in the 1980s. The consensual morality and sense of duty proclaimed by Republicans like Jules Ferry in the last century have given way to moral pluralism and a form of 'soft' ethics.[20] Today's liberal State no longer proclaims a single ethical system which it calls its own, and the values and truth-claims of Enlightenment reason have been denounced by French deconstructionists and by post-modernist intellectuals who otherwise have no links with Catholicism. Parliament no longer has the self-confidence to debate on its own social issues that raise difficult ethical questions, and in order to form an opinion seeks the help of the Comité national d'éthique, on which religious delegates are strongly represented. Secularists bewail the Republic's lack of leader-ship and fear that its failure to find a clear voice to condemn racism and xenophobia will leave the moral high ground to the Churches.[21]

The renewed assertiveness of conservative Catholicism in France is also a consequence of the waning of anti-clericalism as an issue capable of uniting the Left. The failure in 1984 of the Socialists to nationalise private, mainly Catholic, schools and the massive public support mobilised by the Catholic parents' association in defence of the private sector strengthened the hand of the Church in public life. Of course, many supporters of the private school sector were not necessarily practising Catholics, nor even believers, but the decision of the government to back down did give the Church, led by the Archbishop of Paris, Cardinal Lustiger, renewed confidence in itself as a national institution. Lustiger's views on Catholic education were keenly sought by the political class both Right and Left, including President Mitterrand, and the Cardinal and other leading clerics became the objects of increased media attention.

The *école laïque* in turn has been accused of failing to impart a sense of France's religious culture. Many young people, even – paradoxically – those who attend Catholic schools, lack knowledge of France's Christian and Catholic heritage. The possibility of includ-ing religious history in the public school curriculum has been raised by the hierarchy and by Catholic and even lay educationalists. In a secular age, in which memories of Christendom are fading away, they argue that the Church is still able to offer a 'service de la mémoire collective'.[22]

Cardinal Lustiger is strongly identified with the new neo-clericalism or *catholicisme identitaire*. The latter is not to be confused with the old political Catholicism of the Right, more especially that of the *Action française* (AF). Lustiger's intransigence is confined to the moral and religious sphere. He stresses the religious foundation of all morality in contrast to those Christians who are prepared to accord secular morality a degree of autonomy. This is a continuing source of conflict among Catholics and goes to the heart of the Church's identity as an *ecclesia docens*, a teacher of faith and morals. Lustiger argues that the moral crisis of the present age can be traced back to the Enlightenment. Glossing over the Inquisition, he exonerates Christianity of the charge of intolerance and writes: 'Je crois que l'antisémitisme d'Hitler relève de l'antisémitisme des Lumières et non d'un antisémitisme chrétien.'[23]

Lustiger offers a subtle rejection of modernity. He does not attack it head on by calling into question its ideals. Instead, he argues that modernity is incapable in practice of achieving them. He notes the promises that the western world has failed to keep, or only kept imperfectly: class and racial divisions still exist, human rights are routinely abused in many parts of the world and the realisation of social justice seems a distant dream. He turns the project of modernity against itself when he affirms that 'je nomme illusion la pensée que la raison peut être sauvée par la raison'.[24] He argues that the only true liberation is the one that comes from God, and only the Church, the legitimate holder of religious authority and power, knows how fully to achieve it. In the modern cultural maze in which meaning and systems of belief have become fragmented, the Church presents itself as an *institution secours*; in a world of doubt and unbelief, it offers certainties. The Cardinal updates the traditional Catholic claim that the Church is the holder of Truth, which the individual cannot find alone; the believer must submit to an authority that is external to the self.

There have been those Catholics, says Lustiger, who have wanted the Church to evolve from inside just like a trade union, adding that this had always left him ill at ease and that he could never identify with that kind of Left Catholicism. He is against what he calls the 'seduction of Marxism' and Liberation Theology, and speaks out against what he sees as the danger of incorporating theories of social struggle within Christianity. He quotes as an example the novel *Les Saints vont en enfer* (1952) in which Gilbert Cesbron argues that Catholics need to become 'naturalised' among the working class outside the Church in order to find a place in the modern world.[25]

According to Lustiger, Catholics who embrace a theology of secularisation want a Church that is self-effacing to the point of self-obliteration, in the belief that this will enable it to fulfil its mission. They regard the death of the institutional Church as a portent of Redemption. Lustiger regards such a theology as dangerous in so far as it puts itself forward as a general theory of the Church's apostolate. It can be understood as a revulsion against the intransigent and triumphalist Catholicism of the *Syllabus of Errors* (1865), although he regards this view of the nineteenth-century Church as 'une représentation caricaturale et mythique'.[26] According to Lustiger, Catholics who think this way suffer from a sense of guilt at belonging to a Church that in the past spurned the modern age. He speculates that their outlook can also be explained by an unspoken desire to fit into a society in which the visible signs of Christianity are fading away, and that, by merging with the general ethos, they hope to be socially more acceptable. They believe that, since the Church is no longer the strong social and political force it once was, Catholics must reassert their influence in oblique ways and, in order to re-occupy a central position in society, must be prepared to renounce traditional religious identity. Lustiger bemoans the fact that too many Catholics have looked at themselves from a sociological perspective, seeing themselves solely through others' eyes as a 'Catholic party', until the moment when they have no longer been able to bear this reflected image. In order to escape the critical eye of society they have sought to dissolve the boundaries of their group identity, a move which they justify by a theology of self-extinction that celebrates the imminent disappearance of the Church as an institution, deemed oppressive and even sinful, in favour of a hidden, diffuse, secret presence.

Lustiger is particularly critical of May 1968, saying that it transformed the aim of the Vatican II into its exact opposite. Instead of the renewal of the ecclesiastical institution through an effort of interior conversion, there was unleashed a process of radical alienation in which people came to regard all social institutions – including the Church – as instruments of oppression. The events handicapped Vatican II's effort of renewal in France and created the nightmarish scenario of a society in the throes of an identity crisis. The Church had to cope with the tide of cultural revolution that swept along in its wake clergy and laity alike. The impact of May 1968 was deep and far-reaching: some Catholics remained steadfast, many others became caught up in the social and cultural turmoil of the time. May 1968, observes Lustiger, never seriously threatened scientific rationality, but it did call into question the aims and values of French society. The unexpectedness of the events had a disorientating effect and the young especially became so self-absorbed that they were unable to hear the message of Vatican II.

One of the effects of May 1968 was to shake the parish structure even further. The traditional parish was criticised for being ill-adapted to the task of evangelisation and too centred on the life of parishioners. The parish was there to ensure 'ordinary' Christian life: administration of the sacraments, the education of children, the care of the elderly, marriages, burials, worship, catechism and instruction in the faith. Critics of the parish argued that the 'real' apostolate of the Church went on outside it. Lustiger claims that the way the role and function of the parish is perceived has evolved since the 1960s. Active Christians have become acutely conscious of the extent of atheism and religious indifference in France, and they have had second thoughts about splitting off the Church's wider social mission from traditional parish worship. They are less interested in entering into dialogue with secularism and religious indifference than in ensuring their own Christian identity in a secularised world that has lost its religious bearings. Every culture needs the sacred and French secular culture has tried to appropriate Catholicism for its own ends. 'Mais en même temps', observes Lustiger, 'tous les sacrements sont la garantie que cette appropriation ne va pas se refermer sur elle-même'.[27]

Until the 1960s, birth control was the centre of controversy in the Church and the focus of prohibition. From the 1970s, other questions began to emerge: abortion, premarital relations, masturbation, the celibacy of priests, homosexuality and AIDS. On all of these issues, a gap has opened up between, on the one hand, Catholic theologians and many ordinary churchgoers and, on the other, the bishops and a core of conservative laity. Lustiger endorses the Church's prohibition of these practices and seems to want to look back with nostalgia to the nineteenth century which he associates with 'des bonheurs tranquilles et des vertus heureuses'.[28] He believes that the modern culture of individualism, especially since 1968, has generated a moral problem that flows from 'une volonté délibérée de transgression'.[29]

When the loi Veil was voted in 1975, the Catholic hierarchy adopted a discreet approach. While insisting that Catholic women should not seek abortions, they refrained from undertaking a major campaign urging the medical profession to use the conscience clause. The Church was unable to find the right words and arguments to address the concrete issue of abortion. French bishops are still trying to steer a careful path between the thesis of moral orthopraxy and the hypothesis that the Church has to accept the right of governments to enact legislation that may run counter to the Church's moral teaching. This modus vivendi has been put at risk by John Paul II's encyclical Evangelium vitae (1995), which rejects the hypothesis of co-existence. It calls on Catholics to reject all political debate on abortion and has been used as a justification for civil disobedience by those wishing physically to attack abortion clinics.

Lustiger, like his fellow bishops, follows the papal thesis. At the same time, he does not want to abandon the counter-balancing hypothesis, namely the Church's ability to influence public debate on ethical issues – especially those thrown up by advances in medical science. The *Comité national d'éthique* was set up under Mitterrand to address such issues and, in this area too, Lustiger calls for the Catholic moral message to be 'ultra-rigoriste'[30] and for Catholic members of the committee to reflect orthodox teaching. He also cautions against any attempt by the committee to give moral endorsement to political decisions or to take the place of moral conscience.

THE IDENTITY OF A MINORITY: CATHOLIC INTEGRISM

Staunch opposition to the secular State and attachment to Christian social order as embodied in the concept of Christendom are marked characteristics of the contemporary integrist movement. It blames the post-Conciliar Church for throwing in the towel to secularism and ushering in a time of crisis, exemplified by lower Mass attendance, a decline in vocations and a general crisis of Catholic identity. There are around a hundred thousand committed integrists in France, and several million sympathisers.[31] They are adept at exploiting the media, and every year at Pentecost a pilgrimage to Chartres is organised, which attracts between ten and thirty thousand people. However, their significance lies not so much in their numbers as in what they reveal about a certain Catholic psyche, which denounces the secularisation of morality and which longs for the triumphalist certainties of the past.

The integrist current was particularly strong at the beginning of the century, representing the identity of the French Catholic majority until the First World War. It was weakened by the 1926 condemnation of *Action française*, re-emerged in the 1950s as a reaction against the worker-priest experiment and found renewed vigour in its campaign against Vatican II. Catholic integrism is now a world-wide if limited movement, but, given the strong ideological flavour of French Catholicism, it is not surprising that it should have started in France. Apart from the abbé de Nante's *Contre-Réforme catholique*, there is the modern Catholic integrist movement, founded by Archbishop Marcel Lefebvre.

Lefebvre spent thirty years in west Africa, becoming first a bishop, then Metropolitan in Dakar, and finally Apostolic Delegate to all French-speaking Africa. He was highly regarded by Pius XII. In 1962, he was elected Superior-General of the Holy Ghost Congregation and attended Vatican II, where he soon found himself out of sympathy with the Council's support for liturgical reform, collegiality of the bishops with the Pope, ecumenism and adherence to a positive definition of religious freedom. Convinced that the new direction of the Council threatened to undermine orthodoxy, he founded a seminary in the diocese of Ecône in Switzerland, called the *Fraternité Saint-Pie X* and proceeded to ordain seminarists he had trained. While declaring his fidelity to a Rome that stood for unchanging tradition, he steadfastly refused to recognise the authority of the Council. His refusal to stop ordaining priests led to his suspension *a divinis* in 1976 – that is to say, he was no longer allowed to exercise the priestly ministry. In the same year, his supporters took over the church of Saint-Nicolas-du-Chardonnet in Paris. To remove them required the will of both the Church authorities and of the competent civil authority, which happened to be the Right-wing Paris city council. For political motives, the council was reluctant to act, and the Church was embarrassed by the affair, all the more so in the light of falling church attendance and the marked drop in vocations to the priesthood that followed the Council's reforms. From 1983 on, Lefebvre denounced ever more loudly the ecumenical initiatives of Pope John Paul II. The inter-religious gathering which the Pope arranged at Assisi in 1986 was a scandal in the eyes of the rebel Archbishop; he felt so alienated from the Vatican that he decided to ordain his own bishops in 1988, thereby creating a breakaway Church.

Catholic integrism is primarily a religious phenomenon, a reaction against what some feel to be the Protestantising effect of Vatican II on the Church. However, it would be naive to suppose that it does not harbour a political agenda. It is both anti-Masonic and anti-Communist. It finds a voice in the Right-wing press, including the review *Itinéraires* and the daily *Présent*, as well as in *Minute, Rivarol, Aspects de la France,* and in some political monthlies like *Lectures françaises.* The annual Joan of Arc procession in Paris brings together integrists and National Front supporters. The annual National Front party celebration is preceded by a Latin Mass, celebrated according to the rite of Pius V. Just before his death in March 1988, Lefebvre was fined eight thousand francs by the Court of Appeal in Paris for 'racial defamation' and 'incitement to racial hatred', for suggesting publicly that immigrants, beginning with Muslims, should be expelled from Europe. In 1976, he declared his support for Latin American dictatorships. He was an admirer of Maurras and Pétain, and supported the cause of French Algeria. While the racism of the National Front is condemned by all the Churches, some of the Front's personalities like Marie-France Stirbois are vociferous in their support of extremist Catholic groups such as *Chrétienté-solidarité*, and support a platform of 'family values' which recalls the new Right in the United States. Also, while both mainstream and integrist Catholics are anti-abortion, it has been noted that attacks by Catholic 'commandos' on abortion clinics have occurred wherever the Front's vote has increased.[32]

Catholic integrism stands for a radical rejection of secularisation, and of the Council's compromise with secular ideals and principles. The first principle to be condemned is that of democracy, in the form of a collegial model of Church government: namely, the obligation placed on the Pope to share the government of the Church with his fellow bishops, who in turn must reach collective decisions arrived at in the forum of bishops' conferences. The second is the principle of religious freedom, proclaimed by Vatican II, which – according to Lefebvre – gives other religions the right to propagate error. While not going so far as to want to forbid people to follow the religion of their choice, he maintains that religious freedom is not an absolute right but only something to be tolerated. To suppose that Rome is not the sole rock on which the Church is built is somehow to imagine that the truth can exist outside her; to open the door to recognition of other religions and to proclaim freedom of conscience is tantamount to apostasy. Here we can see a clear affiliation with the strictures of the *Syllabus of Errors*, and a deliberate reworking of counter-Revolutionary rhetoric. Lefebvre writes:

> Si l'on y regarde de plus près, c'est bien avec sa devise que la Révolution a pénétré dans l'Église de Dieu. La liberté religieuse … qui donne le droit à l'erreur. L'égalité c'est la collégialité, avec la destruction de l'autorité personnelle, de l'autorité de Dieu, du Pape, des éveques, la loi du nombre. La fraternité est représentée par l'œcuménisme.[33]

The quest for religious liberty at Vatican II is to be explained, according to Lefebvre, by the influence of Catholic liberal or modernist theologians – the two adjectives are interchangeable – who are the enemies within. He levels the accusation that their ideas and principles pervaded the Council's deliberations and documents.

Lefebvre condemns *Gaudium et spes*: its appeal to Catholics to listen to the movement of history smacks of nineteenth-century Hegelianism; it constitutes a syncretic document that adulterates Catholic teaching with the assumptions of a secular age and undermines the eternal truth of Rome.

Lefebvre argues that there is a third principle of modern secular society to which Catholicism has surrendered, namely the principle of separation of Churches and State. The Church of the 1960s moved away from the triumphant Tridentine model, and Paul VI had a certain sense of modernity and pluralism. Lefebvre cannot come to terms with the fact that France is no longer a confessional State, writing that 'l'ordre chrétien se distingue bien sûr des régimes libéraux fondés sur la séparation des Églises et de l'État'.[34] He sees the conflict between the *laïque* State schools and Catholic schools in France as an illustration of how harmful separation can be to the realisation of a national community of faith. He postulates a crusade for the reconstruction of Christendom, built on the Kingship of Christ. There are social, cultural, political and religious dimensions to this enterprise. It involves marginalising the influence of the Protestant Churches and non-Christian religions, especially Islam, combating atheism, Communism and Freemasonry, raising the social and cultural profile of the Church, resurrecting the pomp and splendour of the pre-Conciliar liturgy, reinstating Latin as the language of the Mass and restoring the status and role of the clergy. The latter must abandon the social gospel and revert to their traditional role as Massing priests and dispensers of the sacraments. Lefebvre blames the separation of Churches and State for propagating atheism: since no clear place is assigned to religion, both laity and clergy are left confused and religious belief is eroded. 'Le laïcisme a tout envahi', he laments.[35] The priest is made to feel an alien species and is tempted to 'fit in', by abandoning clerical garb and embracing political or social causes; the secular values of State and society have infected Catholics with relativism, even in matters of faith, whereas doctrine is fixed for all time.

Lefebvre defends the notion of a Christian people and nation and upholds traditional Catholic doctrine, which teaches that the civil power has authority to defend citizens against the spread of religious error. He says that the State has the right to moderate and regulate public manifestations of other faiths which the Church deems a danger to the salvation of souls. He even goes so far as to rehabilitate the Inquisition, whose work he compares with that of anti-narcotics agencies![36] In lieu of the Inquisition, traditionalist pressure groups like the *Fraternité Saint-Pie X* and especially ACRIF (*Association contre le racisme et pour le respect de l'identité française et catholique*) have resorted to the courts to have what they perceive to be blasphemy outlawed: for example, over the representation of Mary in Godard's film, *Je vous salue Marie*.[37]

CONCLUSION

The pluralist nature of contemporary French Catholicism has generated a 'débat identitaire tantôt bruyant, tantôt discret'.[38] There has been a privatisation of belief which has given rise to a spectrum of Catholic identity. It is as a response to this phenomenon that Catholics have attempted to define what it is to be a member of the Church.

Radical theology has tried to bridge religious and secular culture. The result has been a metaphorical reformulation of faith. Theologies of secularisation have called into question the assumption that there should be a Christian nation or State. 'Bref, le but n'est pas pour le chrétien de construire une société chrétienne, mais humaine', writes Guy Coq.[39] Catholicism is no longer linked to the individual's primary sense of social solidarity and has ceased to be a core of French cultural identity. One significant indicator of this is the decline in baptisms: whereas in 1972, 100% of practising Catholics said that they intended to have their child baptised, ten years later they were only 87%.[40]

Another response to the privatisation of belief and to secularisation has been to re-assert traditional Catholic theological and moral teaching. This has come from the French hierarchy, who talk quietly of the need to affirm 'difference'. They argue that the dynamics of the opening-up of the Church to the world has not lived up to its promises, that there has been a decline in vocations and religious practice generally, that doctrinal certainties have evaporated, in short, that the Church has become a pale reflection of its old self. Ignorance of the rudiments of Christianity among French pupils in schools is judged a symptom of the wider decline of the historical, literary and philosophical learning that underpinned French Catholic culture. This is held to be responsible for 'l'affligeant simplisme des idées de Dieu qui circulent avec insistance'.[41]

The blurring of evangelising whole social groups and therefore reconverting the whole of society inspired the *Action catholique* movement earlier in the twentieth century. It had a bipolar view of society, with a Christian community on one side and a secular community on the other. It failed to take into account that Catholics themselves were undergoing a process of secularisation. The 'enemy' was already within the walls. The prospect of national reconversion was gradually abandoned by a post-war French Church that was given over to self-doubt and confusion over its role in the nation. The resulting blurring of identity called into question not just the visibility of the Church but also its missionary dynamism. Why evangelise if people are already considered to be living in good faith?

A conservative theologian like Cardinal Lustiger argues that the Church would be naive to look at secular society through rose-tinted glasses and that it would be mistaken to blend in with the wider social ethos. The Church needs to retain its prophetic witness. 'Cependant, la société', he asks, 'peut-elle être privée de toute référence philosophique ou spirituelle commune pour énoncer le bien moral qui s'impose à toute conscience?'[42] In other words, he affirms that it is the Church which confers meaning on social reality, not the other way round. Catholicism brings all acts and thoughts within a religious reference; it does not relegate the religious within a specified time and space, nor does it separate the individual's religious attitudes from his or her attitudes in other areas. The need to discern the 'signs of the time', to recognise 'the autonomy of earthly reality' would seem to indicate that the Church has absorbed the changes of Vatican II that allowed Catholicism to escape from the logic of *intransigentisme*. However, while the Church rejects the politico–religious intransigence of the *Syllabus of Errors* and its present-day integrist exponents, it is increasingly falling back on a moral intransigence that has the potential to return Catholics to the 'ghetto' mentality of the past. The demand for moral autonomy in human sexuality, which now has a social, cultural and political resonance that it never had in previous generations, is the source of a new divorce between the Church and society.

NOTES

1. Gabriel Le Bras, *Introduction à l'histoire de la pratique religieuse en France*, 2 vols (Paris: Press Universitaires de France, 1942–1945).

2. Michel de Certeau and Jean-Marie Domenach, *Le Christianisme éclaté* (Paris: Seuil, 1974), p. 18.

3. Danièle Hervieu-Léger, *La Religion pour mémoire* (Paris: Cerf, 1993), p. 198.

4. Jean Séguy, 'Religion, modernité, sécularisation', *Archives de sciences sociales et de religion*, 61–62 (1986), 175–85.

5. Jean-Louis Schlegel, 'Revenir de la sécularisation', *Esprit*, 113–14 (1986), 11.

6. John Ardagh, *The New France. A Society in Transition* (Harmondsworth: Penguin, 1973), p. 548.

7. Certeau and Domenach, *Le Christianisme éclaté*, p. 68.

8. Jean-Claude Eslin, Olivier Mongin and Jean-Louis Schlegel, 'La religion, sans retour ni détour', *Esprit*, 152–53 (1989), 89.

9. Certeau and Domenach, *Le Christianisme éclaté*, p. 68.

10. 'Malaise dans le catholicisme. Entretiens avec René Rémond', *Esprit*, 152–53 (1989), 89.

11. Jean Rigal, *L'Église en chantier* (Paris: Cerf, 1994), p. 72.

12. Yves Lambert, 'From Parish to Transcendent Humanism in France', in James A. Beckford and Thomas Luckmann (eds), *The Changing Face of Religion* (London: Sage Publications, 1989), pp. 49–63.

13. Danièle Hervieu-Léger, 'Sécularisation et modernité religieuse: le cas français', in *Beliefs and Identity in Modern France*, ed. Martyn Cornick (Loughborough: ASMCF–ERC, 1990), p. 219.

14. Ibid., p. 218.

15. Ibid., p. 222.

16. Rigal, *L'Église en chantier*, p. 55.

17. Jean-Marie Donegani, *La Liberté de choisir. Pluralisme religieux et pluralisme politique dans le catholicisme français contemporain* (Paris: Presses de la Fondation nationale des sciences politiques, 1993), p. 467.

18. Jean-Marie Lustiger, *Le Choix de Dieu. Entretiens avec Jean-Louis Missika et Dominique Wolton* (Paris: Éditions de Fallois, 1987), p. 375.

19. Patrick Michel, 'Les Chrétiens en France aujourd'hui', *Problèmes politiques et sociaux*, 518 (Paris: La Documentation française, 1985), p. 7.

20. Gilles Lipovetsky, *Le Crépuscule du devoir. Éthique indolore des nouveaux temps démocratiques* (Paris: Gallimard, 1992).

21. 'Simplement, devant la vacuité du discours politique, l'idée, sans être formulée clairement, consciemment, progresse qu'il n'y a plus dans ce pays que les hommes d'Église pour avoir une idée de ce qu'étaient les "valeurs"' (François Reynaert and Francis Zamponi, *Sur la terre comme au ciel. Pour une nouvelle morale laïque* (Paris: Calmann-Lévy, 1990), p. 253).

22. Guy Coq, 'L'Enseignement religieux à l'école?', *Esprit*, 147 (1989), 49.

23. Lustiger, *Le Choix de Dieu*, p. 82.

24. Ibid., p. 116.

25. Ibid., p. 378.

26. Ibid., p. 242.
27. Ibid., p. 335.
28. Ibid., p. 303.
29. Ibid.
30. Ibid., p. 217.
31. Étienne Fouilloux, 'Voyage chez les intégristes catholiques', *L'Histoire*, 135 (1990), 97–98.
32. Adam Sage, 'Catholics Forge Links to the Right in Abortion War', *The Observer*, 18 June 1995, p. 21.
33. Marcel Lefebvre, *Lettre ouverte aux catholiques perplexes* (Paris: Albin Michel, 1985), p. 132.
34. Ibid., p. 203.
35. Ibid., p. 51.
36. Ibid., p. 107.
37. For a discussion of the court ruling in the case of the Godard film, see Claire Waquet, 'Le droit à la liberté de conscience', in *Droit, liberté et foi*, ed. J.-M. Lustiger (Paris; Mame–Cujas, 1993), pp. 95–96.
38. Rigal, *L'Église en chantier*, p. 67.
39. Guy Coq, *Démocratie, religion, éducation* (Paris: Mame, 1993), p. 91.
40. Sondages SOFRES, *Le Pèlerin*, 1 November 1972 and 15 October 1982.
41. Coq, *Démocratie, religion, éducation*, p. 209.
42. Cardinal Lustiger, 'La foi: une liberté et un droit', in *Droit, liberté et foi*, p. 181.

Select bibliography

Atkin, Nicholas and Frank Tallet, eds, *Religion, Society and Politics in France since 1789* (London: The Hambledon Press, 1991)
—— *Catholicism in Britain and France since 1789* (London: The Hambledon Press, 1996)
Azéroual, Yves, *Foi et République* (Paris: P. Banon, 1995)
Barbier, Maurice, *La Laïcité* (Paris: L'Harmattan, 1995)
Baubérot, Jean, *Vers un nouveau pacte laïque?* (Paris: Seuil, 1990)
Bédarida, Renée, *Les Armes de l'esprit, Témoignage chrétien, 1941–1944* (Paris: Éditions ouvrières, 1977)
—— *Les Catholiques dans la guerre* (Paris: Hachette, 1998)
Bedouelle, Guy, *Dictionnaire d'histoire de l'Église* (Chambray: CLD, 1994)
Bedouelle, Guy and Jean-Paul Costa, *Les Laïcités à la française* (Paris: Presses Universitaires de France, 1998)
Behr-Sigel, Elisabeth, *Le Ministère des femmes dans l'Église* (Paris: Cerf, 1987)
Berstein, Serge and Jean-Jacques Becker, *Histoire de l'anti-communisme en France*, 2 vols (Paris: Orban, 1987)
Birnbaum, Pierre, ed., *Histoire politique des juifs de France* (Paris: FNSP, 1990)
Boussinesq, Jean, *La Laïcité française: mémento juridique* (Paris: Seuil, 1994)
Bosworth, William, *Catholicism and Crisis in Modern France* (Princeton: Princeton University Press, 1962)
Boulard, Fernand, *Premiers itinéraires en sociologie religieuse* (Paris: Éditions ouvrières, 1951)
Boulard, Fernand and Jean Rémy, *Pratique religieuse urbaine et régions cultuelles* (Paris: Éditions ouvrières, 1968)
Boulard, Fernand, Gérard Cholvy, Bernard Delpal et al., *Matériaux pour l'histoire religieuse du peuple français*, 4 vols (Paris: EHESS, FNSP, CNRS, 1982–)
Boussinesq, Jean, *La Laïcité française. Mémento juridique* (Paris: Seuil, 1994)
Buchanan, Tom and Martin Conway, eds, *Political Catholicism in Europe, 1918–65* (Oxford: Clarendon Press, 1996)
Calvez, Jean-Yves, P. de Charentenay, René Rémond and C. Théobald, *Cent ans après 'Rerum novarum' (1891). La Tradition sociale du catholicisme français* (Paris: Médiasèvres, 1991)
Cannuyer, Christian, *Les Catholiques français* (Paris: Brepolis, 1992)
Caron, Jeanne, *Le Sillon et la démocratie chrétienne 1894–1910* (Paris: Plon, 1966)

Certeau, Michel de and Jean-Marie Domenach, *Le Christianisme éclaté* (Paris: Seuil, 1974)

Cholvy, Gérard, *Géographie religieuse de l'Hérault contemporain* (Paris: Presses Universitaires de France, 1968)

—— *La Religion en France de la fin du XVIIIe siècle à nos jours* (Paris: Hachette, 1991)

Cholvy, Gérard and Yves-Marie Hilaire, *Histoire religieuse de la France contemporaine*, 3 vols (Toulouse: Privat, 1985–88)

Cholvy, Gérard and Nadine-Josette Chaline, eds, *L'Enseignement catholique en France aux XIXème et XXème siècles* (Paris: Cerf, 1995)

Christophe, Paul, *1936: Les Catholiques et le Front populaire* (Paris: Éditions ouvrières, 1986)

—— *1939–1940: Les Catholiques devant la guerre* (Paris: Éditions ouvrières, 1989)

Cointet, Michèle, *L'Église sous Vichy, 1940–1945. La repentance en question* (Paris: Perrin, 1998)

Comte, Bernard, *L'Honneur et la conscience: catholiques français en résistance, 1940–1944* (Paris: Éditions ouvrières, 1998)

Coq, Guy, *Démocratie, religion, éducation* (Paris: Mame, 1993)

Costa-Lascoux, Jacqueline, *Les trois âges de la laïcité* (Paris: Hachette, 1996)

Curtis, David, *The French Popular Front and the Catholic Discovery of Marx: From Refutation to Revision* (Hull: Hull University Press, 1997)

Dansette, Adrien, *Histoire religieuse de la France contemporaine* (Paris: Flammarion, 1951)

Delbreil, Jean-Claude, *Centrisme et démocratie chrétienne: le Parti démocrate populaire des origines aus MRP, 1919–1944* (Paris: Publications de la Sorbonne, 1990)

Delmaire, Danielle, *Antisémitisme et catholiques dans le Nord pendant l'affaire Dreyfus* (Lille: Presses Universitaires de Lille, 1991)

Delumeau, Jean, *La Religion de ma mère: le rôle des femmes dans la transmission de la foi* (Paris: Cerf, 1992)

Donegani, Jean-Marie, *La Liberté de choisir. Pluralisme religieux et pluralisme politique dans le catholicisme français contemporain* (Paris: FNSP, 1993)

Dufourcq, Elisabeth, *Les Aventurières de Dieu* (Paris: Lattés, 1993)

Dupuy, Bernard and Marie-Thérèse Hoch, *Les Églises devant le judaïsme, documents officiels 1948–1978* (Paris: Cerf, 1980)

Duquesne, Jacques, *Les Catholiques français sous l'occupation* (Paris: Grasset, 1966)

Fabrègues, Jean de, *Le Sillon de Marc Sangnier, un tournant majeur du mouvement social catholique* (Paris: Perrin, 1964)

Fayet-Scribe, Sylvie, *Associations féminines et catholicisme. De la charité à l'action sociale, XIXe–XXe siècle* (Paris: Éditions ouvrières, 1990)

Fouilloux, Étienne, *Au cœur du vingtième siècle religieux* (Paris: Éditions ouvrières, 1993)

—— *Les Chrétiens français entre crise et libération 1937–1947* (Paris: Seuil, 1997)

Gibson, Ralph, *A Social History of French Catholicism 1789–1914* (London: Routledge, 1989)

Godin, Henri and Yves Daniel, *La France, pays de mission?* (Lyon: Éditions de l'Abeille, 1943)

Guerry, Mgr, *L'Église catholique en France sous l'occupation* (Paris: Flammarion, 1947)

Halls, W.D., *Politics, Society and Christianity in Vichy France* (Oxford: Berg, 1995)

Hanotel, Valérie, *Les Cathos* (Paris: Plon, 1995)

Hébrard, Marie, *Les Femmes dans l'Église* (Paris: Le Centurion–Cerf, 1984)

Hervieu-Léger, Danièle, *La Religion au lycée* (Paris: Cerf, 1990)

—— *La Religion pour mémoire* (Paris: Cerf, 1993)

Jackson, Julian, *The Popular Front in France: Defending Democracy, 1934–38* (Cambridge: Cambridge University Press, 1988)

Jamet, Dominique, *Clovis ou le baptême de l'ère: France, qu-as tu fait de ta laïcité?* (Paris: Ramsay, 1996)

Kelly, Michael, *Pioneer of the Catholic Revival. The Ideas and Influence of Emmanuel Mounier* (London: Sheed & Ward, 1979)

—— *Modern French Marxism* (Oxford: Blackwell, 1982)

Landau, Lazare, *De l'aversion à l'estime: juifs et catholiques en France de 1919 à 1939* (Paris: Le Centurion, 1980)

Laot, Laurent, *Catholicisme, politique, laïcité* (Paris: Éditions ouvrières, 1990)

—— *La Laïcité, un défi mondial* (Paris: Éditions ouvrières, 1998)

Larkin, Maurice, *Religion, Politics and Preferment in France since 1890: La Belle Époque and its Legacy* (Cambridge: Cambridge University Press, 1995)

Latreille, André, ed., *Histoire du catholicisme en France*, 3 vols, III, *La Période contemporaine du XVIIe siècle à nos jours* (Paris: Spes–Éditions ouvrières, 1962)

Le Bras, Gabriel, *Études de sociologie religieuse* (Paris: Presses Universitaires de France, 1956)

Lebrun, François, ed., *Histoire des catholiques en France du XVe siècle à nos jours* (Toulouse: Privat, 1980)

Leclerc, Gérard, *La Bataille de l'école, quinze siècles d'histoire, trois ans de combat* (Paris: Denoël, 1985)

Marrus, Michael and Robert Paxton, *Vichy France and the Jews* (New York: Basic Books, 1981)

Maugenest, Denis, ed., *Le Mouvement social catholique en France au XXe siècle* (Paris: Cerf, 1990)

Mauriac, François et al., eds, *Le Communisme et les chrétiens* (Paris: Plon, 1937)

Mayeur, Jean-Marie, *L'Histoire religieuse de la France, 19ème–20ème siècle. Problèmes et méthodes* (Paris: Beauchesne, 1975)

—— *Catholicisme social et démocratie chrétienne. Principes romains, expériences françaises* (Paris: Cerf, 1986)

—— *La question laïque, XIXème–XXème siècle* (Paris: Fayard, 1997)

McLellan, D., *Marxism and Religion. A Description and Assessment of the Marxist Critique of Christianity* (London: Macmillan, 1980)

Millman, Richard, *La Question juive entre deux guerres: ligues de droite et antisémitisme en France* (Paris: Armand Colin, 1992)

Montclos, Xavier de, et al., eds, *Églises et chrétiens dans la IIe guerre mondiale, la région Rhône-Alpes* (Lyon: Presses Universitaires de Lyon, 1978)

—— *Églises et chrétiens dans la IIe guerre mondiale, la France* (Lyon: Presses Universitaires de Lyon, 1982)

Murphy, Francis J., *Communists and Catholics in France 1936–1939. The Politics of the Outstretched Hand* (Gainesville: University of Florida Press, 1989)

Nique, Christian and Claude Lelièvre, *La République n'éduquera plus. La Fin du mythe Ferry* (Paris: Plon, 1993)

Passmore, Kevin, *From Liberalism to Fascism: The Right in a French Province, 1928–1939* (Cambridge: Cambridge University Press, 1997)

Paul, H.W., *The Second Ralliement: The Rapprochement between Church and State in the Twentieth Century* (Washington: Catholic University of America Press, 1967)

Pierrard, Pierre, *L'Église et les ouvriers en France, 1940–1990* (Paris: Hachette, 1991)

—— *Juifs et catholiques français* (Paris: Fayard, 1970); second extended edition published as *Juifs et catholiques français: d'Édouard Drumont à Jacob Kaplan, 1886–1994* (Paris: Cerf, 1997)

Portier, Philippe, *Église et politique en France au XXème siècle* (Paris: Montchrestien, 1993)

Poulat, Émile, *Liberté, laïcité. La Guerre des deux France et le principe de modernité* (Paris: Cujas–Cerf, 1988)

—— *L'Ère postchrétienne. Un monde sorti de Dieu* (Paris: Flammarion, 1994)

Prost, Antoine, *Éducation, société et politique* (Paris: Seuil, 1992)

Ravitch, Norman, *The Catholic Church and the French Nation, 1589–1989* (London: Routledge, 1990)

Rémond, René, *Les Catholiques, le communisme et les crises 1929–39* (Paris: Armand Colin, 1960), rev. as *Les Catholiques dans la France des années 30* (Paris: Éditions Cana, 1979)

—— *Nouveaux enjeux de la laïcité* (Paris: Le Centurion, 1990)

—— *Le Catholicisme français et la société politique: écrits de circonstance, 1947–1991* (Paris: Éditions ouvrières, 1995)

—— ed., *Histoire de la France religieuse*, 4 vols (Paris: Seuil, 1966–92)

Rémond, René, Jean-Pierre Azéma, François Bédarida et al., *Touvier et l'Église: rapport de la commission historique instituée par le cardinal Decourtray* (Paris: Fayard, 1992)

Rigal, Jean, *L'Église en chantier* (Paris: Cerf, 1994)

Sevegrand, Martine, *Les Enfants du bon Dieu. Les Catholiques français et la procréation au XXe siècle* (Paris: Albin Michel, 1995)

Suffert, Georges, *Les Catholiques et la gauche* (Paris: Maspéro, 1960)

Sutter, Jacques, *La Vie religieuse des Français à travers les sondages d'opinion (1944–1976)* (Paris: CNRS, 1984)

Tranvouez, Yvon, *Catholiques d'abord. Approches du mouvement catholique en France. XIXème–XXème siècle* (Paris: Éditions ouvrières, 1988)

Wellers, Georges, André Kaspi and Serge Klarsfeld, *La France et la question juive 1940–1944* (Paris: Messinger, 1979)

Index

Bold type refers to continuous treatment of an entry; several mentions of an entry within a range of pages is indicated by e.g. 121–25. Titles of works are italicised.

Weil, Simone 156
Weill, André 34
Welfare State 146
Wendel, François de 49
Wendel, Guy de 52
white slave trade (traite des Blanches) 42
women's issues 3, **219–40**
women's groups 56, 57, 62, 69, **219–40**
worker-priest movement 13, 109, 157, 158, 272
working class 145, 157, 255, 269

World Peace Day 191
World War I (Grande Guerre) 18, 27, 100, 102, 121–22
World War II (Seconde Guerre mondiale) 30, **32–37**, 43, 131–32, **149–53**

xenophobia 29, 268

Zay, Jean 59
Zirnhald, Jules 99